The Miracle Stories of the Synoptic Gospels

STUDIES IN THE SYNOPTIC GOSPELS

by Herman Hendrickx, CICM

The Infancy Narratives
The Passion Narratives of the Synoptic Gospels
The Resurrection Narratives of the Synoptic Gospels
The Sermon on the Mount
The Parables of Jesus
The Miracle Stories of the Synoptic Gospels

The Miracle Stories of the Synoptic Gospels

Herman Hendrickx

Geoffrey Chapman
London

1817

Harper & Row, Publishers
San Francisco

A Geoffrey Chapman book published by
Cassell Publishers Limited
Artillery House, Artillery Row, London SW1P 1RT

Harper & Row, Publishers, Inc.
Icehouse One-401
151 Union Street
San Francisco, California 94111-1299

First published 1987

ISBN 0 225 66487 9 (Geoffrey Chapman)
      0-06-254851-4 (Harper & Row)

Scripture quotations, unless otherwise indicated, are from the Revised Standard Version Bible (RSV), Catholic Edition, Copyrighted © 1965 and 1966 by the Division of Christian Education of the National Council of the Churches of Christ in the USA. The abbreviations JB, NAB and NEB denote, respectively, the Jerusalem Bible, the New American Bible and the New English Bible.

British Library Cataloguing in Publication Data

Hendrickx, Herman
    The miracle stories of the synoptic Gospels.—
    (Studies in the Synoptic Gospels)
    1. Bible. N.T.—Criticism, interpretation, etc.
    2. Miracles
    I. Title   II. Series
    226'.7   BS2545.M5

Cover illustration: the healing of the paralytic from a North Italian ivory panel, probably first quarter of the fifth century. Reproduced by permission of the Victoria and Albert Museum, London.

Typeset by Scribe Design, Gillingham, Kent
Printed and bound in Great Britain by Biddles Ltd, Guildford

Contents

Preface

Like the other volumes of *Studies in the Synoptic Gospels*, this book had its beginning in several series of lectures and seminars given to groups of theology students, religious and catechists. The positive response of the reading public and the generally kind appreciation expressed in reviews of the previous five books in this series encouraged me to revise my notes on the miracle stories in the light of recent publications, giving special attention to those that include or inspire interesting pastoral considerations.

Pressed for time or space, or both, every teacher and/or author on the New Testament–like, no doubt, teachers in any other field–has to make a crucial choice. Should he cover all the texts that concern the particular area of the New Testament treated and therefore deal rather briefly with each of them, or should he discuss the texts–and their context!–as completely as possible and consequently limit himself to a selection of texts?

As for the parables, the author has again opted for the second approach, thereby possibly disappointing some readers who may not find here an explanation of some of their favourite miracle stories, but hoping somehow to satisfy those who go for a more detailed treatment and so acquire the skills to do their own research on other miracle stories. Since many students and readers tend to consider the miracle stories entirely or mainly in isolation, the author has spent quite a number of pages situating the miracle stories in their respective gospel contexts. In recent years the miracle stories have come again into public interest, especially in Great Britain where they feature quite prominently in a continuing debate. This should make this book rather timely.

It is impossible to account in detail for every idea or formulation for which I am indebted to New Testament scholarship, and such an apparatus would be beyond the scope and format of this book. Nevertheless, compared to the previous volumes in this series, I have increased the number of notes. As before, an extensive bibliography, mainly of books and periodical articles published during the past twenty-five years, is included. I am deeply indebted to the work of many biblical scholars and I wish to record here my appreciation and thanks.

I should like to thank all those who had a share in the publication of this book. I am especially indebted to Rev. John Linskens, CICM, for many valuable insights received during lectures as well as private discussions, first as a student and later as a colleague. I would also like to express here my gratitude to Miss Anne Boyd, Chief Editor, without whose constant interest *Studies in the Synoptic Gospels* and particularly this book on the miracle stories would not have been possible, and Miss Fiona McKenzie, who has been involved in this series since its beginning in 1984, for her highly expert editing.

1 Miracles: the state of the question

The present-day notion of miracle

Many people approach the notion of miracle with great reservation. For many scientists miracles are unknown as such: if an event cannot be explained in the present state of science, it will surely be explainable one day. For the technologist miracles are unthinkable: to believe in miracles is to display remnants of a primitive mentality. For the psychologist miracles are the object of distrust: there are too many cases of hallucination, if not of delirium. At the same time, however, certain sects and faith-healers testify to extraordinary ecstatic phenomena and healings. At Lourdes a special bureau registers healings which cannot be explained by present-day medicine, of which approximately two per cent are later recognized as miraculous.

A similar situation can be observed at grassroots level. Of a group of twenty factory workers who discussed what they understood by 'miracle', fifteen answered: 'an event which cannot be explained by natural science'. Two said that it is an event which cannot be explained naturally, i.e., by our natural intellect. Two others spoke of 'an event which happens unexpectedly', and one of 'divine intervention which goes against the laws of nature'. In all these answers the idea that a miracle is concerned with something *extraordinary* predominates. They differ from each other in determining the nature of the *order* from which a miracle deviates. The great majority apply the standards of natural science and consider as miracle what does not correspond to the scientifically established natural order. A few speak of a miracle where an event cannot be explained by an average human intellect, to which belong the so-called psi-phenomena studied by parapsychology, etc. Another small group speak of a miracle when something does not correspond to normal expectation, e.g., a driver escaping unharmed from a car which is totally wrecked in an accident.

Only one answer mentions 'a special intervention of God', and thereby explicitly posits a connection between God and what is

1

considered a miracle. But the statement reveals a way of thinking in which God's activity is considered as an 'intervention' in the course of events in this world which conform to the laws of nature. God and nature are seen as two basically separate realities. But since God has created the world and its laws, he can interfere in its 'mechanism' in the sense that–unlike a mechanic–God can change the working of one wheel without disturbing the working of the rest of the machinery. This outlook combines (apparently unsatisfactorily) elements of an ancient and medieval image with concepts derived from a view of the world which is strongly influenced by the findings of natural science. But we can no longer take it for granted that what seems to go beyond human power must be divine, since these are not the only possible alternatives. In order to be considered a miracle an event should have religious significance. To be sure, religious significance can be taken in a wider or narrower sense; but in order to be a miracle, an event must definitely have religious significance. Extraordinary events without religious significance are more appropriately referred to as magical or psychic phenomena rather than miracles.

It may be said that the main characteristic of the present-day concept of miracle is its extraordinariness. Those who believe that God has something to do with miracles most of the time understand his activity as an intervention from outside in a course of events in this world. In the face of such a way of thinking it is easily understood that miracles recede more and more into the background. Many things which because of their extraordinariness and inexplicable character could still be considered miracles yesterday, appear perfectly explicable today, and are therefore no longer considered miraculous.

But it was not the extraordinary character of the biblical miracles that gave them special meaning, but the whole religious context in which they fitted. Miracles function within a larger reality. They reveal something of this reality, but are themselves fully understood only in terms of the larger reality, and their significance is primarily theological. To isolate the study of the miracles from this context would inevitably lead to misinterpretation.

Anyone trying to understand and explain the miracle stories of the New Testament must see them first of all as phenomena of *their* time. One can hardly start from a definition of 'miracle', for the ancient and the modern mind think in different ways. The term 'miracle' in our day has come to be used rather carelessly, often with the connotation of 'extraordinary' or 'wonderful'. While this might be acceptable in present-day English usage, it does not adequately express the biblical concept. Any attempt to determine the significance of the miraculous in early Christian thought should carefully distinguish modern ideas on the subject from ancient thinking. For our ancestors, miracles were a confirmation of the faith; for some of our contemporaries they are rather an obstacle to the faith. The former believed because of miracles; the latter sometimes believe in spite of miracles. At any rate, the term 'miracle' must be understood in its biblical sense and not in the modern one, whether it be from the viewpoint of traditional Christian belief or of rationalistic disbelief in its reality. The important question is, therefore, how we present-day people can develop the kind of sensitivity which will allow us to think, hear and see like people of New Testament times.

Miracles in antiquity

The books of the Bible originated in antiquity, in the area of the Near East and the Mediterranean, between 1000 B.C. and A.D. 100. The authors were people of their time, stamped by the culture in which they lived. This is very noticeable in the texts they produced, including the biblical miracle stories. The latter presuppose a definite world view and a particular image of God, as well as a personal relationship to God which is based on this image. Therefore, we should first of all ask ourselves how people in those times understood their world and the working of superhuman forces in it.

The ancient world view

The ancient world view divided the universe into three levels: the upper world, the earth, and the underworld. The solid disc of the earth constituted the centre of the whole. Like a gigantic cheese-cover, the massive firmament arched over it; at the extremities of the earth, it rested on the 'pillars of heaven'. On the inside of the firmament the 'great and small lights' were fixed. The vault was pierced by openings, the 'floodgates of heaven', through which poured the rains. Under the earth were the lower waters, the primeval ocean which washed the rocks on which were fixed the 'pillars of the earth'. The upper world was the place of God, or the gods, and the heavenly beings. The intermediate space between heaven and earth was believed to be inhabited by good spirits, while the underworld was thought of as the realm of death and the habitat of evil powers. In this context the people, not only of the Near East and the Greco-Roman empire in biblical times, but also of the Middle Ages, viewed the world and its powers, and the biblical writers shared this view.

What follows from this for the understanding of miracles in antiquity? Miracles were an integral part of the ancient world view. God, divine powers, good and evil spirits constantly intervened in earthly events. It would not be correct, however, to say that throughout antiquity all people were afflicted by the desire for miracles and by superstition. In fact, in antiquity a number of critical and sceptical voices were also heard. But, generally speaking, the ordinary, normal course of things was not attributed to a worldly set of laws, but to the activity of divine powers which could (and did) at times interrupt this regularity to let things take another course. Or, in the words of Thomas Aquinas: 'God can act apart from the order implanted by him in things' (*Summa Contra Gentiles*, III, 99, 1).

The difference between the ancient and the present-day world view

One of the difficulties present-day people experience with the biblical miracles is the understanding of reality which underlies them.

The chief difference between what people of our times designate as miracle and what people of antiquity called miracles consists especially in the reversal of the importance of the two components, experience of extraordinariness and experience of the divine. At the present time the extraordinariness is so predominant that the experience of the divine hardly plays a part; in antiquity, on the other hand, the experience of divine activity, its 'epiphany', was what constituted a miracle, while extraordinariness played a minor part. When the biblical authors speak of *signs*, they emphasize the *revelatory* power of the events rather than their miraculous character.

These different views are rooted in a different consideration of the world: in the ancient and medieval world view, God, and also good and evil spirits, were thought of as powers which constantly and immediately interfered–or at least could interfere–in the course of world events. The ancient world did not believe in an anonymous nature, and consequently did not have to ask how God, or the gods, intervened in it.

This outlook was replaced by a fundamentally different world view at the beginning of modern times. It began with the researchers whose insights underlie modern physics and modern natural science: Copernicus, Galileo, and Newton. They established that the earth is not the centre of the universe, but only a part of one among many solar systems. They proved in the different realms of nature the validity of the principle of causality, according to which nothing that has happened, happens without a sufficient ground for its happening thus and not otherwise. The findings of classical Newtonian physics were not superseded, but only more exactly defined by the progress of atomic physics, and even by quantum physics. The regrettable conflict in the past between the Church and natural science, that is, between Christian belief in miracles, on the one hand, and the world view of natural science, on the other hand, was possible only because of a failure to distinguish carefully between two basically different levels of experience, thinking, and speaking. Texts from antiquity which were not written from the perspective of natural science were judged from that point of view, while believers selected from the ancient texts statements which seemed to contradict the world view of natural science. Both approaches were wrong.

Miracles in the Bible

Similarities and dissimilarities

When the people of antiquity recognized divine activity in an event in a clearer way than usual, they spoke of a miracle. This was also the case with the biblical writers, but their understanding of miracles distinguished itself from that of their environment in one very important respect. The myths of Israel's neighbours described the origin of the world as the outcome of a struggle with the chaotic elements of nature, from which the gods had also previously originated. In Israel's faith, however, God was sovereign ruler over all powers from the very beginning. Creation was therefore described as a sign of God's power, and was celebrated as such in Israel's liturgy (Ps 136[135]:4–7). In fact, the fundamental miracle for biblical thought is the creation of the world.

Furthermore, except for a few aberrations, and unlike its environment, Israel did not worship the heavenly bodies and forces of nature as gods. God himself cared for the lives of individuals and saved them from dangerous situations (Ps 107[106]). That God's care is concerned in a special way with the whole people was expressed in the miracles found in the Exodus story, the prototype of all miracles. Later on God worked signs through the prophets, notably Elijah and Elisha (I Kgs 17; II Kgs 4 – 5).

A miracle is not an event taking place in the realm of nature alone; it also eminently belongs to the realm of history. It occurs only in the context of human history and God's activity within history. For Israel, God is not only the God of nature, but in the first place the God of history. A miracle is extraordinary because in it God manifests himself as Saviour. The miracle thus becomes a sign which refers to the God who is always near and directing things. In order to understand any event as a sign, a certain form of intuition is needed. To see an event as a sign of salvation requires a salvation-consciousness: historical happenings and even miraculous events can be understood as saving events only through attuned listening and interpretation.

Old and New Testament

Compared with almost two thousand years of Israelite history and the number of biblical books, miracles and miracle stories occupy only a small place in the Old Testament. It is indeed correct to say that when one considers the length of time of the biblical period, the number of miracle stories contained in the biblical books is small.

Of the many sicknesses healed by Jesus and the magicians of his time–fever, blindness, paralysis, etc.–the stories of Moses, Elijah and Elisha say nothing. While we cannot be absolutely certain whether the Old Testament prophets were healers or not, one thing is certain: they are not described as such in the Old Testament. Except for a few rare instances, the Old Testament accounts cannot have served as models for most of the gospel healing stories.

It should not be overlooked, however, that 'our knowledge is limited by the snobbishness of the literary tradition of antiquity. Ancient literature is almost entirely upper-class and rationalistic'.[1]

We may assume, then, that healings and magical practices proliferated especially, though not exclusively, among the lower classes of society. The customers were the same as those who consult healers and clairvoyants today.

In the New Testament, however, and especially in the gospels, miracles play a much more important part than in the Old Testament. In the synoptic gospels seventy-six passages are found which deal with Jesus' miracles. Some of these passages are very lengthy, while others are just brief allusions. Some narrate individual miracles, while others relate summary statements or group miracles. Some are mentioned in only one gospel, while others occur in several gospels and thus constitute several passages. The gospels report approximately thirty miracles performed by Jesus, and Acts twice refers indirectly to Jesus' miracles (Acts 2:22; 10:38); otherwise, the New Testament does not mention them at all. Speaking of the gospels, it may indeed be said that nowhere, throughout the whole Bible, do we find so many miracles performed by a single person. For example, if the miraculous elements were deleted from the first ten chapters of Mark, almost half of these chapters would be gone; more exactly, some 200 out of 425 verses. Miracle stories represent 209 of the 660 verses of Mark, i.e., 31 per cent of the whole gospel.

And yet, if the New Testament as a whole should be understood against the background of the Old Testament, this is especially true for the miracle stories. The similarities in arrangement and vocabulary between some Old and New Testament miracle stories have been pointed out, especially raisings of the dead and multiplications of loaves. The authors of the Old and the New Testament shared the same world view, the same interpretation of history, and their stories are similar in format and in what they intend to affirm. *Miracles are remarkable events which believers understand to be signs of God's saving activity*. The basic difference between Old and New Testament is that in the latter God's saving activity in and through Jesus has a final and definitive (eschatological) character.

It has recently been shown that the miracle stories of the New Testament were more influenced by Old Testament piety than by Hellenistic religiosity, more precisely, that the authors of the miracle stories were influenced by the language and the theology of the Psalms in their presentation as well as their interpretation, and that the same attitude of faith and intention of proclamation underlie both the Psalms and the miracle stories of the New Testament.

Rabbinic and Hellenistic miracle stories

The gospel miracle stories belong to a literary genre which is also found in non-Christian literature. While it is important to point out the peculiarities of biblical miracle stories, it is equally important to consider the more general category to which they belong, to highlight the basic beliefs which they presuppose, and to identify the motifs and the stylistic features which they often share with non-Christian miracle stories. There is no properly Christian *form* of miracle stories. Their formal characteristics are exactly the same as those of the corresponding Jewish and pagan miracle stories.

There are two types of miracle stories current in the ancient world during the period within which the New Testament came into being: the Jewish miracle story recorded in the Talmud, and the Hellenistic miracle story. But both belonged to the same general cultural context and did not exist in total isolation from each other.

(i) Rabbinic miracle stories

Rabbinic literature extends from the second to the fifth centuries A.D., and in some cases even to the eleventh and twelfth centuries. Most of the texts cannot be dated with certainty, but often contain very old tradition. A difficulty which pertains especially to the study of the miracles is the fact that the rabbinic schools manifested a definite distrust of the 'marvellous'. Yet it can be said that by referring to the first miracle of creation and the fundamental miracle of the Exodus, but also to other biblical miracles (Elijah, Elisha), the rabbinic tradition encourages the faithful to wonder before the all-powerful God who alone is capable of liberating his people from desperate situations. The miracles of the Exodus are the prototype of the marvellous things God will do for Israel at the time of the final redemption. Indeed, the rabbinic traditions affirm a parallelism between the events of the Exodus and those of the redemption in the time of the Messiah. This last consideration is very important for the interpretation of the New Testament miracle stories.

It has been noted that miracle-working was fairly common among rabbis but that cases of exorcism are practically unknown in rabbinic literature. Jesus' own reference to exorcistic activities by the 'sons of the Pharisees' (Mt 12:27; Lk 11:19) shows that he was not alone in performing exorcisms, but he seems to have considered them a particularly important aspect of his ministry.

It should be said that the rabbinic miracle stories, e.g., those reported of Rabbi Hanina ben Dosa, who lived in Galilee before and after A.D. 70, are different from the gospel miracles, and it may be concluded that Jesus is not presented with the features of a rabbinic miracle-worker.

(ii) Hellenistic miracle stories

It has been pointed out that the miracle stories of the gospels are more clearly related to the Hellenistic than to the rabbinic miracle stories. One thinks here first of all of the miracles attributed to the healer-god Asclepius (Aesculapius) and Apollonius of Tyana. According to a fourth-century inscription, Asclepius performed about eighty miracles, most of them healings, at the sanctuary of Epidaurus in Greece. In fact, from the time of Homer (eighth century B.C.) to the reign of Constantine (fourth century A.D.) Asclepius was the pre-eminent figure associated with healing in the ancient world. Throughout all these centuries he was considered an agent of divine cures as well as the founder of the medical profession.

Of particular interest are the divine *aretalogies* which proclaim the virtue (*arētē*) or the power (*dunamis*) of Zeus, Apollo, or Asclepius in a particular intervention. The accounts of Asclepius' miracles can as a whole be attributed to this category. The healing stories of Epidaurus are often built on the same threefold schema: (1) the presentation of the sick person and his illness; (2) the intervention of the god during an incubation period at the sanctuary (a night passed in a dormitory); and (3) the healing. It is clear that a similar threefold schema is found, e.g., in the healing of Peter's mother-in-law (Mk 1:29–31 and par.). Given a definition of aretalogy as 'a formal account of the remarkable career of an impressive teacher that was used as a basis for moral instruction', its application to the study of the gospels becomes readily apparent. Attempts have even been made to establish a 'divine-man Christology' on this basis.

In view of the tendency of Hellenistic Jewish religious propaganda to represent great figures of Jewish history, especially Moses, as 'divine men', *theioi andres*, the question has been raised whether the early Christian tradition also used the hermeneutical device of 'divine men' in interpreting the figure of Jesus. Here a study of Philostratus' *Life of Apollonius*, a disciple of Pythagoras (sixth century B.C.) who lived in the first century A.D., is of foremost importance. The work contains about twenty miracle stories, among which are one raising from the dead, five healings, and four exorcisms. Some of these stories contain undeniable similarities to the gospel miracle stories. While some exegetes think that the *Life of Apollonius* is the best parallel to the gospel miracles, others say that a simple enumeration of the miracles contained in this work sufficiently shows the enormous difference which separates them from the miracles of Jesus.

How much influence did the *theios anēr* figure exert on the gospels' picture of Jesus? No unanimity has been reached. It has been pointed out that 'if the apostles tend increasingly to be pictured in popular Hellenistic terms as a divine man, a tendency begun in canonical Acts, the same cannot be said of Jesus'.[2] While it can be said without hesitation that the *historical Jesus* did not understand his role in terms of a 'divine man' in the Hellenistic sense, his image in the *gospels* nevertheless shows at times striking similarity to the Hellenistic type of 'divine man'. But then it should be noted that there is no uniform pre-Christian type of the *theios anēr* figure. Moreover, the phrase occurs rather seldom in Hellenistic writings, and it has been used with far too much imprecision, so that it may be concluded that the influence of this motif on the gospels remains questionable. Indeed the concepts of aretalogy and of 'divine man' have not been clearly defined and suffer a degree of imprecision which makes firm conclusions nearly impossible.

A different vocabulary

The present-day idea of miracle is too closely connected with that of the extraordinary. The Hebrew Old Testament has no word corresponding to the Greek word *phusis*, 'nature', which, remarkably, occurs only in the deutero-canonical writings from Hellenistic,

Greek-speaking Judaism, e.g. Wisdom. Accordingly, Hebrew has no idea that would correspond to 'miracle' in our common conception of it as 'something that goes against or beyond the laws of nature'. The Old Testament most often uses the term *ot*, 'sign', which has a very broad meaning and can also refer to non-miraculous events. It emphasizes the revelatory character of an event. The Hebrew Bible also uses the term *geburah*, 'powerful act', which apparently focuses on the divine power manifested in an event, and *mofet*, 'portent', which is most of the time found in hymns and confessions of faith. Of all three terms the last is closest to our concept of 'miracle', without, however, coinciding with it.

For the evangelists, Jesus' miracles were certainly acts which provoked special attention. But they avoided talking about them as 'prodigies' (*thaumata*; *thaumasia* is used once in Mt 21:15). They preferred to qualify them as 'acts of power' (*dunameis*),[3] or 'signs' (*sēmeia*),[4] 'wonders' (*terata*, always used together with *sēmeia*), and 'works' (*erga*). These terms turn our attention away from the wondrous element as such and emphasize the theological and symbolic character of Jesus' earthly ministry once it is understood in the light of the resurrection.

While it has often been maintained that early Christians distinguished the miracles in their tradition from non-Christian miracles by calling them *sēmeia* or *dunameis* rather than *terata*, which would carry with it connotations of magic and the mythical,

> the miracle terminology is generally more fluid than many interpreters have notices or are willing to allow and ... *sēmeion* and *teras* are often not sharply distinguished and on occasion function as synonymous ... . The grounds are tenuous for asserting that in denoting extraordinary phenomena *sēmeion* is *eo ipso* distinct from *teras* and is, indeed, a distinctive term for Christian miracles ... . The conflict between pagan and Christian over miracle in the book of Revelation is not signaled by any terminological distinction between pagan and Christian miracles; *sēmeion* designates both ... . The distinctions pagans and Christians draw between miracle claims lie in the eyes of the beholders, and represent communal and cultural judgements.[5]

It has been observed that ideas and terminology usually assume importance when social groups provide them with the power to influence behaviour. A closer scrutiny of the social cradle and cultural dimensions of miracle terms not only clarifies the way in which those terms are used but also provides a better understanding of the individuals and groups using them.

As the evangelists saw it, everything that happened was either an act of God, or a deed of man, or both. They saw the world not as a *physical* structure but as a *power* structure. They asked, not 'what was the cause?', but 'who is responsible?' They thought in terms of personal will rather than mechanical cause and effect. Hence one should always bear in mind that the meaning of a miracle story, i.e., a miracle as told by an evangelist, is not simply its explanation in terms of 'cause', but rather its explanation in terms of 'purpose' or 'meaning for us'.

Nowadays people speak of miracles in terms of a 'violation of the laws of nature'. The more important this 'violation', the greater the miracle. But Jesus and his contemporaries would not have understood this way of thinking and speaking. They were not familiar with our concept of 'laws of nature'. To them, the only 'law of nature' was the faithful love of God for his people. People of biblical times saw God's love at work in a good rainfall, as well as in a victory in battle, or a healing. Certainly, they distinguished degrees in different divine interventions, but they never split them up into two categories, the natural and the supernatural. They did not look at the universe as a closed system following inflexible physical laws, but as completely open and responsive to God. To distinguish between natural and supernatural events would have been foreign to their outlook.

We may conclude, then, that *our* word 'miracle' does not express adequately what the *gospels* want to tell us about Jesus' activity. Miracles in the biblical sense do happen when one believes in Jesus, and it is faith in Jesus which recognizes a miracle and by that faith a miracle becomes a sign. In a biblical perspective, therefore, one cannot speak of a miracle as a 'violation of nature'.

The miracles: signs of the kingdom

Jesus gave a radically new meaning to the 'language' of the miracles: they are signs of the kingdom, signs of what God wants to do and is already doing for humankind in Jesus. They 'signify' that the powers of the kingdom, the powers of God's love are at work: 'the time is fulfilled' (Mk 1:15). The miracles of Jesus are also part of his message of salvation. Jesus' miracles are an integral part of his ministry of announcing and establishing the kingdom. If this interrelationship between the miracles of Jesus and his message of the kingdom of God is disregarded, neither the miracles nor the message of the kingdom will be understood correctly. The connection between healings and the kingdom of God is particularly clear: 'heal the sick in it and say to them, "The Kingdom of God has come near to you"' (Lk 10:9). The miracles do not stand by themselves. Detached from the message of the kingdom, they would be like missiles launched without a target.

Jesus' miracles are as much an integral part of his message as his words: he does not just announce the kingdom; he *is* the kingdom. His actions are signs of the Father's love giving people an opportunity to live a new life. The kingdom of God manifests itself as a power of love. In the New Testament sickness is understood in a wider context: Jesus' healing ministry was one aspect of the manifestation of the presence of the kingdom (Mt 12:28). Since disease was understood to be part of the disobedience of creation against its creator, healing meant that God's plan for the redress of humankind was being activated. But, in a sense, this divine power is at work only proleptically in Jesus' earthly ministry, i.e., before the resurrection. Therefore, Jesus' signs—for instance, the healing of the leper and the stilling of the storm—cannot be understood except *in the light of the resurrection*, which is the total realization of the covenant: the man Jesus totally lives the life of God and opens up for his brothers and sisters the access to this new life. The resurrection is the sign *par excellence* which gives meaning to all Jesus' signs. In this sense the Easter faith can be called 'the fulfilment of the miracle of faith'. It is in the light of the resurrection of Christ and in an atmosphere of participation in this resurrection that the gospel traditions have reached their present form, and it would be very surprising if this 'formation' left no traces in the synoptic miracle stories. The Easter faith is also the realization of the expectation of God's people. This explains why the miracle stories of the gospels are at the same time re-read *in the light of the Old Testament*: they are the fulfilment of the Old Testament.

This does not mean, however, that by simply relating some of Jesus' miracles to Old Testament prophecies we have explained them as a whole. We should not think that we can accomplish what the evangelists were apparently unable to do, that is, to bring all the miracles of Jesus under one common denominator and to give them all the same interpretation. The material is far too varied and heterogeneous to fit into such a simple and comprehensive explanation. We should not allow ourselves to be led into making facile statements such as that Jesus, in his mighty works, 'anticipated the new age', or 'inaugurated a new period of history', given the fact that, by the ordinary criteria of historians, history seems to have continued in pretty much the same way before and after Jesus' earthly ministry.

The meaningful and eventful context of Jesus' 'powerful deeds' is expressed in Mt 11:2–6, where in reply to John the Baptist's question, 'Are you he who is to come, or shall we look for another?'

(Mt 11:3), Jesus gives an answer which is basically a quotation from Isa 35:5–6; 61:1, and which reminds us of the programmatic text of Lk 4:18–19. Instead of answering, 'Yes, I am the one to come', Jesus refers to his works which can be *seen*, and his message which can be *heard* (cf. Mt 11:4, expressing the close relationship between Jesus' miracles and his message), which should enable the questioners to form their own conclusion: In Jesus, God's kingdom has come near. The time of salvation, of which Isaiah spoke, is here. In the synoptic gospels, then, Jesus' miracles are clearly related to the coming of the kingdom. But it is also clear that at least for Jesus himself the miracles did not primarily have the character of proof or credential. Their connection with the coming of the kingdom lies elsewhere. They were not so much an external guarantee of the coming of the kingdom as one of the means by which the kingdom came.

In the activity of Jesus, God completes his creative activity. In this connection we should note the very interesting reaction of the bystanders: 'He has done all things well' (Mk 7:37). Where else in the Bible did we hear about all things being good? In Gen 1, speaking of God's creation! Several scholars have therefore made the plausible suggestion that the frequency of miracles performed on the sabbath should not be understood simply as the raising of test cases for the law, but also as emphasizing Jesus' powerful works as a resumed, renewed creativity. He continues or resumes God's creative work: 'My Father is working still, and I am working' (Jn 5:17). In the fourth gospel, Jesus repeatedly refers to his miracles as 'works', *erga*, a term the Septuagint used for 'creation' in Gen 2:2, 'And on the seventh day God finished his work (*ta erga*) which he had done, and he rested on the seventh day from all his work (*apo pantōn tōn ergōn*) which he had done'. The Jews believed that for the whole of time God continued his constant creative activity every day–not merely sustaining the world, but creating each new day of history–even though Gen 2:2 describes him as 'resting' on the sabbath. In Jn 5:16–17 Jesus links his miracles of healing, his 'works', with the creative activity of the Father. The healings constitute a new creation, a victory over the rule of Satan.

This creative activity does not go unopposed. Thus the New Testament miracles are also *power* struggles: Jesus is indignant, inveighs against somebody, and speaks a commanding word. In short, this is the reason why the New Testament miracles are so often presented as exorcisms. Let us compare two such *power* stories (*dunameis*) in Mark:

Man with unclean spirit (1:23–27)	Stilling of the storm (4:35–41)
25 But Jesus *rebuked* him, saying,	39 And he *rebuked* the wind and *said*,
'*Be silent*, and come out...'.	'Peace, *be still*!...

27 *And they were all amazed...*
saying, 'What is this?...
With authority he commands
even the unclean spirits
and they obey him.'

41 *And they were filled with awe*
and said, 'Who then is this
that   .
even wind and sea
obey him?'

As this example shows, the division of miracle stories into healings/exorcisms and nature miracles is not without problems. On the other hand, it should not necessarily be supposed that the evangelists always thought everywhere of equally active hostile demonic powers. But the language of conflict found in a good number of miracle stories should not be treated as merely symbolic imagery. Jesus' ministry was a life-and-death struggle with the forces of evil which had seized the world. This should not be dismissed as just the expression of a naive and totally outdated world view. The food that is available in today's world is overabundant in some countries and almost non-existent in others. This is the work of demonic forces which have taken over the world and exploit it to their own enslaving ends. The stark contrast between the 'it is good' of the creation account and the reality of contemporary suffering cannot be ignored. It is the manifestation of corporate and structural evil in all its harshness and perversity.

How the gospel exorcisms are to be understood is very clear from the Beelzebul controversy (Mk 3:22–30; Mt 12:24–32; Lk 11:15–23). The two kingdoms are, as it were, pitted against each other. Jesus' miracle-working is the coming and the victory of the kingdom of God. Lk 11:20 says: 'But if it is by the finger of God that I cast out demons, then the kingdom of God has come upon you'. The idea of working powerful deeds 'by the finger of God' occurs in Ex 8:19, 'And the magicians said to Pharaoh, "This is the finger of God" ... '. Jesus acts as the new Moses establishing the kingdom of God.[6]

Yet the miracles do not merely disclose the fact that the rule of God is *breaking in* with the person and ministry of Jesus. They show also *the way in which this happens*: where God establishes his rule, people become 'healed'. This does not only mean 'healed' in a spiritual sense as, for instance, in the forgiveness of sins, but also denotes that the *entire person*, including his/her corporality, has been received by Christ and led to salvation. But just as the kingdom of God has indeed begun but has not yet reached its final fulfilment, so too Christ's healing activity has indeed started but is not yet completed. Jesus' works are the fully valid (in German: *vollgültig*) confirmation of his message; they are as valid as his word. But they are not the final, definitive (in German: *endgültig*) act of God in the bodily realm. The totally new creation which begins with the resurrection will be definitive. The miracles are not just prefigurations of salvation but a real gift of salvation at the present time. Jesus' healings are neither legitimation miracles nor mere omens: rather they are themselves already eschatological salvation. The 'already' of the salvation offered now is the presupposition and basis of the 'not yet' of the definitive, total salvation.

In fact, the eschatological understanding of miracle has been considered a specific feature of Jesus' proclamation. Some have called it the decisive distinction between the miracles of the New Testament and those reported in other contemporary literature. 'Perhaps the clearest difference is the eschatological interpretation and the subservience of miracle account to proclamation in the Gospel accounts of Jesus.'[7]

In this sense it may be said that in the pair *word* and *sign* the word predominates. In reference to the gospel of Matthew it has been said that the miracles are presented under the emblem of the compassion of God which is unveiling itself in the last days and visits God's people in mercy. Mt 9 – 10 contains in a topical arrangement examples of what, in answer to John the Baptist's question, are referred to in Mt 11:5 as signs of the age to come. Matthew is thus interested in the miracles of Jesus from the standpoint of his own particular eschatology.

Since God's kingdom is not yet completed by Jesus, suffering and death are not yet dispelled, but through him God's saving word has been spoken once and for all, and in his saving activity the definitive realization of salvation by God has been introduced. Therefore, Jesus' miracles have according to the gospels a definitive or eschatological character. They are like lights in the night: when the light-beams of a car fall on a road-sign, one recognizes the direction one is following. This knowledge still guides the driver long after the road-sign has again disappeared in the dark. This understanding of miracle and the miracle-worker is not found outside the New Testament.

For Jesus his miracles, while not unique in themselves, are nevertheless unique in their relation to his proclamation of the dawning of the kingdom of God. They challenge our faith in the redemptive intervention of God in and through the person of Jesus, his words and his deeds. But they are not proofs. Rather, they invite people to a decision. Those who witness Jesus' exorcisms and healings are entirely free to decide that 'he is possessed by Beelzebul, and by the prince of demons he casts out the demons' (Mk 3:22). But they may also decide that they are real miracles and that 'it is by the finger of God' (Lk 11:20) that Jesus performs them. As soon as the miracles are separated from the person of Jesus they also lose their function of referring to the one who should be recognized through these signs.

Miracle and faith

The miracles point to something (in German: *hinweisen*) but do not prove anything (in German: *beweisen*). They do not have the function of proofs in Jesus' activity, nor can the miracle stories today serve as conclusive proofs. In the light of our present understanding of the miracle stories, it is not possible to argue as follows: Jesus performed healings and exorcisms, etc. which cannot be explained by the laws and forces of nature known to us. Therefore, he is the absolute, definitive revealer and mediator of salvation, even God in person, as necessarily and indisputably as two plus two make four.

Notwithstanding their witnessing power, Jesus' powerful acts must be *believed* as much as his word about the dawning of the kingdom of God. This follows from their character as signs as well as from the gospel texts: a sign accomplishes its goal only when it is understood. However, not every sign is understood. Whether it is understood and accepted depends on how clearly it refers to what is signified and with what presuppositions it is viewed. We can allow the sign to lead us to the reality or the person signified, but we can also refuse to let the sign do its work. Both attitudes were adopted towards Jesus' signs. Some said: 'by the prince of demons he casts out the demons' (Mk 3:22); others: 'Lord, to whom shall we go? You have the words of eternal life' (Jn 6:68). Both groups were eyewitnesses of the events, but the second meaning did not force itself upon them. This meaning is grasped only by those who approach the signs with an attitude of faith.

The evangelists were apparently less concerned about the historical character of the miracles, i.e., whether they actually happened–though they would probably not have had any difficulty in stating that they did happen–than with the question of faith in Jesus as he is proclaimed in the gospels. It is clear that for the evangelists the miracles did not force people to believe in Jesus and they should not now be used as if they did.

As regards the relationship between faith and miracle, it is surprising that in many cases faith is clearly considered a prerequisite for a miracle. Mark reports, e.g., that since Jesus did not find faith in Nazareth, 'he could do no mighty works there' (Mk 6:5). After several healings Jesus says 'your faith has made you well' (Mk 10:52; Lk 17:19). In other cases, however, it is the miracle that leads people to faith, e.g., in Matthew's report of the walking on the water (Mt 14:33).

Is faith a prerequisite for the miracle, or does the miracle lead to faith? A statement in Mark may help us reach an answer to this question. When Jesus told the father of an epileptic boy that if he believed his son would be healed, the father exclaimed, 'I believe, help my unbelief' (Mk 9:24). Faith is not something acquired once and for all. Jesus looks for a faith that allows itself to be carried further by the sign. His opponents did not have this openness. To them the miracles were not signs. They wanted proofs. Therefore, Jesus said, 'no sign shall be given to this generation' (Mk 8:12).

With regards to the demand for faith, the seventy-six miracle texts of the synoptic gospels can be divided as follows:

(1) narratives where faith is specifically mentioned, sought, described as rewarded, etc.: 20 narratives; (2) narratives where faith is not explicitly mentioned, but where it is obviously demonstrated in some explicit manner (e.g., 'they brought to him all who were sick ... ' in Mark 1:32; ' ... besought him that they might only touch the fringe of his garment ... ' in Matthew 14:36): 25 narratives; (3) narratives where faith prior to the miracle is neither mentioned, nor even implicitly demonstrated: 31 narratives, our largest category therefore. So we cannot say that 'Jesus always required faith.' The most we can say is this: in crucial miracle passages Jesus is described as demanding faith. In numerous other passages no such requirement is stated.[8]

On the other hand, it should not be overlooked that in the synoptic gospels almost two-thirds of the uses of 'believe' (*pisteuein*) and related terms occur in relation to miracles. Faith here is understood as trust in God's power, an openness and sensitivity to God's power to perform mighty works. Faith is, therefore, obviously neither a psychological disposition which facilitates the healing, nor a religious act by a person who thereby earns ('merits') healing.

It may be concluded, then, that the relationship between miracle and faith cannot be expressed in a smooth statement. On the one hand, Jesus' miracles intend to elicit faith, not to force it. They can never force faith because, on the other hand, most of the time they implicitly or explicitly presuppose this very faith. Faith is here understood as the belief that with Jesus the definitive rule of God has been inaugurated and that Jesus reveals in his miracles that he is the one whom the Christian community subsequently confesses and proclaims. Jesus' miracles possess the character of a call and decision. This is also true for today. Only those who take salvation history as a whole into consideration can adequately assess the importance and significance of Jesus' miracles. But without faith one cannot see the effect of God's healing intervention in history. Today, too, without faith there is no real access to the miracles.

Miracle and faith belong together in ancient thinking. And yet one can see in the mutual relation of faith and miracle the uniqueness of the New Testament's faith in miracles. Generally speaking–making allowance for a few (apparent) exceptions on both sides–it can be said that while in the ancient world in general faith followed the miracle, in the New Testament it is a prerequisite or condition for the miracle, where it is mentioned or referred to.

The miracles are eschatological signs which have meaning only in so far as they refer to the message and the person of Jesus Christ. Faith in miracles is in the last resort not faith in this or that particular miracle, but in the Lord who reveals himself in and through all these particular events.

Miracles and the historian

The question

At this stage the question may arise: are the miracles historical? In a case as, for instance, the stilling of the storm (Mk 4:35–41; Mt 8:23–27; Lk 8:22–25), can one still find out exactly what happened? The answer to this question calls for some preliminary clarifying remarks.

First remark

To speak of 'exactly what happened' is ambiguous. The human sciences have taught us that there are no merely 'objective' events, but only events which are grasped and interpreted: the reality of an event can come to us only through the repercussions it had on a human consciousness, individual or collective. Language is the privileged medium of this interpretation. Even when a story is based on an actual occurrence, the story is not simply a record of that occurrence. Rather it creates an impression of what the precipitating occasion meant to the storyteller and what it can mean to one who listens to the story today. As we consider a miracle story, then, the question we face is not 'What actually happened?' What we can establish is the impression produced by the miracle on the eyewitnesses and the stylized editing to which the early Christian tradition subjected it. This is all we can discover by historical research. Except for a few narratives of a factual and undeniably historical character, the extent and way in which the early Christian tradition reflects genuine facts in each of its aspects can be established only vaguely. Historical criticism of the gospels, therefore, deliberately orients itself to the study of the Christian tradition seen as dedicated testimony and as an expression of faith and religious experience.

There are two approaches or methods to determine the historicity of an event in a critically justified way, and these two (can) complement each other. The first consists of the critical investigation of the origin and import of the testimonies: one tries to show that the testimony intends to affirm the event as a fact, that it can reach back to the event, and that it is competent as well as trustworthy. The second consists of the critical investigation of the internal and external possibility or probability of what the witnesses testify to. However, to establish the possibility of an event—a miracle—does not amount to establishing that it actually happened. One may also ask whether the *whole* reality is sufficiently known to assert confidently what is possible or impossible. Many people are afflicted with a sense of the impossible, and that may be precisely why miracles do not seem to happen. Nevertheless the second method can reinforce the results of the first.

Finally and most importantly, it should be noted that the miracle *story* is not to be confused with the miracle *event*. In fact, the actual event of the miracle and the miracle story should be clearly distinguished. The miracle stories are not on-the-spot reports or historical documents which give us an objective and complete description of the circumstances, the fact and the details of the past miraculous event. They are rather accounts of how the time of salvation which dawns in Jesus' words and deeds takes shape and realizes itself in actual situations of distress. They therefore do not give a direct answer to the question of exactly what happened. The relation between miracle *story* and miracle *event* cannot be fully clarified by literary and tradition-historical methods. The ultimate standard for the 'wonderful things' attested can only be the analogy of related and similar experiences in one's own life, in the present Christian world and in the Christian faith-tradition.

Second remark

Taking, e.g., the stilling of the storm, exegetes agree in seeing in the present accounts 're-readings' (in French: *relectures*) of an event, produced by the early Christian community, with the Old Testament as their starting-point, in this particular case probably the book of Jonah, and in the light of the Easter faith. Indeed, many gospel miracle stories show signs of editing and even repeated reworking, indicating that they originated in early Christian communities and were handed down by long tradition, first oral, then written. Form criticism has demonstrated this beyond reasonable doubt. At the same time the Palestinian background of most of the miracle stories is firmly established. It cannot reasonably be questioned that a number of miracle stories of Jesus as wonder-worker were already circulating during his lifetime and that his disciples remembered and repeated them after his death. How much they were expanded by repetition or by invention, and which of the details, or whole stories, reflect original facts, are questions which often cannot be answered.

In fact, the accounts of Jesus' miracles *as we have them now* originated mainly after Easter, but they are based on historically reliable tradition. This is supported first of all by the observation that we find references to Jesus' miracles in statements which are generally believed to be authentic sayings of Jesus: (a) the Beelzebul controversy (Mk 3:22ff.; Mt 12:24ff.; Lk 11:15ff.); (b) the woes pronounced over Chorazin, Bethsaida and Capernaum (Mt 11:20–24; Lk 10:13–15); (c) Jesus' reply to the inquiry by John the Baptist (Mt 11:4ff.; Lk 7:22f.); (d) the blessing addressed to Jesus' disciples (Mt 13:16f.; Lk 10:23f.); (e) Jesus' reply to Herod (Lk 13:32). Further, there are many features in the miracle stories which belong to a Palestinian environment.

Can the event as such still be recovered? Here the opinions of the specialists diverge: for some, Jesus actually manifested an extraordinary power over the storm; others, on the other hand, stress that Jesus always refused to perform spectacular wonders (see, e.g., Mt 4:5–7; Mk 8:11–12). The present state of the accounts does not allow us to settle the question definitively. But their profound meaning is to be sought in the experience of a real saving act by the disciples and related to the presence of Jesus.

The historian should not fail to point out that Jesus acted as if he exerted extraordinary power over the natural and supernatural realm, and that this power went unchallenged by both friends and opponents. Jesus acted with spiritual authority, and this fact is attested by those who said 'he is possessed by Beelzebul' (Mk 3:22) as by those who narrated and recorded the baptism and temptation accounts. The question whether Jesus really worked miracles should not be separated from the more fundamental question who Jesus really is, since the only accounts we have of his life, words and deeds reflect the deeper understanding which his followers gained after and in the light of Easter. There are no purely objective and factual accounts of Jesus' actions, but only accounts interpreted in the light of the resurrection and preached to communicate the Easter faith.

Third remark

In the present stage of research the Bible is no longer treated as a single piece of writing. Each book is studied for itself. The same can even be said for the pericopes or individual passages within a particular book. This is also the case with the miracle stories: before they reached their present place in the gospels, they led an autonomous existence. No up-to-date scholars would make a blanket statement on the historicity of the miracle stories as such. They accept the *global fact of miracle*, that is, that Jesus did perform miracles, but this does not necessarily amount to acceptance of the historicity of all *miracle stories*, still less all the details of these stories. As is true of the gospel tradition as a whole, the tradition of Jesus' miracles is uneven with regard to historicity, but part of it can definitely be considered as having firm grounds in the life of Jesus. Thus not all the miracle stories in the gospels should be given equal historical weight. One has to allow for the possibility that some miracle stories have grown in the telling, perhaps even for the possibility that some are mis-recollections of sayings or symbolic actions of Jesus, e.g., the cursing of the fig tree in Mk 11:12–14, 20–25 and Mt 21:18–22; cf. Lk 13:6–9. But even when a number of miracle stories have been excluded for these and other reasons, there remains an impressive body of material which attributes to Jesus a number of miracles which have no close parallel in the ancient world and which testifies to the amazement and wonder which Jesus provoked on many occasions.

But the acceptance of the general observation that Jesus did perform miracles does not finally settle the problem for exegetes and theologians. The study of individual miracle stories shows that while many of them contain features which convince everyone, others are considerably less convincing and are wholly or partly rejected even by moderate scholars. It should be noted that raising questions about the historicity of *some* miracle stories or some of their details is not (necessarily) equivalent to putting into question *the miracles* of Jesus, i.e., the fact of miracles as such. It has become pointless to discuss whether the miracle stories are true or false as a whole, since they do not form a monolithic unity. It is far more useful to determine what is probably true in each one of them taken separately.

It should also be noted that the *isolated fact* is important only in so far as it refers to the decisive meaning of the *person of Jesus Christ*. Although the miracle tradition of the New Testament takes the view that Jesus did perform many miracles, and although most of the miracle stories of Jesus are based on historical events, the *theological* meaning of each and every miracle story does not depend in the first place on whether it happened exactly as it is narrated, but on the fact that Jesus is still the one he was then: the Saviour and helper of all people in any kind of need. The miracle tradition is narrated from the perspective of the experience that in Jesus' deeds God's nearness to the community manifests itself.

It is indeed clear that what is in the forefront now is no longer questions about the historical factuality of the recorded miracles, or about their 'physical' or 'supernatural' character, or about the relation between miracles and science, but rather questions about the kerygma or message which they have in view: what do these stories mean for the faith? If we are convinced that by the resurrection from the dead Jesus of Nazareth was established as the Son of God, the one who brings definitive salvation, then the question of the historicity of a *particular* miracle in the life of the earthly Jesus is no longer decisive for the Christian faith. Ultimately, faith is not based on every miracle narrated in the gospel actually having happened or on a miracle's happening exactly the way it is presented in the gospel. The real basis of our faith is that Christ has been raised from the dead.

The fact of miracles as such

If for each individual miracle we cannot reach back to an event as such, can we be sure of the general fact that Jesus indeed performed miracles? Yes, we can be sure that *Jesus performed real signs which were interpreted by his contemporaries as experiences of an extraordinary power*. If Jesus had not performed any signs, he would not have been recognized as a religious man of his time. He would not have been able to raise the questions concerning his person or progressively reveal his mission. To proclaim a religious message without supporting it by any signs was considered unusual (see Jn 10:41 for John the Baptist).

Notice the formulation of the issue. To many people it is: if Jesus performed miracles he must be God; but can we believe in the historicity of the gospel miracles? This question should rather be formulated as follows: Jesus performed miracles, in the first place because it belonged to the religious 'language' of his time. The miracle story is a 'way of speaking' (in German: *Sprachform*) alongside others; in early Christianity, as in antiquity in general, it was not thought of as indisputably valid always and everywhere. Rabbinic material demonstrates that the world in which Jesus lived was such that no one who knows this environment is surprised when the gospels also display the marks of their origin by narrating miracles attributed to Jesus.

But Jesus gave his miracles a new dimension by *who he is*. Hence, 'who do you say that I am?' In other words: It is not that Jesus' contemporaries immediately saw the uniqueness of his miracles and then drew the conclusion from this that he must be unique, i.e., divine. Rather, the early Christians discovered the true uniqueness of Jesus' person after and in the light of Easter. 'Re-reading' the miracles in this light, they discovered their true uniqueness and formulated them in such a way as to express this post-Easter discovery.

Without his ambiguous signs, however, Jesus could not have raised the essential question concerning his person, and the Christian community could not have formulated the answer already contained in a veiled way in these signs. At the *general level*, there does not seem to be any reason to dispute Jesus' miracles. The miracle stories of the gospels are sufficiently 'solid' not to be classified as mere inventions. The so-called nature miracles may appear suspect to some, but there is little doubt among biblical scholars that Jesus performed healing miracles, and no doubt at all that his contemporaries considered him capable of curing certain diseases and cases of demonic possession.

As to the *material content* of the miracles: has there been a violation of the laws of nature, i.e., a 'miracle' as it is often understood nowadays? The question must remain unanswered, because it does not correspond to the perspective of antiquity in general and the evangelists in particular. Jesus' signs really revealed to them God's extraordinary power at work in him, but this does not necessarily mean that they discovered it in the extraordinariness of the event as such, where it would often be situated today. Again, their world view was not the same as ours. Nevertheless, we know Jesus' miracles only through their testimony. The true question, then, is not that of the material content of the miracles, but that of their meaning.

The fundamental originality of Jesus' miracles

Comparing the miracle accounts of the New Testament with the general phenomenon of miracle in the history of religions, we cannot start from the assumption that all statements about miracles outside the Bible are unhistorical (based on imagination and deceit), and that only the Old and New Testament accounts are based on facts. In other words, we cannot without further ado declare Jesus' miracles authentic and historical and deny the same qualities to others. We can hardly say of the miracles at Epidaurus that 'none of our readers will find in these cases anything but some purely natural phenomenon' (L. Monden), or that 'it can and should be affirmed that none of the "wonderful facts" of the hellenistic and rabbinic documentation presents a sufficient guarantee of authenticity that the characteristics of a single true miracle can be discerned in them' (L. Sabourin). We cannot limit God's activity to biblical miracles. If we claim to approach the biblical miracles with 'critical realism', we will also have to reckon with the possibility of miraculous phenomena in other cultural and religious realms.

It has also been pointed out that the connection between miracle and teaching is found throughout antiquity, and that therefore it cannot be presented as a distinctive feature of the gospel miracles. The fact, then, that Jesus performed miracles does not yet make him unique. The history of religions reports many miracles, including walking on the water and raising from the dead. The power to perform miracles might give Jesus some authority, but not unique authority. In fact, critical research has come up with such an impressive number of Jewish and Hellenistic parallels to particular biblical miracles that we cannot avoid the question whether we are dealing here with historical events of Jesus' life, or whether the miracle stories constitute a later faith-image of Christ which has been retrojected into the accounts of the life of the earthly Jesus.

But notwithstanding all parallels from religious history, Jesus occupies a unique place as an apocalyptic miracle-worker. He brings together two spiritual worlds which had never before been connected in this way: apocalyptic expectation of universal salvation, and realization in individual cases of present miraculous salvation.

The originality of Jesus' miracles does not so much consist in the fact that they are *miracles*, as in their being miracles *of Jesus*. Indeed, the unique element in the miracle stories of the gospels is not the marvellous event as such, but the person of Jesus who stands at the centre of the account. Their radical newness, compared with other miracles of the time, does not consist in their form, even if real differences from the miracles reported of Jesus' contemporaries can be observed. To the evangelists, the real difference consists in the fact that these miracles were performed *by Jesus*, the Son of God who inaugurated the kingdom. Their radical newness is *Jesus himself, dead and risen*.

The miracles: acts of liberation

Jesus' redemptive activity may be briefly characterized as 'liberation' from demonic powers, from disease, death and natural catastrophes, and even from famine.

Liberation of the poor

To the two disciples sent by John the Baptist Jesus said: 'Go and tell John what you hear and see: the blind receive their sight and the lame walk, lepers are cleansed and the deaf hear, and the dead are raised up, and the poor have good news preached to them' (Mt 11:4–5). What the prophets had promised is now being fulfilled (Isa 29:18–19; 35:5–6; 61:1). Even the dead are being raised to life. But even that is not the greatest miracle. The most important stands at the end: 'and the poor have good news preached to them'. The poor are the first beneficiaries of the proclamation and the inchoative realization of the kingdom.

Jesus did not just promulgate theories about liberation. He brought concrete salvation reaching the most fundamental needs of people. Jesus proclaimed the good news to the poor not only in words but also in mighty deeds, in healings and exorcisms. The latter indicated the end of Satan's rule. Explaining their significance, Jesus said: 'How can one enter a strong man's house and plunder his goods, unless he first binds the strong man? Then indeed he may plunder his house' (Mt 12:29). The exorcisms Jesus performed were signs that Jesus was binding the power, the stronghold of Satan and all evil powers and establishing God's rule among people. He was liberating the poor who were under the tyranny of evil. His miracles announced the dawning of God's rule when the poor would be liberated from their poverty.

> Gerd Theissen...sees the miracle stories in the oral tradition reflecting the preoccupation of the lower social classes with the limitations imposed on their lifestyle. The miracle stories describe the confidence that the enslaving powers of the old order, the hostile realities of the world, have been broken. The lower classes are then freed to claim a new life.[9]

> The narrative tells a marvelous breakthrough in the struggle against oppressive restrictions of human life. Exorcisms tell the overthrow of arbitrary, violent and total oppression, controversy miracles the exposé of violent moral and social restriction, provision stories a break in oppression of want and human resignation to it and demand stories the initiative that breaks out of physical and psychological impotence.[10]

Jesus' miracles are in the first place a sign of the dawning of the *eschaton*, the kingdom of God in our world of misery and injustice, and its immediate radiation on people, in particular, in favour of the poor of all kinds.

This message of salvation is addressed first of all to the poorest, to those who cannot wait because their needs concern their very lives. If people are in a desperate situation, they ask for a 'miracle', and nobody has the right to disapprove of this request. Paralytics and lepers lived in such a situation: no medical hope, no social security to assure them a minimum of livelihood. Moreover, they were in total religious insecurity because they were considered sinners. Physically, morally, socially, they were outcasts. Jesus came to restore their taste of life.

This is the sign of the kingdom: it concerns first of all those who are abandoned to their fate, who cannot defend their rights, who have no rights (the 'little ones' or 'the least of my brethren' in Mt 18:6, 10, 14; 25:40, 45). And this is the most authentic signature of God in Jesus' life: in him God takes up the cause of the poor (Mt 5:3; 11:5). Hence Jesus' fury against a religious system that (with the best of intentions!) made it impossible for the poor to live the good news. Jesus' healings on the sabbath are a sign that the sole criterion for a religious law is that it is at the service of man; liberation and not enslavement! 'The sabbath was made for man, not man for the sabbath' (Mk 2:27). It was on a sabbath that Jesus said to 'a woman who had a spirit of infirmity' (Lk 13:11), 'Woman, you are freed (liberated) from your infirmity' (Lk 13:12). And while the ruler of the synagogue and his cronies were indignant because of this act of liberation performed on a sabbath (Lk 13:14), 'all the people (the masses) rejoiced at all the glorious things that were done by him' (Lk 13:17). Jesus' healings and exorcisms were mainly performed for outcasts or marginals. Here there appears a commitment and an involvement which is unknown in other miracle stories. It should be recognized how much Jesus wanted to challenge and change the order and criteria of existing society.

Salvation which starts from the elementary needs of people moves towards deeper liberation from sin, offered to everyone personally. This is the irruption in people's life of the unexpected, which opens up for them a new possibility of existence, and invites them to a life which makes them come out of their closed world of sin, law and death. Thus the miracles reported in the synoptic gospels provoke a movement much deeper, much more radical than just physical healing: they insist on the *conversion of being*. Through faith they call people to follow Jesus. And yet the fact should still be stressed that redemption for Jesus was much more than something merely internal, something infinitely greater than a theological proposition limited to the forgiveness of sins. The forgiveness of sins is a narrower, concentric circle within the wider reality of cosmic redemption, of the transformation of the world.

Liberation of humanity

This liberation goes beyond the individual. Miracles speak of hope. What the miracles do to individual people gives hope to all, as can be seen from the conclusion of the healing of the deaf-mute: 'He has done all things well; he even makes the deaf hear and the dumb speak' (Mk 7:37). Beyond physical suffering and death, the New Testament authors discover a much more dangerous alienation: hardness of heart, sin, and beyond them an adversary called Satan. The struggle with Satan occupies an essential place in the synoptics. This means that the alienation mentioned above is not only an individual alienation, but has a 'cosmic' dimension affecting the whole of humanity. The miracles of Jesus are part of a great multi-dimensional process of liberation from all forms of evil (cosmic, physical, psychic, social, religious) which Jesus comes to announce and realize. As features of this total liberation the miracles are saving events. The 'kingdom' achieves the total liberation from all forms of unfreedom (cosmic, social, personal) which constrain people. Jesus' miracles 'tell' us that the 'kingdom' is total salvation of the whole of humanity. The New Testament view of health embraces the whole person—physical health, but also religious-ethical life in accordance with God's will for humanity. In accordance with this total view of humanity, the final fulfilment is presented as a condition free from sickness and death (Rev 21:4), or, for that matter, whatever oppresses and burdens humanity.

God—and therefore Jesus—is on the side of the poor. This, however, does not set him against the rest of humanity. No, God shows his concern for the whole of humanity there where it is most threatened, in its poor and oppressed, in those who are forced to live in subhuman conditions. God's—Jesus'—and our struggle for the poor and the oppressed is ultimately a struggle for the survival of humanity and human values. This struggle will entail action against oppressive and dehumanizing structures and situations and those who represent and uphold them.

The miracles are signs that this liberation which is already at work among people is not simply *their* work. It is first of all the work of *God* in Jesus, the only one who can liberate humanity from hatred and death. People are to accept this *gift* of the Father (Lk 12:32), a gift which they cannot acquire by themselves but which, far from immobilizing or 'infantilizing' them, makes them *responsible for their destiny*.

The miracles point toward the collective future of humanity; beyond personal cases, the gospel healings are *preceding signs* of what the reconciled world, inaugurated by the resurrection, will be. This introduces a radical newness, a breakthrough into the closed world of death. In Jesus, creation finds accomplishment. But this accomplishment must become a reality *for all people*. Jesus' miracles announce this state of humanity where 'death shall be no more, neither shall there be mourning nor crying nor pain any more, for the former things have passed away' (Rev 21:4).

Jesus calls his disciples to be the signs of this accomplishment. The disciples received his powers to realize this salvation. In the accounts of Acts, the miracles performed by the apostles are like carbon copies of those performed by Jesus: they are worked by the same Spirit. For Paul, and progressively in the whole primitive Church, the 'charisms', the gifts of the Spirit for the edification of the Body of Christ, become more important than the 'miracles' (I Cor 12:27–28). The greatest of them all is love (I Cor 13).

This 'hierarchy of values' is an indication of how the miracles should be actualized. To raise the question of miracle today is perhaps for the Church to seek and posit *concrete signs* 'speaking' to today's world of a total liberation, personal as well as collective. What are the *loci* of the miracles today? They are as vast as the dimensions of humanity and the world: the domains of health, interpersonal relations, cultural, social, economic, and political realms. They may be called: respect for the person, human dignity, struggle for justice, freedom. In his miracles, Jesus used the language of his time, which is different from ours. We must therefore 'translate' it into our language. Now today's language of salvation expresses itself in terms of 'struggle' for justice, for dignity, true human relationships. We should seek in this language and in these realms the concrete realization of God's will for people today.

Ambiguous, just as they were in Jesus' time, the true signs today are those which constitute a *breakthrough into our closed world* in order to call humanity to a life of true and total freedom. This is a life of which human beings will never become absolute owners, but which they should receive as the Father's gift which moves them forward and makes them truly responsible for their future.

Different approaches to the miracles

The miracles occupy an important place in the gospels and the Acts of the Apostles. It is impossible to omit the miracle stories from the picture of Jesus presented by these documents.

The 'naive' approach

For centuries, the miracle stories have been favourite topics in preaching, catechetics, and Christian devotion. In these colourful stories, with their often vivid reactions of persons involved, the personality of Jesus is set in relief in an astonishing manner. Two features are highlighted: on the one hand, Jesus' immense mercy, his profound compassion and, on the other hand, Jesus' power, his sovereign authority over illness, death, nature. For those who approach the gospels 'naively', the miracle stories contribute to situate Jesus' personality both close to us because of his mercy, and close to God because of his authority and power. It should be noted here that purely human sentiments cannot possibly be considered the main point of Jesus' miracles.

The apologetic approach

The previous approach easily leads to a simplistic apologetic reasoning which was and still is very popular: Jesus performed miracles; therefore he must be the Son of God. Or, as stated by Cardinal Ottaviani in *Osservatore Romano*: 'The divine mission and nature of Christ are proved by the many and great miracles the Lord performed on earth'. But, e.g., Origen could accept the attribution of healings to Asclepius without conceding that those actions in any way supported claims to divinity.

Indeed, the apologetic approach poses a number of problems.

> From the time that Quadratus made apologetic use of the Gospel miracles in his *Apology to Hadrian* (*c.* A.D. 125) the interpretation of the miracles seems to have been inextricably bound up with the defense of the Christian faith. While the apologetic usefulness of the miracles has had the advantage of leading the best theological minds in the Church to study and comment on it, this constant apologetic coloring of the exegesis of the Gospel miracles has been a mixed blessing.[11]

In the gospels themselves we sense at times a certain distrust of miracles. Texts like Mt 7:22–23 and Mt 24:23–25 seem to suggest that miracles by themselves do not prove anything. In fact, the miracles are not primarily meant to prove, but to reveal and to explain. Moreover, Jesus did not claim to have a monopoly of miracle-working, even though—after and in the light of the resurrection—the evangelists make him appear unique (Mk 2:12; Mt 9:33: Jn 9:32). According to Mt 12:27 and Lk 11:19, he recognized other Jewish exorcists in his time.

Furthermore, Jesus' own attitude towards miracles is rather complex. On the one hand, he sees them as constituting a sign and a call (Mt 11:2–6, 20–24). On the other hand, Jesus tries to avoid too much publicity, and categorically refuses to perform the spectacular prodigies which Satan or people expect from him (see the temptation narrative, Mt 4:1–11; the refusal of a sign from heaven, Mt

12:38–40). And when he is asked to perform a miracle to confirm his claim that God is with him, Jesus again refuses categorically (Mk 8:11–13). The reactions of those who witnessed the miracles were likewise far from uniform. Thus, in the gospels themselves, a certain 'ambiguity' can be noted in the appreciation of the miracles. They do not contain a uniform, monolithic doctrine on the 'miracles of Jesus'. They caution us, therefore, against setting out on the road of an apologetic whereby the miracles would be 'proofs' of Jesus' divinity.

We must learn to understand Jesus' powerful deeds in the perspective of the cross. Paul (I Cor 1:2–4), Mark (Mk 15:39), Luke (Acts 4:8–20), and the other New Testament writings as well, do not try to prove Jesus' divinity from the miracles. They rather try to express the meaning of Jesus' miracles starting from the cross.

The critical approach

To many people today, the miracle stories seem incredible, and a certain repugnance is experienced against accepting that they really happened as they are told. For this repugnance there may be different reasons, of unequal value. Some may react by saying that today miracles are rare; for instance, there is David Hume's remark: 'It is strange...that such prodigious events never happen in our days!' If in his time Jesus cured so many people, why does he not cure me now? The mentality of others may be influenced by scientific rationalism, and they may find it hard to accept that God's action might interfere in the chain of causality in this world. Still others may stress that the gospel texts express a culture very different from ours; an ancient culture may 'produce' miracles stories just as a modern culture 'produces' novels. Finally, it must be taken into account that there is a 'history' of the gospel tradition, and a 'history' of the redaction or editing of the gospels. Therefore, many Christians today recognize their own thoughts in the words of a contemporary writer: 'I do believe, not because of the miracles, but notwithstanding the miracles!' Indeed, for many of our contemporaries, the miracles of Jesus are more an obstacle than a road to faith in Christ.

The possible consequences of this critical approach are the following. Firstly, as a kind of defensive reflex, some may be tempted to impose on themselves, or even on others, a 'naive' approach to the miracles, saying that they do not care about the critical doubt. If God is almighty, why question any of the miracles related in the gospels? Secondly, at the other end of the spectrum, critical doubt may lead to a radical rejection of the whole gospel tradition as worthless. How can a tradition be taken seriously which tells such incredible things as miracles about its founder?

But those who truly believe in Jesus and nevertheless refuse to disregard critical doubt because they want to be intellectually honest, are not without resources to 'save' the miracle stories. Either they may accept that the events which the miracle stories refer to did not really constitute 'miracles' in the strict sense. Instantaneous healings could be given a natural explanation, and so on. Or they may accept that the miracle stories, or at least some of them, do not refer to actual events, but constitute symbolic ways of making us understand the present actions of the risen Christ and the Spirit. To explain that the risen Christ introduces us to a life which even death cannot swallow up, Jesus would have been presented as raising Lazarus from the tomb. To make us understand that a baptized person has access to a deeper perception of the mystery of God, Jesus would have been presented as healing the man born blind, etc. This solution may be ingenious, but is it acceptable when it is applied to *all* miracle stories?

It is by no means intellectually honest and effective systematically to ignore critical doubt. The history of the Church (think, e.g., of the case of Galileo) shows this beyond any doubt. On the other hand, it is useful and necessary to *question the critical doubt*. It is all too easy to get rid of ancient texts on the simple ground that they tell us incredible things. One should also try to *explain why the texts are what they are, why miracle stories are presented the way they are*.

The collection of miracle stories, and the way in which they are inserted into the totality of the accounts concerning Jesus of Nazareth, have profoundly original aspects. At this point one has the right to question the critical doubt.

Would our texts be what they are if the first Christians had clothed in the form of miracle stories facts which were not at all miraculous in themselves? The fact that a miraculous feature is found in the texts should be given serious attention. This is done only when the significance of the miraculous element is studied in the context of the material in which it is found. Would the miracle stories be what they are if the first Christians had taken the initiative to translate a 'doctrine' on the risen Christ and the action of the Spirit into miracle stories? It is hard to explain the originality of the collection of miracle stories unless we admit that the texts reflect at least to some extent Jesus' own somewhat ambiguous attitude towards miracles. We can hardly escape the impression that if it had been only the faith of the early Christian community which shaped the miracle stories, the result would not have been what we read now in the gospels. This is confirmed by a reading of the apocryphal gospels, which contain miracle stories of a quite different kind.

The prophetic approach

The renewal of exegetical studies invites us to search for the meaning of the miracle stories by studying them in the totality of the gospel message. Jesus announced the coming of the kingdom of God. By his parables he gave us an idea of what the coming of the kingdom is like. In the Sermon on the Mount we have the great orientations of the life of the kingdom. Jesus also disclosed *his unique role* in the coming of the kingdom. He not only announced 'a kingdom to come', but also inaugurated it as 'a kingdom already here'.

In this perspective, the miracles of which we find the accounts in the gospels should be understood as 'announcements in act' of the coming and nearness of the kingdom. They are 'prophetic actions' performed by Jesus, which permit us to discern the 'face' of this kingdom, as well as Jesus' role in the coming of this kingdom. In the prophetic approach to the miracle stories, the reader's attention is not concerned in the first place with the 'material fact' of the miracle (what actually happened?), but rather with the *salvific and spiritual meaning* of what is narrated (what is here and now the action of Christ's Spirit announced by the miracle stories?).

The miracle stories confront us with the prophetic gestures of Jesus which, in a symbolic way, announce the action of the Spirit in the kingdom. In the kingdom life is stronger than death, people are not blind but have insight, people are not paralysed but on the march in the freedom of the Spirit, and true hunger and thirst are allayed.

In conclusion, we may say that confronting the critical doubt which almost necessarily accompanies our reading of the miracle stories leads us to the question: 'Who is this man?' Our answer to this question is not provoked by the miracle stories as such. It is brought about by the Easter message, 'He has risen, God has made him Christ and Lord'. If we believe this Easter message, then we will answer the question 'Who is this man?' by saying 'He is the Son of God in power according to the Spirit of holiness by his resurrection from the dead' (Rom 1:4).

If we accept the Easter message, then we believe that the announcement of the coming of the kingdom by Jesus has been confirmed by God himself. We believe that the Spirit of God is at work in the life of people. And the prophetic reading of the miracle stories may then help us to discern the action of the Spirit in our own lives. The miracle stories of the New Testament are not yet really true for us when what they *tell* us really happened in Jesus' time, but only when what they *proclaim* happens today.

Recent interdisciplinary approaches

In recent years the miracle stories have been studied against the background of discussions on structuralism, phenomenology, etc. In one such study, Gerd Theissen,[12] in a 'synchronic' effort, draws up an elaborate inventory of seven roles, thirty-three motifs, and six themes which are found in the New Testament miracle stories in order to list the variables. He maintains that no matter what these variables are, the structure of the 'field' of the stories remains the same. Situating humankind in the disputed realm between divine and demonic powers, the miracle stories function as symbolic events by which the human experience of limitation is transcended. In a 'diachronic' effort Theissen then lists the modifications and transformations of the form in order to show how the miracle stories are 'reproduced' in new literary contexts. Finally, Theissen deals with the social, religious-historical and existential functions of the miracle stories as symbolic acts, demonstrating the new insights which the sociology of knowledge can bring to form criticism of the miracle stories. He shows convincingly that in narrating a miracle story, the narrator merely actualizes any number of roles and motifs from a limited stock belonging to the miracle genre. As to the miracle stories' social function, it is especially worth noting here that while ancient sites of healing and oracle supported the established order, and sorcery and magic constitute an individualistic response to increasing social disintegration, the early Christian miracle stories make a claim for a new lifestyle.

Another important attempt at an interdisciplinary approach to the miracle stories is found in the work directed by Xavier Léon-Dufour.[13] The second part of this volume contains three chapters which exemplify the use of different methods of analysing a miracle story, pointing out the strengths and the weaknesses of each. The psychoanalytic method shows that a text has more than one meaning. The classical approach (i.e., form criticism, tradition criticism, redaction criticism) affirms the continuity of the written text and the underlying levels of tradition. Semiotic analyses demonstrate the need for active participation on the part of the reader to reach the depth of communication inherent in the story as communicative experience. Léon-Dufour's comprehensive overview dealing with the structure (based on G. Theissen), the production, and the function of miracle stories in antiquity (socio-economic and socio-cultural factors), and in Christianity, as well as their existential function, incorporates findings from sociology, structuralism and generative poetics to formulate a theological definition of miracle.

Several of the disciplines mentioned above will no doubt still further the study of the miracle stories. Personally, I expect most from the sociological approach.

2 The healing of a demoniac at the synagogue

Mark 1:21–28	*Luke 4:31–37*
21 And they went into Capernaum;	31 And he went down to Capernaum, a city of Galilee.
and immediately on the sabbath he entered the synagogue and taught.	And he was teaching them on the sabbath;
22 And they were astonished at his teaching, for he taught them as one who had authority, and not as the scribes.	32 and they were astonished at his teaching, for his word was with authority.
23 And immediately there was in their synagogue a man with an unclean spirit;	33 And in the synagogue there was a man who had the spirit of an unclean demon; and he cried out with a loud voice,
24 and he cried out,	
'What have you to do with us, Jesus of Nazareth? Have you come to destroy us? I know who you are, the Holy One of God.'	34 'Ah! What have you to do with us, Jesus of Nazareth? Have you come to destroy us? I know who you are, the Holy One of God.'
25 But Jesus rebuked him, saying, 'Be silent, and come out of him!'	35 But Jesus rebuked him, saying, 'Be silent, and come out of him!' And when the demon had thrown him down in the midst,
26 And the unclean spirit, convulsing him and crying with a loud voice, came out of him.	he came out of him, having done him no harm.
27 And they were all amazed, so that they questioned among themselves, saying, 'What is this? A new teaching! With authority he commands even the unclean spirits, and they obey him.'	36 And they were all amazed and said to one another, 'What is this word? For with authority and power he commands the unclean spirits, and they come out.'
28 And at once his fame spread everywhere throughout all the surrounding region of Galilee.	37 And reports of him went out into every place in the surrounding region.

Mark 1:21–28

The context

After the first summary of Jesus' activity (Mk 1:14–15), followed by the calling of the first four disciples (Mk 1:16–20). Mark emphatically presents the 'coming' of Jesus in Galilee and its impact on the proclamation of the gospel.[14]

The evangelist has linked the originally independent story of the healing of Peter's mother-in-law with the context, in particular with Mk 1:21–28, by placing the original introduction of the healing before Mk 1:21b–28, and connecting Mk 1:29 with that same passage by means of a new indication of situation, 'and immediately leaving the synagogue'. This editorial activity not only creates a narrative transition from one story to the other, but also diminishes the importance of the single account which, by its insertion into the gospel, becomes now just one episode in Jesus' life, and can no longer be considered a comprehensive report of Jesus' activity in Galilee.

By the reformulation of verse 29 Mark links the healing of the mother-in-law of Peter not only with Mk 1:21–28, but also with Mk 1:16–20, because he repeats the names of the disciples whose calling has been narrated in the latter pericope. The witnesses of the healing are thus reduced to the intimate circle of Jesus' disciples. The original account did not know this limitation, and possibly Mk 1:32–34 was originally the reaction of the 'whole city' to the miracle which happened in the 'house of Simon'. The whole account is presented in the form of a typical day of Jesus, and is therefore often called a 'day at Capernaum'.

But this 'day at Capernaum' leads to a following day in the whole of Galilee (Mk 1:35–45), and according to a number of scholars, Mk 1:21–45 constitutes a literary as well as a theological unity. This account may be divided into two phases: first, Jesus' stay at Capernaum (Mk 1:21–34), and second, Jesus' mission in Galilee (Mk 1:35–45). In both phases Simon and his companions, that is, the first four disciples, act as intermediaries (Mk 1:29–31 and Mk 1:35–38). Moreover, Mark's account is constructed according to an alternating pattern of particular scenes (a) and generalizing notes (b):

(a) Mk 1:21–27: In the synagogue of Capernaum, on a sabbath, Jesus teaches and expels an unclean spirit (imposition of silence).

(b) Mk 1:28: Jesus' fame spreads throughout the *whole of Galilee*.

(a) Mk 1:29–31: in Simon's house, Jesus heals the former's mother-in-law at the intervention of Simon, Andrew, James and John.

(b) Mk 1:32–34: At the door/gate, at the end of the sabbath, the *whole city* gathers around Jesus; healing and exorcism (imposition of silence).

(a) Mk 1:35–38: In the morning (leaving Capernaum), Jesus goes to a lonely place where Simon and his companions join him.

(b) Mk 1:39: Jesus proclaims the gospel and casts out demons *throughout all Galilee.*

(a) Mk 1:40–45: Jesus cleanses a leper who comes to him (imposition of silence). Then he withdraws to the countryside.

As such this composition has no equivalent in Matthew or Luke. Its progression is determined by a succession of indications of time and place, a closer study of which indicates that Mark's account at Capernaum is not limited to one day (the sabbath), but opens up into the whole of Galilee on the following day, i.e., the first day of a new week.

The transition from the first to the second phase of the account is found in Mk 1:32–34. If the two phases of the account are compared, the following parallels appear: firstly, the exorcism of an unclean spirit in the synagogue of Capernaum (Mk 1:21–27) is parallel with the cleansing of the leper in Galilee (Mk 1:40–45); secondly, there is the double intervention of Simon and his companions, in the house in Capernaum (Mk 1:29–31), and outside the city in a lonely place (Mk 1:35–38); finally, Jesus' fame spreads from Capernaum to the surrounding region (Mk 1:28), as a prelude to his actual activity in the whole of Galilee.

The two healings found at the extremities of this composition constitute close parallels.[15] In fact, these two accounts have a formally identical structure:

(1) situation: the man and his unclean condition (Mk 1:23 and 40).
(2) dialogue with Jesus (Mk 1:24–25 and 40–41).
(3) Jesus' intervention and cure (with repetition of the same verbs; Mk 1:25–26 and 41–42).
(4) severe expression of Jesus ('rebuked': Mk 1:25; 'sternly charged': Mk 1:43).
(5) imposition of silence (Mk 1:25 and 44).
(6) consequence of the episode ('so that...': Mk 1:27 and 45).

One should also note the following 'inclusion' or framing repetition between Mk 1:21 and Mk 1:45:

Mk 1:21 —And they went into Capernaum
        —and entered the synagogue
        —Jesus was teaching

Mk 1:45 —He could no longer enter
        —(openly) into a town
        —Jesus was out in the country

A similar 'inclusion' frames the following literary unit in Mk 2:1 and 3:1.[16]

The only passage in Mk 1:21–45 which has no parallel is Mk 1:32–34 which seems to constitute the centre of the composition and the pivot of a concentric composition. In this central pericope (Mk 1:32–34), the spatial indication 'about the door' (Mk 1:32) marks the transition from the city of Capernaum with its synagogue and the house of Simon (Mk 1:21–31) to the rest of Galilee with its towns and lonely places (Mk 1:35–45). Similarly, the temporal indication 'that evening, at sundown' (Mk 1:32) marks the end of the day spent at Capernaum (Mk 1:21–31) and inaugurates the next day open to the whole of Galilee, to which Jesus is going to extend his activity from early morning onwards (Mk 1:35–45). In this manner, Mk 1:32–34 really widens the spatial and temporal framework in which the historical 'coming' of Jesus is situated. Moreover, Mk 1:32–34 also seems to explain the impositions of silence which are found in Mk 1:21–27 and 1:40–45: 'he would not permit the demons to speak, because they knew him' (Mk 1:34). Thus as regards both the progression of the account and the parallels discovered, Mk 1:32–34 seems to constitute the centre of intelligibility of the whole text on the literary as well as the theological plane.[17]

A comparison with the Matthean sequence confirms that Mk 1:29–31 was not originally connected with the preceding pericope. Matthew ignores the episode at the synagogue. On the other hand, there are curious analogies: Mk 1:21 speaks of entering Capernaum, like Mt 4:14, 'and leaving Nazareth he went and dwelt in Capernaum', and Mk 1:22 summarizes the effect produced by Jesus in terms almost identical with Mt 7:28–29.

Matthew 7	*Mark 1*
28 And when Jesus finished these sayings,	22 And
the crowds *were astonished*	they *were astonished*
at his teaching,	*at his teaching,*
29 *for he taught them*	*for he taught them*
as one who had authority,	*as one who had authority,*
and not as their *scribes.*	*and not as* the *scribes.*

The two traditions (Matthew and Mark/Luke) agree in connecting Jesus' teaching and his deeds; the motif of the people's admiration is specified by Mark/Luke at the end of the account of the healing in the synagogue:

Mark 1:27	Luke 4:36
What is this?	What is this word?
A new teaching!	
With authority	For with authority
he commands	and power he commands
even the unclean spirits,	the unclean spirits,
and they obey him.	and they come out.

Similarly Matthew ends the Sermon on the Mount (Mt 5:1–7:29) by referring to the admiration of the crowds because of Jesus' teaching (Mt 7:28–29). This is followed by the miracle accounts which we are studying (Mt 8:1–17).

It may be said, therefore, that the connection between the accounts of the exorcism in the synagogue (Mk 1:21–28) and the healing of Peter's mother-in-law (Mk 1:29–31) is not original and does not correspond to a historical sequence. The 'day at Capernaum' is a theological composition. The fact that the accounts were not connected in the tradition makes their present connection in the Marcan redaction even more important. Indeed, in his present redaction Mark connects Mk 1:29–31 not only with the episode in the synagogue (Mk 1:21–28), but also with the calling of the first disciples (Mk 1:16–20). Again, the calling of the first disciples cannot be separated from the first preaching in Galilee (Mk 1:14–15, 'preaching the gospel'; 'believe in the gospel'), and finally the title verse of Mark, 'The beginning of the gospel of Jesus Christ, the Son of God' (Mk 1:1). *Euangelion*, 'gospel', means the preaching *of* Jesus as well as the preaching *about* Jesus Christ. The miracle stories of this section have to be seen in this Christological perspective, and are for Mark part of the unfolding of the 'gospel'. In his gospel Jesus is no longer just a miracle-worker, but 'Jesus Christ, the Son of God' (Mk 1:1), whose miracles are an integral part of his message. The insertion of Mk 1:29–31 in the present context establishes a close connection with the statement, 'he taught them as one who had authority' (Mk 1:22). A close relationship between word and deed is thereby expressed as well as an original understanding of Jesus' miracles.

It was said above that the 'day of Capernaum' is a theological composition. Does this mean that all the units contained in it originally only existed separately? It seems that the healing of Peter's mother-in-law was connected at a very early stage with the account of the healings performed in the evening (Mk 1:32–34). The agreement with Matthew, who presents the same sequence, is the first indication for this early connection: a partial agreement within a large disagreement. Moreover, the text contains two expressions which are relatively rare in Mark: 'all who were sick' (*pantas tous kakōs echontas*, only here and in Mk 2:17; 6:55), and 'demoniacs' (*daimonizomenous*, only here and in Mk 5:15–18). Probably Mark received Mk 1:29–31 and 1:32–34 already combined by the tradition. He inserted this grouping into its present context by means of the initial seam, 'and immediately he left the synagogue' (Mk 1:29), and by the theological finale on the messianic secret, 'and he would not permit the demons to speak, because they knew him' (Mk 1:34). The literary structure of Mk 1:21–45 is then as follows:

(***) And they went into Capernaum (= 1:21a) ... on the sabbath ...

A: *Mk 1:22–27*
And they were *astonished* at his *teaching*
for he taught them as one who had *authority*, ...
And immediately there was in their synagogue
a man with an UNCLEAN spirit; and he cried out,
'What have you to do with us, Jesus of Nazareth? ...
I know who you are, the HOLY One of God.'
But Jesus **rebuked** him, saying,
'Be silent, and *come out of him*!'
And the UNCLEAN spirit ... *came out of him*.
And they were all amazed,
SO THAT THEY questioned among themselves, ...
'What is this? A new *teaching*!
With *authority* he commands even the UNCLEAN spirits,
and they obey him.'

  B: *Mk 1:28*
And at once his fame spread (*kai exēlthen*) everywhere
throughout **all** the surrounding region **of Galilee**.

  C: *Mk 1:29–31*
And immediately he/they left (*ex-elthontes*) the synagogue, and entered (*ēlthon*) the house
of SIMON and Andrew, WITH James and John.
Now SIMON's mother-in-law lay sick with a fever,
and immediately *they told him* of her.
and he came (*pros-elthōn*) and took her by the hand
and lifted her up,
and the fever left her; and she served them.

D: *Centre: Mk 1:32-34*
That evening, at sundown, they brought to him
all who were *sick* or *possessed with demons*.
And THE WHOLE CITY was gathered together ABOUT THE DOOR.
And he healed many who were *sick* with various diseases,
and cast out many *demons*;
and he would not permit the *demons* to speak,
because they knew him.

C': *Mk 1:35–38*
And in the morning, a great while before day,
he rose and went out (*ex-ēlthen kai ap-ēlthen*)
to a lonely place, and there he prayed.
And SIMON and those who were WITH him pursued him,
and they found him and *said to him*,
'Every one is searching for you.'
And he said to them, 'Let us go on to the next towns,
that I may preach there also;
for that is why I came out (*ex-ēlthen*).'

B': *Mk 1:39*
And he went (*kai ēlthen*) throughout **all Galilee**,
preaching in their synagogues and casting out *demons*.

A': *Mk 1:40–45*
And a leper *came to him* beseeching him,
and kneeling said to him,
'If *you will*, you can make me CLEAN.'
Moved with pity, he stretched out his hand and touched him,
and said to him, '*I will*, be CLEAN.'
And immediately the leprosy left him,
and he was made CLEAN.
And he **sternly charged** him,
and sent him away at once,
and said to him, 'See that you say nothing to any one;
but go, show yourself to the priest,
and offer for your CLEANSING what Moses commanded,
for a proof to the people.'
But he went out and began to talk freely about it,
and to spread the news,
SO THAT JESUS could no longer openly enter a town,
but he was out in the country;
and people *came to him* from every quarter.

(***) And when he returned to Capernaum (= 2:1a) ... a paralytic ...

The pericope proper

It is clear that Mark presents 1:21–28 as a self-contained pericope. This appears from the single localization in the synagogue of Capernaum and from the redactional connection of verse 27c, 'with authority he commands even the unclean spirits', with verse 22, especially, 'for he taught them as one who had authority', and finally, the twofold use of the formula-like 'and immediately' within the same pericope, thus indicating only two 'acts', as in Mk 1:29, 30.[18]

Mark's choice of Mk 1:21–28 as the first miracle to be narrated in his gospel indicates that the whole of Jesus' ministry is going to be a confrontation with the powers of evil. But Mark does not intend merely to relate past events of Jesus' life; he affirms that what Jesus was for people during his earthly ministry, he is also for the evangelist's contemporaries and for today.[19]

> **Verse 21:** And they went into Capernaum; and immediately on the sabbath he entered the synagogue and taught.

This verse introduces the encounter. On the sabbath, Jesus teaches in the synagogue; except for this information, the account is narrated without indication of time and place. Verse 21a, 'and they went into Capernaum', is probably traditional. But since it does not fit well in the present pericope, it may originally have been found in another place, namely the introduction to the healing of Peter's mother-in-law, where it connects easily with the plural 'they entered' (rather than 'he entered', as in RSV, JB, NAB, but correctly in NEB): 'And they went to Capernaum and entered ... '. When Mark composed the 'day at Capernaum', he placed the phrase at the very beginning, so that Mk 1:21a functions now as the main introduction to Mk 1:21–34, followed now by the two miracle stories, Mk 1:21b–28 and 1:29–31.

Verse 21b situates the whole story in the synagogue, thus connecting the two 'acts' each introduced by 'and immediately' (Mk 1:21b and 23a). Except for this 'immediately' which may be redactional and serves as the transition from 'and they went into Capernaum', which is now placed in front, verse 21b is pre-Marcan tradition. That Jesus worked on the sabbath in the Galilean synagogues is a solid traditional datum, and an analysis of verses 21b–22 shows that the present location is likewise traditional. Only *edidasken*, 'he taught', could make one suspect that verse 21b is redactional, but this is not as strong as the possibility, or rather the necessity that verse 21b stood in the pre-Marcan tradition as the introduction to the exorcism, which cannot have started with verse 23. However, on the basis of a comparison of Mk 1:21–22 and Mk

11:15–18, where *edidasken*, 'he taught', in Mk 11:17 is clearly redactional, and the conviction that Mark wanted to present the 'day at Capernaum' and the 'day at Jerusalem' in the same way, some scholars attribute 'immediately' and 'he taught' to the Marcan redaction.

> **Verse 22:** And they were astonished at his teaching, for he taught them as one who had authority, and not as the scribes.

The unidentified hearers 'were astonished'. *Ekplēsesthai* is used five times in Mark. In Mk 6:2; 7:37; 10:26 the verb is possibly, and in Mk 11:18 certainly, redactional. The formulation of Mk 11:18, 'all the multitude was astonished at his teaching', suggests that Mk 1:22a too is redactional. This is further supported by the fact that *didachē*, 'teaching' (Mk 1:22, 27; 4:2; 11:18; 12:38) is always redactional in Mark, and, except for Mk 1:27, always referred to as '*his* teaching' (*didachē autou*).

Literally, verse 22b begins with the periphrastic 'for he was teaching'. A study of the Marcan vocabulary shows that verse 22b may have been composed with an eye to Mk 2:10, 'But that you may know *that the Son of man has authority ...*' . The scribes are Jesus' main opponents and appear for the first time where the *exousia*, 'power, authority', of the Son of man is discussed. As a whole, verse 22 is to be considered redactional.

> **Verse 23:** And immediately there was in their synagogue a man with an unclean spirit;

In the present context the exorcism begins with verse 23 since, by the insertion of verse 22, verse 21b is developed into an 'act' of its own. Verse 23 is again introduced by the formula-like 'and immediately'. Some feel that 'immediately' can also fit after verse 21b, and say that it may therefore be traditional. But others think that it is redactional since it constitutes a link between the teaching in the synagogue and the exorcism of the unclean spirit. If verse 21b was the original introduction of the account, the mention of 'synagogue' in verse 23 was made necessary by the insertion of verse 22. Mk 3:1a and b offers an interesting parallel: 'Again he entered the synagogue' (1a), 'and a man was there ... ' (1b). Mk 3:1b immediately follows 3:1a; the indication of place in 1b consists simply of the adverb 'there'. Mk 1:21b, however, is separated from Mk 1:23a by verse 22, which forces Mark clearly to repeat the place, 'in the synagogue', and to establish a link with the audience of verse 22 by adding 'their'. It seems, therefore, that instead of 'their synagogue', the original account may simply have had 'there'. The possessive *'their* synagogue' anticipates the 'chorus' of the concluding verse who function as witnesses of the miracle.

Verse 23 contains a number of Semitizing features which may have originated in a Hellenistic-Jewish milieu. The expression 'a man with an unclean spirit' is reminiscent of Mk 5:2, 'there met him out of the tombs a man with an unclean spirit'. Like Mk 7:24–30 and 9:14–29, Mk 5:1–20 has many points of contact in vocabulary and topic with Mk 1:23–27. Jesus' opponent is pointedly mentioned at the end of the verse: an unclean spirit. The hearers' or readers' attention is called to the development of this opposition. Except for 'immediately' and 'their synagogue' there are no signs of Marcan intervention in verse 23.

Verse 24: and he cried out, 'What have you to do with us, Jesus of Nazareth? Have you come to destroy us? I know who you are, the Holy One of God.'

The unclean spirit cried out through the possessed man. The verb *anakrazein*, 'to cry out', occurs also in Mk 6:49 where it describes the reaction of the disciples when they see someone walking on the water whom they think to be a ghost. The cry of the demon consists of three parts: a defensive gesture and a 'confession' frame the central piece which speaks of Jesus' role, his coming in the sight of the unclean spirits. The plural 'us' refers to the fact that as a whole they are threatened with annihilation. Jesus' coming from God, and in his place, means the decisive annihilation of everything unclean in the present hour. The statement about the comprehensive threat to the demons enhances the image of the exorcist, who is the Holy One of God.

The spirit flings a defence formula at Jesus, 'What have you to do with us?' This defensive question has an exact parallel in Mk 5:7. Such formula often contains the mention of a name, here 'Jesus of Nazareth'. A perusal of the Old Testament occurrences of the formula shows that the text has been formulated with the help of I Kgs 17:18, 'What have you against me, O man of God? You have come to me to bring my sin to remembrance, and to cause the death of my son'. The phrase 'man of God' is replaced by 'Jesus of Nazareth', but is again taken up in a slightly different form at the end of the verse in the predicate 'the Holy One of God' which is patterned after Judg 13:7; 16:17. This is combined with a reference to Jesus' menacing 'coming' and the recognition formula, 'I know who you are'. The clause 'have you come to destroy us?'

does not refer simply to the coming of Jesus from Nazareth to the synagogue of Capernaum, but describes Jesus' coming to earth as a heavenly mission to destroy the demons, and thus reflects the cosmic scope of the struggle. Here the loftiness of Jesus' person is seen not as end in itself, but in its significance for the historical struggle in which he is involved.[20]

The hostility between Jesus and the demons is accentuated by Jesus' 'destroying', to be compared with 'tormenting' in Mk 5:7, and by the opening statement, 'What have you to do with us?' The dramatic shift from the plural 'us' to the singular 'I know' is striking; as is the fact that after this overt statement of Jesus' name and origin the gospel will still speak of the secret (mystery) of his person. This may indicate one of the special concerns of the account.

It is not excluded that the rare phrase 'Holy One of God' is an allusion to Jesus as the bearer of the 'Holy Spirit' (Mk 1:8) as against the 'unclean spirit' (Mk 1:23, 26–27). Such a contrast between two kinds of 'spirit' is explicit in Mk 3:29–30.

While some scholars think that verse 24 shows no certain signs of Marcan redaction (R. Pesch), others think that the verse can be attributed to the evangelist, on the grounds that the formulation of Mk 1:24 and 5:7 is too uniform to be attributed to the tradition, and that the formulation of the account is influenced by I Kgs 17:18–24 as well as the Marcan reinterpretation of the original exorcism story (P. Guillemette).

Verse 25: But Jesus rebuked him, saying, 'Be silent, and come out of him!'

For the first time Jesus is here explicitly mentioned as subject. The verb *epitimaō*, 'to rebuke', is used for the reprimand of demons or demonic powers in Mk 3:12; 4:39; 8:32f.; 9:25; compare Mk 10:13, 48. The first four instances are found in redactional contexts, but the verb does belong to the traditional language of exorcisms. This allows us to attribute *epitimaō* in Mk 1:25 and 9:25 to the tradition. It is one of the principal verbs used with *Iēsous* in Mark. *Epetimēsen* should not simply be understood as a reproach, but rather as a command by which the demon as representative of the forces of evil is defeated. This explains the reaction of the demon in Mk 1:24, expressing not merely that *he* is defeated (therefore not: 'have you come to destroy *me*?'), but that the cosmic struggle between God and the demonic powers is going to end in total defeat (therefore: 'have you come to destroy *us*?').[21] Jesus' threat, which corresponds to the traditional way of narrating a miracle account, obtains new weight through

Jesus' presentation as the Holy One of God. In the Septuagint *epitimaō* is a technical term for the powerful divine word of rebuke and threat, e.g., Zech 3:2, 'The Lord rebuke you, O Satan! The Lord who has chosen Jerusalem rebuke you!' The Holy One of God performs the function of God; in his activity God's rule—and thereby the destruction of the rule of Satan—dawns.

Verse 25 should be read as *two* commands separated by 'and': 'Be still' and 'Come out of him'. The first command refers back to the defensive statement of the demon, while the second, the harsh imposition of silence, belongs to the ritual of this kind of account (compare Mk 4:39).

As a whole verse 25 gives a very traditional impression, but the expression 'be silent' may be by the hand of the evangelist.

> **Verse 26:** And the unclean spirit, convulsing him and crying with a loud voice, came out of him.

Verse 26 describes the execution of Jesus' command and the departure of the unclean spirit. To the command 'Come out of him' corresponds the mention of the departure, 'he came out of him'. But first the verse mentions the last signs of the resistance which is broken by the mere word of Jesus: the unclean spirit shakes the sick person and utters a loud cry. The verb *sparassein*, 'to convulse', occurs also in the healing of the epileptic boy (Mk 9:20, 26, together with *krazein*, 'to cry out'). The phrase 'with a loud cry' characterizes the demonic utterance (cf. Mk 5:7 and Lk 8:28). The loud cry of the departing demon suggests the intensity of the conflict and the extent of the victory. Except for Acts 19:12, the same verb, *exerchomai*, 'to come out' or 'to go out', is used in all exorcism stories to describe the departure of demons or evil spirits, and, except for Mk 7:29, 30 and Lk 4:41, the verb is always in the aorist tense. Practically all scholars agree that the whole of verse 26 belongs to the pre-Marcan tradition.

> **Verse 27:** And they were all amazed, so they questioned among themselves, saying, 'What is this? A new teaching! With authority he commands even the unclean spirits, and they obey him.'

Verse 27a, 'and they were all amazed', belongs to the typical style of traditional miracle stories. The verb *thambeisthai*, 'to be amazed', however, is used in Mark alone (Mk 1:27; 10:24, 32). The term also serves to indicate the accreditation of the miracle by the spectators.

Verse 27b, 'so that they questioned among themselves', is considered traditional by some. Others, however, point out that the construction of the Greek text (*hōste* with infinitive) is Marcan, and that the verb *suzētein*, 'to question', is always used in redactional contexts in the rest of the gospel (Mk 8:11; 9:10, 14, 16; 12:28).

But almost everybody agrees that verse 27c, 'a new teaching with authority', was inserted by the evangelist. In the Greek text these words belong together, although this no longer appears so in the RSV (different in JB and NAB). In the light of Mk 1:22 and other similar cases, e.g., Mk 4:41, it can hardly be doubted that 'teaching' and 'with authority' belong together.

Is the rest of the crowd's reaction ancient tradition? If 'a new teaching with authority' is omitted, the question 'what is this?' loses its meaning. Therefore, several exegetes attribute the question to Mark. But on the grounds of a comparison with the very similar pericope, Mk 4:35–41, and particularly by analogy with Mk 4:41, Pesch reckons with the possibility of an original '*who* is this?', which Mark changed because of the redactional insertion of 'a new teaching with authority'. But some scholars object that it is improbable that Mark changed 'Who is this?' into 'What is this?' because the first part of the gospel (Mk 1:14–8:26) is concerned with the person of Jesus and attempts to answer the question 'Who is Jesus?'

The expression 'unclean spirits' picks up the key word of the introduction (verse 23), but because of verse 24 it is here used in the plural. Those who consider verse 24 redactional say, therefore, that originally verse 27 mentioned only one spirit, but the insertion of verse 24 forced Mark to speak of 'spirits' and to put the verb 'obey' in the plural. *Epitassein*, 'to command', occurs also in Mk 6:27, 39 and in an exorcism, Mk 9:25. *Hupakouein*, 'to obey', occurs in Mark only here and in the closely related Mk 4:41. The pre-Marcan text of verse 27 will then have been:

> Who is this?/What is this?
> He commands even unclean spirits/an unclean spirit,
> and they obey him/he obeys him.

The story could end here. The epiphany of 'the Holy One of God' has taken place. That the following 'chorus-ending' (in German: *Chorschluss*) does not as in other miracle stories (see Mk 2:12) constitute an acclamation but poses a question may betray the missionary interest of the account (together with verse 24?). By its question the 'chorus-ending' alters the amazement of verse 27a. The exorcism raises the question concerning the person of the exorcist. The answer to this question, however, has already been given by the unclean spirit: Jesus is the Holy One of God.

Verse 28: And at once his fame spread everywhere throughout all the surrounding region of Galilee.

The adverbs 'at once' and 'everywhere' emphasize the fact that 'his fame spread'. The verb *exerchomai*, 'to spread', literally, 'to go out', occurs frequently in Mark, but only here in combination with *akoē*, 'fame'. The adjective 'all' or 'whole' (*holos*) is also found in a good number of instances, some of which are redactional. 'Everywhere' (*pantachou*) and 'surrounding region' (*perichōros*) occur only here in Mark (but see *pantachou* in the 'longer ending' of Mark, Mk 16:20). The fact that 'of Galilee' is so clumsily added by the redactor, according to Pesch, confirms the traditional character of the rest of the verse. The exorcism which occurred in a synagogue thus concludes with a progress report on the expanding fame of the miracle-worker.

Verse 28 relates the success of the miracle-worker. The question concerning his person is spread throughout the surrounding region. The missionary purpose of the account which probably belonged to a cycle of miracle stories appears again: the news concerning Jesus should be spread, the question concerning Jesus should be raised everywhere and should lead to confessing him as the Holy One of God. The hyperbolic conclusion 'everywhere throughout all the surrounding region' underlines the propagandistic tendency of the account.

Besides Mk 1:21a, which some consider the original introduction to Mk 1:29–31, the following can be identified as pre-Marcan tradition (seriously disputed phrases or clauses are bracketed):

21b And on the sabbath he entered the synagogue and taught.
23a And (immediately) there was in their synagogue a man with an
    unclean spirit,
  b and he cried out,
(24a saying, 'What have you to do with me, Jesus of Nazareth?
  b Have you come to destroy us?
  c I know who you are, the Holy One of God.')
25a And Jesus rebuked him, saying,
  b ('Be silent,' and) 'come out of him!'
26a And the unclean spirit, convulsing him,
  b and crying with a loud voice, came out of him.
27a And they were amazed,
 (b so that they questioned among themselves,)
  c saying, 'Who is this? (What is this?)
  d He commands even the unclean spirits,
  e and they obey him.'
(28a And at once his fame spread everywhere
  b throughout all the surrounding region.)

The pericope corresponds to the following schema:
(1) Encounter in the synagogue (verses 21b, 23a).
(2) Defensive formula of the demon (verses 23b–24).
(3) Threat (verse 25a).
(4) Imposition of silence (verse 25b).
(5) Order to leave (verse 25b).
(6) Final reaction and exit of demon (verse 26).
(7) Amazement of the crowd (verse 27a).
(8) 'Chorus-ending' (verse 27b–e).
(9) Success of the miracle-worker (verse 28).

The meaning of the original account

The numerous linguistic and topical parallels with the other four Marcan exorcism stories confirm that Mk 1:21–28 is a genuine exorcism story. As regards the schema of the ancient miracle stories, two features call for special attention: firstly, the formulation of the unclean spirit's defence which becomes a 'confession', and secondly, the missionary-minded conclusion of the account, especially the 'chorus'. Here we seem to be in touch with the specifically Christian elements of the account; here too should be found the motives which led to the origin and the spread of the story. The presentation of Jesus as 'the Holy One of God' in verse 24, and the reply to the astonished question of verse 27a with a statement about Jesus in verse 27b are not accretions on a later level of tradition, between the original account and the Marcan redaction (against Schille), but simply the motifs of the very first account.

The chorus-ending of a miracle story may have various functions. It is obvious that its narrative goal may be the question concerning the person of the miracle-worker, since the chorus-ending is presented in the form of a question. But the possibility should always be left open that the account may already have answered the question. And it may be the specific feature of this Christian exorcism story that it does exactly that.

The narrator's aim will best be arrived at by trying to understand the story starting from the chorus-ending. Here the listeners/readers should ask themselves: 'Who is this?' The account wants to direct our attention to Jesus. As a whole it has the character of a reference, since what is stressed is not what is actually told but what is brought about in the listeners/readers. The 'yield'. of the account, its reference- and demonstration-effect, is summed up in the continuation of the chorus: 'he commands the unclean spirits, and they obey him'. This exorcist is lord over the unclean spirits. He rules over them and expels them by a mere word. But the obedience of the unclean spirits also shows that they know Jesus as one who is superior to them. Since they obey his command (and since they have 'supernatural' knowledge) their involuntary 'confession' deserves the confidence of the hearers who ask 'Who is this?' The narrator thus refers the hearers for an answer to their question to the cry of the unclean spirit(s) in verse 24.

That this confession is presented in the form of a defensive gesture by unclean spirits, as befits an exorcism, gives it authenticity. The narrator has skilfully used the schema of the narration for his special concern.

To the question 'Who is this?' (verse 27) corresponds, according to the purpose of the narrator, 'I know who you are' (verse 24). Verse 24 contains the key to the understanding of the account: Jesus is presented as 'the Holy One of God'. 'The Holy One of God' may correspond to '(Jesus) the Nazarene' (RSV: of Nazareth) by way of a pun on 'Nazirite' and 'Nazarene'. Even without presupposing an Aramaic substratum, such a pun may be supported even in Greek by the interchange of 'Nazirite of God' and 'holy one of God' in the Septuagint versions of Judg 13:7 A and B and 16:17 A and B. The title 'the Holy One of God' could be the early Christian community's explanation of the name 'Nazarene' (= man of Nazareth). This explanation by the community will have preceded the formulation of the account.

I Kgs 17:18 served as the basis and, by way of the defensive gesture, as an appropriate stylistic feature for an exorcism which allowed the introduction of the community's explanation of Jesus' origin. The reference to I Kgs 17:18 may have been because the stories of Elijah, the Old Testament charismatic man of God to whom this text refers, played an important role in early Christian miracle tradition. If 'the Holy One of God' was considered by the narrator as a description of Jesus, the man of God, and therefore as his designation as a charismatic figure, then the quotation and the formulation of the unclean spirit's words are easily explained. This can be supported by a reference to Jer 1:5 and especially II Kgs 4:9 where Elijah is called a 'holy man of God'.

It should also be noted that Jesus is referred to as *the* Holy One of God. Jesus is presented as the eschatological prophet and charismatic who supersedes the men of God in the Old Testament (as well as the Hellenistic 'divine men'?), and whose name already betrays his nature. As man of God, Jesus threatens the unclean spirits (plural in verses 24 and 27) with total annihilation. He commands them and they obey him. The superiority of Jesus over other miracle-workers is especially expressed in bringing together Jesus' name and his nature. The name by which the unclean spirit addresses

Jesus betrays his nature and thereby the power of the one addressed: he is the Holy One of God.

The healing of the Gerasene demoniac (Mk 5:1–20) and especially Mk 5:7 shows that the description of Jesus by demonic speech in this first exorcism story can still be enhanced. Nevertheless, in Mk 1:21b, 23ff., the story gives the combination of the name 'Jesus' with the title 'the Holy One of God', as well as the statement about Jesus' 'coming', its unique missionary power. To this and the narrator's certainty of Jesus' undoubtedly unusual exorcistic activity, the story owes its origin.

The place of origin should be sought in the Hellenistic-Jewish mission of the early Church. By means of such a story the missionaries could make maximum use of their knowledge of Jesus' exorcistic activity and show his superiority to be the superiority of the 'Holy One of God'.

By changing the question 'Who is this?' into 'What is this?' Mark removed the point of the original exorcism story. What did he make of this miracle story?

The meaning of the exorcism on the level of the Marcan redaction

Mark has adapted the story and inserted it in a precise context in his gospel. The story has therefore undergone a considerable amount of re-interpretation.

At the beginning of his gospel the evangelist presents a 'day' of Jesus' activity in Capernaum, a day in which Jesus heals many sick people and expels many demons. Mark thus makes the exorcism in the synagogue an 'example' of Jesus' works. As such, the exorcism is 'historicized' in the framework of the gospel. This is done by means of its location ('in Capernaum', and by placing verse 21a in front of the pericope) and by its vague yet sufficient temporal fixation, i.e., on the same day that Peter's mother-in-law was cured in Capernaum. The exorcism is transferred from its unlocalized and timeless sphere (except for the mention of the sabbath and the synagogue) in the framework of Mark's gospel, which attempts to give a geographical-chronological sketch of Jesus' activity. The character of the exorcism is thereby changed: it now occupies a precise position in Mark's total presentation of Jesus' activity. In Mark's gospel this exorcism story now becomes *the first miracle of Jesus*. That Mark chooses an exorcism as the first miracle corresponds to the role which the exorcistic activity of Jesus occupies in his gospel (Mk 1:34; 3:11f.; 3:22–30; 5:1–20: 7:24–30; 9:14–29; compare also Mk 6:7, 13; 9:38–40).

Granted that Mark intends to illustrate Jesus' proclamation of the dawning of the kingdom of God (Mk 1:14–15)—which is preceded by Jesus' confrontation with the devil (Mk 1:12–13)—it is still possible to ask whether Mark had a particular reason for choosing *this* particular exorcism rather than another for the beginning of his gospel. Nazareth is mentioned in this gospel only in Mk 1:9, 'In those days Jesus came from Nazareth ...'. Here and only here did Mark find the combination of Jesus' *coming* from *Nazareth*. These terms are digested in the words of the unclean spirit (verse 24) which, by way of a pun, allude to Jesus' origin from Nazareth and interpret his coming as a comprehensive threat to the demonic world. The comprehensive claim which is here expressed in Jesus' activity made the story suitable to illustrate the beginning of his ministry.

One may also reckon with the probability that the evangelist did not know of any exorcisms other than the four he included in his gospel, since the later gospel tradition presents no other exorcism passages. If this supposition is correct, it is easy to see that in fact only the pericope chosen by Mark was suitable for the beginning.

It may also have been of importance to Mark that the exorcism story situated in the synagogue belongs to a Jewish environment and thus in the first part of the gospel (Mk 1:2–3:6), while the exorcism in the land of Gerasa (Mk 5:1–20), which leads to the proclamation of the good news in the Decapolis (Mk 5:20), must be situated at least at the transition of the proclamation from a Jewish to a Gentile environment. The two titles, 'the Holy One of God' (Mk 1:24) and 'the Son of the Most High God' (Mk 5:7), could serve such a consideration.

But how did Mark edit this exorcism story which he placed at the beginning of Jesus' activity? To the advanced introduction (verse 21a) Mark attached the traditional introduction of the exorcism story (verse 21b), which mentioned (only) an encounter in the synagogue on a sabbath. The traditional note of Jesus' teaching activity in the synagogue was used by Mark as a theological datum which depicts Jesus' activity explicitly as proclamation and teaching (insertion of verse 22).

While, according to Mark, John the Baptist, Jesus, the twelve *preach* repentance and good news, Jesus alone *teaches* (fifteen times, always indicating a continuous activity. The only apparent exception, Mk 6:30, expresses a single momentary action). Jesus' *teaching* is, therefore, clearly distinguished from the general preaching done by others before and after him. Most of the time the content of Jesus' teaching is not indicated.[22] Mark may have felt that this had been sufficiently expressed in Mk 1:14–15.

First the evangelist attaches to verse 21b a notice concerning the reaction of the (unnamed) audience, which provides the opportunity to depict Jesus' teaching as so exceptional that people were astonished (verse 22a). This is then followed by a justification (*gar*, 'for'): the strong reaction of the crowd is due to the fact that Jesus teaches as one who has authority (verse 22a). The periphrastic 'for he was teaching' expresses Mark's tendency to generalizing expansion; Jesus' activity is comprehensively characterized.

Exousia, 'authority', is the important key word which is repeated in the insertion in verse 27, 'with authority' (Mk 1:27c). The positive characterization of Jesus' teaching as 'with authority' is followed by a negative comparison, 'and not as the scribes' (verse 22c). The exceptional character of Jesus is thus again emphasized, while the statement also anticipates the conflict which will arise precisely because of Jesus' teaching with authority (and will lead to Jesus' death and thereby to the conclusion and climax of Mark's gospel).

A closer look at the different motifs shows that Mark especially emphasizes Jesus' teaching activity in the redactional sections of his gospel (Mk 2:13; 4:1ff., at the lake; 6:6, round about in the villages; 6:34, in a lonely place, before the multiplication of the loaves; 8:31; 9:31, instructions concerning the suffering and raising of the Son of man; 10:1; 11:17; 12:35; 14:49, in the temple of Jerusalem). Since in Jerusalem Jesus is no longer performing miracles, the general 'scaffolding' of his activity in Mark's gospel is his teaching. Mark, therefore, has a programmatic interest in letting Jesus start his activity with teaching. Mark does not intend to present Jesus primarily as a miracle-worker, but as a powerful proclaimer of the dawning rule of God and a teacher with authority who calls people to follow him (Mk 1:14–20). Therefore, right at the beginning of his presentation of Jesus' activity Mark uses a miracle story to stress the special dimension of Jesus' teaching. Traditional miracle stories are inserted into Mark's gospel with a specific function. The first miracle is a good example of this procedure.

The framing of the exorcism story by the redactional additions of verse 22 and part of verse 27 shows that in Mark the exorcism serves as an illustration of Jesus' teaching with authority, which caused the hearers to be beside themselves with astonishment, which divides them into a group to whom 'has been given the secret of the kingdom of God' and 'those outside' who 'see but not perceive' and 'hear but not understand, lest they should turn again, and be forgiven' (Mk 4:11–12). One could also say that people are divided into those who follow the call to *metanoia* and faith, and those who refuse to follow Jesus, or into those who see in Jesus' miracles a sign of his authority and accept him as teacher, and those who accuse him of a pact with the devil (Mk 3:20–35).

Even if the exorcism story demonstrates Jesus' authority/power, *exousia* should not be understood here merely as the pneumatic power of the miracle-worker. Jesus' *exousia* is inseparable from the proclamation that the kingdom of God is near. The authority of Jesus is a comprehensive characteristic of his activity (cf. Mk 2:1–12; 11:28–33). To be sure, this authority cannot be based on the content or on the special style of his teaching.

> Jesus was distinguished from others not because he taught something completely different, but because he taught with such authority that things happened. Men were moved to action and sick persons were healed.[23]

Even more: sinners receive forgiveness (Mk 2:1–12). The nearness of God's kingdom appears in Jesus' teaching with authority. Accordingly the exorcism story becomes an illustration and therewith a function of Mark's gospel.

> It is in the exorcism that the authority of Jesus is supremely manifest, and it is through the exorcisms that the kingdom can be seen as having drawn near (1:15). In the exorcisms, the authority of Jesus' word and the authority of his action are united.[24]

Although, at least in the first half of the gospel, Mark makes plenty of room for Jesus' miraculous activity, he does not simply reproduce traditional miracle stories, but rather uses them to illustrate the kerygma, his gospel, the person and message of Jesus. Mark is not concerned simply to record miracles as such but to relate them to what the gospel says about Jesus.

This is confirmed by the special function Mark gave to the exorcism story which he worked into his gospel in Mk 1:21–28. Mark deliberately does not yet admit here (unlike Mk 4:41) the question 'Who is this?' In Mk 1:27 the question 'What is this?' refers to the teaching with authority which triggers off the conflict between Jesus and the scribes, as Mk 2:1–12, the first of the five so-called Galilean controversies, shows. Not for nothing does Mark add in Mk 1:22c that Jesus did not teach like the scribes. According to the citation from Isa 29:13 in Mk 7:7, the latter teach human traditions and leave the commandment of God, and therefore teach without authority, since they do not instruct people in the fulfilment of God's will (see also Mk 3:25; 12:28–34).

The scribes doubt Jesus' authority and suspect him of an alliance with the devil (Mk 3:22–30), and say: 'He has an unclean spirit' (Mk 3:30). But he controls the unclean spirits so much that they obey his word spoken in the power of the Holy Spirit (Mk 1:9f.; 3:29). His is the authority of the Spirit of God, he is the 'Holy One of God' (Mk 1:24), as the unclean spirits themselves admit. The accusation of alliance with the devil falls back on those who accuse him. He does not teach like the scribes. In Mark's understanding this is clear from the beginning of Jesus' activity.

In the first part of his gospel (Mk 1:2–3:6) the evangelist aims to present Jesus as appearing and acting with authority throughout Galilee. Jesus' appearance and activity leads to conflict with his opponents, to separation from and division within families (Mk 3:20–35), and among the listeners in general (Mk 4:1–12). Only after this division can the question about Jesus' person, in whom we should believe (Mk 4:40f.), be brought to the fore.

Precisely for this reason, Mark changes the chorus-ending in Mk 1:27 from 'Who is this?' to 'What is this?', as already indicated. The question about Jesus' teaching with authority should be asked first. Mark does not seem to worry about the fact that this change causes a tension within the exorcism story, which normally leads to the question about the person of the exorcist. Apparently it was more important to him to provoke by his interpretation the question about Jesus' teaching with authority; through his consistent emphasis on that teaching, the evangelist also wants to pose this question by his gospel as a whole. Mark knew very well that one cannot be absolved from answering this question by the demonstrative power of the miracle stories (Mk 11:28–33). It is also possible that the evangelist did not experience this tension to the same extent we do. It should be remembered that Mark composed a 'day' in Capernaum. And in the summary, Mk 1:32–34, he has given an important hint for the understanding of the exorcism story. As the redactional conclusion Mk 1:34 (compare also 3:11–12) shows, Mark intended to interpret the confession of the unclean spirit (Mk 1:24) and the subsequent imposition of silence (Mk 1:25) in line with his theory of the messianic secret. Mk 1:34 is undoubtedly composed in reference to Mk 1:24–25. The tension which the chorus-ending (Mk 1:27) generates is deflected and thereby integrated by Mark in so far as he understands both the demonic confession and Jesus' imposition of silence in a new way, particularly in the sense which he expresses in a generalizing phrase in Mk 1:34, 'and he would not permit the demons to speak, because they knew him'. That in Mk 1:24 the unclean spirit did express what he knew apparently does not worry Mark. His point is more explicitly expressed in the general statement of Mk 1:34. To the latter corresponds the fact that in the chorus-ending (Mk 1:27) the demonic confession (Mk 1:24) is no longer used, but the question 'Who is this?' is transformed into a question concerning the new teaching with authority.

Mark calls Jesus' teaching with authority 'new'. Unlike *neos*, which means 'what was not there before', *kainos* means 'what is new in nature, different from the usual, impressive, better than the old, superior in value or attraction'. Jesus' teaching is new because it is done with authority, because Jesus works through the Spirit of God, because he does not teach like the scribes, but especially because he is the Son of God (Mk 1:11; 3:11; 5:7; 9:7, 'listen to him'). It is also new because it touches people and frees them from demons, sin, and false burdens (Mk 7:1–16). It is new because it is constantly transformed in act, especially in the predictions of the passion and resurrection which are characterized as 'teaching'. By the framework of Mk 1:22 and 1:27d, and the reference in Mk 1:34, the evangelist has re-interpreted the traditional exorcism story. For Mark it now has more of a character of teaching and proclamation than was the case in the strongly missionary tradition.

Mark concludes his re-interpretation by adding in verse 28 'of Galilee'. According to the evangelist Jesus' initial activity took place in Galilee (Mk 1:9). Here, at the lake and in the synagogue, Jesus proclaims and teaches, expels demons and heals sick people. Jesus' call rings through the whole of Galilee (Mk 1:28; 1:39). The first 'day' in Capernaum shows a 'successful' Jesus. When after a successful preaching tour (Mk 1:35–45) he returns to Capernaum, he triggers off the opposition of those from whose teaching Jesus' teaching with authority is so clearly distinguished, namely the scribes (Mk 2:1, 6). The opposition is aroused by Jesus' teaching (Mk 2:5) with authority (Mk 2:10). Mark subordinates the miracle stories of his first section (Mk 1:2 – 3:6) to the principal idea of Jesus' teaching with authority and the corresponding resistance. Looking beyond Mk 3:6 ('how to destroy him') to the end of his account, it can be seen that Mark has not hesitated to highlight the 'scandal' already in his first account of Jesus' initial activity in the synagogue of Capernaum. This 'scandal' leads to the excited astonishment of some as well as to the decision of others to kill him (see also Mk 11:17ff.). But it leads the faithful to following in suffering and glory.

Luke 4:31–37[25]

The context

The 'premature' reference to Capernaum as a typical place of Jesus' saving activity (Lk 4:23) enables Luke to present a different picture of the beginning of Jesus' public ministry. Mk 1:14–15 is followed by the call of the first disciples (Mk 1:16–20). Luke, however, turns right away to the account of 'the day of Jesus' powerful activity in

Capernaum' (Mk 1:21–39). This allows him to connect the first account of Jesus' powerful work directly with the Nazareth pericope (Lk 4:16–30). The note that Capernaum is 'a city of Galilee' is also intended to connect the two pericopes geographically. The same redactional intention characterizes the concluding verse, Lk 4:44. In contrast to Mk 1:39, Luke concludes his narration with the general note that Jesus continues his preaching activity in the synagogues of Judea. Against the beginning in Galilee there stands the continuation of the mission in Judea. This intentional distinction of region does not, however, bring about any noticeable change within Jesus' mission. The characteristic circumstances of Jesus' missionary activity, such as his sabbatical preaching in the synagogues, are retained. In this respect beginning and end (Lk 4:14–15 and Lk 4:44) correspond to each other.

In fact, the whole account of Jesus' initial activity (Lk 4:14–44) presents Jesus' word as an eschatological, powerful word (see especially Lk 4:14–15, 42–44). Lk 4:31–37 should be seen in this context. Jesus' word, which in the Nazareth pericope (Lk 4:16–30) is announced as 'fulfilment event' (Lk 4:21), now comes to the fore with its special dynamism. Lk 4:38–41 develops this theme further, until it is summarily rounded off in Lk 4:42–44 (compare Lk 4:14–15).

With Lk 4:31 there begins the first great Marcan section of the third gospel.[26] A look at the synopsis shows that in Lk 4:31–44 Luke depends closely on Mark. Luke places the pericope of Jesus' activity in the synagogue of Capernaum right after the programmatic declaration in the synagogue of Nazareth (Lk 4:16–30). Against Jesus' activity in his native town, which is characterized by contrasts (Lk 4:22, 'all wondered ...', and Lk 4:29–30 which describes a violent reaction), Luke sets the events in Capernaum which in the first account are already characterized by the twofold amazed reaction of the people (verses 32 and 36–37). As in Mark, the text consists of two elements which are closely related. The summary note on Jesus' teaching (Lk 4:31–32) is followed by the presentation of the exorcism in the synagogue (Lk 4:33–37). By means of the key words *exousia*, 'authority', and *logos*, 'word', the paragraphs are closely connected, but a new development is clearly recognizable in the change of subject in Lk 4:33 (from 'Jesus' in verses 31–32 to 'a man'). .

The pericope proper

Verse 31: And he went down to Capernaum, a city of Galilee. And he was teaching them on the sabbath;

The introductory verses 31–32 describe the situation in Capernaum in a way which is very similar to Lk 4:15. Instead of Mark's 'they', Luke has 'he' for the simple reason that while Mark has already related the calling of the disciples (Mk 1:16–20), in Luke this will follow only in Lk 5:1–11. Capernaum is described as 'a city of Galilee' (compare Lk 1:26, 39; 2:4; 7:11; 9:10, 52; compare also Lk 8:26 with Mk 5:1), since Luke's readers were not familiar with the geography of Palestine. In Lk 4:23, where Capernaum appeared for the first time in the gospel, this clarification could not be given, and Luke therefore adds it to the second mention of Capernaum, which is in fact the first in a narrative context.

By the sentence structure Luke emphasizes what is for him the most important aspect of Jesus' activity: 'He was teaching'. The same expression is found in Lk 5:17; 13:10; 19:47; 21:37. Luke does not mention any precise location: he seems to take it for granted that Jesus teaches in the synagogue (cf. Lk 4:15; 6:6; 13:10). The time-indication 'on the sabbath' does not seem to have any special importance (unlike 13:10; 14:1). The choice of the plural *sabbasin* seems to be deliberate. 'Apparently when Luke found *sabbasin* in Mark he changed it to *sabbatōi* when it really meant one special sabbath, but retained *sabbasin* when it meant on the sabbath day in general.'[27] By retaining the plural here Luke confirms the information of Lk 4:16 that Jesus taught in the synagogues on the sabbath 'as his custom was'. Luke thus presents Jesus' activity as typical and in both 4:16–30 and 4:31–37 starts from the same assumptions. By this note, framed by the generalizing verses 14–15 and 44, the Capernaum pericope is made part of the typical activity of Jesus at the beginning of his public ministry.

Verse 32: and they were astonished at his teaching, for his word was with authority.

Luke simplifies Mk 1:22 in that he introduces the comprehensive concept 'his word' (*ho logos autou*; see also Lk 4:36) and omits the polemical comparison with the scribes. The basic meaning of *logos* is expressed in Lk 1:2, 4. 'The word' (*ho logos*) in Luke obviously refers to the kerygma. Authority is attributed to the word. Indeed the subject of the sentence is not Jesus, but the word (compare Lk 5:15, as against Mk 1:45), which was already mentioned in Lk 4:22. Lk 4:32 may be considered as a kind of doublet of 4:22. The redactor returns once more to this word in 4:36. This shows again how important Jesus' teaching activity is for Luke, who is here developing Mark's concept. This is underlined by the fact that *ho logos* is the only subject mentioned 'by name' in verses 31–32. While Mark speaks only of Jesus' *didachē* ('teaching'; the word *didachē* occurs only in this pericope in all three synoptics: Mk 1:22; Lk 4:32; Mt 7:28), Luke brings in 'the word' in Lk 4:32 and 36. The 'word' of God's rule is the presupposition for Jesus' powerful activity.

Verses 31–32 speak of Jesus' teaching 'with authority'. Verse 32b, 'for his word was with authority', has been called 'a redactional subtitle for the following episodes', of which the Capernaum episode is the first. The *exousia* which Luke takes over from Mark is understood as a quality of Jesus' word. While Mark speaks of Jesus' authority/power, Jesus' word appears in Luke as an independent powerful reality, and while at other times Luke speaks of 'the word of God', he has 'his word' here: Jesus speaks this word on which is based his 'being different' (cf. Lk 4:16–20) which provokes 'fear and trembling' (Lk 4:15, 22, 36; see below, commentary on verse 36). This characterization of Jesus' word as a powerful/authoritative word should not be based only on Lk 4:36. Rather, reference should also be made to Lk 4:14–15 and Lk 4:21: Jesus' word in the power of the Spirit addresses to people the 'today' of fulfilment.

> **Verse 33:** And in the synagogue there was a man who had the spirit of an unclean demon; and he cried out with a loud voice,

Luke's first exorcism story is developed against the background of the information given in verses 31–32. Luke connects verse 33 with verses 31–32 without any noticeable seam. A second important figure enters the scene: 'there was a man'. He is further described as having 'the spirit of an unclean demon' (compare Mark's 'with an unclean spirit'), an expression found only here in the New Testament. The spirit of the man is caused by a 'demon', who as such is a neutral figure for Luke's Hellenistic readers, and is therefore further described as 'unclean', and therefore negative. Luke intensifies the man's/spirit's cry by adding 'with a loud voice'. In Luke there is no longer room for such a reaction after the command to leave the man (compare Lk 4:35 and Mk 1:26).

> **Verse 34:** 'Ah! What have you to do with us, Jesus of Nazareth? Have you come to destroy us? I know who you are, the Holy One of God.'

Luke begins the direct speech with an exclamation of fear (*ea*; RSV: 'Ah!'; not an imperative, 'leave us alone!', as in NAB). With this exclamation the demon expresses his resignation in the face of Jesus' authority (compare Lk 10:17ff.). The texts of Mark and Luke are almost identical. The demon recognizes in his conqueror the Son or Holy One of God. Already in Lk 1:35 Jesus is referred to as 'holy, the

Son of God', and in Lk 1:32 the angel foretells that Jesus 'will be called the Son of the Most High'. For Luke the titles 'Son of God' and 'the Holy One of God' are equivalent to 'Messiah'. This equivalence is confirmed in Lk 22:67–70. There the question of the high priest whether Jesus is 'the Christ, the Son of the Blessed' (Mk 14:61) is transformed into two questions (Lk 22:67 and 70) in which Messiahship is clearly the presupposition for the recognition of Jesus' Sonship. Luke, therefore, understands the titles in Lk 4:34 (and 4:41) in a messianic sense.

> **Verse 35:** But Jesus rebuked him, saying, 'Be silent, and come out of him!' And when the demon had thrown him down in the midst, he came out of him, having done him no harm.

Jesus' reply is the same as in Mark. Verse 35b, however, is quite different from Mk 1:26. The demon threw the man down. Except for Lk 4:35 the verb *riptein*, 'to throw down', always refers to human action (Lk 17:2; Mt 9:36; 15:30; 27:5; Acts 22:23; 27:19, 29). For Luke, the demonstration is important; he therefore stresses that the demon left the man 'in the midst', that is, in full view of all (compare also Lk 5:19 and Mk 2:4; Lk 6:8 and Mk 3:3). The demon's action should not be understood as a final threat. After Jesus' word the demon had no more power. In fact, Luke insists that the demon went out 'having done him no harm'. Besides the powerlessness of the demon Luke also emphasizes Jesus' mercy for the afflicted man. The departing demon is not allowed to harm him.

> **Verse 36:** And they were all amazed and said to one another, 'What is this word? For with authority and power he commands the unclean spirits and they come out.'

The beginning of this verse reads literally: 'And fear came on all ...'. The 'amazement' (*thambos*; see Lk 5:9; Acts 3:10, each time in reaction to a miraculous event) which falls on all those present, expresses 'fear and trembling' because of the unexpected confrontation with the divine. This 'fear' is also expressed in the ensuing conversation among the onlookers, as is skilfully suggested by the alliteration of the Greek text, *sunelaloun pros allēlous legontes*, literally, 'they spoke to one another saying'. This is expressed more concretely in direct speech in verse 36b. Luke anticipates the answer by formulating the question, 'What is this word?' He formulates similar questions in Lk 1:66; 7:49; 8:25; 9:9. The tendency to define things more precisely appears especially in Lk 5:21, 'Who is this that speaks ...?' compared with Mk 2:7, 'Why does this man speak thus?' The reference to Lk 4:22, 'for his word was with authority', is obvious in verse 36c, 'for with authority and power he commands'. It is a distinct possibility that the subject of the verb 'to command' is 'the word' rather than Jesus himself.

In Mark, the 'amazement' of the crowd concerns the miracle (cf. Mk 1:27, 'What is this?'), but in Luke it bears directly on Jesus' word ('What is this word?'). Thus it becomes clear that this word transcends all other speaking by men and hence is different from other human words. The typical Lucan change of *didachē*, 'teaching' (Mk 1:22, 27) into *logos* (*autou*) connects verse 32 with verse 36 and indicates an aspect of the theology of the word typical of Luke: proclamation and powerful act are not two different things. As fulfilment event Jesus' word comprises both.

Jesus commands 'with authority and power', two attributes which are exclusively ascribed to God's, or Jesus', activity. In Lk 4:14 we learn that 'in the power of the Spirit' Jesus returned to Galilee and began to teach, 'being glorified by all' (Lk 4:15b). The reason for this popular reaction is expressed in Lk 4:32, 36, 'with authority'. In Lk 9:1 the disciples receive 'power and authority over all demons and to cure all diseases'. Luke likes to combine 'power and authority' in describing Jesus' activity. In fact, in the gospels this combination occurs only in Luke. The question about 'this word' is thereby answered once more: Jesus' word comprises his teaching as well as his powerful word against the demons as illustrated by Lk 4:31–37.

Verse 37: And reports of him went out into every place in the surrounding region.

In a concluding note the author summarizes the 'echo' of the event. Only here does Luke use the word *ēchos* for information about Jesus. In Lk 21:25; Acts 2:2 (and Heb 12:19) it has another meaning. Elsewhere Luke uses *phēmē* (Lk 4:14) or *ho logos* (Lk 5:15; 7:17). By substituting 'into every place' for Mark's 'everywhere', Luke makes the expression 'in the surrounding region' recede into the background. What is important is not the 'spreading throughout all the surrounding region' (cf. Mk 1:28), but the fact that each place in the region receives the report. Luke is certainly thinking of the region at the Lake of Genesareth around Capernaum. The exact location is already given by Lk 4:14 and 31.

The Lucan redaction

A comparison with Mk 1:21–28 shows clearly that the latter was the basic text for Lk 4:31–37, but Luke has given it many features of his own.[28] His style clearly reflects a conscious imitation of the Septuagint. Moreover, he has used his Marcan source in an associative manner: he takes up many textual elements of Mark and gives them another grammatical function or uses them with a different accentuation. These many interventions in the basic text indicate that Luke is placing special emphases. It is striking that Lk 4:34–35a is an almost literal parallel to Mk 1:24–25, while elsewhere the text is extensively edited. Apparently the author was not especially interested in the details of the exorcism as such. Only the departure of the demon receives two special notes important for Luke: on the one hand, the power of the demon appears broken; on the other hand, the stressing that the man is unharmed expresses Luke's concern for the latter.

But Luke devotes more attention to the initial and concluding verses. Here he consciously emphasizes Jesus' teaching as well as the characterization of his word as spoken with authority (Lk 4:31–32). The whole pericope is ultimately conceived as a text which by means of the word proclaimed sheds light on Jesus himself and his powerful word. The most important feature is the teaching activity, to which Jesus' activity as the exemplification of this comprehensive reality is oriented. This idea has been prepared in Lk 4:22. Unlike what happened in Nazareth, 'fear and trembling' (*thambos*) falls on the people (Lk 4:36).

Through the Lucan redaction of the pericope it can be seen that for Luke the exorcism which he takes from Mark is not in the first line of interest. It serves him as an opportunity to express his understanding of Jesus' activity. The exorcism itself thus recedes into the background.

While in Mark the story may be plainly designated as an exorcism, Luke's pericope should rather be called a 'catechetical Jesus-story' (Kirchenschläger). Luke's goal is to present the person and activity of Jesus, not just a single event. The exorcism narrated is a literary vehicle for a statement about Jesus which Luke wants to express clearly in consideration of his own community and in agreement with Lk 1:3–4. In the forefront are two elements which the author describes extensively and which he uses to characterize the person of Jesus: by his *word* Jesus proclaims his message, which in his *activity* is seen to be endowed with authority and power.

The power of Jesus' 'word' over the demons remains the theme of Luke's redactional treatment of the 'day of powerful activity in Capernaum'. Thus the whole Capernaum pericope fits in harmoniously with the beginning in Galilee. Luke unfolds the contents of the 'word' (see Lk 4:22, 'words of grace', RSV: 'gracious words') in

3 The healing of Peter's mother-in-law

Mt 8:14–15	Mk 1:29–31	Lk 4:38–39
	29 And immediately he left the synagogue, and entered the house of Simon and Andrew, with James and John.	38 And he arose and left the synagogue, and entered Simon's house.
14 And when Jesus entered Peter's house,		
he saw his mother-in-law	30 Now Simon's mother-in-law	Now Simon's mother-in-law
lying sick with a fever;	lay sick with a fever, and immediately they told him of her.	was ill with a high fever, and they besought him for her.
	31 And he came	39 And he stood over her
15 he touched her hand,	and took her by the hand and lifted her up,	
		and rebuked the fever,
and the fever left her,	and the fever left her;	and it left her; and immediately
and she rose and served him.	and she served them.	she rose and served them.

The original text

Starting from Mark, which is almost generally considered the oldest of the three synoptic texts, we will try to reconstruct the oldest text.

The clause 'and immediately he/they left the synagogue' (Mk 1:29a; literally, 'and immediately leaving the synagogue') is certainly redactional, for it connects the account of the healing with Mk 1:21–28, and thus connects the two accounts chronologically and topographically. Since Mk 1:21b, 23–27 has been identified as originally an independent pericope, this connection must be attributed to the evangelist. Moreover, Mark has connected the two accounts by placing the original introductory formula of Mk 1:29–31 at the beginning of the healing of the possessed man, Mk 1:21a, 'And

63

he went into Capernaum'. If this is so, then the plural, 'they entered', in Mk 1:29 must be the original reading.

The mention of James and John should be attributed to the evangelist. Their inclusion by means of 'with' is rather awkward; the same construction occurs in Mk 15:1; 15:31, and Mark shows a clear interest in the pair of brothers (Mk 1:19; 5:37; 9:2; 13:3; 14:33). In Mk 1:29 the evangelist refers to the people mentioned in Mk 1:16–20, thereby connecting Mk 1:29–31 with that pericope. Thus by means of topographical notes (Mk 1:21a, 29a, 33, 35) and the deliberate recollection of the circle of people (Mk 1:16–20, 29b, 36), the evangelist creates a redactional unit in Mk 1:(14–15)16–39. For similar reasons the mention of Andrew must be attributed to Mark. 'Simon and Andrew' are mentioned together because Mark had found this traditional pair in Mk 1:16–20.

The original introduction to the account must therefore have been: 'And they went into Capernaum and entered the house of Simon'.

In Mk 1:30–31 the evangelist's intervention has been minimal. The second mention of Simon may have to be attributed to him: in the original account, which did not include the names of the other disciples, a simple 'his' must have sufficed. 'Immediately' in verse 31 is also possibly Marcan. But these two points are uncertain.

That the cured person entertained those who stayed at her home, i.e., that she waited at table, may be a traditional feature intended to demonstrate the healing (compare Mk 2:12; 5:15; 5:42f.). But such features are not always necessary (compare Mk 3:5; 5:25–34; 10:52), and in a very concise story like Mk 1:29–31 the remark 'and the fever left her' can suffice. Moreover, the clause 'and she served them' introduces a new aspect of the story: Jesus stays in the house for a meal. This could not be inferred from the original introduction in verse 29, where no special reason was given for Jesus' entering Simon's house. It served apparently to prepare the reader/listener for the *healing* of Simon's mother-in-law. It should also be noted that in Mk 15:41 the 'service' of women to Jesus is emphasized and related to their discipleship. Some scholars conclude from this that, according to Mark, service was 'the specific manner of discipleship for a woman' (E. Schweizer). But it seems rather that the evangelist considers discipleship in general as 'service' (Mk 9:35; 10:43; compare 10:45). If, moreover, it is remembered that by the insertion of the names of the disciples in Mk 1:29 the evangelist shaped the account into a *disciple story*, it cannot be excluded that he was responsible for the insertion of 'and she served them'. His theological intention would then be to present 'service' as the task of the disciple in general, and, as in Mk 14:7–9, a woman as an example of true discipleship.

The traditional account of the healing may then have run:

21a   And they went into Capernaum,
29   and entered the house of Simon.
30   (His) mother-in-law lay sick with a fever,
      and they told him of her.
31   And he came and took her by the hand,
      and lifted her up;
      and the fever left her.

It has often been said that the account of the healing of Peter's mother-in-law can be traced back to historical recollection, and even that it comes from Peter himself. To agree with the first conjecture is not necessarily to support the second. There is no real ground for accepting that the account came straight from Peter and that originally it was perhaps in the 'we'-form. Nevertheless, the solid localization of the account in Capernaum and 'in the house of Simon', and especially the identification of the sick person as the mother-in-law of Peter support the thesis that we are dealing here with historical recollection.

But this does not yet make the account a historical document. From a very early stage of the tradition the account has been narrated according to the fixed schema of a Hellenistic miracle story. However, compliance with a well-known literary schema and the presence of a historical core are not mutually exclusive. The schema is as follows:

(1) Statement of illness (verse 30a);
(2) request for healing (verse 30b);
(3) healing gesture (verse 31a);
(4) result: healing (verse 31b).

The localization of the account in Capernaum and 'in the house of Simon', together with Mk 1:38 which concludes this section, assures us that we are dealing with ancient Galilean tradition. The Galilean community looks back on a widespread activity of Jesus, possibly originating in Capernaum (compare Lk 4:31; Mt 11:23 and parallel). This tradition serves then as ground for the Christian mission proceeding from Capernaum. The situation in life of this tradition is therefore the reflection of the early Christian community on its own origin and on the Galilean mission.

The synoptic accounts of the healing of Peter's mother-in-law no longer allow us to determine exactly what was the intention of Jesus when he accomplished this healing, nor what precise significance the very first witnesses attributed to it. We know, however, that the Jews considered fever as a punishment by God, associated with consumption (Deut 28:22; 32:24; Lev 26:16), or the plague (Hab

3:5). At a later time fever was commonly attributed to a demon. In this perspective, the miraculous healing of Peter's mother-in-law must have meant to people that Jesus was the One sent by God as promised by Isaiah, who would come to free them from their afflictions, consequences of moral evil (Isa 26:19; 29:18; 32:3; 35:5).

Mark 1:29–31

> **Verse 29:** And immediately he (they) left the synagogue and entered the house of Simon and Andrew, with James and John.

Two details in Mk 1:29 have no parallel in the other accounts: the use of 'immediately' (*euthus*) to make the connection with the preceding narrative, and the mention of Andrew, James and John in addition to Peter. The first of these is a well-known characteristic of the gospel of Mark (cf. Mk 1:10, 12, 18, 21, 23, 28, 30, 42, 43, etc.). The second may be seen as an agreement between Matthew and Luke against Mark, but it should also be noted that the inclusion of proper names not found in the other gospels is another characteristic of the gospel of Mark, e.g., the mention of Alexander and Rufus in Mk 15:21 (compare Mt 27:32; Lk 23:26). The meaning of *euthus* may be 'so then', but it is also possible that the intention is to say that the first thing Jesus did upon leaving the synagogue was to enter the house of Simon and Andrew. It has also been thought that *euthus* suggests here that Jesus wanted to withdraw from the crowd. The account is connected to the previous one by means of the catchphrase construction 'and immediately ... (in) the synagogue' (Mk 1:23) ... 'And immediately ... (out of) the synagogue' (Mk 1:29).

Some ancient authorities read 'they left' instead of 'he left'. If we accept the reading 'they left', we get a very awkward sentence. Why are James and John not included in the 'they'? By way of explanation it has been suggested that Mark got the story directly from Peter in the form '*we* went out and came into *our* house, together with James and John'. But for several reasons 'it seems more likely that the story reached Mark, like the rest of his material, as part of the oral tradition of the Church'.[29]

The house into which Jesus withdraws and where he gives his disciples privileged instruction is almost always a redactional localization. Mk 1:29, 2:1, 15 and 14:3, however, probably represent a traditional use of the word. Here the house is that of Simon and Andrew. Matthew and Luke mention Simon only (Matthew: Peter); Mark alone alludes to James and John. Simon's house seems to have been a rendezvous of Jesus and his disciples during this period of

Jesus' ministry. Several commentators, e.g., Weiss, Klostermann, and Bultmann, suggest that the three names peculiar to Mark are a later addition.

Verse 30: Now Simon's mother-in-law lay sick with a fever, and immediately they told him of her.

Peter was married at the time of his call. From Paul we know that his wife later accompanied him on his missionary journeys: 'Do we not have the right to be accompanied by a wife, as the other apostles ... and Cephas' (I Cor 9:5). The early Christians did not take offence at the fact that the first disciples and the 'rock' of the Church (cf. Mk 3:15, 'Simon whom he surnamed Peter') did not live in celibacy. Peter's mother-in-law lay sick with a fever. 'Although the data are inadequate to identify the disease, various scholars feel themselves capable of giving a possible diagnosis ... nothing can be said for certain about the disease.'[30]

Again Mark uses *euthus*, here undoubtedly with the meaning 'at once', 'immediately'. To tell Jesus of the sufferer was the first thing they did. It seems best to interpret this as an implied request that Jesus would use his healing power on her. This at least is Luke's interpretation: 'and they besought him for her' (Lk 4:38).

Verse 31: And he came and took her by the hand and lifted her up, and the fever left her; and she served them.

In the Greek, the grammatical construction of verse 31 presents an anomaly. Inverting the chronological order of the actions of Jesus, who must first have approached, then taken her by the hand, and finally lifted her up, Mark places the act of lifting up in the centre: coming, *he lifted her up*, taking her by the hand. Undoubtedly the point of the account is to be sought in the principal verb framed by two participles.

The verb used to refer to the lifting-up of the sick woman is the same as the verb used for the resurrection of the dead: *egeirein*. Mark is very well aware of this meaning of the verb, as appears from the resurrection of Jesus. 'And as for the dead being raised (*egeirontai* ...', Mk 12:26). 'You seek Jesus of Nazareth, who was crucified. He has risen (*ēgerthē* ...', Mk 16:6; see also Mk 6:14, 16; 14:28). Beside these passive forms, the verb is also found in the active voice, especially in the early Christian preaching as related by Luke: Acts 3:15, 'Whom God raised (*egeiren*) from the dead'; cf. Acts 4:10; 5:30; 10:40; etc. But, while the word has different meanings ('to lift up' and 'to raise'), can it really be assumed that Mark was aware of and intended to refer to this second meaning? The following points may help us to define Mark's thought clearly.

Several New Testament authors have observed the connection between the different meanings of the verb so that a symbolic use of the word may be considered habitual in the apostolic period. This understanding of the verb *egeirein* is found in Jn 2:19–22, but also in the liturgical hymn quoted in the epistle to the Ephesians which describes the *baptismal* resurrection: 'Awake (*egeire*), O sleeper, and arise (*anasta*) from the dead' (Eph 5:14). Luke parallels David raised by God to be king (Acts 13:22) and the risen Christ (Acts 13:30, 37), by way of the deliberate middle term of Jesus 'brought' (*ēgagen*) by God (Acts 13:23). It may safely be accepted that this point of view was not unknown to Mark.

Moreover, we find at least two texts in Mark which seem to reveal a clearly established connection between the gesture of lifting up and the resurrection. In Mk 5:41f., addressing a dead girl, Jesus says 'arise' (*egeire*). 'And immediately the girl got up' (*anestē*). Note also that here, as in Mk 1:31, it is said that he took her by the hand. In Mk 9:26f., it is an epileptic who 'was like a corpse; so that most of them said, "He is dead"' whom Jesus lifted up (*ēgeiren*), and he arose (*anestē*). In these two passages it is difficult not to interpret the gesture of lifting up as referring to resurrection.

Should it therefore be concluded that in Mk 1:31, Mark wanted to describe a (baptismal) resurrection? To affirm this would, in our opinion, force the text and deform Mark's thought. Undoubtedly, it is not by chance that there is not found in Mark any punning on or real transformation of the verb *egeirein*. In Mk 5:41f. and 9:26f. we found rather a dynamic passage from one meaning to another, which corresponds perfectly to Mark's usual way of thinking. We must therefore conserve the concrete, historic, particular and determined value of the scene described. But at the same time, we should let ourselves be carried by the movement of thought which, by means of a healing, especially expressed by the verb *egeirein*, necessarily moves toward the contemplation of resurrection and full salvation. In this sense we may say that the expression is here almost certainly intended to draw the attention of the reader to the 'baptismal resurrection' of which Jesus' gesture becomes a lasting symbol.[31]

Miracle stories often end with the motif of the amazement and awe of the crowd or the testimony of the healed person, but here, as in a number of other miracle stories, the final motif stresses the completeness of the healing: Peter's mother-in-law serves Jesus and his companions.[32] But to stop here would be a misjudgement of Mark's thought. The imperfect tense *diēkonei* indicates continued activity. This is the woman's response to what Jesus' *exousia gure for preaching*

(authority, power; Mk 1:22, 27) has done for her. It is striking that her service concerns not Jesus alone, but all those present. The service to which Jesus' *exousia* calls us is the service to our fellow human beings. While it is true that *diakonein* retains its basic meaning in the New Testament, including Mk 1:31, the word also underwent considerable development and was given important theological overtones. The service here described is a beginning; it inaugurates the service of all people healed by Christ. It is a lasting service, as the imperfect tense indicates, and is directed toward the Lord as well as to the ecclesial community.

Looking back now at the beginning of the account, 'he (they) left the synagogue and entered the house of Simon', it seems that here too one should not try to transpose everything allegorically; but the movement referred to presents a 'sense', i.e., an orientation of thought which urges us to expand and generalize this simple topographical note. Admittedly Mark may not have been fully aware of the symbolic import of Jesus' move, leaving the synagogue and making of Peter's house a church of salvation, but it remains true that the image possesses of itself a dynamism which can go beyond the clear zone of what is consciously perceived. Therefore, Mark did not have to be fully conscious of all that he reported. It suffices that he sensed, and made his readers sense, that the images of Jesus' terrestrial life are valid not only for Capernaum, but for the whole world.[33]

Luke 4:38–39

The context

First, Luke presents the pericope in the same sequence as Mark, as far as the 'day at Capernaum' is concerned (Mk 1:21–39; Lk 4:31–44). However, while Mark immediately adds the healing of the leper (Mk 1:40–45), Luke inserts the account of the miraculous catch of fish with the calling of Peter (Lk 5:1–11) before the healing of the leper (Lk 5:12–16). An equivalent of the calling story is found in Mark before the 'day at Capernaum' (Mk 1:16–20). Consequently, in Mark Jesus is no longer alone but already followed by his disciples, Simon, Andrew, James and John. In Luke, on the other hand, Jesus' relation with his disciples is very different. After the inaugural scene at Nazareth (Lk 4:16–30), Luke narrates the journey of Jesus alone to Capernaum. Similarly, when Jesus leaves Capernaum, he is followed by the crowds (Lk 4:42), and not by Simon and his companions as in Mark (Mk 1:36).

On the other hand, contrary to Mark (Mk 1:39), Jesus' journey to Capernaum is not presented by Luke as the prototype of the mission in Galilee. Instead, he writes, rather strangely, 'he was preaching in the synagogues of Judea' (Lk 4:44; he also omits Mark's 'casting out demons'). While in Mark it is in Galilee that the leper comes to Jesus to be cleansed (Mk 1:39–40; 2:1), the episode is situated by Luke in a vague context: after the account of the miraculous catch of fish and the calling of Peter 'by the lake of Gennesaret' (Lk 5:1), 'he was in one of the cities' (Lk 5:12; of Judea?; see Lk 4:44) where he cured the leper. Finally the healing of the paralytic is no longer situated by Luke in Capernaum (Lk 5:17–26).

That the present context of the healing of Peter's mother-in-law is due to Lucan redaction may be supported by similar instances in Acts. The parallelism has been pointed out between Lk 4:38–41 and Acts 28:7–10, both consisting of two short miracle stories, the healing of an individual followed by that of a group. In both instances the individual is an unnamed relative of the host, Simon and Publius respectively, and is suffering from a fever (compare Lk 4:38 and Acts 28:8). Both groups are healed of their illnesses (Lk 4:40, *asthenountas*; Acts 28:9, *astheneias*), and both passages mention the laying-on of hands (Lk 4:40, *tas cheiras epititheis*; Acts 28:8, *epitheis tas cheiras*).[34]

These few features suffice to indicate that, even if at first sight Luke seems to present an account which is parallel to Mark's, differences appear in several instances: the role of the disciples, insertion of the healing in Jesus' activity in Galilee, etc.

The account proper

Verse 38: And he arose and left the synagogue, and entered Simon's house. Now Simon's mother-in-law was ill with a high fever, and they besought him for her.

Lk 4:38a is much more closely parallel, both in context and language, to Mk 1:29 than Mt 8:14a. Only Mark and Luke mention that Jesus came out of the synagogue. Mark and Luke use the name 'Simon', whereas Matthew writes 'Peter'. Luke cannot imagine that any Christian reader would not know right away who this Simon was. Since Luke does not copy Mk 1:16–20 but has his own account of the call of the first disciples (Lk 5:1–11), he omits the other three names here.

In both Mark and Luke, but not in Matthew, the reference to Peter's mother-in-law begins a new sentence. Luke's description of the illness is different from that of Mark, but the comment that the disciples spoke to Jesus about the sick woman is very similar in Mark and Luke. The differences between Lk 4:38b and Mk 1:30 are differences of style, not of meaning.

Simon's mother-in-law was ill with a 'high fever'. Instead of Mark's *puressousa*, 'fever-stricken', Luke writes *sunechomenē puretōi megalōi*, 'being seized with a great fever'. Galen writes that it was customary for physicians to distinguish fevers by the terms *megas*, 'great', 'high', and *smikros*, 'small', 'low'. The adjective *megas*, 'great', with *puretos*, 'fever', seems to appear only in medical writings. Here the notice certainly intends to suggest the quality of the miracle.

'And they besought him for her.' On the one hand, Luke omits the names of secondary figures, throwing into relief the principal characters; on the other hand, he retains two plurals, *'they* besought' and 'she served *them'*. Does this indicate that Luke was using a tradition which originally mentioned the disciples? This may be so, but it should also be considered that the evangelist *intentionally* retained these plurals: it is the Christian community of yesterday and today who must pray for the salvation of the sick and sinners (cf. Jas 5:14–15; Acts 8:15). It would be mistaken to overlook this typically Lucan perspective and to translate this communitarian plural by an anonymous 'one besought him'.

Verse 39: And he stood over her and rebuked the fever, and it left her; and immediately she rose and served them.

Jesus approached the sleeping mat on which the sick woman lay so that 'he stood over her'. This was the typical attitude of the exorcist. Mark's clause, 'and he came and took her by the hand', has no parallel in Luke, who writes instead 'he rebuked the fever'. The expression 'stood over' (*epistas epanō*) together with 'rebuked' (*epetimēsen*) illustrates the sovereign authority of Jesus which the fever demon cannot resist. Nobody in the demonic realm is capable of resisting Jesus even for a moment (note: 'immediately'). The Lucan redaction is interested in showing the healing power of Jesus. He did not address the sick woman but 'rebuked the fever' as he would rebuke a demon. 'Rebuking' seems to personify an impersonal evil, but rather, it reflects the conviction that behind all sickness is the working of Satan. Jesus rebuked an ordinary fever which was considered evidence of demonic activity. In the contemporary view Satan ruled the world. Thus the kingdom's advance was assured as the rule of the demon was being broken. It was assured, directly, as the demons were routed and destroyed, and indirectly, as the varying manifestations of demonic power were destroyed. One of the ways in which Satan ruled his captured realm was through diseases. Thus when Jesus healed disease he was pushing back the kingdom of Satan. The demonic character of the fever may be suggested by the phrase 'and the fever left her' (*aphēken*; compare Mk 1:31; Mt 8:15; Jn 4:52).

Jesus did not take the sick person by the hand, but 'rebuked (*epetimēsen*) the fever', a formula which is very dear to Luke. He has used it for the demoniac in the synagogue (Lk 4:35 = Mk 1:25); he repeats it immediately after this healing account for the demons who want to proclaim Jesus' divine sonship (Lk 4:41). The same formula recurs in the stilling of the storm (Lk 8:24). Jesus also 'rebukes' the unclean spirit of the epileptic (Lk 9:42) and James and John for their misplaced zeal (Lk 9:55). If Luke is interested in the sick person, he does not forget that he/she is under the influence of the devil. We can still speak of a miracle story, but of a miracle story which is oriented to exorcisms. Jesus appears as the Saviour going about doing good and liberating those who are in the power of the devil. 'The verb *epetimēsen* ... is used as a catchword bond with vv. 35, 41. The three episodes thus linked, depict Jesus making use of the commanding word of salvation and deliverance.'[35]

The healing of Peter's mother-in-law is here unmistakably presented with exorcistic features. The change is probably determined by the context. While Mark emphasizes the astounding 'teaching' of Jesus (Mk 1:22, 27), Luke speaks in both instances of the 'word' (Lk 4:32, 36). The tension between teaching and miracle which is clearly present in Mark is thus lifted. The authoritative word is identified with the exorcistic command. Luke goes on to shape the healing of Peter's mother-in-law in line with this motif. While in Mark she is healed by touch, in Luke the healing is brought about by threatening the fever, as if it were a demon to be dispelled by an exorcistic word. By the insertion of exorcistic features Luke has brought together two grounds for the authority of the exorcistic word. Even so, the healing of Peter's mother-in-law is not an exorcism proper. It is simply provided with exorcistic features. A decisive feature, the departure of the demon, is absent. In a real exorcism the demon does not just affect one or another function of a person, but takes over his personality completely. In such cases of 'possession', the demon has to depart. Form-critically expressed: the demon must be the opponent, not just a secondary character hidden in the background.

Even in the least spectacular of his miracles Jesus revealed a kindness and power which were amplified and actualized in the glorious Christ. Thus without transforming the past event symbolically, Luke makes his readers think of Christ who is now their Saviour.

The middle term consists of the two qualities of kindness and power which are both necessary for the salvation of people. Luke is especially interested in the union of these two qualities in the Christ of yesterday and today. He seems to underline this double aspect in Peter's speech in the house of Cornelius: 'How God anointed Jesus of Nazareth with the Holy Spirit and with power; how he went about doing good and healing all that were oppressed by the devil, for God was with him' (Acts 10:38). This double aspect underlies the characteristic phrases of Lk 4:39: bending over the sick person, Jesus expresses his kindness; rebuking the fever in such a way that his order is immediately effective, he reveals his power. παραχρημα

'And immediately she rose.' Luke inserted 'immediately' (*parachrēma*) to emphasize the miraculous nature of the cure. The word occurs also in Mt 21:19, 20; otherwise it is confined in the New Testament to Luke, who uses it ten times in the gospel and six times in Acts. 'And immediately he rose before them ...' (Lk 5:25). 'And immediately her flow of blood ceased' (Lk 8:44). '... how she had been immediately healed' (Lk 8:47). 'And she got up immediately' (Lk 8:55). 'And immediately she was made straight' (Lk 13:13). 'And immediately he received his sight' (Lk 18:43). 'And immediately his feet and ankles were made strong' (Acts 3:7).

Luke has substituted the discrete participle *anastasa*, 'rising', for Mark's more important and suggestive *egeirein*. The narrator is interested in and explicitly develops the attitude of Jesus who bent over her and rebuked the fever: Jesus' power and mercy are immediately effective. In this final clause Mark and Luke agree in writing that 'she served *them*', while Matthew has 'him'. Peter's mother-in-law is immediately so completely cured that she can serve them, a clear sign of the cure, but also a reference to the new task of women in the life of the Christian community.

Matthew 8:14–15

The context

In comparison with the accounts of Mark and Luke, Matthew does not present a sequence of parallels, since he does not narrate the 'day at Capernaum'. Nevertheless, several elements of it can be found in Matthew, particularly in two places in his gospel. Firstly, the Matthean summary, after the account of the calling of the 'brothers' (Mt 4:18–22), summing up Jesus' activity and presenting large crowds following him (Mt 4:23–25), echoes several verses of Mark (Mk 1:28, 32, 34, 39). Secondly, after the Sermon on the Mount (Mt 5:1–7:29), where Matthew shows the authority of the kingdom in the person of Jesus the teacher, Mt 8–9 shows this same authority in the person of

Jesus the healer. In these chapters Matthew presents ten miracle stories, among which we find the following parallels to Mark's account, underlining the link of Mt 8:14–15 and 16, comparable only to that of Mk 1:29–31 and 32–34:

—astonishment of the crowds in the face of Jesus' authority (Mt 7:28–29);
—the cleansing of the leper (Mt 8:1–4);
—......
—healing of Peter's mother-in-law (Mt 8:14–15);
—many healings at evening time (Mt 8:16).

While telling the story of the cleansing of the leper (Mt 8:1–4 = Mk 1:40–45), Matthew had passed over Mark's account of the healing of Peter's mother-in-law, and of the many sick people in the evening, and the departure of Jesus from Capernaum in the early morning. Now Matthew returns to the first two paragraphs in the section of Mark which he has not used so far (Mk 1:29–34), and reproduces them with omissions as well as additions of his own. Especially noteworthy is Matthew's omission of 'at sundown' (Mk 1:32), which Mark had specifically mentioned because the previous events happened on the sabbath (Mk 1:21–28), and the law forbidding work on the sabbath would end at sundown; from that moment on people could begin to carry the sick to Jesus.

The wider context of Mt 8 – 9 extends from Mt 4:17, 'From that time Jesus began to preach, saying "Repent, for the kingdom of heaven is at hand"', to Mt 11:1–6, 'And when Jesus had finished instructing his twelve disciples, he went on from there to teach and preach in their cities ...'. Three important summary passages assure the unity of this wider context, i.e., Mt 4:23; 9:35; and 11:1, in which Jesus' ministry in Galilee is described as including teaching (*didaskein*), preaching (*kērussein*), and healing (*therapein*). Jesus' teaching is found in the Sermon on the Mount (Mt 5:1 – 7:29), while his ministry of healing is described in Mt 8:1 – 9:38 (although in these chapters Jesus does much more than heal, or even perform miracles; see Mt 8:18–20, 21–22; 9:9, 10–13, 14–17).

The narrower context is indicated by the almost identical summary passages, Mt 4:23, 'And he went about all Galilee, teaching in their synagogues and preaching the gospel of the kingdom and healing every disease and every infirmity among the people', and Mt 9:35, 'And Jesus went about all the cities and villages, teaching in their synagogues and preaching the gospel of the kingdom, and healing every disease and every infirmity'. It should be noted that Mt 4:23 belongs together with Mt 4:24–25, which refers to Jesus' healing ministry (verse 24) and the fact that Jesus was followed by great crowds from all Israel (verse 25), two points extensively dealt with in Mt 8 – 9. In fact, Mt 8:1 recalls Mt 4:25, for both say that 'great crowds followed him'. And Mt 8:16, 'they brought to him many who were possessed with demons; and he cast out the spirits with a word, and healed all who were sick', picks up Mt 4:24, '... and they brought him all the sick, those afflicted with various diseases and pains, demoniacs, epileptics, and paralytics, and he healed them'. Moreover, a good number of words and expressions found throughout Mt 8 – 9 recall Mt 4:24–25.

In recent years many scholars have followed the classic study of Heinz Joachim Held,[36] according to which Matthew compiled in Mt 8 – 9 a cycle of miracle stories and other materials which deal successively with the themes of Christology (Mt 8:2–17), discipleship (Mt 8:18 – 9:17), and faith (Mt 9:18–31). But this view overlooks the fact that the long central section, Mt 8:18 – 9:17, should be divided into a travel section (Mt 8:18–34) and a section dealing with debates (Mt 9:1–17).

It is better, therefore, to follow Christof Burger[37] who says that Mt 8 – 9 should be seen as a section composed of four subsections arranged thematically to deal with Christology (Mt 8:1–17), discipleship (Mt 8:18–34), questions concerning the separation of Jesus and his disciples from Israel (Mt 9:1–17), and faith (Mt 9:18–34). These four subsections may be considered as Matthew's commentary on and illustration of Mt 4:24–25, referring to Jesus' healing ministry and his being followed by crowds coming from all Israel and the Decapolis. In both Mt 4:24–25 and Mt 8 – 9 the theme of following is expressed by the verb *akolouthein*, 'to follow' (Mt 8:1, 10, 19, 22, 23; 9:9, 27). While carrying out his healing ministry Jesus also gathers followers (Mt 8:18–20, 21–22; 9:9, 10–14). Each of the four subsections mentioned above contributes something to this overall picture of Mt 8 – 9.[38]

The account proper

Attention has been drawn to the highly stylized character of the Matthean version of this account, which is said to have a 'strictly executed inclusion structure':

And when Jesus entered Peter's house,
　he saw his mother-in-law
　　lying sick
　　　with a fever.
　　　　He touched her hand,
　　　and the fever left her,
　　and she rose
　and served him.

It has further been observed that the two verses of the pericope (in Greek) have the same number of words (fifteen) and even the same number of syllables (thirty).

> **Verse 14:** And when Jesus entered Peter's house, he saw his mother-in-law lying sick with a fever;

An open-minded reader of the Matthean version gets the impression that Jesus entered the house alone. The disciples are not mentioned, although the use of the expression 'Peter's house' makes the presence of Peter probable. Further, there is no mention of the 'people' (Mk 1:30b; Lk 4:38b). The less important characters are absent and everything points to the fact that Matthew's interest is concentrated on the major figure alone, namely Jesus. This is already clear from the fact that, purely as a matter of grammar, Jesus (*ho Iēsous*) is the only subject in the incident of the healing. The change of subject (Jesus—the mother-in-law—'they'—Jesus), which gives a certain liveliness to the Marcan account, is deleted. Instead of this we read: 'And when Jesus entered ... he saw ... and he touched her hand'. The further development of the narrative reveals that the occurrence takes place between Jesus and the mother-in-law alone, for the concluding clause reads 'and she served *him*' instead of 'and she served *them*' (Mk 1:31b; Lk 4:39b). No mention of 'telling Jesus' (Mark), still less of 'beseeching him for her' (Luke). Jesus 'entered and saw' as later in the house of Jairus (Mt 9:23). According to his well-known technique, Matthew reduces the proceedings to two partners—Jesus and the person or the group in front of him: Jesus and the demons (Mt 8:28–34), Jesus and the scribes (Mt 9:2–8), Jesus and the miraculously cured (Mt 9:18–26), Jesus and the crowd (Mt 12:15–21). Such a reduction of anecdotic elements strongly emphasizes the person of Jesus.

Matthew no longer speaks of 'Simon', the Galilean fisherman, but of 'Peter', whose community name is announced at his calling (Mt 4:18) and is later on proclaimed by Jesus (Mt 16:17–18). It is no longer possible here to think of a straightforward account of an eyewitness. Rather, we are dealing with the testimony of a community which lives its faith while remembering the events of Jesus' time.

> **Verse 15:** he touched her hand, and the fever left her, and she rose and served him.

Like Mark, Matthew writes that Jesus 'touched' the woman as he healed her. The second half of Mt 8:15 is almost exactly parallel to

Mark. Matthew's 'she rose' (*ēgerthē*) may be related to Mark's 'and he lifted her up', or 'he raised her up' (*ēgeiren*). Instead of Mark's 'she served them', Matthew has 'she served him'.

Jesus acts with sovereign independence: he comes, he sees, he touches; and through the contact of his hand (or garment) the fever of Peter's mother-in-law, the leprosy of the leper (Mt 8:3; Jesus here adds: 'I will, be clean'), the haemorrhage of the woman (Mt 9:22), the blindness of the two blind men (Mt 9:29), the fear of the witnesses at the transfiguration (Mt 17:7) all disappear.

Jesus does not help the sick woman to get up by taking her by the hand (unlike Mk 1:31), but by a simple touch he gives her new strength: 'she rose' by herself. The elimination of all the other people present in the parallel account shows that Matthew wants to stress the symbolic import of the healing gesture. The sick woman is lying down, as if she were paralysed (*beblēmenēn*; the same expression is used for the centurion's servant, Mt 8:6, and for the paralytic, Mt 9:2). Then, rising (*ēgerthē*), she becomes the figure of someone paralysed by sin who is raised by Jesus and devotes herself to his service (cf. Mt 20:28; 25:44; 27:55).

All these indications invite us to understand the term *ēgerthē*, 'she rose', in the strongest possible sense. As the ruler's daughter rose up (Mt 9:25), and especially as Jesus rose (Mt 28:6, 7), so this sick woman is raised by Christ. In this perspective, even more clearly than in Mark and Luke, the attitude of the healed person who 'served' Christ is given a religious meaning. In this light, it may be asked whether by replacing 'Simon' by 'Peter' Matthew is intending to underline the community value of his house. Moreover, is it merely accidental that, because of a difference in context from Mark and Luke, Jesus is not said to leave the synagogue? For Matthew, indeed, Jesus and his followers constitute the true Israel, and hence do not have to leave the synagogue. Did Matthew deliberately choose another context for this reason? Present methods of investigation and analysis do not permit us to give the final answer to such a question.

Jesus' healing miracles depict the salvation which he brings to the world. This salvation is likened to life from death (e.g., 'you have been raised with Christ', Col 3:1), and those who have received it are expected to serve Jesus (e.g., 'you are serving the Lord Christ', Col 3:24). The actual description of the miracle may have been influenced by the teaching of the early Church.

What then is the literary genre of this account? It is no longer a miracle story as such. The notice of the healings performed on that same evening (Mt 8:16, 'that evening they brought to him many …') no longer has the character of a local event as in Mark, who describes the whole city gathered at the door of Simon's house. In Matthew,

Jesus alone acts; the illness is only an opportunity for Jesus' action. There is no dialogue climaxed by a (healing) word of Jesus, contrary to most of Matthew's miracle stories: Jesus speaks to the leper (Mt 8:2–4), to the centurion (Mt 8:5–13), to Jairus, the woman with the haemorrhage and the two blind men (Mt 9:18–30), to the Canaanite woman (Mt 15:21–28), to the blind men of Jericho (Mt 20:29–34). Mt 8:14–15 seems to be a 'catechetical account' of the effect of the redemption symbolically performed by Jesus.

Matthew, witness of the catechetical tradition, is not satisfied with simply integrating into his redaction the collection of miracles which are symbolic of the resurrection. By means of examples he shows how Jesus confirms by deeds his teaching of the Sermon on the Mount (Mt 5:1 – 7:29), and already foreshadows the answer given to the disciples of John the Baptist. All the miracles invite us to turn towards this man who saves; 'and blessed is he who takes no offence at me' (Mt 11:2–6). The movement of actualization already begun in the early Christian community here reaches its completion. Christians serve Christ; by their redemption they have passed from the impotence of sickness to the position of servants standing before the living God.

Another indication of Matthew's transposition is found in the immediate context. Like Mark and Luke, Matthew refers to the many healings Jesus performed that same evening; but he adds: 'This was to fulfil what was spoken by the prophet Isaiah, "He took our infirmities and bore our diseases"' (Mt 8:17; quoting Isa 53:4). Here we have the exact Hebrew text, where in the Septuagint and the Targum it is given a more spiritual interpretation. We should take it as Matthew's own rendition of the Hebrew, which was certainly correct, but may nevertheless be regarded as an *ad hoc* interpretation, since it differs from the Greek and Aramaic interpretations known to us. This quotation thus presented by Matthew in this particular context reveals his understanding of the miraculous healings that precede it. If Matthew applies this quotation to the healing miracles rather than to the passion of Jesus, these healings must symbolize for him the salvation obtained by that passion; through these healings he sees Christ suffering and dying for us in order to heal us from sin and death.

> The healing of Peter's mother-in-law is obviously conceived as an immediate example of the quotation from scripture about the vocation of Christ (Mt 8:17), and is correspondingly given Christological emphasis by Matthew.[39]

Indeed, the incorporation of this healing into the section Mt 8:2–17 points to a Christological purpose. Three miracles (the healings of a leper, the centurion's servant, and Peter's mother-in-law) stand alongside each other and reach their clearly recognizable conclusion in the summary report and the quotation from the Old Testament in Mt 8:16–17. By this healing activity Jesus fulfils the prophecies (Isa 53:4). There he was 'announced' as the One who would free us from our illnesses. Correspondingly, Mt 8:14–15 presents Jesus as answering of his own accord (no request in Matthew!) this call laid upon him by God. Matthew's abbreviation of the Marcan version, therefore, does not have merely formal causes. His revision amounts to a re-interpretation by means of which he expresses more clearly a theological perspective which was already present in Mark, though in a more subdued manner.

4   The healing of the leper

Mt 8:1–4	Mk 1:40–45	Lk 5:12–16
1 When he came down from the mountain, great crowds followed him;		12 While he was in one of the cities, there
2 and behold, a leper came to him	40 And a leper came to him beseeching him,	came a man full of leprosy; and when he saw Jesus,
and knelt before him, saying, 'Lord, if you will, you can make me clean.'	and kneeling said to him, 'If you will, you can make me clean.'	he fell on his face and besought him, 'Lord, if you will, you can make me clean.'
3 And he stretched out his hand and touched him, saying, 'I will; be clean.' And immediately his leprosy was cleansed.	41 Moved with pity, he stretched out his hand and touched him, and said to him, 'I will; be clean.' 42 And immediately the leprosy left him, and he was made clean.	13 And he stretched out his hand, and touched him, saying, 'I will; be clean.' And immediately the leprosy left him.
	43 And he sternly charged him, and sent him away at once,	14 And he charged him
4 And Jesus said to him, 'See that you say nothing to any one;	44 and said to him, 'See that you say nothing to any one;	to tell no one; but 'go and show yourself
but go, show yourself to the priest, and offer	but go, show yourself to the priest, and offer for your cleansing	to the priest, and make an offering for your cleansing,
the gift that Moses commanded, for a proof to the people.'	what Moses commanded, for a proof to the people.'	as Moses commanded, for a proof to the people.'
	45 But he went out and began to talk freely about it, and to spread the news,	15 But so much the more the report went abroad concerning him;

80

> so that Jesus could no
> longer openly enter a
> town,
> but was out in the
> country;
> and people came to him and great multitudes
> from every quarter. gathered to hear
> and to be healed
> of their infirmities.
> 16 But he withdrew
> to the wilderness
> and prayed.

The pre-Marcan account

Mk 1:40–45 cannot be the original form of the account; it cannot be
doubted that Mark edited the original story. Some obvious tensions
occur, especially in the second part of the account. In verse 44 we find
side by side the command to be silent, 'see that you say nothing to
any one' (Mk 1:44a), and the request to 'show yourself to the priest
... for a proof to the people' (Mk 1:44b). The concluding verse 45
which, on the one hand, depicts the breaking of the imposition of
silence and, on the other hand, does not mention the execution of the
request to go to the priest, again stands in tension with Mk 1:44ab.
This tension has been explained as the result of a combination of two
versions of the same story in Mk 1:40–45, of which one contained the
imposition of silence and its breach, and the other the request to
show himself to the priest. This analysis is too ingenious to be
probable. Mk 1:40–45 is not the combination of two versions of an
account, but a consistent traditional story which was redactionally
expanded by means of certain motifs which caused a number of
tensions in the present account.

Reconstruction of the pre-Marcan form of the account[40]

Usually the evangelist intervenes most in the initial and final verses of
a traditional account. But in this particular case verse 40 has not
really been edited so as to connect the healing of the leper with the
preceding context. This happens only at the end of the story, in verse
45 which also prepares for the next verse, the introduction to the
healing of the paralytic. Mark inserts the healing of the leper into the
context without any introductory notice giving its setting, and simply
attaches it to Jesus' proclamation in Galilee described in Mk 1:39, so
that it appears still to belong to the context created by the evangelist
in Mk 1:14–39, which seemed to have ended with the recapitulation
of Mk 1:39. This is confirmed by the fact that characteristic features

of Mk 1:14–39 appear once more: *kērussein*, 'to announce, proclaim', and *erēmos topos*, 'lonely place, out in the country'. The relation of the cleansing account to the preceding context is therefore clear, even without any introductory notice by the evangelist.

What exactly should be attributed to Mark? Verses 40–43 have most probably remained substantially unchanged. Verse 40 contains an ancient introduction to an isolated tradition without indication of time or place: it presents the leper and his request. Verses 41–42 narrate the cleansing in the style of the pre-Marcan miracle tradition. The difficult verse 43 is certainly not to be attributed to Mark. The evangelist has taken over the miracle story proper without any detectable changes.

Mark's intervention can be detected only in verses 44–45. The injunction to silence in verse 44a, 'see that you say nothing to any one', is judged in different ways. Some take it to be a traditional feature; others consider it a redactional insertion. The apparent absence of explicit injunctions to silence in the tradition raises the possibility that Mark formulated verse 44a, but since he likes to fall back on pre-existing catchwords, formulations and images, Mk 1:44a could actually be the traditional source of Mark's redactional injunctions to silence. Still, the imposition of silence, 'see that you say nothing to any one', is probably redactional. Its formulation argues against the attempt to understand it as a traditional 'command to be silent, which was limited until such time as the healing was confirmed by the priest'.[41] The command is absolute and so stands in tension with the request to show himself to a priest. This will not have been part of the original account. That the command to be silent is a foreign element in the story is also suggested by the fact that the typical dismissal 'go' (*hupage*; compare Mk 2:11; 5:19; 5:34; 7:29; 10:52) links up very well with 'and he said to him' in Mk 1:44a.

Comparison with similar secondary commands to be silent (Mk 5:43; 7:36; 8:30; 9:9) shows that here too the evangelist is responsible for its insertion. Mk 16:8, where it is said of the fleeing women that 'they said nothing to any one' is a close redactional parallel to 'say nothing to any one' in Mk 1:44a. So everything seems to indicate the redactional nature of the clause. And yet it is not excluded that the command to be silent was present in some form in the original account as part of the (exorcistic) activity of the healer. Mark would then have interpreted this command in line with his 'messianic secret' theory.

Verse 45 stands in double tension to verse 44. Attempts to solve the problem by suggesting that there is no change of subject and the whole statement applies to Jesus are contradicted by the initial words of verse 45, 'but he' (*ho de*) which can only refer to the healed leper.

Many scholars, then, consider verse 45 a Marcan addition. This is supported by the presence of several typically Marcan features, i.e., the words *kērussein* and *polla* ('to proclaim many things') and the clause 'so that he could no longer enter a town, but'. The rest of the verse, however, is considered original by several exegetes. This opinion is supported by its vocabulary. Moreover, it is form-critically probable that the account did not end with verse 44, but had a conclusion which reported the effect of Jesus' healing (compare Mk 1:27; 2:12; 5:15, 20; 7:37). This could have been contained in verse 45, which was then redactionally expanded by the evangelist. Originally the traditional core of the concluding verse may have read: 'but he went out and began to spread the news, and people came to him from every quarter'.

The expansion of the verse by the evangelist indicates why he allowed the tension between the inserted command to be silent and the final verse. The reason is not his alleged interest in the breach of the command, but the extant tradition which already contained the public announcement of the cleansing in verse 45. The reconstructed short conclusion does not stand in tension with the request to the cured man to show himself to the priest. In fact, it may have meant that he started spreading the news already while *on his way* to the priest. The present tension between verses 44 and 45 is due to the expansion and new interpretation of the latter by the evangelist, who now focuses especially on the cured man's actions. The pre-Marcan text may have been as follows:

40 And a leper came to him beseeching him,
  and kneeling said to him,
  'If you will, you can make me clean.'
41 Moved with pity/anger,
  he stretched out his hand and touched him,
  and said to him, 'I will; be clean.'
42 And immediately the leprosy left him,
  and he was made clean.
43 And he sternly charged him,
  and sent him away (at once),
44 and said to him,
  ('See that you say nothing to any one;
  but) go, show yourself to the priest,
  and offer for your cleansing what Moses commanded,
  for a proof to the people (literally: to them).'
45 But he went out and began to spread the news,
  and people came to him from every quarter.

Interpretation of the pre-Marcan account[42]

The schema of the traditional healing miracle and its contacts with Hellenistic narrative style are easily recognized. The schema consists of five features:

(1) indication of situation with mention of disease and request (verse 40);
(2) healing with gesture and word (verse 41);
(3) the healing is established (verse 42);
(4) demonstration of the healing (verses 43–44);
(5) 'progress report' with missionary thrust (verse 45).

> **Verse 40:** And a leper came to him beseeching him, and kneeling said to him, 'If you will, you can make me clean.'

As usual, the story is handed down without indication of time and place; not even Jesus' name is mentioned. Typically, the narrator says literally that the leper 'comes to him'. Compare:

Mk 2:3:   And they come, bringing to him a paralytic …
Mk 5:22: Then comes one of the rulers of the synagogue …
Mk 7:32: And they bring to him a man who is deaf …
Mk 8:22: And they bring to him a blind man …

Such expressions are stereotyped. That the leper is not 'brought' but 'comes' to Jesus, is because he must avoid human company.

The words 'leper' and 'leprosy' here and elsewhere in the gospels are used of several kinds of skin disease, but almost certainly not of what we now call leprosy (Hansen's disease) which seems to have been extremely rare in Palestine at that time. The cleansing of leprosy was one of the signs expected during the messianic era (cf. Mt 11:5).

The request for healing is also conventionally described: 'beseeching him and kneeling'. Compare (in literal translation):

Mk 5:23: he falls at his feet, and beseeches him saying …
Mk 7:32: and they beseech him …
Mk 8:22: and they beseech him …

The first element of the pericope which is not prescribed by the narrative schema is the formulation of the request: 'If you will, you can make me clean'. The leper confesses his confidence in Jesus' will and helping power. His words should definitely not be interpreted as an expression of hesitation or doubt. Elsewhere the requests are not so explicit (compare Mk 5:23; 9:22; 10:47ff.). In Mk 1:40, Jesus' power by which he performs his powerful acts (compare Mk 5:30; 6:2, 5, 14; 9:39) is identified with his will. Jesus' will is sufficient to perform a miracle like the cleansing of the leper, which to his contemporaries was almost as unusual as raising somebody from the dead. Here the narrator seems to be making a Christological point, because the words of the leper characterize Jesus' will as God's will, and his power as God's power.

The leper (equivalent to a dead man!) acknowledges Jesus' divine power, which is confirmed by Jesus' powerful word in verse 41. The leper requests an act of power which, according to the Old Testament and contemporary Jewish understanding, only God could perform. The healing of a leper was almost equated with raising from the dead (II Kgs 5:7; Job 18:13, where leprosy is called 'the first-born of death'). The leper's request ascribes this power to Jesus. The narrator apparently formulates the account against the background of a Christology which proclaims Jesus as the prophet of the endtime: 'that there is a prophet in Israel' (II Kgs 5:8), and one who is greater than Elisha who cured the leper Naaman (II Kgs 5). Jesus has God's power.

> **Verse 41:** Moved with pity [anger], he stretched out his hand and touched him, and said to him, 'I will; be clean.'

Jesus' healing activity is described in line with the conventional schema and vocabulary of miracle stories, but taking into account the particular request of the leper and its Christological import. The original reading is most probably 'moved with anger', as found in Codex Bezae and some other manuscripts, rather than 'moved with pity', as RSV, JB and NAB have (but see NEB: 'in warm indignation'). Psychological explanations are not in order. The text contains nothing to suggest that Jesus was angry because the leper approached him and thus transgressed the law of Lev 13:45–46. The same should be said of the suggestion that Jesus was angry because of 'the horror of the misery which accompanied the disease', or because of the power of the evil one or sin shown in the disease, or because the mission he had just begun was interrupted. Neither is Jesus angry at the injustice committed against lepers in Israel. The text is not about Jesus' anger *against anything*, but rather about Jesus' miracle-working.

The meaning of 'moved with anger' (*orgistheis*) must be determined in this particular context and in connection with the verbs 'to beseech', 'will', 'can', and the healing gesture. The cleansing of the leper is equivalent to a raising from the dead. The exact meaning of 'moved with anger' can be gathered from parallel materials and was established long ago. 'The best explanation is that the wonder-worker has to work up his emotions in preparation for the difficult deed of healing, as in Jn 11:35, 38.'[43] In the expression 'moved with anger' we are dealing with a technical term for a kind of 'prophetic frenzy' traces of which have been pointed out in the New Testament. Therefore, 'moved with anger' must be understood in parallel with Jn 11:33, 'deeply moved in spirit and troubled', and 11:38, 'deeply moved again', as preparation of the wonder-worker for an especially difficult miracle.

Then follows the healing gesture: 'he stretched out his hand and touched him'. Touching with the hand is a typical feature, a common healing gesture. It symbolizes the transfer of power to the sick person (compare Mk 3:10; 5:27, 28, 31; 6:56). Jesus touches the tongue of the deaf-mute (Mk 7:33), and the companions of the blind man request Jesus to touch him (Mk 8:22). The narrator does not seem to give any special thought to the fact that the person Jesus touches here is a leper, that is, an 'untouchable'. The means of transfer of power is the hand: 'What mighty works are wrought by his hands!' (Mk 6:2). Extending the hand is a powerful gesture. The healing gesture related in Mk 1:41 belongs to a series of traditional, conventional pictures. Compare:

Mk 1:31: He took her by the hand and lifted her up ...
Mk 5:41: Taking her by the hand he said ...
Mk 8:25: Then again he laid his hands upon his eyes ...
Mk 9:27: But Jesus took him by the hand and lifted him up

In Mk 1:41 the gesture receives its special importance, that is, its Christological point, from the special formulation 'stretched out his hand' and the words of Jesus which follow. The gesture can indeed have different meanings according to the will of the one acting. In association with the leper's request in verse 40, the gesture in verse 41 is to be interpreted as an expression of Jesus' divine will and power. But the extension of the hand is not only a divine gesture; it is also the gesture of the miracle-worker Moses (and Aaron; Ex 4:4; 7:19; 8:5 [8.1]; 9:22f.; 14:16, 21, 26f.), and thus of the type of the endtime prophet Jesus. By this gesture Jesus indicates his power which, in close connection with the leper's request, he also expresses in the statement, 'I will; be clean'. As an answer to the request, 'If you will, you can make me clean', this statement gives special significance to Jesus' action as the execution of a liberating power. Jesus speaks the word of power: 'I will' (compare Mk 9:25, 'I command you'). The healing word 'be clean' (compare II Kgs 5:13, 'wash, and be clean') constitutes a bridge between the establishment of the healing (verse 42) and the demonstration which is associated with the cultic cleansing (verse 44). Elisha could only promise Naaman that he would be clean if he would wash himself in the Jordan (II Kgs 5:10), and the command in the servants' version (II Kgs 5:13) is only an abbreviation of this promise. Jesus however, commands by his own will. The intended intensification of the image of the endtime prophet is unmistakable.

If the healing word here is compared with the other healing words found in Mark (Mk 2:11; 3:5; 5:41; 7:34; 10:52), it is easy to note the peculiarity of Mk 1:41, which is closely related to the formulation of the leper's request. By means of the singular word of power the narrator again breaks through the conventional picture, thus making a Christological point. All depends on the presentation of Jesus as the mighty endtime prophet who acts in the power of God.

Verse 42: And immediately the leprosy left him, and he was made clean.

The healing is established. In view of Jesus' healing word, the narrator adds: 'and he was made clean' (compare II Kgs 5:14, 'and he was clean'). The establishment of the healing, often the *immediate* healing, is most of the time stated briefly. The narrator speaks as if he were an eye-witness, although only Jesus and the cleansed person were present (compare Mk 1:31; 3:5; 5:29; 7:35; 8:25; 10:52). Comparison with the other texts shows that only fever (Mk 1:31) and leprosy (Mk 1:42) are considered as diseases which befall and 'leave' a person. Nevertheless they are not necessarily considered as diseases of demonic origin.

The use of 'immediately' is intended to stress the instantaneous character of the healing, and therefore its miraculous nature. The addition of 'and he was made clean' makes clear that the healing is complete. The formulaic expression (compare Lev 13 – 14) states that the man is again able to join activities of public worship. In the present context it stresses the saving power of Jesus, whose word (Mk 1:41) is immediately fulfilled. The Christological point of the story continues to operate.

Verses 43–44: And he sternly charged him, and sent him away (at once), (44) and said to him, ('See that you say nothing to any one; but) go, show yourself to the priest, offer for your cleansing what Moses commanded, for a proof to the people.'

Verses 43–44 depict the demonstration of the healing. Miracle stories regularly demonstrate that the previously sick person is really cured. Simon's mother-in-law who was lying sick with a fever serves the guests (Mk 1:31); the paralytic gets up and carries his stretcher home

(Mk 2:12); the man with the withered hand can stretch out his hand (Mk 3:5); the Gerasene demoniac sits there clothed and in his right mind (Mk 5:15); the daughter of Jairus can eat (Mk 5:43); the man who was previously dumb speaks plainly (Mk 7:35); the man who was blind now sees everything clearly (Mk 8:25).

The only way of demonstrating the cleansing of a leper in a story which does not mention any eye-witnesses is to refer to the law which regulated the healing of a leper (Lev 13 – 14). Only the priests could establish the cleansing from leprosy and therefore, in the present account, the miracle. The vocabulary of verse 44, which piles up features found in Lev 13 – 14, presupposes knowledge of the Jewish law on the question and indicates, therefore, the Jewish-Christian origin of the account.

The sending of the cured person to the priest also demonstrates the reality of the healing: 'Go, show yourself to the priest, and offer for your cleansing what Moses commanded'. The introductory 'go', which appears repeatedly in miracle stories, not only enlivens the account but also prepares the way for the specific direction to show himself to the priest, and reinforces its import by building up expectation. Compare:

Mk   2:11: Go home.
Mk   5:19: Go home to your friends ...
Mk   5:34: Go in peace, and be healed of your disease.
Mk   7:29: For this saying you may go your way ...
Mk 10:52: Go your way; your faith has made you well.

Compare also II Kgs 5:19, 'Go in peace'. Mk 1:44 also belongs to this series. The command 'go' brings the healing to the fore. It should be compared first of all with the commission given to the healed man of Gerasa (Mk 5:19). This comparison is a help to understanding the injunction of silence: the man should not say anything to any one, but his ritual cleansing before the priest should be 'a proof for them' (Greek text: *eis marturion autois*, 'as a testimony for them'). *Marturion* could mean 'proof' that the leper is cured, or 'testimony' that Jesus has cured the leper. In the pre-Marcan tradition this expression should not, as in Mk 6:11; 13:9, be understood as 'evidence against them', and is not directed against the priests, but means a positive testimony.[44] It means a proof or testimony of the healing of the leper (Jesus' action) to those to whom the leper should not say anything, namely his environment. This is clearly indicated by the syntax: say nothing ... but perform the ritual cleansing before the priest for a testimony, a proof to them. Jesus' action should speak for itself.

The command to remain silent is preceded by the clause 'and he sternly charged him, and sent him away (at once)'. In Mt 9:30f., which could be the oldest direct interpretation of our text, the context is rightly explained: 'And their eyes were opened. And Jesus sternly charged them, "See that no one knows it". But they went away and spread his fame through all that district'. Jesus cannot remain hidden. But why has the narrator used such a harsh and offensive phrase? The expression 'he sternly charged him', has here, i.e., *after* the cleansing, no thaumaturgic meaning. It cannot be a remnant of an exorcism either, since then too the verse would be in the wrong place. *Ekballein* means here, as in Mk 1:12, 'to drive out', 'to send away'. Is Jesus furious because he foresees that the cleansed man will be 'disobedient', or that many will be led by this to a superficial belief in miracles? Here, as in Mk 1:41, alleged ideas or feelings entertained by Jesus should not be read into the text. One should rather try to understand the purpose of the narrator. What could 'he sternly charged him' mean? A number of parallel passages may help us.

It has already been said that Mt 9:30–31 points us in the right direction. The contrast between Jesus' injunction of silence and the fact that the man speaks openly should be emphasized. Other injunctions of silence, whether redactional or not, are also formulated in a harsh way, by means of the verb *epitiman*, 'to rebuke', 'to order strictly', 'to charge'; Mk 3:12; 8:30; 10:48). Once it is seen that *epitiman* fulfils the same function as *embrimasthai* does here (compare Mk 10:13, 'and the disciples *rebuked* them'; Mk 14:5, 'And they *reproached* her'), then the formulation of Mk 1:43 no longer appears as an isolated case. The narrator emphasizes the injunction of silence so strongly in order to make full use of its being broken at the end of the account. That this is the right interpretation of the original account is confirmed by Mark, the interpreter, himself, inasmuch as the injunctions to silence in Mk 5:43 and especially in Mk 7:36 are his own work. Mk 7:36 reads: 'And he charged them to tell no one; but the more he charged them, the more zealously they proclaimed it'. Finally, there is also the conclusion of the account of the healing of the blind man of Bethsaida in Mk 8:26, which shows that the motif of secrecy at the end of the narrative is rooted in the pre-Marcan tradition. Thus again a kerygmatic concern is connected with the demonstration of the cure, as becomes clear in the conclusion of the account.

> **Verse 45:** But he went out and began to talk freely about it, and to spread the news, (so that Jesus could no longer openly enter a town, but was out in the country;) and people came to him from every quarter.

One should not ask whether or not the 'missionary propaganda conclusion' of the account presupposes the cleansing ceremony before the priest. The account does not intend to answer such questions. It is concerned only with the fact that the cured person makes the healing known and thereby attracts people to the miracle-worker. Such 'propaganda conclusions' indeed betray the missionary interest of the Christian miracle stories. They belong to the repertory of the narrator (compare Mk 1:28; contrast Mk 3:6).

It has been suggested that 'openly' (*phanerōs*) was added by Mark to smooth the transition to Mk 2:1, which would otherwise stand in tension with Mk 1:45, but Jn 7:10, stating that Jesus went up to Jerusalem for the feast of Tabernacles 'not publicly (*phanerōs*) but in private', following Jn 7:1, 'because the Jews sought to kill him', suggests that Jesus was not trying to avoid the crowds so much as the hostile Jewish leaders. Thus understood, the 'many' mentioned in Mk 2:2 do not constitute a problem, and the plan to 'go on to the next towns' (Mk 1:38) can be further implemented.[45]

Finally, the effect of the healed man's action is mentioned: 'and people came to him from every quarter'. The imperfect tense suggests a continual stream of people: 'people kept coming to him'. Perhaps this feature takes the place of the 'chorus-ending' mentioned elsewhere in which 'all' acclaim Jesus (compare, e.g. Mk 2:12). The extent of Jesus' power, which is manifested in his action, is met by the concourse of the multitudes. The narrative is rounded off.

Summing up, one may say that in its pre-Marcan form the account of the cleansing of the leper follows the usual pattern of the healing story. The motif of the healing of a *leper* conditions the special form of the demonstration of the cure. In the leper's request and in Jesus' healing gesture and word we find striking theological, i.e. Christological accents. The account receives a strongly missionary emphasis through the contrast between the injunction to silence and the spreading of Jesus' fame.

The origin of the pre-Marcan account[46]

The question of the possible influence of Old Testament texts, especially Num 12:9–15, the leprosy of Miriam, and II Kgs 5, the cure of Naaman, is very important for determining the origin of the account. Is Jesus presented as the prophet who supersedes Moses and Elijah-Elisha, i.e., the endtime prophet? Mk 1:40–45 belongs indeed to that tradition-historical stage of the early Christian proclamation in which Jesus was proclaimed as the endtime prophet and miracles exceeding those of the great men of God in the Old Testament were told of him to that end. The miracle stories which belong to this group do not represent the oldest stage of the Jesus tradition. They owe their existence not so much to the historical

tradition about Jesus as to the proclamation of Christ and the
missionary needs of the early Church. In other words, the narrators
were not so much guided by the immediate impression made by
miracles like the one narrated in Mk 1:40–45, as by the interests of
the missionary proclamation of Christ.

Neither the place nor the time of the action nor the name of the
person cured is mentioned. No feature of the account is so individual
that it allows one to reach back to historical tradition. Positively, one
can only say that the author is clearly familiar with the Old
Testament, its laws concerning the clean and the unclean (Lev 13 –
14; Mk 1:44), the story of Naaman (II Kgs 5; Mk 1:41, 44f.), and
other features, like the gestures of Moses and the theology of God's
will and power. He is also familiar with the Hellenistic terminology of
wonder-working.

Strictly speaking, in order to be able to tell this story, the
narrator needed only the assessment of Jesus as the endtime prophet
who supersedes the Old Testament prophets, not a historical
tradition that Jesus actually healed this leper, or lepers. The
Christology of the early Church, based on Jesus' general behaviour
and on his death and resurrection, is sufficient basis for this account.

Mark 1:40–45

The context[47]

Mk 1:40–45 is situated in between two sections of the gospel: the first
presents Jesus' authority over the powers of evil (Mk 1:21–39), the
second describes the growing opposition to Jesus on the part of the
Jewish authorities (Mk 2:1 – 3:6). The two sections are generally
considered to constitute a unity in themselves. The cleansing of the
leper is situated in between these two sections, which are at the same
time independent and yet connected with each other so as to form
together a great narrative unit (Mk 1:[14–20]21 – 3:6). The isolated
position of Mk 1:40–45 appears also from the fact that no indications
of time or place are found at the beginning of the account (Mk 1:40).
The initial situation is abrupt and contrasts with the spatial and
temporal indications found in the surrounding sections.

Compared with the previous section, in terms of *dramatis
personae* Mk 1:40–45 contains an entirely new element, the Jewish
authorities: 'but go, show yourself *to the priest*, and offer for your
cleansing what Moses commanded, *for a proof to them*' (Mk 1:44;
RSV: 'for a proof to the people'). The healing concerns not only
Jesus and the leper, but also a third party. The continuation (verse
45) does not mention the reaction of the priest or those for whom the

testimony or proof was intended. We hear only of the indirect consequences which the healing has for Jesus. Until now there has been no direct confrontation between Jesus and his opponents. This will happen only in the next pericope, Mk 2:1–12, the first of five controversies which constitute a section of their own (Mk 2:1 – 3:6). The sending of the cleansed leper is a preparation for the next section. It is true that a few scholars take Mk 1:40–45 to be a controversy, the first in a group of six (M. Herranz Marco), but the great majority of exegetes consider Mk 2:1 – 3:6 a self-contained collection of five controversies to which Mk 1:40–45 constitutes a transition. It is especially from the dramatic point of view that the transitional function of Mk 1:40–45 clearly appears. For its relation to the preceding context see Chapter 2 above, particularly the discussion of the context of Mk 1:21–28. As for verbal contacts, we limit ourselves here to mentioning the use of the expression *exebalen* (Mk 1:43; RSV: 'he sent away'; literally 'expelled', a quasi-technical term for the expulsion of demons; compare Mk 1:34, 39), and the curious repetition of *ton logon*, 'the word' in Mk 1:45 (RSV: 'the news') and Mk 2:2, a term which is rarely used elsewhere in the narrative sections of Mark.

The intermediate position between two sections, the dramatic character of the account, and its particular way of sharing various features with the preceding and following context, make the cleansing of the leper into the literary transition between Mk 1:21–39 and Mk 2:1 – 3:6.

According to his plan, the evangelist has spread throughout the whole gospel the miracles handed down to him by the early Christian tradition. The place of the cleansing of the leper is determined by two factors. Firstly, the account allowed Mark to lead Jesus' activity in Galilee to a first climax. Secondly, this account, which shows Jesus in accord with the Mosaic law (verse 44), occupies a suitable place right before the Galilean controversies (Mk 2:1 – 3:6), which present Jesus in conflict with the advocates of the Jewish law. Finally, the insertion of an account without any definite indication of time or place after the summary statement of Mk 1:38–39 was rather easy.

The account proper[48]

The account is 'historicized' by its insertion into Mark's gospel. Instead of an independent tradition with its own Christological import, it now becomes an episode in Jesus' life, a station on Jesus' way which Mark interprets as the way of the (risen) Son of God (cf. Mk 12:6). The story no longer has any importance on its own, but only in the totality of Mark's presentation of Jesus' life as a way from

Galilee to Jerusalem and the cross. Only in the light of cross and resurrection can the story be understood correctly.

Negatively, this conclusion is confirmed by the redactional insertion of the injunction to silence in verse 44. In the context of the other impositions of silence found in Mark this means that Jesus does not want his miracles to be known, since they lead time and again to misinterpretation of his person and mission (compare Mk 1:35ff.; 3:7–12; 6:53–56). They did not lead to faith in Jesus, but only attracted people who craved for miracles. In other words, Jesus' miracles did not lead to his recognition as Son of God, as shown by the cross. For Mark, then, the miracles are only *signs* which can refer to the greatness of the One who really revealed himself as the Son of God in the cross and resurrection. Thus a miracle does not have conclusive force, but only limited Christological importance. It remains always a *hidden* sign which can only be understood from the perspective of the cross and resurrection. Until that time, however, the injunction to silence remains (Mk 9:9).

The regular breach of the injunction to silence (Mk 1:45; 7:36) is given as little thought by the evangelist as its actual pointlessness in the historicizing setting (Mk 5:43; 7:36; 8:26). How could, e.g., the raising of the ruler's daughter remain a secret? How could a blind man go home cured and keep it a secret? The historically inconsistent presentation is imposed on the evangelist by the tradition which he has received. The mission-oriented miracle stories reported in conventional terms the impression Jesus' miracles made on those who witnessed them. The evangelist is not concerned with the actual observance of the command, but he uses the injunction to silence in order to highlight the true function of Jesus' miracles in the history of the revelation of Christ. The breach of the injunction, as it is found in two miracle stories (Mk 1:45; 7:36) which originally already contained an extensive note on the effect of the miracle on the witnesses, should therefore not be given too much importance. As such, this does not represent the outlook of the evangelist. Much more important to him is the fact that by his rejection and cross the end of Jesus' earthly life shows that even in the miracles people had not recognized who he was, even though this had been made public against his will. By the Marcan injunctions to silence, the miracles are denied paramount importance for the revelation of Jesus and so for the Christological proclamation of the Christian community.

By means of the particle *alla*, 'but', the evangelist connects the redactional injunction to silence with the original command to the man to go and show himself to the priest. This could mean that while the *miracle* must remain hidden, the priest should nevertheless establish the *healing*. Whereas in the original account the thought of verse 44 was that through the priestly assessment of the healing and the prescribed offering the miracle would be established and would publicly testify to Jesus, Mark has blotted out this idea by the imposition of silence. Nobody should know that Jesus performed the healing by means of a miracle.

The evangelist widens the 'propaganda' conclusion of the account (verse 45) by means of the addition 'and he began to talk freely' (*kērussein polla*, literally, 'to proclaim many things'). The healed man joins the movement of Jesus' proclamation (Mk 1:14, 38, 39) and promotes it (compare Mk 5:19f). He is made the first missionary of Mark's gospel.[49] Mark gives, as it were, a miniature picture of the mission. The proclamation by the missionaries consists of the spreading of Jesus' actions. This redactional addition further develops a tendency which was already present in the traditional account.

The breach of the injunction to silence does not detract from the fact that Jesus did not want his miracles to be made public. This is first of all supported by the redactional *hōste*-clause, 'so that...', which Mark inserts in verse 45. This clause serves as link between this scene and the preceding and following contexts. It serves especially as development of a theme which was introduced in the central part (Mk 1:35–45) of the first section of the gospel (Mk 1:1 – 3:6). Jesus has withdrawn from Capernaum to a lonely place (Mk 1:35) because of the masses' craving for miracles (Mk 1:37), to proclaim his message in the whole of Galilee (Mk 1:38–39). Now the cured leper makes Jesus so widely known that he can hardly find a place to hide: he can no longer openly enter a town (anticipating Mk 2:1), and he is out in the country (a generalization referring back to Mk 1:35). In this way the conclusion of the traditional miracle story is heightened: 'people came to him from every quarter'. The evangelist thus brings to a climax (compare Mk 1:28, 33f., 38f.) Jesus' appearance with power and authority (Mk 1:22, 27).

The redactional insertion shows the consequences for Jesus of the breach of the injunction to silence: he can no longer enter a town, but is out in the country. Mark thus refers to Mk 1:35ff., where he shows Jesus withdrawing from the masses who crave for miracles. The same idea may be found in Mk 1:45b: to avoid misinterpretation of his mission and person by the miracle-seekers, Jesus must hide. It thus becomes finally clear that the miracles are only veiled signs which can be misinterpreted and which were and are inadequate to make the person and mission of Jesus fully understood. This hiddenness of Jesus can be lifted only when there is no longer any danger of misunderstanding, when in his death and resurrection Jesus has been revealed as Son of God. From that time too Jesus' miracles

obtain their true function as signs of faith for the community
following the crucified and risen Lord.

Matthew 8:1–4

The context

The general Matthean context of this miracle story has been
discussed in the study of the healing of Peter's mother-in-law (Mt
8:14–15). Unlike the other two synoptics, Matthew has carefully
linked the cleansing of the leper, the first healing miracle he presents,
with the conclusion of the Sermon on the Mount (Mt 5:1 – 7:29). We
hear again of the 'mountain' of Mt 5:1 and the 'crowds' of Mt 5:1 and
7:28. Thus Matthew makes the crowds not only hearers of Jesus'
words but also witnesses of his powerful deeds. He does not intend to
provide us with precise biographical details so much as to underline a
theological connection: he who proclaims the 'new law' is also the
one who commands the leprosy (Mt 8:3). To the 'I say to you' of Mt
5:21–48 there corresponds the 'I will' of the present healing miracle.

Matthew, who left his Marcan source at Mk 1:21, now takes up
the thread of Mark again at Mk 1:40–45, after Jesus has come down
from the mountain (Mt 8:1). Nevertheless he does not follow the
Marcan order schematically. One may wonder why he places the
healing of the leper first after the Sermon on the Mount, particularly
since with the healing of Peter's mother-in-law (Mt 8:14–15 = Mk
1:29–31) he is taking up earlier Marcan material. The content and
intrinsic value of the account itself, the nature of its revision by
Matthew, and its place in the context (Mt 8:2–17) answer this
question.

Matthew, who is considered the most systematic and catechetical
of the evangelists, is not concerned with a historical precision which
would him make correct Mark, but with theological, especially
Christological, and didactic considerations. He 'abbreviates the
descriptive part almost completely. Generally he substitutes formal
expressions for it which are not illustrative at all but typical. Thus in
Matt. 8:2a ... and likewise Matt. 8:3b ...'.[50]

The account proper

Matthew's version of the healing of the leper neatly divides into
introduction (verse 1), exposition (verse 2), miraculous healing
(verse 3), and conclusion (verse 4).

Verse 1: When he came down from the mountain, great
crowds followed him;

This whole verse is an editorial addition linking the teaching on the mountain to the cleansing of the leper. 'When he came down from the mountain' corresponds to 'He went up on the mountain' in Mt 5:1, and the 'mountain' mentioned here is therefore the mountain of the Sermon. The clause is reminiscent of statements about Moses' descent from Mount Sinai (Ex 19:14; 32:1, 15; 34:29).

The 'crowds', which were last mentioned in the conclusion of the Sermon on the Mount (Mt 7:28–29), and will remain in sight in the continuation (Mt 8:18; 9:8, 33, 36), 'follow' Jesus. This does not simply mean that they accompany him, but that, through their hearing and acknowledgement of his power (*exousia*, Mt 7:29), they follow him as people who have heard him and want to learn from him. Jesus is therefore presented as the Lord of his community at its beginning. ϭχλοι πολλοι

'Great crowds' is a favourite expression of Matthew's. It occurs in Mt 4:25, just before the Sermon on the Mount, and here again right after the Sermon. The phrase is always used in favourable contexts: 'and great crowds followed him' (Mt 4:25); 'great crowds followed him' (Mt 8:1); 'Jesus saw great crowds around him' (Mt 8:18); 'great crowds gathered about him' (Mt 13:2); 'great crowds came to him' (Mt 15:30); 'and large crowds followed him' (Mt 19:2). The phrase is always used in a context of following Jesus or gathering around him.

Matthew inserts the account, which was narrated in Mark without any reference to time or place, into the context of a continuous narrative, but he does not eliminate the tensions which thus arise. Jesus is on his way from the mountain (Mt 8:1) to Capernaum (Mt 8:5) when the leper approaches him. Since Jesus is accompanied by the crowds, the injunction to silence which Mt 8:4 takes over from Mk 1:44 becomes meaningless. The command can therefore yield only a theological meaning.

Verse 2: and behold, a leper came to him and knelt before him, saying, 'Lord, if you will, you can make me clean.'

καὶ ἰδου

'And behold' (*kai idou*, not in Mark at this point) is a favourite expression of Matthew, who uses (the emphatic) *idou* more than fifty times.

The expression 'come and kneel' often occurs in the Old Testament, referring to cultic adoration. The first of the two terms, 'to come' (*proserchesthai*) is used forty-one times by Matthew to describe the usually respectful approach of people to Jesus (e.g. Mt 8:5; 9:18, 20). Matthew rewrites Mk 1:40 in such a way that the leper 'knelt *before him*' instead of 'said *to him*', i.e., Jesus. Moreover, he

ΠΡΟΣΕΚΥΝΕΣ *imperfect*

changes Mark's 'falling on his knees' (*gonupetōn*) into 'knelt down', 'worshipped him' (*proskunei*). Thus Matthew emphasizes that Jesus is worthy of worship. This is also suggested by the insertion of 'Lord' at the beginning of the leper's appeal to Jesus. The addition is all the more notable, because Matthew has a tendency to abbreviate. He uses the title 'Lord' only in the speech of those who believe in Jesus (Mt 8:6; 15:22; 17:15; 20:30–31). Others address him as, e.g., 'teacher' (Mt 12:38) or 'rabbi' (Mt 26:49). The verb *proskunein*, 'to kneel before', is one of Matthew's favourite terms (thirteen times, as against twice each in Mark and Luke), always used in the sense of genuine worship or supplication (Mt 2:2, 8, 11; 14:33; 18:26; 28:9, 17), also when it is found in the introduction of miracle stories (Mt 8:2; 9:18; 15:25; 20:20). The latter use focuses the attention of the reader on the adoring petition, an attitude which can also still be adopted by the believing community in the presence of the risen Lord.[51] Wherever some form of address occurs in the healing miracles the petitioners invariably address Jesus as *kurios* (Mt 8:2, 6, 8, etc.), thus expressing a positive faith in Jesus, saviour and lord, who has the power to help them.[52]

The supplication itself, 'if you will, you can make me clean', is literally copied from Mark. But its situation in the gospel of Matthew makes clear what is still hidden in Mark at this stage: Jesus' power (Mt 7:29), which has been shown in his teaching (Mt 5:1 – 7:29), shines forth in his healing work (cf. Mt 8:9; 9:6). Jesus can do what he wills.

> **Verse 3:** And he stretched out his hand and touched him, saying, 'I will; be clean.' And immediately his leprosy was cleansed.

Jesus touches the leper as a method of curing him, and as a sign of his power over the disease. For other instances of cure by touching, see Mt 8:15; 9:20–21, 29; 14:36. The parallelism has been noted between 'came to him, knelt down before him, and said' and 'reached out his hand and touched him and said'. In all three gospels Jesus' words echo the petition of the leper, but by means of his abbreviated presentation, Matthew has strongly highlighted, through the use of catchwords already present in Mark, the firm connection between the leper's request, Jesus' healing saying, and the actual healing:

Mt 8:2:	if you will, you can	make me clean.
Mt 8:3a:	I will	be clean.
Mt 8:3b:	and immediately	was cleansed his leprosy.

The verb *katharizein* occurs several times in Lev 13 – 14, indicating both the priest's declaration that a person is clean and the condition of the person concerned. Matthew's expression 'his leprosy was cleansed' with 'leprosy' as subject is unusual and probably caused by Matthew's editing of Mk 1:42 which avoids Mark's duplicate expression 'the leprosy left him, and he was made clean', and retains the catchword *katharizein*.[53]

Matthew's editorial activity results above all in locating the centre of gravity in Jesus' touching the leper, to which the other actions of stretching out his hand and speaking to the leper are subordinated.

Mark's 'moved with pity' is surprisingly omitted. Elsewhere Matthew retains such expressions (Mt 9:36; 14:14; 15:32; 18:27; 20:34). But the omission could easily be accounted for if instead of 'moved with pity' Matthew read in Mark 'moved with anger', which is almost certainly original, since the change from 'moved with anger' to 'moved with pity' is easily comprehensible, whereas the opposite is almost unthinkable.

Faith is not mentioned, but the brevity of the petition and the instant echo of Jesus' answer illustrate the faith of the leper and the healing power of Jesus. Whenever the theme of faith explicitly occurs in Matthew's miracle stories it refers to the faith expressed in the petitioner's request, to which Jesus reacts in a way which corresponds to that faith. Even where an explicit reference to faith is absent the correspondence of request and response indicates the same relationship, expressing that what is expected in faith is granted.[54]

> **Verse 4:** And Jesus said to him, 'See that you say nothing to any one; but go, show yourself to the priest, and offer the gift that Moses commanded, for a proof to the people.'

The final verse agrees by and large with Mark. Matthew omits the Marcan phrase 'for your cleansing' (Mk 1:44), possibly because in his gospel Jesus cleansed the leper immediately. On the other hand, Matthew adds 'the gift' (cf. Mt 2:11; 5:23, 24). Matthew does not tell us what the cleansed man did; in fact, he omits the whole of Mk 1:45.

Of the numerous injunctions to silence found in Mark, Matthew has retained only a few (Mt 8:4; 9:30; 12:16; 16:20; 17:9), two of them at the end of a miracle story (Mt 8:4; 9:30). The great crowds who follow Jesus (Mt 8:1) are witnesses to the event, so that the command not to say anything to anyone seems absurd. However, Matthew appears to intend to say that nobody outside the community should hear this. The people who follow Jesus are the eschatological community who understand his eschatological activity.

The second part of the command, 'but go, show yourself to the priest ...', is not intended to contradict the command to tell no one. The prohibitions against divulging a miracle are one of the fundamental themes of the synoptic tradition, while the order to show himself to the priest is probably the point of the story. It shows that Jesus is willing to observe the law which he comes to fulfil (Mt 5:17).

The clause 'for a proof to the people' reads literally 'as a testimony to them'. Its meaning is disputed. Some think that since there is mention of only one priest, 'them' must refer to the people. Others believe that 'them' refers to the priests. Jesus' sending the leper to the priest is evidence that he keeps the law and teaches others to keep it. Or else the fact that the leper comes to them cured—a fact which they themselves can establish—testifies to Jesus' messianic power. Theoretically, *autois* might be translated 'against them' (cf. Mk 6:11; Lk 9:5), but the present context does not favour a negative connotation, and elsewhere in Matthew the phrase 'for a witness to them' apparently has a positive connotation (Mt 10:18; 24:14).

Matthew has chosen to place this healing at the head of his miracle collection (Mt 8 – 9), probably because he interprets it as an illustration of the earlier statement that Jesus did not come to abolish the law, but to fulfil it (Mt 5:17). Thus Jesus breaks through a law which can only exclude a leper, not heal him. Matthew also uses the healing story to call people to worship the 'Lord' who reaches out to everyone who comes to him with faith and presents a petition to him.

Luke 5:12–16[55]

The context

After the opening sermon at Nazareth, which is placed programmatically at the beginning of Jesus' activity (Lk 4:16–30), Luke has followed the thread of Mk 1:21–34, and has presented his day in Capernaum (Lk 4:31–41). Lk 4:42–44 has remodelled Mk 1:35–39 into an exposition of the following scenes. Then, in Lk 5:1–11, Luke has inserted his version of the calling story (compare Mk 1:16–20) which had previously been passed over in Lk 4:30. With the healing of the leper Luke resumes the thread of the Marcan account which he had briefly left in the calling story of Lk 5:1–11. From Lk 5:12 on he again follows his Marcan source (Lk 5:12 – 6:19 = Mk 1:40 – 3:19). Essentially Luke stays close to Mark. At any rate, all changes and redactional intervention witness to Luke's theological design. In Lk 5:12ff. the evangelist picks up again the thread of the account developed in Lk 4:43f.: Jesus continues his proclamation in the other cities of Judea. By combining the healing of the leper with the calling of the first disciples, Luke suggests that the calling of the first 'apostles' is followed by the calling and healing of outcasts and sinners. The actual connection of both stories is indicated by the insertion at the beginning of Lk 5:12 of one of Luke's favourite formulas, 'and it came to pass as ...' (*kai egeneto en tōi*, as usual not rendered in most English translations). Luke's first readers must also have understood this story as closely connected with the following account, the healing and forgiving of the paralytic, Lk 5:17–26. The combined accounts must have reminded them of the cleansing and forgiveness communicated by the Lord in baptism. Gentile Christians in particular must have heard here a reference to the 'promise' of Lk 4:27, 'And there were many lepers in Israel in the time of the prophet Elisha; and none of them was cleansed, but only Naaman the Syrian'. This is being fulfilled in that Christ now takes away the 'leprosy' of the Gentiles. What Jesus once did on earth demonstrates what he does now again and again after Easter.

The account proper

> **Verse 12:** While he was in one of the cities, there came a man full of leprosy; and when he saw Jesus, he fell on his face and besought him, 'Lord, if you will, you can make me clean.'

Luke situates the healing story in his typical general and vague manner, 'in one of the cities'. Similar expressions are found in Lk 13:10, 'in one of the synagogues'; Lk 5:17; 8:22; 20:1, 'on one of those days'. The word 'city' is here derived from the programmatic indication. 'I must preach the good news of the kingdom of God to the other cities also; for I was sent for this purpose' (Lk 4:43) to which Luke is referring here.

In the style of the Septuagint Luke introduces the leper with the expression 'and behold', not rendered in most English translations. Luke then changes Mark's 'leper' into 'a man full of leprosy', thus conforming to the Old Testament practice of indicating the subject of 'behold'-clauses as 'a man' or 'a woman'. 'Full of leprosy' intensifies the Marcan tradition and thereby prepares for the greatness of the following miracle (compare Lk 4:38, 'high fever', as against Mk 1:30, 'fever').

The reformulation of the introductory clauses leads to another addition which resumes the action of the leper, 'and when he saw Jesus'. This rephrasing also allows Luke to mention Jesus (not mentioned by name since Lk 5:10), and thus he can introduce the name into an account which was handed on 'anonymously' by Mark.

Again in line with the Septuagint, Luke writes that the leper 'fell on his face' (see, e.g., Gen 17:3, 17; Lev 9:24, etc.; compare Lk 17:16), a frequently found expression for respectful greeting or veneration. As in Mt 8:2, Luke inserts the address 'Lord' which he also adds elsewhere in a number of passages taken from Mark as well as from Q (see below, note 28). In Luke, the address expresses submission to the sovereign person of Jesus. The request itself is identical with that in Mark. The words of the leper suggest that Jesus can heal him by an act of his will alone.

> **Verse 13:** And he stretched out his hand, and touched him, saying 'I will; be clean.' And immediately the leprosy left him.

Verse 13 summarizes three Marcan verses (Mk 1:41–43). Luke avoids all references to Jesus' emotions mentioned in Mk 1:41, 43; he omits 'moved with pity/anger', 'sternly', 'sent him away'. By a slight change of word order Luke underlines that it is Jesus (not just his hand, Mk 1:41; not discernible in RSV translation) who touches the leper. As was the case with the leper's request, Luke reproduces Jesus' healing words literally. As in Lk 4:39, the disease 'leaves' almost like a demonic being, and in fact immediately. Luke's word order emphasizes the greatness of the miracle more than Mark's does. Leprosy was indeed considered a deadly disease (II Kgs 7:3; 15:5) and a divine punishment (II Kgs 5:19–27; 15:1ff.) which could be healed only by a miracle performed by God himself (II Kgs 5:7). The final clause of Mk 1:42, 'and he was made clean', was most probably considered redundant and therefore omitted.

> **Verse 14:** And he charged him to tell no one; but 'go and show yourself to the priest, and make an offering for your cleansing, as Moses commanded, for a proof to the people.'

Luke reproduces Mk 1:44 almost exactly except for turning the first clause, 'see that you say nothing to any one', into indirect speech, and a few minor stylistic changes which do not show in English translation. The injunction to silence is derived from Mark where it fits into the theme of the messianic secret (compare Lk 8:56 and Mk 5:43). It is not a particularly significant feature in Luke, where it is to be considered vestigial, and should not be given much weight in the interpretation of the Lucan account. Jesus' words 'Go and show ...' allude to the regulation of Lev 13:49 (compare Lk 17:14). The final clause 'for a proof to the people', literally, 'as a testimony to them', was most probably already difficult for Luke. 'Them' probably refers to the priests rather than to the people.

> **Verse 15:** But so much the more the report went abroad concerning him; and great multitudes gathered to hear and to be healed of their infirmities.

Verse 15 is considerably edited. Luke omits the leper's disregard for Jesus' injunction to silence as well as the statement that as a consequence Jesus could no longer enter a city (Mk 1:45). But he mentions the spreading of Jesus' fame and the coming of the multitudes in another, no less impressive way. As at the beginning of the account, Luke refers here again to Lk 4:42–43, '... and the people sought him and came to him'. 'The report concerning him' (cf. Lk 7:17) is the subject of verse 15a, so that in Luke's presentation it spreads, as it were, independently, and even more than before. Then, it spread in Galilee (Lk 4:14) and the environment of Capernaum (Lk 4:37). But now it goes beyond this region, not only in Judea (cf. Lk 4:44), but as far as Jerusalem (Lk 5:17). *Dierchomai*, 'to spread', is one of Luke's favourite terms; the imperfect tense expresses the constant, progressive spreading of Jesus' fame. 'In Luke's version (5,12–16), the "report" of the event simply "goes out" (v 15) thus lifting the responsibility for disobedience from the leper.'[56]

Luke describes the coming of the multitudes in reference not only to Mk 1:45, but also to Mk 2:2, '... and many were gathered together', which will be passed over in Lk 5:17. Similarly, Luke's often repeated motif of the people's readiness to listen is derived from Mk 2:2, 'and he was preaching the word to them'. Luke sees in these multitudes the masses of the *oikoumenē* ('the inhabited world', the Roman Empire) of his time who were ready for the mission. They were eager to hear the word (Mk 2:2) and expected healing (preparing for the following story, Lk 5:17–26), two features characteristic of Jesus' mission in Luke, namely the power to preach and the power to heal.

> **Verse 16:** But he withdrew to the wilderness and prayed.

Jesus withdrew (*hupochōrōn*, only here and in Lk 9:10 in the New Testament but frequent in classical literature) to the wilderness, seeking the stillness of prayer. Luke omitted the mention of prayer in Lk 4:42 (compare Mk 1:35) because of the programmatic statement in Lk 4:43, and possibly also because Luke considered it improper for Jesus' prayer to be interrupted by the people.

Luke places the notice about prayer in between two summary

statements (Lk 5:15 and 17), in which, on the one hand, the desire of the people for salvation and, on the other hand, the twofold activity of Jesus in word and deed are summarily presented. Together with Lk 5:16 these two summary statements are found in between two pericopes (Lk 5:12–14 and 5:18–26) which not only illustrate Jesus' powerful activity, but also interpret it. The texts speak in general terms of his being and praying in a solitary place as well as of his activity. The evangelist thus considers them not as isolated episodes in Jesus' life, but as expressions of his activity as a whole.

Lk 5:12–14 and 5:18–26, which illustrate the summary statements concerning Jesus' activity, ultimately deal with the forgiveness of sins and so with a theme which occupies an important place in the third gospel and should be considered one of its characteristic themes. According to Luke's understanding, the forgiveness of sins is salvation which will benefit both the people of God and all other peoples (Lk 1:77; 24:47).

Lk 5:12–14 and 5:18–26 deal with God's power as well as Jesus'. According to Jewish interpretation, God alone can cure people of leprosy and forgive sins. While Jesus' critics deny him this power which belongs to God alone, it is acknowledged by the people who come to him for help and healing (Lk 5:12, 18f.). As praying Messiah Jesus acts in God's authority for the salvation of people. Through his prayer he is totally directed both towards God and towards people. The theocentric and anthropocentric directions of his person are united in his prayer. In the prayer 'occasioned' by his baptism (Lk 3:21f.) at the beginning of his ministry Jesus expressed a fundamental and comprehensive 'yes' to the saving will of the Father. During his public ministry—as illustrated in Lk 5:12—he has constantly executed this 'yes' so that through Jesus' prayer God can always continue his saving work through Jesus.

Luke has given a generalizing and typical presentation of Jesus' ministry and prayer. At the same time he has made use of a terminology which is borrowed from the language of the missionary Church and alludes to its situation. In so doing he has freed Jesus' prayer from the limitations of the time of Jesus' public ministry. He has placed Jesus and his prayer in the situation of the post-Easter Church and thus indicated the universal meaning of Jesus' prayer in the history of salvation.[57]

Compared with Mark, Luke underlines Jesus' sovereignty and miraculous power: the leper addresses Jesus as Lord, he falls on his face; the masses come to Jesus to hear his word and to be cured from their infirmities. Jesus' miraculous activity continues; it is instanced in the healing of *one* leper, which thus receives exemplary significance. The miracle, then, is only a concrete demonstration of what has been said in verses 15–16.

5 The healing of the paralytic

Mt 9:1–8	Mk 2:1–12	Lk 5:17–26
1 And getting into a boat he crossed over and came to his own city.	1 And when he returned to Capernaum after some days, it was reported that he was at home. 2 And many were gathered together, so that there was no longer room for them, not even about the door; and he was preaching the word to them.	17 On one of those days, as he was teaching, there were Pharisees and teachers of the law sitting by, who had come from every village of Galilee and Judea and from Jerusalem; and the power of the Lord was with him to heal.
2 And behold, they brought to him a paralytic lying on his bed,	3 And they came, bringing to him a paralytic carried by four men.	18 And behold, men were bringing on a bed a man who was paralysed, and they sought to bring him in and lay him before Jesus;
	4 And when they could not get near him because of the crowd, they removed the roof above him; and when they had made an opening, they let down the pallet on which the paralytic lay.	19 but finding no way to bring him in, because of the crowd, they went up on the roof and let him down with his bed through the tiles into the midst before Jesus.
and when Jesus saw their faith he said to the paralytic, 'Take heart, my son; your sins are forgiven.' 3 And behold,	5 And when Jesus saw their faith, he said to the paralytic, 'My son, your sins are forgiven.'	20 And when he saw their faith he said, 'Man, your sins are forgiven you.'

104

some of the scribes	6 Now some of the scribes were sitting there, questioning in their hearts,	21 And the scribes and the Pharisees
said to themselves,		began to question, saying,
'This man is	7 'Why does this man speak thus? It is blasphemy! Who can forgive sins but God alone?'	'Who is this that speaks blasphemies? Who can forgive sins but God only?'
blaspheming,'		
4 But Jesus, knowing	8 And immediately Jesus, perceiving in his spirit that they thus questioned within themselves,	22 When Jesus perceived
their thoughts,		their questionings,
said, 'Why do you think evil in your hearts?	said to them, 'Why do you question thus in your hearts?	he answered them, 'Why do you question in your hearts?
5 For which is easier, to say,	9 Which is easier, to say to the paralytic,	23 Which is easier, to say,
"Your sins are forgiven," or to say, "Rise	"Your sins are forgiven," or to say, "Rise, take up your pallet,	"Your sins are forgiven," or to say, "Rise
and walk"?	and walk"?	and walk"?
6 But that you may know that the Son of man has authority on earth to forgive sins' — he then said to the paralytic —	10 But that you may know that the Son of man has authority on earth to forgive sins' — he said to the paralytic —	24 But that you may know that the Son of man has authority on earth to forgive sins' — he said to the man who was paralysed —
'Rise, take up your bed and go home.'	11 'I say to you, rise, take up your pallet and go home.'	'I say to you, rise, take up your bed and go home.'
7 And he rose	12 And he rose, and immediately took up the pallet	25 And immediately he rose before them, and took up that on which he lay, and went home, glorifying God.
and went home.	and went out before them all;	
8 When the crowds saw it, they were afraid, and they glorified God, who had given such authority to men.	so that they were all amazed and glorified God,	26 And amazement seized them all, and they glorified God
	saying, 'We never saw anything like this!'	and were filled with awe, saying, 'We have seen strange things today.'

Mark 2:1–12

The context

The majority of exegetes consider Mk 2:1 – 3:6 entirely or partly a pre-Marcan collection or part of such a (larger) collection. An important reason for this assumption is the thematic and formal compactness of Mk 2:1 – 3:6. Many also give a lot of weight to Mk 3:6 in establishing Mk 2:1 – 3:6 as a pre-Marcan tradition. Again in reference to Mk 3:6, there is often mention of an intensification of conflict in the course of Mk 2:1 – 3:6. The tradition of the collection is seen as the result not so much of historical events but rather of a well-planned composition. The intention of this collection is mostly considered to be to present an explanation for the anti-Jesus attitude of the Jews and for Jesus' death.

Mk 2:1 – 3:6 is clearly distinguished from both the preceding and following sections, in which the crowds are presented as coming to Jesus, and in which there is no mention of conflict. As shown below, Mk 2:1 – 3:6 is a self-contained and well-constructed unit set in a frame (Mk 1:45 and 3:7–8) which contrasts sharply with it. All these indications point in the direction of a Marcan insertion of Mk 2:1 – 3:6 into a wider context.[58]

The common theme of the five pericopes which constitute this section is liberation by Jesus: liberation from sin and illness (the healing of the paralytic, Mk 2:1–12), liberation from isolation (the meal with tax collectors and sinners, Mk 2:13–17), liberation from a rigoristic practice of fasting (Mk 2:18–22), liberation from the slavery of the sabbath command (plucking ears of corn, Mk 2:23–28), and liberation from illness and legalism (healing of the withered hand, Mk 3:1–6).

The five pericopes are arranged in a chiastic pattern according to content:

A   The healing of the paralytic (Mk 2:1–12; a healing of the resurrection type; threefold use of *egeirein*, 'to rise').
  B   The eating with tax collectors and sinners (Mk 2:13–17 concerns eating).
    C   The question about fasting (Mk 2:18–22).
  B'   Plucking ears of grain on the sabbath (Mk 2:23–28 concerns eating).
A'   The healing of the man with the withered hand (Mk 3:1–6; a healing of the resurrection type; *egeire* in Mk 3:3).

The first and last accounts are constructed along parallel lines. They have almost identical introductions (translated literally): 'and having again entered into' (Mk 2:1) and 'and again he entered into ' (Mk 3:1). They have the same form: a controversy *apophthegm*, i.e., a short, pithy saying of Jesus set in a brief narrative context, embedded in a healing miracle. Both miracles are of the resurrection type, not exorcisms. In both stories the controversy apophthegm is embedded in the miracle and at the same time clearly distinguished from it by means of the repetition of Jesus' address to the person being cured: 'he said to the paralytic',in Mk 2:5 and 2:10; 'he said to the man' in Mk 3:3 and 3:5. In both stories we are told that Jesus' opponents do not express their objections openly; in the first, Jesus knows that they question in their *hearts*; in the last, Jesus grieves at their hardness of *heart*. These are the first uses of 'heart' in Mark and the word is not used again until Mk 6:52. In both stories, Jesus replies to the silent opposition in controversy style with a counter-question: 'which is easier to say ...' (Mk 2:9) and 'is it lawful on the sabbath to do good or to do harm?' (Mk 3:4). In both cases, the stories return to the miracle form by means of Jesus' again addressing the person to be cured. It may be concluded that Mk 3:1-6 seems to have been so formulated as to balance the healing of the paralytic (Mk 2:1-12).

The middle three pericopes, eating with tax collectors and sinners (Mk 2:13-17), on fasting (Mk 2:18-22), and plucking grain on the sabbath (Mk 2:23-28) contain several characteristics which distinguish them from Mk 2:1-12 and 3:1-6. They do not contain any miraculous features, but on the other hand contain wisdom sayings and proverbs. In Mk 2:1-12 and Mk 3:1-6 the cast of characters consists of Jesus, his opponents, and the sick person. In the middle three pericopes, it consists of Jesus, his opponents, and his disciples, and in all three the behaviour of Jesus or the disciples is questioned.

The first two stories are related to each other. The first deals with the issue of forgiveness of *sins*. The second revolves around Jesus' association with *sinners*. The two accounts are linked by the catchwords *sins* and *sinners*, each used four times.

The fourth and fifth stories deal with the sabbath law. In the fourth, the Pharisees ask why the disciples do what is not lawful on the sabbath (Mk 2:24); and in the fifth, 'they' are watching to see if Jesus will heal on the sabbath (Mk 3:2), and Jesus asks if it is lawful on the sabbath to do good or evil (Mk 3:4). These two accounts are linked by the catchwords *sabbath(s)* and *it is lawful* (*exestin*), used seven and three times respectively.

Whereas in content Mk 2:1-12 and 2:13-17 belong together (sins-sinners), in structure and form Mk 2:13-17 and Mk 2:23-28 are parallel. At the beginning of Mk 2:13-17 Jesus is out of doors, beside the sea, calling Levi, a sinner, from his tax office, an environment of sin (Mk 2:13-14). The account ends with a proverb: 'Those who are well have no need of a physician, but those who are sick', followed immediately by an implied Christological statement, 'I came not to call the righteous, but sinners' (Mk 2:17). Similarly, Mk 2:23–28 presents Jesus out of doors, in the fields, with the disciples breaking the sabbath law by plucking ears of grain (Mk 2:23). The account ends with the proverb, 'The sabbath was made for man, not man for the sabbath', followed by the Christological statement, 'So the Son of man is lord even of the sabbath' (Mk 2:27–28).

Mk 2:13–17 and Mk 2:23–28 do not deal with *sinners* or the *sabbath*, but with *eating*. In the first, the verb 'to eat' is used twice in the present tense. In Mk 2:23–28 'to eat' is used twice in the aorist.

> The literary interrelationships and correlations of the first two and the last two stories seem sufficiently numerous and precise to establish that Mark 2:1 – 3:6 is a well-worked-out deliberate chiastic structure. This leaves C, the question about fasting, as the middle section of the structure by definition. Story C is set apart from the pattern of the other stories. Each of the other four stories has an explicit setting; C is completely without any indication of setting. In the other four, the opponents are named; in story C, they are not specified .... In terms of content, C fits very well as the center of the chiastic structure. It is concerned with fasting, set between B and B' which are concerned with eating. Vs. 20, with its allusion to the crucifixion, is the center not only of C but of the entire controversy section. It is set over against the two outside stories, A and A', with their 'resurrection' type healings.[59]

The literary structure of Mk 2:1 – 3:6 is then as follows:

(1:45 But he went out and began to talk freely about it,
    and to spread the news (*ton logon*),
    so that Jesus could no longer (*hōste mēketi*)
    openly enter (*eiselthein*) a town, but was out in the country;
    and people came to him from every quarter.)

A. *Mk 2:1–12*
2:1 And when he returned (*eiselthōn*) to Capernaum after some days, it was reported that he was at home.
  2 And many were gathered together,
    so that there was no longer (*hōste mēketi*) room for them,
    not even about the door;
    and he was preaching the word (*ton logon*) to them.
  3 And they came,

bringing to him a paralytic carried by four men.
4 And when they could not get near him because of the crowd,
   they removed the roof above him;
   and when they had made an opening,
   they let down the pallet on which the paralytic lay.
5 And when Jesus saw their faith,
   he said to the paralytic,
   'My son, your *sins* are forgiven.'
6 Now some of the scribes were sitting there,
   questioning in their HEARTS,
7 'Why does this man speak thus?
   It is blasphemy!
   Who can forgive *sins* but God alone?'
8 And immediately Jesus, perceiving in his spirit
   that they thus questioned within themselves, said to them,
   'Why do you question thus in your HEARTS?
9 Which is easier, *to say to the paralytic,*
   "Your *sins* are forgiven," or to say,
   "Rise (*egeire*), take up your pallet and walk"?
10 But that you may know that the Son of man
   has authority on earth to forgive *sins'*—
   he said to the paralytic—
11 'I say to you,
   rise (*egeire*), take up your pallet and go home.'
12 And he rose (*ēgerthē*), and immediately took up his pallet
   and went out before them all;
   so that they were all amazed and glorified God, saying,
   'We never saw anything like this!'

B. *Mk 2:13–17*
13 He went out again beside the sea,
   and all the crowd gathered about him,
   and he taught them.
14 And as he passed on,
   he saw Levi the son of Alphaeus sitting at the tax office,
   and he said to him, 'Follow me.'
   And he rose (*anastas*) and followed him.
15 And as he sat at table in his house,
   many tax collectors and *sinners* were sitting with Jesus
   and his disciples;
   for there were many who followed him.
16 And the scribes of the Pharisees,
   when they saw that he was *eating* with *sinners* and tax
   collectors,

said to the disciples,
'Why does he *eat* with tax collectors and *sinners*?'
17 And when Jesus heard it, he said to them,
'Those who are well have no need of a physician,
but those who are sick.
I came not to call the righteous
but *sinners*.'

C. *Centre: Mk 2:18–22*
18 Now John's disciples and the Pharisees were *fasting*;
and people came to him and said,
'Why do John's disciples
and the disciples of the Pharisees *fast*,
but your disciples do not *fast*?'
19 And Jesus said to them,
'Can the wedding guests *fast*
while the bridegroom is with them?
As long as they have the bridegroom with them,
they cannot *fast*.
20 The days will come,
when the bridegroom is taken away from them,
and then they will *fast* in that day.
21 No one sews a piece of unshrunk cloth on an old garment;
if he does, the patch tears away from it,
the new from the old,
and a worse tear is made.
22 And no one puts new wine into old wineskins;
if he does, the wine will burst the skins,
and the wine is lost, and so are the skins;
but new wine is for fresh skins.'

B'. *Mk 2:23–28*
23 One *sabbath* he was going through the grainfields;
and as they made their way
his disciples began to pluck ears of grain.
24 And the Pharisees said to him,
'Look, why are they doing ***what is not lawful*** on the *sabbath*?'
25 And he said to them,
'Have you never read what David did,
when he was in need and was hungry,
he and those who were with him:
26 how he entered the house of God,
when Abiathar was high priest,
and *ate* the bread of the Presence,

which *it is not lawful* for any but the priests to *eat*,
and also gave it to those who were with him?'
27 And he said to them,
'The *sabbath* was made for man,
not man for the *sabbath*;
28 so the Son of man is lord even of the *sabbath*.'

A'. *Mk 3:1–6*
1 Again he entered the synagogue,
and a man was there who had a withered hand.
2 And they watched him,
to see whether he would heal on the *sabbath*,
so that they might accuse him.
3 And *he said to the man who had the withered hand*,
'Come here (*egeire eis to meson*).'
4 And he said to them,
'*Is it lawful* on the *sabbath* to do good or to do harm,
to save life or to kill?'
But they were silent.
5 And he looked around at them with anger,
grieved at their hardness of HEART,
and *said to the man*, 'Stretch out your hand.'
He stretched it out, and his hand was restored.
6 The Pharisees went out,
and immediately held council with the Herodians against him,
how to destroy him.

(7 Jesus withdrew with his disciples to the sea,
and a great multitude from Galilee followed;
also from Judea
8 and Jerusalem and Idumea and from beyond the Jordan
and from about Tyre and Sidon a great multitude,
hearing all that he did,
came to him.)

The five stories, which presuppose a Galilean milieu, were used in
the defence of some community concerns (controversies) as well as
for preaching (paradigms). But while the term 'controversy' may be
appropriate for the origin of the separate pericopes in the community, it no longer fits the pre-Marcan collection as a whole, which is not
just a compilation of controversies, nor the Marcan redaction. In
their present setting, the opposition of Jesus' adversaries in Mk
2:1 – 3:6 is only the negative of the film; the developed film shows the
faith of the community in Jesus as the Christ. Though the

Christological weight of Jesus' activity in the five scenes is not the same, the Christological implications of none of the five can be overlooked. They contain the 'otherness' and 'newness' of Jesus' teaching, which can be understood only from the vantage point of his death and resurrection. Jesus is the one who in his death and resurrection has inaugurated the new era in which people are liberated from sin and legalism.[60]

The pericope proper

Analysis of the text

> **Verse 1:** And when he returned to Capernaum after some days, it was reported that he was at home.

(Literally: And entering again into Capernaum after some days, it was heard that he was in the house.) On the one hand, the start of the account constitutes a sudden break in the story line. The preceding healing of the leper (Mk 1:40–45) ends with the leper spreading the news 'so that Jesus could no longer openly enter a town, but was out in the country; and people came to him from every quarter' (Mk 1:45b). Mk 2:1 has Jesus returning to Capernaum. According to Mark, then, the first thing Jesus does after becoming unable to enter a city is to enter a city! The evangelist seems to be making an entirely new beginning.

On the other hand, Mk 2:1–2 is judiciously connected with Mk 1:45 by means of three catchwords or phrases which occur in chiastic order:

Mk 1:45: the word (RSV: news), so that ... no longer, ... enter.
Mk 2:1–2: he returned (entering), so that ... no longer, ... the word.

'Again' is undoubtedly one of Mark's favourite adverbs by means of which he often links a story with an event or a place already known from the preceding narrative. Here 'again' obviously refers to Mk 1:21, 'they went into Capernaum', from which Mark probably also borrows the location 'Capernaum' for a story which had no such indication in the tradition (compare Mt 8:1; Lk 5:17). By inserting this location, Mark created some inconsistency with Mk 1:45, which he tries to smooth out by adding the phrase 'after some days'. Mk 2:1a also forms an inclusion with Mk 2:13, 'he went out again beside the sea'.

Some scholars prefer to link 'after some days' to 'it was reported' rather than to 'he returned', resulting in the meaning: '(only) after some days it became known that he was in the house'. For a parallel they refer to Mk 7:24f., 'And he entered a house, and would not have

any one know it; yet he could not be hid. But immediately a woman
… heard of him … and came' (see also Mk 6:55, 'to any place where
they heard he was').

'The house' as Jesus' whereabouts occurs often in Mark (Mk
1:29; 2:15; 3:20; 5:38; 14:3), and the motif of separation is repeatedly
underlined (Mk 7:17; 9:28; 10:10). The expression is often redactional and is then opposed to 'outside (the house)'. The former is the
place of secret revelation for the disciples, the latter for public
proclamation to the crowds (compare, e.g., Mk 1:21 and 1:29; 7:14
and 7:17; 10:1 and 10:10). Here 'the house' is most probably
traditional and refers to the house of Simon and Andrew mentioned
in Mk 1:29. The pre-redactional form of verse 1 was presumably:
'And it was heard that he was in the house', or, in RSV's words: 'It
was reported that he was at home'.

Verse 2: And many were gathered together, so that there was
no longer room for them, not even about the door; and he
was preaching the word to them.

The transition from Mk 2:1 to 2:2 is similar to Mk 3:20, 'Then he
went home; and the crowd came together again, so that they could
not even eat'.

The clause 'and many were gathered' is probably pre-Marcan,
for in similar redactional phrases Mark always says explicitly in which
place they came together (Mk 4:1; 5:21; 6:30; 7:1). Furthermore,
'many' for an undetermined number of people is also pre-redactional,
for Mark's favourite expression is 'crowd', which he will, in fact,
substitute for the pre-redactional 'many' in Mk 2:4.

'So that there was no longer room for them, not even about the
door' is a crescendo resumption of Mk 1:33, 'and the whole city was
gathered together about the door'. The same theme is found in
redactional verses like Mk 3:7–9, where it is said that the crowd is so
big that Jesus has to get into a boat (cf. Mk 4:1). In Mk 3:20 so many
people gather together that Jesus and his disciples do not have time to
eat. It seems that in Mk 2:2, too, Mark has expanded his source.

'And he preached the word to them' is typically Marcan. The
absolute 'the word' became an early Christian technical term for the
kerygma, equivalent to the absolute 'the gospel' (*euangelion*), which
Mark alone uses. Mark also uses the absolute 'the word' several times
(Mk 1:45; 2:2; 4:14, 15, 16, 17, 18, 19, 20, 33; 8:32; 10:22). Besides,
the expression 'to preach the word' (*lalein ton logon*) is also typically
Marcan (Mk 2:2; 4:33; 8:32, all redactional). The content of Jesus'
'word' is rarely specified: the power of Jesus' word can be derived
only from the reaction of the listeners. In Mk 2:2 no such indication

occurs, since 'preaching the word' does not have any meaning of its own, but merely belongs to the description of the situation of the following scene (compare Mk 2:12). The pre-redactional form of the verse would be: 'And many were gathered together'.

> **Verse 3:** And they came, bringing to him a paralytic carried by four men.

The phrase 'to him' is probably a redactional addition. In the pre-redactional tradition such explicit indication was most probably lacking. Compare Mk 7:32, 'and they brought to him a man who was deaf', and Mk 8:22, 'and some people brought to him a blind man'. The phrase 'carried by four' is peculiar to Mark.

> **Verse 4:** And when they could not get near him because of the crowd, they removed the roof above him; and when they had made an opening, they let down the pallet on which the paralytic lay.

(Literally: And not being able to carry him near him because of the crowd, they removed the roof above him, and digging through it, they let down the pallet on which the paralytic lay.) The word 'crowd' (*ochlos*) occurs here for the first time in Mark. Thirty-two out of thirty-seven times Mark uses it to indicate a further unspecified group of people around Jesus. He uses the term in the singular, not in the plural as Matthew and Luke do. Most often it appears somewhere in the beginning of a story and provides the setting for it. As elsewhere, Mark changes the pre-redactional 'many' used previously into 'crowd'. The phrase 'because of the crowd' is therefore a Marcan addition (compare Mk 3:9). The crowd do not play any part in the continuation of the account, but of course at the very end they stand in good stead for the 'chorus-ending' of the miracle story (Mk 2:12).
    The clause 'they removed the roof above him' is also redactional. Properly speaking, the text says that they took the tiles off the roof. Originally it must have referred to digging through the dried-mud flat roof of the Palestinian house. Mark apparently clarified the matter for his non-Palestinian readers, who had tile-roofed houses and to whom 'digging through the roof' would sound rather strange. Besides, Mark loves such duplicate expressions indicating time or place.

Summing up, it appears that Mk 2:1–4 underwent considerable redactional expansion. The original, pre-Marcan tradition must have looked more or less as follows:

1 And it was heard that he was at home.
2 And many gathered together.
3 And they came bringing a paralytic carried by four.
4 And not being able to carry him near him,
  they dug through the roof,
  and let down the pallet on which the paralytic was lying.
The original account had a very concise introduction of the situation
(Mk 2:1–2), as is still found in Mk 7:32 and 8:22. All the other data
are superfluous in an independent pericope and become useful only
in the context of a continuous gospel account. In verse 3 the miracle
story proper begins.

Verse 5: And when Jesus saw their faith, he said to the
paralytic, 'My son, your sins are forgiven.'

From verse 5 on we discover very little redactional activity. By the
remark that 'Jesus saw their faith' (compare Acts 14:9, 'Paul ...
seeing that he had faith to be made well ...') the narrator interprets
the unusual effort, the overcoming of obstacles as 'miracle faith'
(compare Mk 11:22f.). The action of the bearers is a non-verbal
request and expression of trust. The address 'son' (*teknon*; literally,
'child') is found only here in Mark's gospel.

That a sick person is assured of forgiveness in the context of a
miracle story is unique. 'Your sins are forgiven' is a divine passive,
i.e., a veiled hint at an action on the part of God, and therefore
means '*God* forgives your sins'. The fact that in the ensuing
controversy (Mk 2:6–10) the power to forgive sins is attributed to *the
Son of man*, clearly indicates the secondary character of this
controversy. In the miracle story, Jesus' words of comfort in verse 5b
should not be interpreted as an act of forgiveness, but rather as
encouragement of the one who seeks help: God forgives his sins and,
therefore, Jesus can and will cure him. The faith of the bearers
appears therefore not only as trust in the miracle-worker, but also as
faith in God who forgives sins, i.e., the merciful Father, whom Jesus
proclaims.[61]

Verse 6: Now some of the scribes were sitting there,
questioning in their hearts,

Verse 6 presents an abrupt shift of plot. The account is interrupted to
let the reader know that there are some scribes present in the house
who wonder to themselves about Jesus' words. For the time being the
paralytic seems to be forgotten, as Jesus is entering into a theological
debate with the scribes, here considered as representatives of a

caste, 'some of the scribes'. In their hearts (cf. Mk 7:21) they think the objection against Jesus which the narrator formulates in verse 7. The phrase 'questioning in their hearts (within themselves)' occurs three times (Mk 2:6b, 8b, 8d).

> **Verse 7:** 'Why does this man speak thus? It is blasphemy! Who can forgive sins but God alone?'

The clause 'why does this man speak (*lalei*) thus?' resumes 'preaching (literally, 'speaking'; *elalei*) the word' of verse 2c, and applies it to the forgiveness of sins. It may be redactional. While Jesus speaks 'the word', i.e., the gospel message or good news, the scribes hear 'blasphemy'. For the first time in Mark's gospel the reader realizes that there is opposition to Jesus and his message.[62]

In their hearts, the scribes accuse Jesus of blasphemy, the charge upon which the Sanhedrin eventually condemns Jesus to death (Mk 14:64). The first and the last confrontation of Jesus with the Jewish authorities concern the issue of blasphemy. The reproach presupposes forgiveness of sins by Jesus himself, whereas in verse 5b Jesus spoke of *God's* forgiveness.

> **Verse 8:** And immediately Jesus, perceiving in his spirit that they thus questioned within themselves, said to them, 'Why do you question thus in your hearts?

Verse 8a, whose content seems to be derived from verses 6b and 8b, has merely a connecting function and may be redactional. As well as an easier transition, the emphasis on the sovereignty of Jesus, who sees into the hearts of his opponents, may have led to the insertion. The clause has a parallel in Mk 5:30, 'And Jesus, perceiving in himself ...'. The transition from verse 6b, 'questioning in their hearts' to 'perceiving (*epignous*)' in verse 8a is also found in Mk 8:16., 'And they discussed it with one another ... and being aware of it (*gnous*) ...'. Jesus is presented as knowing the secret thoughts of the scribes ('within themselves'), as a result of the application of the theological concept of God as the 'heart-knower' (*kardiognōstēs*; Acts 1:24; 15:8) to the Son of man.

> **Verse 9:** Which is easier, to say to the paralytic, 'Your sins are forgiven,' or to say, 'Rise, take up your pallet and walk'?

The use of a counter-question in controversies recurs elsewhere in Mark (Mk 3:4; 11:30; 12:37). Jesus asks the scribes if it is easier to *say* 'your sins are forgiven' or to *say* 'rise ...'. He does not ask which is

easier to accomplish. In the understanding of the evangelist the
forgiveness of sins is undoubtedly the more difficult thing to do. The
scribes, however, presumably think that it is easy to *say* 'your sins
are forgiven' if there is no need to prove that it really happened.[63]
Jesus' counter-question challenges the scribes' assumption that he has
spoken lightly without any basis in fact; it also leads to the healing
word which demonstrates that the man has actually been forgiven.[64]

Verse 10: But that you may know that the Son of man has
authority on earth to forgive sins—he said to the paralytic—

The clause, 'that you may know', addressed to the scribes, suggests
that they witness the healing described in verses 11–12a, and so
belong to the 'all' who respond to the miracle.

The phrase 'Son of man' occurs here for the first time in Mark,
without any preparation or explanation. Mk 2:10 and 2:28 are the
only instances in the synoptic gospels which deal with the earthly
authority of the Son of man. The term does not occur again in Mark
until Mk 8:31, the first prediction of the passion. The clause 'the Son
of man has authority on earth to forgive sins' is couched in a context
consisting entirely of materials already mentioned several times, so
that as the only new element the clause stands out and Jesus' claim
cannot be missed by the scribes within the account or by the readers
who are confronted by the choice between accepting Jesus' claim or
labelling it blasphemy.[65]

The opinion that 'but that you may know that the Son of man has
authority on earth to forgive sins' is a parenthetical aside by Mark to
his Christian readers over the heads of the scribes (Cranfield, Lane,
Mally, Perrin, Trocmé) is to be rejected because 'the saying forms an
integral part of the rhetorical structure of the debate with the scribes
found in vv. 6–10a. It directly answers both questions posed by the
scribes in v. 7, and is therefore addressed to them'.[66]

The last clause literally repeats Mk 2:5b, 'he said to the
paralytic'. This inclusion has been considered an important argument
for the thesis that verses 5c–10b were inserted into a pre-existent
healing story, Mk 2:1–5b, 11–12.

Verse 11: 'I say to you, rise, take up your pallet and go
home.'

The emphatic and repeated 'I say to you' emphasizes Jesus' speaking.
Since the paralytic does get up and take his pallet, Jesus' words are
indeed words of power.[67]

The authoritative 'I tell you' will have been introduced into the text because of the separation of address and healing by the insertion of verses 6–10, in order to emphasize the change of addressees (verse 10: 'you [plural] may know'; verse 11: 'I tell you [singular]'). The words 'I say to you, rise' occur also in Mk 5:41.

The healing is achieved merely by Jesus' word: 'rise' (see Mk 1:31; compare Acts 9:40; 14:10). This is followed by a *demonstration* command: the healed man carries home the mat on which he lay and thus demonstrates his healing before the eyes of all (verse 12). Finally there follows the dismissal of the cured man to his home (compare Mk 5:19), i.e., the return to his family circle.

> **Verse 12:** And he rose and immediately took up the pallet and went out before them all; so that they were all amazed and glorified God, saying, 'We never saw anything like this!'

The phrase 'immediately' is probably a Marcan addition. It underlines the immediacy with which the paralytic regains his strength.

By the exact execution of the command, underlined by the nearly literal correspondence of command and execution, the reality of the healing is accurately stated. The recognition of the miracle, 'he rose', corresponds to the healing word.

The healing is verified by the onlookers ('before them all') who by their amazement, their 'ecstasy' (*hōste existasthai pantes*; compare Mk 5:42; 6:51) confirm the miracle. The reaction of 'all' seems to be a typical reaction of the crowd to a miracle found in many miracle stories. Apparently, the scribes are no longer in the narrator's mind.

The crowds give testimony to the manifestation of divine power (possibly introduced together with the insertion of verses 6–10 in view of verse 7c, 'who can forgive sins but God alone?'), giving praise to God, and place the miraculous healing and the miracle-worker in the right light: 'we never saw anything like this!' The acclamation serves the missionary point of the account.

Mark 2:1–12: a composite text

All the efforts to prove the unity of the pre-redactional version of Mk 2:1–12 have failed. On the other hand, the evidence for the compositional nature of this pericope and for the fact that it consists of at least two levels of tradition are manifold and convincing.

Firstly, there is a break in the narration in Mk 2:10. In the middle of the verse the addressees suddenly change: '"But that you (plural = scribes?) may know that the Son of man has authority on earth to forgive sins"—he said to the paralytic—"I say to you (singular), rise, take up your pallet and go home"'. It is clear that in the clause 'he said to the paralytic' the narrator takes over. For a smooth sequence we should have read something like: 'But that you may know that the Son of man has authority on earth to forgive sins, listen to what I am going to say to the paralytic, "I tell you, rise ..."'.

Secondly, the clause found towards the end of Mk 2:10, 'he said to the paralytic', also occurs as the introduction to the direct speech in Mk 2:5. The words we would have expected to follow this clause in Mk 2:5 are now found in Mk 2:11, 'I say to you, rise, take up your pallet and go home'. The words about forgiveness now found in Mk 2:5b are rather surprising.

Thirdly, the statement about forgiveness of sins appears abruptly. The same is the case with the scribes in Mk 2:6, who are suddenly on the scene and later disappear equally mysteriously. They play no part whatsoever in the conclusion where we would have expected them, e.g., to go away as frustrated and defeated antagonists.

Fourthly, in Mk 2:11-12 we find the classical conclusion of a miracle story, i.e., command of healing, healing, recognition of the miracle, and reaction of the crowd. This is a perfect conclusion of the story as far as it has been developed down to Mk 2:5. As said above, the scribes have disappeared. So has the theme of forgiveness of sins. As we shall see, Matthew made up for that anomaly. He realized that forgiveness of sins was the main point of the combined account and should not be left unconsidered in the conclusion.

Fifthly, the remark in Mk 2:12 that 'they were all amazed' certainly does not take into account the scribes who in Mk 2:6-10 were not happy at all.

Sixthly, the story as it now stands has two very clearly distinguished points: the healing of the paralytic and the power to forgive sins.

Seventhly, the attribution of forgiveness of sins to the earthly Jesus himself is unique in the gospels. The only possible exception is Lk 7:47-49, but the passage is probably a secondary formation attached to the story of the woman sinner in Lk 7:36-50 and in friction with the content of Lk 7:36-46. In all other texts Jesus urges people to repent so that *God* may forgive them, or, more specifically, he demands that their repentance should take the form of forgiving their brothers in order that God may forgive them. The power to forgive sins is ascribed to Jesus on the basis of his resurrection. But the remarkable thing in this pericope is that not only does the earthly Jesus claim the power to forgive sins, but he also performs a miracle to legitimate that power, while elsewhere he refuses to perform legitimation miracles. He even explicitly rejects such an idea (Mk 8:11f.). Originally Jesus' miracles as well as his words were revelations of the inaugurated kingdom of God appealing to faith. To use miracles for legitimation is called a temptation. It is clear from the whole gospel tradition that only in later stages were the miracles used as apologetic evidence. We do not say that such use is altogether illegitimate, but that it is a later development. And, in fact, if we look at the miracle story itself, that is, without the intervening verses dealing with forgiveness of sins (Mk 2:5b–10), it is not a legitimation miracle. In other word, the passage about the forgiveness of sins represents a later level of the apostolic tradition which made the miracle into a legitimation and was inserted into the existing miracle story which then became the setting of the passage about Jesus' power to forgive sins.

Finally, verses 1–5a, 11–12 form a perfect miracle story with all the classic themes thereof. But in its present form it is affected by the insertion of a text (verses 5b–10) which is of a very different character. Thus it has become a mixed literary form. A possible objection against this last argument could be: if the whole story were not an original unit, and if there was a strong interest in connecting forgiveness of sins with an existing miracle story, why was this not done more often in the tradition? The answer is: (1) Not every miracle story was suited for this treatment. The person to be cured should be in a situation in which he can be addressed. This excludes stories about the raising of a dead person, a healing from a distance, and the healing of a person possessed by a demon. (2) The healing should not have been narrated from the beginning for another special purpose, e.g., a healing on a sabbath. This again eliminates a good number of healing stories. But the healing of the paralytic provided a nearly ideal scene for such a development. Here a didactic text on Jesus' power to forgive sins could be inserted into an existing miracle story in such a way that the latter was subordinated to the former.[68]

The extent of the insertion is debatable. The actual point at issue is the position of Mk 2:5c, 'My son, your sins are forgiven'. According to some authors it belongs to the insertion, while others attribute it to the earlier miracle story. But if the forgiveness of sins was already part of the original miracle story, it is hard to explain why this feature plays no part in the conclusion of the text (Mk 2:11–12). The repeated 'he said to the paralytic' argues in favour of the delimitation of Mk 2:5c–10, but upon closer scrutiny it becomes clear that this does not result in a smooth transition, for the sequence of 'he said to the paralytic' (Mk 2:5b or 10d) and 'I tell you' (Mk 2:11a) is awkward. Not for nothing do we find in Mk 5:41 'Talitha cumi' in between 'he said to her' and 'I say to you', and in Lk 7:14, in a similar position, 'young man'. Either 'I say to you' must be omitted from the original miracle story, or 'My son' retained in it, but then the postulate must be abandoned of the insertion of Mk 2:5c–10 in between the double 'he said to the paralytic'. A smooth text is obtained by reading: 'He said to the paralytic: "My son, your sins are forgiven. I say to you …".' That just this particular miracle story was combined with a debate about forgiveness of sins can be understood against the background of Old Testament thinking concerning the connection between sin, illness, healing and forgiveness. But the procedure gains in plausibility if Mk 2:5c, 'My son, your sins are forgiven', occurred in the original miracle story and provided a juncture.[69]

The most important objection to this view is undoubtedly that Mk 2:5c breaks out of the structure of the miracle story, but is it necessary for all miracle stories to correspond in all their features to a stereotyped format?

Against the background of Old Testament and Targum considerations about forgiveness of sins, the Jesus-saying of Mk 2:5c looks as follows: the statement is formulated in the present passive: Your sins are forgiven right here and now. The passive is a periphrasis indicating divine action: God forgives. The present indicates absolute certainty of God's forgiveness as an event happening now. The nearness of God's rule links healing and forgiveness. For the eschatological dimension of the healing of a paralytic, see Isa 35:3, 6, '… make firm the feeble knees … then shall the lame man leap like a hart' (cf. Mt 11:5; Lk 7:22). On the other hand, forgiveness of sins is referred to as God's ultimate act of salvation (e.g., Jer 31:31–34). In this eschatological perspective the juxtaposition of assurance of forgiveness and healing word should not surprise us.[70] In Mk 2:1–5, 11–12 too the peculiarity of Jesus' miracles is realized; this consists in the combination of 'two conceptual worlds which had never been combined in this way before, the apocalyptic expectation of universal salvation in the future and the episodic realisation of salvation in the present through miracles'.[71]

The meaning of the original pre-Marcan miracle story

The text of the original story runs as follows:[72]

1 And it was heard that he was at home.
2 And many were gathered together.
3 And they came bringing a paralytic carried by four.
4 And not being able to carry him near him, they dug through the roof, and let down the pallet on which the paralytic lay.
5 And Jesus seeing their faith said to the paralytic,
  'My son, your sins are forgiven.
11 I say to you, rise, take up your pallet and go home.'

12 And he rose, and taking up his pallet went out before them all;
   so that they were all amazed and glorified God, saying,
   'We never saw anything like this!'

Attention should be paid to some details of this apparently very
simple and realistic story before going on to tackle the question of its
literary form and its main point, which can be derived from its form
and structure.

In its pre-Marcan form the miracle story was not connected with
Mk 1. The introduction (Mk 2:1–2) is very simple and general.
Nothing is said about the precise setting or location. Only the most
necessary characters are mentioned. The name of Jesus is not
mentioned, which for an isolated, independent unit is rather
surprising. But it is, of course, possible that Mark omitted the name,
since in his sequence it was sufficiently clear of whom he was
speaking, whereas quite often Matthew mentions Jesus' name
explicitly at the beginning of a miracle story, most probably
influenced by its use in the liturgy of the community.

That Jesus was 'at home' (in the house), without any further
indication as to which house he was in, may indicate a certain
measure of secrecy. 'The many' who will play an important part in the
conclusion are also mentioned here.

Then the second principal actor appears, the paralytic carried by
four, a feature illustrating his total helplessness. He was lying on a
pallet, the poor man's bed, which could easily be carried (see Mk
2:12). He certainly enters in a very strange way: the bearers dug a
hole through the wattle of which the Palestinian roof was made. They
presumably carried the paralytic up to the flat mud roof along the
outside stairs which every Palestinian house had. We are dealing here
with a real Palestinian feature which, as Mark apparently realized,
the Roman readers did not understand.

The question may be raised why, on the very first level of the
story, the bearers entered the house in such a strange way, since on
that level there was no mention yet of such a large crowd that 'there
was no place any more, not even about the door'. Orginally, this
feature could have been an exorcistic motif. Once expelled, the
demon who supposedly caused the paralysis would have to get out of
the house through the only 'entrance' he knew, namely the hole in
the roof, which would obviously be closed up after the incident.
Hence he would not know how to enter the house again afterwards. It
could be argued that such an explanation is too fantastic and without
basis in the text, but the hypothesis is not without grounds. The
feature is certainly anomalous and even impossible if interpreted in
the present text as a historical detail. Jesus, the disciples and the

crowd are packed into the house; and all of a sudden the four bearers start digging a hole through the roof big enough to lower a man lying on a stretcher. Chunks of mud must have fallen on all the people present! And Jesus continued preaching. Isn't this more fantastic and improbable than the hypothesis presented above? So, originally, the entrance through the roof may have nothing to do with the blocking of the doorway by the crowd, but rather with an intention to *avoid* the door.

Next, the text speaks of Jesus seeing the faith of these people, including that of the paralytic. This is apparently the focus of the miracle story. Most commentators speak here of confidence in Jesus' readiness and capability to help him, but faith is here more than trust in the miracle-worker; it is the adequate correlative to the forgiveness of sins, which exceeds the faith in miracles found in antiquity. The name 'Jesus' appears here for the first and only time in the miracle story.

And so we move on to Mk 2:11 in which we find the healing word consisting of an address, 'my son', a word of authority, 'I say to you', and a command, 'rise, take up your pallet and go home'. This is the powerful, divine answer to the faith shown by the bearers and the paralytic. The efficacy of the powerful word is indicated in its effects which correspond perfectly to the command in all its parts:

rise (*egeire*)   — and he rose (*ēgerthē*)
take up your pallet   — and he took up his pallet
and go home   — and went out before them all.

The man no longer needs the help of his bearers and the healing takes effect immediately. The demonstration occurs in front of all the people present. The concluding chorus of acclamation is, therefore, also expressed by all. These 'all' are, of course, the 'many' of Mk 2:2. This reaction to the miracle by all those present is a typical feature of the miracle stories. They were all amazed or 'besides themselves' (*existasthai*), which points to a kind of intervention from above. They give glory to God because of his divine intervention. And finally they exclaim 'We never saw anything like this!' This conclusion is implicitly Christological, not only in the context of Mark's composition, where it leads to the great question concerning Jesus' person in Mk 8:27–30, but also already in the pre-Marcan miracle story.

The structure of the story is clear. It is a concentric structure, the focus appearing in the centre. Looking at the *persons involved*, we discover the following concentric structure:

(Jesus and) the many (Mk 2:1–2)
   The paralytic (Mk 2:3–4)
      Jesus (Mk 2:5, 11), only here mentioned explicitly
   The paralytic (Mk 2:12a)
(Jesus and) the many (Mk 2:12b).

Looking at the theme of *faith*, the following concentric structure appears:

Exposition
  demonstration of faith
    recognition of this faith (Mk 2:5)
  response to this faith
Conclusion.

We see that in both instances *Jesus and faith* are the central themes. Reducing it to a brief and simple schema, we have:

Exposition: many gather
Corpus: the paralytic is brought to Jesus
           Jesus and faith
           healing word and demonstration
Conclusion: reaction of the crowd.

Comparison with other biblical as well as extra-biblical accounts of healings of paralytics should highlight the literary form, and above all, it should reveal what is unique in our story compared with other healing stories of the same kind. An analysis of non-biblical stories associated with the sanctuary of Asclepius in Epidaurus as well as pre-Lucan stories of healings of paralytics in Acts (Acts 3:1–10; 9:32–35; 14:8–11) reveals many parallels with our pre-Marcan miracle story. The form is the same and the features follow the same sequence. The following features are essentially parallel:
—the paralytic is brought in on a pallet;
—the healing word is a command;
—the healing is demonstrated by the fact that the man rises and walks away;
—quite often he carries his own pallet;
—the bystanders are amazed.

The literary *form* of these stories derives from the Hellenistic world. This does not mean that the synoptic miracle story is dependent on any one of these Hellenistic stories as far as its *content* is concerned.

It is important to note that in the Hellenistic miracle there is no explicit emphasis on faith. Of course, the paralytic taken to the sanctuary of Asclepius in Epidaurus also believes in the healing power of the god, but this is not made a point for special reflection in the miracle story. In the pre-Marcan story, on the other hand, this feature is emphasized. The paralytic's faith is mentioned by Jesus himself. This is unique, and the theological affirmation should be formulated from the starting point of this feature.[73]

The theological affirmation of the pre-Marcan miracle story

The unique feature of the pre-Marcan miracle story is the explicit mention of faith. The question now is what kind of faith this story is talking about. Many commentators refer here to initial faith in Jesus as the wonder-worker. But in dealing with a miracle story which was given its format in the post-Easter tradition, how can the level of the historical Jesus be reached? Dealing with a miracle story which revolved around an epiphany of God in Jesus, the early Christian community thought of faith on that same level. That is the implication of the chorus of acclamation, of the 'being beyond themselves', of the glorifying, and of the implicit Christological confession, 'We never saw anything like this!' So the faith mentioned at the beginning cannot be simply a vague initial confidence in the wonder-worker. It is faith in the post-Easter kerygma that the narrator has in mind. What it was on the level of fact is largely irrelevant as far as the explanation of the story under consideration is concerned. That our story is implicitly Christological and speaks of a truly Christian faith means, to put it paradoxically, that such faith is faith in Jesus dead and risen. It is faith in the actual, present Christ, expressed in a story about the past.

So the story came into being and was used as an example story of what Christian faith is all about. It shows that such faith knows no obstacles. It leads people to Christ, no matter what problems arise. And the addressees of the story should recognize how Jesus encounters the person who comes to him with such faith. A story with such a message was meaningful only for people who already believed in Jesus, for those who could identify themselves with the man of the story and with his faith. We are, therefore, inclined to think that the situation in life of the pericope was not missionary preaching to outsiders, as is held by a number of scholars, but rather the instruction of the Christian community. Certain features of the story point to Palestine, but the structure suggests a place with strong Hellenistic influence. The origin of the story should therefore be sought in a Christian community in Galilee. Mark's location seems to be in accord with the origin of the story.

The miracle story expanded by the forgiveness of sins[74]

We deal now with the next stage of the pre-Marcan tradition and its meaning. The expanded text must have looked as follows:

1 And it was heard that he was at home.
2 And many were gathered together.

3 And they came bringing a paralytic carried by four.

4 And not being able to carry him near him, they dug through the roof and let down the pallet on which the paralytic lay.

5 And Jesus seeing their faith said to the paralytic, 'My son, your sins are forgiven.'

6 *Now some of the scribes were sitting there, questioning in their hearts,*

7 *'Why does this man speak thus? It is blasphemy! Who can forgive sins but God alone?'*

8 *And immediately Jesus, perceiving in his spirit that they thus questioned within themselves, said to them, 'Why do you question thus in your hearts?*

9 *Which is easier, to say to the paralytic, "Your sins are forgiven," or to say, "Rise, take up your pallet, and walk"?*

10 *But that you may know that the Son of man has authority to forgive sins—he said to the paralytic—*

11 'I say to you, rise, take up your pallet and go home.'

12 And he rose, and immediately took up the pallet and went out before them all; so that they were all amazed and glorified God, saying, 'We never saw anything like this!'

Where did the composer of this expanded version get the text about forgiveness of sins? Some scholars think that it was a pre-existent independent text which was inserted into Mk 2:1–5, 11–12 at this stage of the tradition. But Mk 2:6–10 cannot have existed as an independent unit, since in their isolated form the verses would have lacked any 'hanger'. They are irrevocably dependent on the framework of the miracle story. Therefore, many scholars say that the original setting of Mk 2:6–10, in which the circumstances of time and place were indicated, was lost and replaced by a new frame constituted by the miracle story split up for this purpose. But this too is improbable, for if the early Church had known such a pericope, would it have dealt so casually with it? Does not the very subordination of the miracle-story to the text about forgiveness of sins prove how important this issue of forgiveness was to the early Church?

On the present level of the tradition the central piece (Mk 2:6–10) perfectly corresponds to and presupposes the frame story (Mk 2:1–5, 11–12). There is 'carried' (*airomenon*; Mk 2:3), 'carry' (*aron*; Mk 2:9), 'carry' (*aron*; Mk 2:11), and 'carrying' (*aras*; Mk 2:12). Such a play on words throughout the whole text must be the work of an author who constructed the central piece in consideration of and out of the elements of the frame story of the healing of the paralytic. Besides, in Mk 2:9, 'your sins are forgiven' is a literal quotation of Mk 2:5. Then there is the fact that the central piece (Mk 2:9) as well as the miracle story speak of a paralytic, whereas the synoptic tradition elsewhere hardly ever mentions paralytics. Moreover, there is the very rare word 'pallet' (*krabbatos*) which occurs in the frame story as well as in the central section (Mk 2:4, 9, 11). The term is so rare that both Matthew and Luke omitted it. It would be remarkable if both the frame story and an allegedly pre-existent text about forgiveness had contained this very rare word. The conclusion suggests itself: the central section on the forgiveness of sins was composed by a Christian author in view of and with elements of the story of the paralytic, into which he inserted this composition.

The author created two 'peaks' in which, if we take them together, the real point of the text appears. First, the scribes disdainfully ask themselves: 'Why does this fellow (*houtos*) speak like this (*houtōs*)?' This creates a certain tension for the reader. Then the scribes think to themselves: 'It is blasphemy!' This clarifies the objection the scribes have in mind. They accuse Jesus of claiming divine prerogatives. Finally, it is stated precisely what this blasphemy consists of: 'Who can forgive sins but God alone?' They accuse Jesus of claiming the power to forgive sins. That is the first peak.

Then we find the same kind of development in Jesus' answer. First, he asks why they think to themselves like that. Secondly, he introduces an *a fortiori* argument, or rather he sets the scene for such an argument: 'Which is easier ...?' And finally, we get the challenging answer to the objection of the scribes. They were indeed right; only God can forgive sins. Their objection would be to the point if Jesus were just a man, but he legitimates himself as the Son of man who has the authority to forgive sins. That is the second peak.

The effect of the insertion of the central section is clear:

(1) The originally independent miracle story is reduced to the level of a framework.

(2) Jesus' answer to faith is no longer the expected healing, but the forgiveness of sins.

(3) The miracle in which Jesus revealed himself to the people who came to him in faith now plays only a subordinate part.

(4) The miracle about which all were beside themselves becomes the easier, less important thing.

(5) The healing is no longer performed for the sake of faith, but to legitimate Jesus' power to forgive sins.

(6) The miracle which was originally a *sign* of God's nearness, becomes a reality that can be verified.

(7) The healing is no longer performed for the sake of the paralytic, but to refute the adversaries.

(8) The encounter of Jesus and the believing man is out of focus. The focus now becomes the 'controversy' with the adversaries.

(9) The miracle story, which was at first an example story, becomes now a 'controversy'.

The point of the new story, the general thesis, is Jesus' power as the Son of man. In fact, the forgiving of the personal sins of the paralytic is only a starting point for a general affirmation. The scribes raise the issue to a general level: 'Who can forgive sins but God alone?' And Jesus finally also answers in this very general sense. The specific story is only an occasion for the general question.

We have already seen that we should look for the real point in the two 'peaks' of the expanded story: Mk 2:7, the question, and Mk 2:10, the answer. The scribes who appear in Mk 2:6 are not the real, historical adversaries of the historical Jesus. Thus it is beside the point to raise questions such as where those scribes come from at this very moment, etc. They could be representatives of the Jews who at the time of the composition of this story objected to the Christian claim that sins could be forgiven in the name of Jesus. Once we see that the scribes are no more than lay figures for the Christian author, we need not ask why these scribes do not voice their feelings at the end of the story, and how Jesus discerned their feelings which, after all, were not expressed. The story does not tell us anything, therefore, of the consciousness of Jesus. It speaks of the faith of the early Christians. They know who Jesus is and express this in this very story.

Many scholars, following R. Bultmann, have characterized this story as a controversy (*Streitgespräch*), but we wonder whether this is correct. First, it is not Jesus' words about the power to forgive sins which are the basis on which the frame story has been composed. The frame existed first as a miracle story, and the central part has been composed by means of the frame story. Secondly, properly speaking, we do not have a controversy with questions and answers, but a crescendo monologue in answer to the thoughts of the scribes. Moreover, Jesus' decisive answer does not occur at the very end of the story, as we would expect in an authentic controversy. As it is now, the decisive statement of the whole composition is found in Mk 2:10, 'that you may know that the Son of man has authority to forgive sins'. We conclude, therefore, that the expanded story should be called an instruction (*Lehrgespräch*) rather than a controversy (*Streitgespräch*).

The theological meaning of the expanded account

We have identified the expanded narrative as an instruction whose point is expressed in the two 'peaks' of Mk 2:7 and 2:10. On the level on which this composition came into being, Mk 2:7 expresses the question of the instruction, 'Who can forgive sins but God alone?', which finds its answer in Mk 2:10, 'Jesus as the Son of man can', of course, because in him, as the Son of man, God's forgiveness is bestowed upon people.

Apparently, the early Christian community was no longer fully satisfied with the theology of the earlier miracle story. While it was once thought that the encounter with God took place in the miracle, now the salvific gift, the response to faith, is the forgiveness of sins through Jesus as the Son of man. The former miracle story is made to legitimate Jesus' power to forgive the sins of the one who encounters him in faith.

In no other text is the forgiveness of sins ascribed to the earthly Jesus and, in fact, the early Christian kerygma connects forgiveness of sins with Jesus' death and resurrection (I Cor 15:3; Gal 1:4). Do we have in Mk 2:1–12 a legitimate interpretation of the activity of the earthly Jesus in the light of his death and resurrection? Or, in other words, what can we legitimately ascribe to the earthly Jesus when we speak of the forgiveness of sins? Firstly, Jesus made clear that all people were sinners, that there were only two categories of people: those who knew that they were sinners, and those who did not. All people need mercy and he showed his preference for those who were aware of the need of divine mercy in the light of Jesus' call for conversion. He did not so much talk about forgiveness as show the realization of God's forgiving mercy by not separating himself from public sinners, such as tax collectors and prostitutes, but going to the extent of eating with them and even inviting them. Thus he entered into communion with them, and showed that God had accepted them, that they had already been forgiven. It was to such practices that the Jewish authorities objected (see Lk 15:1–2), and Jesus defended himself against them in a number of parables, e.g., Lk 15:3–32.

The enlarged story of Mk 2:1–12 is a homogeneous and legitimate development of the original material. The instruction says that he who accepted sinners during his life on earth and gained forgiveness through his death and resurrection is now the Lord who in his divine glory and authority actually forgives sins. Transferring this post-Easter article of faith to the earthly Jesus was legitimate on the ground of Jesus' dealings with sinners during his ministry. It was only in the light of the resurrection that Jesus' followers became aware of the divine power of Jesus, of which nobody would even have dreamed during his public ministry. It is this post-resurrectional insight which is ultimately expressed in its most definite form on the level of the composition of the enlarged story: The Son of man has the power to forgive sins.

The question still remains about the situation of this text in the life of the early Christian community. Quite a few scholars think that with this text the early Church wanted to justify its practice and right to forgive sins. In fact, Matthew certainly develops this perspective (Mt 9:8). However, we think that Mark's text is not yet explicitly ecclesial in this sense. Besides, the Church's authority to forgive sins is mostly expressed in the form of a commission of the risen Lord to his disciples (Lk 24:47ff.; Jn 20:22f.). Mark is explicitly *Christological*, expressing the authority of *Jesus*, his divine right to forgive sins, a right whereby, as it were, he takes God's place. Nobody can forgive sins but God. That is true. But by his death and resurrection Jesus entered the divine existence, and so he can forgive sins in God's place.

When we say that the text of the expanded story is first of all explicitly *Christological*, we do not intend to say that a later *ecclesial* development such as that found in Matthew would be illegitimate. The power of Jesus to forgive sins is described in Mk 2:10 as the power of the *Son of man*. We subscribe to the opinion that the title 'Son of man' cannot be interpreted in a merely individual sense. Like all Christological titles, and even more than the others, 'Son of man' points to Jesus as the inclusive representative and embodiment of God's people. The representative function is already clear in Dan 7:13ff., but appears clearly in a number of New Testament texts as, e.g., Mt 25:31ff. Therefore, ascribing to Jesus as Son of man the power to forgive sins has ecclesial implications. If not, how could Mark ever have written what he does write about the power of man over the sabbath, and the power of the Son of man (the Man) over the sabbath (Mk 2:27–28)?

There is one more question to be answered. Why is Mark at this point in his gospel already using the Christological title 'Son of man' which he begins to use purposely only from Mk 8:31 on? The answer is: the title was already found in the pre-Marcan tradition. The healing story provided the later author with a unique opportunity to develop the text into an instruction about Jesus' power to forgive sins and, on that ground, he ascribed to him the Christological title 'Son of man'. Mark apparently liked the story too much to omit it, or even to transfer it to a place after Mk 8:31. Besides, it is difficult to see where he could have placed it after Mk 8:33. Once he had decided to place the story at the beginning of his gospel, he could not omit the title mentioned in the verse which expressed the real point of the story.

Mark 2:1–12 on the level of the Marcan redaction

We still have to deal with the meaning of the pericope on the level of the Marcan redaction. In what sense did Mark reinterpret the pericope when he placed it here in the context of his gospel? We can immediately say two things. First, recalling what we said above about the editorial additions in Mk 2:1-4, he provided the text with an expanded introduction, and second, he placed it in the context of a series of 'controversies' in Mk 2:1 - 3:6. What consequences did this entail for the interpretation of the pericope?

By expanding the introduction, Mark inserted the pericope into the total sequence of Jesus' earthly ministry. By the phrase 'again entering into Capernaum' he refers back to the 'day at Capernaum' (Mk 1:21-35). The day at Capernaum had been a day of Jesus' preaching with power, casting out demons, healing Peter's mother-in-law, and healing many sick people. That day the crowd had been impressed by Jesus' power and authority (Mk 1:22, 27). Now Mark continues and, by way of a crescendo, concludes that this power is a divine power (Mk 2:10). By saying 'there was no longer room for them, not even about the door', Mark refers again to the day at Capernaum. Mark thus emphasizes how Jesus' audience, and in a way his success, increases. At the same time he brings out more strongly the impossibility for the men carrying the paralytic of getting near Jesus.

At the same time Mark emphasizes a theme which is very prominent in his gospel: the tension between revelation (in front of the crowd) and hiddenness (in the house). In fact, this 'messianic secret' is fully preserved.[75] Jesus reveals that he is the Son of man who has the power to forgive sins, but at the same time he does not reveal this identity directly. He does not say directly that he is the Son of man; only those to whom it is given can understand (Mk 4:11).

Mark says also that Jesus preaches *the word*. He uses the absolute, Christian kerygmatic term which means the same as 'gospel', the joyful message about Jesus dead and risen. Mark does not mention the content of Jesus' preaching, but he certainly means that what follows is a demonstration of that content: the power of Jesus dead and risen to forgive sins in those who believe. This explains why Mark, even more than the previous authors, focuses on Jesus. In Mk 2:3 he specifies that they bring the paralytic *to him*. He also says that Jesus knows *immediately* what the scribes were thinking (Mk 2:8), and that the man took up his pallet *immediately* and went away in front of them all (Mk 2:12).

Mark's context makes this text what it was not by itself, namely, a polemic controversy. That is apparently the way he wanted to see it, though he did not for that purpose change the form of the story itself. For Mark, the scribes, who had been no more than 'literary' figures, became real adversaries. The controversy concerns the Jewish theological principle that God alone can forgive sins (Mk 2:7), and

Jesus opposes to this his claim of divine power. In this perspective, we get a kind of polemic, though the form is not perfect:
(1) Expanded description of the scene (Mk 2:1–4);
(2) the offending statement of Jesus (Mk 2:5);
(3) polemic question by the adversaries (Mk 2:6–7);
(4) Jesus' answer: (a) counter-question (Mk 2:8–9);
                            (b) the point (Mk 2:10);
(5) legitimation of Jesus' claim through a miracle (Mk 2:11–12).

But what is the exact function of Mk 2:1–12 in the context of Mk 2:1 – 3:6 in which it is now found? Many scholars hold that Mk 2:1 – 3:6 in its entirety is a pre-Marcan collection. We would rather be inclined to think that the pre-Marcan collection ran from Mk 2:15 to 3:6. Why? Several pre-synoptic collections were built up on the basis of identity of form. Now, from Mk 2:15 we have indeed concise controversies with Pharisees (not with scribes!). On the basis of the form principle, Mk 2:1–12 with its extensive miracle story as a frame simply cannot have been part of the collection. Besides, the real controversies deal with questions of orthodox doctrine, not of miracle working. Moreover, some scholars speak of a pre-Marcan *Galilean* controversy collection. But it seems that all Galilean features are redactional, that is, from Mark's hand. So we certainly cannot make that setting a criterion of a pre-Marcan collection. Besides, clearly Galilean features are found only in Mk 2:1–12 and 2:13–14. So, it seems that Mark himself created the beginning of the 'Galilean controversy collection'. He placed the expanded miracle story in front of the collection of controversies.

But questions have also been raised about the end of the pre-Marcan collection of controversies. The questions revolve particularly around the origin of Mk 3:6. We think that Mk 3:6 is the pre-Marcan conclusion of the controversy collection which started with Mk 2:15. Mk 3:6 cannot simply be the conclusion of Mk 3:1–5, because the Pharisees as adversaries are not mentioned in Mk 3:1–5, but they are the adversaries of the controversies from Mk 2:15 on. Neither is Mk 3:6 Marcan, to be aligned with Mk 11:18; 12:12 and 14:1f., and in that sense pointing forward to the passion, for in all these verses the driving force is not the Pharisees but the chief priests and the scribes, and everywhere except in Mk 3:6 we find the typical expression, 'they tried to arrest him', or 'they sought a way to destroy him'.

We conclude, therefore, that a pre-Marcan collector put four controversies together (starting from Mk 2:15), all beginning with a very general introduction, 'and it happened' (Mk 2:15), 'and there were' (Mk 2:18), 'and it happened' (Mk 2:23), 'and he entered' (Mk

3:1). This collector wanted to highlight the hostility of the Pharisees, an interest which is not prominent in the Marcan redaction. In a final comment (Mk 3:6) he wanted to emphasize who these adversaries were and the extent of their hostility: 'the Pharisees went out, and immediately held counsel (with the Herodians) against him, how to destroy him'. 'With the Herodians' is most probably Marcan (cf. Mk 8:15 and 12:13).

What was the content and purpose of this pre-Marcan collection of Mk 2:15 – 3:6, directed so explicitly against the Pharisees? It seems that the last two pericopes were the first to be combined. Both of them deal with a violation of the *sabbath* (use of catchword). But the adversaries of the last controversy but one (Mk 2:23–28) were the *Pharisees*, and that seems to have been the catchword of the other controversies which were put in front of the two concerning the sabbath. So we get the following arrangement:

$$\text{sabbath} \left\{ \begin{array}{l} \text{Mk 2:15–17} \\ \text{Mk 2:18–22} \\ \text{Mk 2:23–28} \\ \text{Mk 3:1–5} \end{array} \right. \quad \left. \begin{array}{l} \\ \end{array} \right\} \text{Pharisees}$$

The controversy about plucking ears of corn on the sabbath (Mk 2:23–28) is the axis of the collection. There is no increase in tension in the course of the series of pericopes which, as it is, simply stand next to each other, linked by catchwords. But the pre-Marcan collector provided the collection with a conclusion in Mk 3:6 in which he highlighted the implacable hostility of the Pharisees. Jesus' 'failure' is to be explained by this hostility, and his rejection by the leaders of the people ultimately leads to his death.

Mark only slightly edited this pre-Marcan collection itself (Mk 2:13–14; 2:27–28; 3:1). The most important redactional intervention consists in the fact that Mark put the expanded story of the paralytic in front of the whole collection, while at the same time introducing a few editorial changes in the story itself, as we saw above. In Mark, the peak of the series of controversies is reached right at the beginning, in the verse that stands at the centre of the first pericope, namely Mk 2:7, 'Who ... but God?' Jesus claims divine prerogatives. After that all the other violations of commands and laws are no longer a surprise; they can be understood very well in the light of the first claim. What, then, is the point of the total composition of Mk 2:1 – 3:6 which is so emphatically prefaced by Mark with Mk 2:1–12?

Mark deals with a secret, mysterious revelation of the Christ, a revelation of Jesus' glory hidden in his humility, which reaches its climax in his passion and death. His 'glory' and 'divinity' shine through specifically in the miracles. Both elements, glory and humiliation, are present in almost all miracle stories: there is a revelation of Jesus' glory, but it is counterbalanced by the fact that this revelation is 'secret'. In the story of the paralytic, too, the element of revelation of Jesus' glory and 'divinity' is found. As the healer he does not put to shame the faith of the paralytic. He heals him with a powerful command (Mk 2:11). The same feature is alluded to when it is stated that he knows the secret thoughts of people (Mk 2:8). The context also contributes to this effect. Jesus easily defeats his adversaries. Then there is, of course, the title 'Son of man'. The Son of man has the power to forgive sins.

But there are also elements of lowliness and humility. This is even true of Mk 2:1–12 itself. The 'revelation' still takes place 'in the house', that is, not fully publicly. Moreover, Jesus does not state directly 'I am the Son of man and as such I have the power to forgive sins'. Mark strengthened this element of hiddenness and humility by placing the pericope at the head of the series of controversies. We saw that the pre-Marcan collection already had its climax in Mk 3:6, the Pharisees taking counsel how they could destroy him. In other words, even this pre-Marcan collection was already dominated and controlled by the passion theme. For Mark, the controversy about divine power becomes also and very specifically a feature which will lead to Jesus' death. Despite his triumph over his adversaries, this controversy takes him one step closer to his destiny, death.

So the two themes of Mark's Christology found throughout the gospel are also connected in Mk 2:1 – 3:6. In the Marcan perspective, Jesus is not only the unique wonder-worker, the Son of man with power to forgive sins; the glory of the Marcan Jesus is completed and fulfilled on the way to the cross which he travels with full consciousness and freedom.[76]

Matthew 9:1–8

The context

For the study of the context in Matthew of the healing of the paralytic we refer to our comments on the context of the healing of Peter's mother-in-law, Mt 8:14–15, in Chapter 3. Mt 9:1–8 occurs in the third section of Mt 8:1 – 9:34, namely Mt 9:1–17, which deals with questions about the separation of Jesus and his disciples from Israel.

The text proper

Let us see how Matthew edits the Marcan story in his own context. He does not show any interest in the concrete, anecdotal details which made the Marcan story so lively. If we did not have the text of Mark, many details of Matthew's introductory verses would be obscure. But here as elsewhere Matthew shows little interest in the anecdotal content, showing all the more interest in the doctrinal. In this particular case this means little interest in the miracle story and all attention focused on the instruction or, as others prefer to call it, the controversy about Jesus' power to forgive sins. Again within this section Matthew pays special attention to what Jesus says.

Verses 1–2a: And getting into a boat he crossed over and came to his own city. (2a) And behold, they brought to him a paralytic lying on his bed;

Let us see how drastically Matthew abbreviated Mark's text:

Matthew 9	Mark 2
1 And getting into a boat he crossed over and came to his own city.	1 And when he returned to Capernaum after some days, it was reported that he was at home.
	2 And many were gathered together, so that there was no longer room for them, not even about the door; and he was preaching the word to them.
2 And behold, they brought to him a paralytic lying on his bed.	3 And they came, bringing to him a paralytic carried by four men.
	4 And when they could not get near him because of the crowd, they removed the roof above him; and when they had made an opening, they let down the pallet on which the paralytic lay.

Matthew adapts the opening verses to the context in which he presents the story, namely after the healing of the Gadarene demoniac at the eastern shore of the lake. So, in Matthew, Jesus comes from the eastern shore and crosses the lake to his hometown, Capernaum (Mt 4:13). Matthew says nothing about being in a house or about many gathering at the door. Matthew omitted many Marcan details because to his mind they distracted the readers' attention away from the basic storyline. He kept only the absolutely necessary. He does not even tell us where Jesus worked the miracle.

'They' (impersonal) brought him a paralytic lying on a bed. Since Matthew did not mention the crowd at the door, the whole event could be something between Jesus and the paralytic. Nothing is said about the strange way in which the paralytic reached Jesus. He does not use the rare word *krabbatos*, 'pallet'. Instead he uses the usual word for 'bed'. Does he mean a real bed, or rather a stretcher? As in Mt 8:6, 14, he uses a strong term for 'lying' on a bed. Literally, the text says that he was 'thrown' (*beblēmenon*) on the bed. This is a rather violent term and most probably has a connotation of demonic possession. Matthew moves as quickly as possible to the encounter of Jesus and the paralytic.

Verse 2b: and when Jesus saw their faith he said to the paralytic, 'Take heart, my son; your sins are forgiven.'

As can be seen, Matthew is no longer abbreviating Mark; he even has an additional expression, 'take heart'. By maintaining this verse in its entirety, Matthew creates a clear unevenness in the text. In Mark it was clear how Jesus could see their faith, that is, by their climbing on to the roof and letting the paralytic down through the roof. But Matthew does not mention this. Their simple arrival with the paralytic was apparently sufficient for Matthew. Moreover, Jesus did not need those external manifestations. He could see the faith of the paralytic as he could read the unexpressed thoughts of the scribes. The theme of faith is certainly no less important than in Mark. In fact, it is precisely the theme of faith which Matthew develops in many miracle stories (Mt 8:13; 9:22, 28–29; 15:28). He thinks in terms of a Christian faith in the early Christian kerygma, which is demonstrated, and to which Jesus is going to respond here, in the first place by the forgiveness of sins. In the Acts of the Apostles faith is the first requirement for forgiveness of sins (Acts 10:43; 13:38; 26:18).

It is a bit surprising that Matthew writes '*their* faith'. Mark referred to the faith of the four bearers and the paralytic who went through so many difficulties to reach Jesus. But in Matthew neither the bearers nor their difficulties have been mentioned. The story seems to revolve entirely around Jesus and the paralytic. To be sure, he has said that 'they' carried the paralytic, but the phrase is to be taken very impersonally, as elsewhere in a number of miracle stories. So it is possible that Matthew overlooked this aspect of his drastic redactional intervention in the opening verses and inadvertently wrote 'they'. Or did he deliberately keep 'they' because he was looking beyond this specific story and its setting, as clearly appears in the conclusion of his story (Mt 9:8)?

Very typically for Matthew, Jesus' words are scrupulously maintained. In fact, he adds 'take heart'. It is a consoling word which is also found in Mt 9:22, whereas he omits it in Mt 20:32 (compare Mk 10:49), most probably because in Mark it was pronounced by the crowd. So, for Matthew, 'take heart' seems to be a typical expression used by Jesus, whom Matthew regularly presents as the risen Christ, the Lord of the community, as is very clearly seen in the stilling of the storm (Mt 8:18–27). In this light, the imperative 'take heart' understood as a word spoken by the risen Christ became very significant. The point already found in Mark, the encounter between faith and forgiveness of sins, becomes even more predominant in Matthew. The disciples should find their real consolation in that encounter rather than in a miraculous response by Christ. The features of the miracle story are therefore reduced to the barest minimum, while the verses dealing with forgiveness are even slightly expanded.

Verse 3: And behold, some of the scribes said to themselves, 'This man is blaspheming.'

Again we should closely compare the texts of Matthew and Mark.

Matthew 9	*Mark 2*
3 And behold, some of the scribes said to themselves, 'This man is blaspheming.'	6 Now some of the scribes were sitting there, questioning
	7 in their hearts, 'Why does this man speak thus? It is blasphemy! Who can forgive sins but God alone?'

It is immediately clear that the words spoken by the scribes are also abbreviated. The crescendo structure of Mark which had its climax in the third clause is gone. In Mark the appearance of the scribes had still a minimum of probability: they happened to be *sitting* there. In Matthew they just begin to 'say to themselves' without any introduction. He indicates that a new development begins: 'and behold, some of the scribes said ...'. Matthew retains only the accusation of blasphemy, since the third clause, 'Who can forgive sins but God alone?', is also omitted. Alone, the accusation of blasphemy becomes more forceful.

The charge of blasphemy in verse 3 is perhaps even more important for Matthew than for Mark, because he expressly repeats it in the context of Jesus' trial (26:65), where Jesus also refers to himself as the Son of Man (vs. 64; but cf. also Mark 13:64, 62).[77]

As in Mark, Jesus' statement is interpreted by the scribes not as forgiveness granted by God, but as forgiveness granted by Jesus himself.

Verse 4: But Jesus, knowing their thoughts, said, 'Why do you think evil in your hearts?

Matthew 9	Mark 2
4 But Jesus, knowing their thoughts,	8 And immediately Jesus, perceiving in his spirit that they thus questioned within themselves,
said, 'Why do you think evil in your hearts?'	said to them, 'Why do you question thus in your hearts?'

Once more we see that everything is abbreviated except Jesus' words. Matthew often omits 'immediately'. Instead of 'knowing in his spirit', Matthew simply says that Jesus 'knew', or, according to some manuscripts, that he 'saw'. The Lord simply knows everything. Just as he saw the faith of the paralytic, so here he knows the scribes' thoughts. The expression is an almost literal translation of an Old Testament formula found in Job 21:27, 'I know your thoughts', and in Ps 94:11, 'the Lord knows the thoughts of man'. This needs no elaboration for Matthew; it is a foregone conclusion: Jesus knew their thoughts. For 'thoughts' Matthew uses a very specific term which is repeated in the second part of this verse, and which indicates their ill will: *enthumēseis*. Jesus' reply is in direct speech. The object of the scribes' thoughts is evil. They appear in a worse light in Matthew than in Mark. According to Matthew, there is something wrong with their fundamental orientation, and this orientation is born from the heart. Instead of 'to question' (*dialogizesthai*; Mk 2:8), which like *dialogismos* implies reprehensible uncertainty (Mt 15:19; 16:7; 21:25), Matthew uses the words 'thoughts' (*enthumēseis*) and 'to think' (*enthumeisthai*) which are not found in the other gospels and imply determined thinking (Mt 1:20; 9:4; and 12:25, the first part of which is closely parallel to 9:4). Hence Matthew judges the scribes more severely, since their thoughts as well as their accusations are without any doubt.[78]

Verse 5: For which is easier, to say, 'Your sins are forgiven,' or to say, 'Rise and walk'?

Matthew 9	Mark 2
5 For which is easier, to say, 'Your sins are forgiven,' or to say, 'Rise and walk'?	9 Which is easier, to say to the paralytic, 'Your sins are forgiven,' or to say, 'Rise, take up your pallet, and walk'?

Once again Matthew abbreviates Mark's text so that the real point comes to the fore. The paralytic is, as it were, all but forgotten, or at least removed from the picture as much as possible. He is not even mentioned as the addressee of the command, 'rise'. The command to take up his pallet/bed is also omitted, though it is mentioned in Mt 9:6b.

Presumably, Jesus formulates the question from the standpoint of the scribes and does not imply that he considers granting God's pardon to a person easier than curing him.[79]

Verse 6a: But that you may know that the Son of man has authority on earth to forgive sins'—he then said to the paralytic—

Except for 'then', Matthew follows Mark very closely. This is the climax of the Matthean text. It was already so for Mark, but it is even more so for Matthew, who reduces the features of the miracle story to their bare minimum. No wonder, therefore, that there is no abbreviation at all in this verse (compare Mk 2:10). The meaning is basically the same as in Mark, but we should refer to the 'key to the gospel of Matthew' (Mt 28:18–20) which speaks even more clearly about the power (of the Son of man; allusion to Dan 7:14) given to him at his resurrection. Besides, in Matthew the Son of man is described as the supreme judge who is to reward everybody according to his deeds (Mt 25:31ff.). He already anticipates this judgement, not by punishing sins, but by forgiving them. Quite naturally, then, 'on earth' is emphasized. The same expression appears in Mt 16:19 and 18:18 where the power to loose and to bind is entrusted to Peter and to the community respectively. The heavenly, Danielic Son of man exercises his power already here on earth when he forgives sins, and he does so on the basis of his resurrection. Matthew does not present Jesus as challenging the scribes' conviction that God alone can forgive sins, but as claiming that God has empowered him to exercise this authority on earth.[80]

Verse 6b: 'Rise, take up your bed and go home.'

Except for the phrase 'I say to you', which is omitted, possibly because Matthew wants to achieve a closer parallelism between Jesus' command and its execution in the next verse, and the substitution of 'bed' for 'pallet', Matthew's text is the same as Mark's.

Verse 7: And he rose and went home.

Matthew 9		*Mark 2*
7 And he rose (*egertheis*)	12a	And he rose (*ēgerthē*), and immediately took up the pallet, and went out before them all;
and went home.		

There are two important differences. First, the carrying of the pallet/bed has disappeared. Second, instead of going out 'before

them all', which prepared for the reaction of 'all' to the miracle in
Mark, Matthew says simply that 'he went home'. Thus we get the
following parallelism in Matthew:

6b Rise ... and go home.
7   Risen, he went home.

Thus the execution corresponds perfectly to the command, especially
that 'and he went home' in Mt 9:7b. There is no doubt that we find
this feature very often in Matthew. Could it be that Matthew gave a
very specific meaning to the phrase 'and went home'? Indeed, rising
(in participle form) becomes, as it were, subordinate to 'going home',
and literally the text says 'he went *away* home'. Is it possible that
Matthew thinks of the 'going home' of the man whose sins have been
forgiven? In fact, as will appear from the next verse, this remains the
main thing in Matthew's mind. 'He went away' (*apēlthen*) is typically
Matthean and constitutes a link with Mt 8:18, 19, 21, 32, 33. Matthew
rephrases and abbreviates the verse in such a way that it suggests that
the man's rising and going home is an expression of obedient
discipleship much in the same way as going to the other side of the sea
was (Mt 8:18–27).[81]

> **Verse 8:** When the crowds saw it, they were afraid, and they
> glorified God, who had given such authority to men.

In the concluding verse Matthew remoulds his Marcan source
entirely.

Matthew 9	Mark 2
8 When the crowds saw it, they were afraid, and they glorified God, who had given such authority to men.	12b so that they were all amazed and glorified God, saying, 'We never saw anything like this!'

From Mk 2:11 on, Mark resumed the text of the miracle story. In Mk
2:11–12 the scribes and the question concerning forgiveness seem to
disappear entirely, and there is no specific reaction in the concluding
verse to what ultimately is for Mark too the most important 'miracle',
namely the forgiveness of sins. In Mark the question of forgiveness
ended where the inserted text came to an end, that is, at the end of
verse 10. In Mk 2:12 we have only an acclamation of the healing
miracle.

In Matthew things are very different. The forgiveness of sins,
which is clearly the most important feature, spills over at the end of
the whole story: it is to the miracle of forgiveness that the crowds
react. As such, this is hardly observable. But the point of their

admiration is expressed in that they glorify God 'who had given such authority to men'. The word *exousia, 'power'*, 'authority', is obviously derived from Mk 9:6a, the power of the Son of man to forgive sins. It is surprising, however, that the crowds glorify God for having given such power to *men*. We said above that on the level of the pre-Marcan enlarged story as well as on that of the Marcan redaction the situation in life was perhaps the power of the Church to forgive sins. At that stage we said that we felt that the Marcan text is Christological and not ecclesial. We cautioned, however, against entirely separating these two aspects; certainly so in a text which speaks of the power of the *Son of man*. Such texts are at least implicitly ecclesial. What was implicit in Mark becomes explicit in Matthew. His point is that the power of the Son of man to forgive sins rests now in the Church. Matthew's reformulation of the statement to the effect that the crowds now glorify God for giving 'such authority to men', no longer reflects the controversy between Jesus and the scribes as such, but rather the contemporary opposition between the Matthean community, which claimed the power to forgive sins, and the synagogue.[82]

We are not surprised by this Matthean interpretation. In Mt 28:18–20 we read: 'All authority in heaven and on earth has been given to me. Go *therefore* and make disciples of all nations, baptizing them in the name of the Father ... teaching them to observe all that I have commanded you ...'. It is the disciples who have to make this general, universal power of the Son of man a reality on earth for all nations. Baptism is among other things forgiveness of sins in response to faith. Thus God's creative presence with his people, through the Son of man, is realized in the history of the Church: 'I am with you always, to the close of the age' (Mt 28:20).

In Mt 16:18–19 it is the Son of man who confers on Peter the position of being the rock of the Church, of having the keys of the kingdom; and what he will bind on earth will be bound in heaven and what he will loose on earth will be loosed in heaven (compare Mt 18:18). Though the meaning of the expression may not be limited to it, the saying about binding and loosing certainly also implies the power to forgive sins. In Mt 18:18 the same power is given to the group of the Twelve and therefore, in a sense, to the community, of which Peter is the centre.

Mt 19:28 states that 'in the new world, when the Son of man shall sit on his glorious throne, you who have followed me will also sit on twelve thrones, judging the twelve tribes of Israel'. The power they will share with the Son of man is already theirs here on earth in the form in which it exists here, namely, the power to forgive sins. This explanation of Mt 9:8 also fits in the Matthean context of Mt 8 – 9 which speaks of the power of Christ which is going to be shared by those who follow him (Mt 10:1). So Matthew tells his readers not only to glorify and thank God for having bestowed such power on the Son of man, but also for having made people share this power so that it is now exercised in the Church.

There is no need, therefore, to wonder where Matthew got those 'crowds' all of a sudden at the end of his story. In a sense they are indeed unexpected. But we have the same feature at the end of the Matthean version of the stilling of the storm (Mt 8:27). There too Matthew thought of the people, the Christians who should be amazed and give thanks. Where Matthew thinks of the praise Christians should give to God he easily creates the 'literary crowds' giving thanks within the narrative.

Luke 5:17–26

The context

Generally speaking, Luke presents the healing of the paralytic in the same context as Mark, that is, after the cleansing of the leper (Mk 1:40–45; Lk 5:12–16). But his presentation is coloured by his own distinctive opening of the gospel, especially the programmatic scene of Lk 4:16–30. From Lk 4:31 on Luke presents Jesus as implementing his programme. Lk 5:17–26 should be seen in the context of the narrative framework stated in Lk 4:43–44, 'but he said to them, "I must preach the good news of the kingdom of God to the other cities also; for I was sent for this purpose". And he was preaching in the synagogues of Judea'. In line with Luke's development of Jesus' ministry in the form of a journey, Jesus has left Nazareth and Capernaum behind and is now working in 'the other cities'. In the light of Lk 4:16–30, where Jesus' mission was presented as a comprehensively liberating approach to whatever burdens or oppresses people, the present healing and forgiveness of sins should also be understood as an act of liberation. Through the constant presence of Pharisees and scribes, their eagerness for debate, especially about sin in all its aspects, Lk 5:17–39 appears as a self-contained section.

On the other hand, Lk 5:12–26 may be seen as describing in two episodes the kind of person who called Levi in Lk 5:27–28. Levi's response (Lk 5:28) is based on Jesus' being one who restores social outcasts to community (Lk 5:12–14) and who forgives sinners (Lk 5:17–26). In Lk 5:29–32 Jesus is depicted as one who not only restores and forgives individuals, but also associates with the many who are in need.[83]

The text proper

Verse 17: On one of those days, as he was teaching, there were Pharisees and teachers of the law sitting by, who had come from every village of Galilee and Judea and from Jerusalem; and the power of the Lord was with him to heal.

In the style typical of the Septuagint Luke begins the narrative with the expression. '(And it happened) on one of those days'. While Luke seems to consider Lk 5:17a the heading of the whole section Lk 5:17–39, Lk 5:17b is the special heading of the healing of the paralytic. Every single word of this verse is redactional. As in Lk 8:22, the expression 'on one of those days' defines a precise period of time. Here Luke refers to the period of journeying mentioned above. Luke does not mention Capernaum, since Jesus has left this city behind. 'As he was teaching' depicts 'the continuing progress of his teaching .... It stresses the context of teaching in which the controversy is to take place'.[84]

'There were Pharisees and teachers of the law sitting by.' Luke removes the anomaly of Mark's and Matthew's version in which the scribes appear without any introduction (Mk 2:6 par.). From the very beginning Luke introduces the characters who are going to play a part in the further development of the story. It is clear, however, that he gets his material from Mk 2:6, for even the expression 'sitting by' is retained. Luke writes 'teachers of the law' instead of 'scribes', for his Greek readers would understand 'scribe' as meaning 'secretary'. The term 'teachers of the law' (*nomodidaskaloi*; only in Lk 5:17; Acts 5:34; I Tim 1:7) probably means a specific group within the Pharisees to be equated with the 'scribes' of Lk 5:21, which undoubtedly belongs to the traditional story, while here in the redactional introduction to the story Luke uses his own term.[85] Luke adds the Pharisees and even places them first. He anticipates the appearance of the Pharisees in Mk 2:16, 24 par. Lk 5:30; 6:2.

These opponents come from Galilee, Judea and Jerusalem, a typically Lucan feature: Jesus' way from Galilee to Jerusalem in reverse! As a result of this redactional intervention Lk 5:17 becomes the heading for all the following controversies, which are also knit more closely together, as appears clearly from Lk 5:27, which links the healing of the paralytic and the call of Levi. Luke views Jesus' adversaries as a group, as he also does in Lk 11:53 and 15:2. Towards the end of the drama the chief priests will be added (Lk 9:22; 19:47; 20:1, 19; 22:2, 66; 23:10).

'From every village of Galilee and Judea and from Jerusalem' should be interpreted in the light of Luke's journey theme: from

Galilee (Nazareth) to Jerusalem. Jesus does not deviate from this line. Instead there is a centripetal movement toward Jesus: people gather from everywhere to the point where he happens to be on that line from Galilee to Jerusalem. But at the same time the end of the journey is already mentioned: Jerusalem, where the hostility of the Pharisees and the teachers of the law will reach its climax. The direction towards Jerusalem will be expressed more definitely in Lk 9:51, 'he set his face to go to Jerusalem'.

'And the power of the Lord was with him to heal.' In Lk 4:14 it has already been said that 'Jesus returned in the power of the Spirit into Galilee', the Spirit who had come upon him while he was at prayer after his baptism (Lk 3:22). In Lk 4:18, Jesus declared: 'The Spirit of the Lord is upon me'. From the outset of the story Luke wants his readers to know that the healing and forgiveness of sins that follows is done in 'the power of the Lord'.

> **Verses 18–19:** And behold, men were bringing on a bed a man who was paralysed, and they sought to bring him in and lay him before Jesus; (19) but finding no way to bring him in, because of the crowd, they went up on the roof and let him down with his bed through the tiles into the midst before Jesus.

Omitting the number 'four', Luke elaborates on the Marcan presentation of the persistence of the people who take the paralytic to Jesus. He first says that they made a vain effort to get to Jesus (Lk 5:18b), and then comments that they found no way to reach him. Then he relates how they managed to get the man on the roof. Luke seems to stress the faith of the bearers even more emphatically than Mark.

In Lk 5:19 Luke clearly is thinking of a Greek house with a tile roof, because he speaks of letting the man down through the tiles. Then he very emphatically says that they let him down 'into the midst before Jesus'. The expression 'in the midst' is also found in Lk 4:35 and 6:8, where it was no doubt a favourite Lucan phrase. But here he adds 'before Jesus'. Already in Lk 5:18 we were told that they intended to bring the man in and lay him 'before Jesus'. Could this have something to do with the Lucan Christological feature of Christ, the merciful Saviour of the sick? Luke does indeed call attention to Christ the healer (Lk 5:17).

> **Verse 20:** And when he saw their faith he said, 'Man, your sins are forgiven you.'

Generally speaking, Luke follows Mark closely. The address 'man' seems to express more distance than the term *teknon*, 'child', 'son', in Mark and Matthew. We find the latter term in Lk 2:48, where Mary addresses Jesus, and Lk 15:31, the father addressing the elder son. The vocative 'man' occurs again in Lk 12:14, in the introduction to the parable of the rich fool, and in Lk 22:58, in Peter's reply to someone who told him that he too was with Jesus.

In the continuation Luke will bring out very strongly Jesus' forgiving mercy. He does so particularly in his special material. Lk 7:36–50, about 'a woman of the city, who was a sinner', speaks in its redactional conclusion of the earthly Jesus forgiving her sins. Then there is the whole of Lk 15, where from the very beginning (Lk 15:1–2), Luke clearly states the theme of the chapter. We also have Lk 18:10–14; 19:8–10; 23:40–43. Jesus is the one who offers God's forgiveness to sinners.

We should also call attention to the remarkable perfect tense, 'your sins *have been* forgiven you'. It is a process which started in the past and lasts until the present. In fact, it seems that Luke, who describes Jesus' life and ministry as a 'way', also thinks of people, represented by this 'man', as being on the way of metanoia and forgiveness. This is, of course, important for an evangelist who thinks of the Christian life as being lived *in* the world.

Verse 21: And the scribes and the Pharisees began to question, saying, 'Who is this that speaks blasphemies? Who can forgive sins but God only?'

Those called 'teachers of the law' in verse 17 now become 'scribes' (*grammateis*, derived from Mk 2:6). The scribes and the Pharisees do not just 'question in their hearts' or 'question within themselves' as in Mark, but express their objections, which is more in keeping with the real form of a controversy. Their question concerns the identity of Jesus: Who is this? This is the right question but raised here with a malicious purpose. It is the question which prepares for the final answer: he is the Son of man (Lk 5:24).

Verse 22: When Jesus perceived their questionings, he answered them, 'Why do you question in your hearts?

ἐπιγνούς

The aorist participle *epignous* suggests that Jesus knew their minds through and through. Here it seems as if Luke, like Mark, is referring to thoughts which have not been expressed. Nevertheless, we think that Luke is referring to words that have actually been expressed, for Lk 5:22 is correlative to Lk 5:21, in which we feel that he is thinking of an explicit expression of the objection. But why then does he speak of Jesus knowing their thoughts (questionings)? This can easily be explained. The question, as it was expressed, was quite legitimate and was, indeed, the real question, namely the question about Jesus' identity. The problem with the scribes and the Pharisees was the *intention* of their question. Without waiting for an answer, they have already qualified Jesus as a blasphemer. Jesus' knowledge (*epignous*) of the scribes' reaction means a clear perception of people's attitude towards him (compare Lk 4:23; 6:8; 9:47). The verse need not be interpreted as referring to Jesus' 'divine wisdom' (H. Schürmann) or his 'prophetic knowledge' (G. Schneider).[86]

> **Verse 23:** Which is easier, to say, 'Your sins are forgiven you,' or to say, 'Rise and walk'?

This is one of the many agreements in wording between Matthew and Luke against Mark in the triple tradition, except for the perfect tense of the verb 'to forgive' which Luke also uses in Lk 5:20. Luke omits any reference to the specific situation and thus may be generalizing Jesus' claim.

Jesus' statement is made from the standpoint of the scribes and Pharisees, who would consider it easier to say 'your sins are forgiven you', the effect of which cannot be checked, than to heal the paralytic with a word, which can be verified. By curing the man Jesus will manifest his power to heal (cf. Lk 5:17), and thus do what his opponents consider more difficult, while by both curing the paralytic and forgiving his sins Jesus exercises the mission for which he has been sent (Lk 4:18).[87]

> **Verse 24:** But that you may know that the Son of man has authority on earth to forgive sins'—he said to the man who was paralysed—'I say to you, rise, take up your bed and go home.'

Here again we notice that Luke's fidelity to his source is much greater where Jesus' words are concerned. There is only one editorial change we should draw attention to. At the end Jesus says literally to the paralytic: 'journey (travel) to your home'. This is a favourite Lucan term and he certainly does not use it without reason. For Luke, discipleship is realized in the form of a journey which is determined by Jesus. The faithful disciple and, in fact, all who believe in Jesus' word depart from the master only at his express command and in order to carry out his will (Lk 8:39; 9:60; 19:32; 22:13). Otherwise, going away from him means apostasy.[88] This is important, especially for what Luke says about healing in the following verse. The paralytic is made totally active: he must rise, take up the bed on which he was carried in passively, and go home.

Verse 25: And immediately he rose before them, and took up that on which he lay, and went home, glorifying God.

Luke emphasizes that the man rose 'immediately' (*parachrēma*). He rose 'before them'. They will become the witnesses in the final acclamation. Strikingly, Luke speaks of 'that on which he lay'. Why not simply 'pallet' or 'bed'? Is Luke having difficulties with that bed here because he had no notion of the Palestinian pallet? The bed known in the Greco-Roman world was in fact quite a heavy piece of furniture. In Lk 5:18 the evangelist simply speaks of a 'bed' (*klinē*); then in Lk 5:24, Jesus' command, he writes 'small bed' (*klinidion*); and finally he says that the man actually carried 'that on which he lay'. It is as if Luke is saying: whatever that *krabbatos* in Mark was, the man, once he was healed, carried it. But another explanation is possible: the man now *carries* that upon which he once *lay*. This points to Jesus as his great benefactor.

Then Luke, as Matthew, says that he went away home. In Luke this expression certainly has its own special meaning. In Lk 5:24 Jesus had told him to *journey home*, which is Luke's favourite expression for the Christian life as a way with Jesus. Going *away* from the master can only be done on his command in order to go *to* others and there carry out his will. Luke therefore thinks of the Christian life as following upon and being a result of forgiveness. This life should also be a constant glorification of God. This theme is very prominent in the Acts of the Apostles. Luke

> draws a sharper distinction: the one who was cured glorifies God freely ...; the others are struck with fear because they have seen a 'paradox' (the literal sense of the Greek), i.e., something that goes beyond all familiar knowledge and thus points to the one who acts contrary to all expectations: God.[89]

Verse 26: And amazement seized them all, and they glorified God and were filled with awe, saying, 'We have seen strange things today'.

Just as the first verse of the pericope, so the last verse is composed by Luke according to his own schema. All react in an ecstatic way; literally 'ecstasy took all'. They react by giving glory to God and are filled with awe. The reason for all this is that they have seen *paradoxa* (plural), i.e., things that go against all expectations. This has apparently a bearing on the whole story, that is, the forgiveness of sins as well as the healing. And they have seen all these things 'today'. This is Luke's 'eschatological today', as found also in Lk 2:11; 4:21; 19:9; 23:43. The eschatological reality of forgiveness of sins has become a reality today through Jesus, the Son of man. That means also that for Luke the glory to be given to God has an ecclesial dimension.

The situation of this pericope is not so much the missionary preaching as the community instruction in which the forgiveness received and at work now (see the perfect tenses in Lk 5:20, 23) is praised, and for which glory is given to God. Luke's editorial interventions result in presenting this single instance of forgiveness as typical of Jesus' ministry.

The pericope, which is embedded in a wider section consisting of controversies of the scribes and the Pharisees with Jesus, specifies the mission of Jesus initially presented in Lk 4:18ff. The forgiveness of sins also belongs to the saving mission of Jesus to the poor and the oppressed. This is demonstrated by a saving act extended to a paralytic who was bound to his bed. By the insertion of the information given in Lk 5:17b, that Jesus is endowed with God's saving power, the emphasis is shifted from the controversy to Jesus' powerful act. The latter indicates that the idea of forgiveness together with the motif of conversion has soteriological meaning for Luke. Salvation does not presuppose a self-chosen penance, but in communion with Jesus, God offers his salvation to sinners. While the idea of conversion is closely related to the nearness of the kingdom, Luke develops a specific eschatology. From a historical perspective he formulates a 'present-day eschatology' and thereby dislodges the previously prevailing 'future eschatology'. His model of a historicized 'present-day eschatology', in which divine salvation is present in Jesus, provides him with the possibility of reflecting further on the continuing opportunity of God's eschatological salvation in the Acts of the Apostles.[90]

6   The healing of the man with the withered hand

Mt 12:9–14	Mk 3:1–6	Lk 6:6–11
9 And he went on from there, and entered their synagogue.	1 Again he entered the synagogue,	6 On another sabbath, when he entered the synagogue and taught,
10 And behold, there was a man with a withered hand. And they asked him, 'Is it lawful to heal on the sabbath?' so that they might accuse him.	and a man was there who had a withered hand. 2 And they watched him, to see whether he would heal him on the sabbath, so that they might accuse him.	a man was there whose right hand was withered. 7 And the scribes and the Pharisees watched him, to see whether he would heal on the sabbath, so that they might find an accusation against him. 8 But he knew their thoughts,
	3 And he said to the man who had the withered hand, 'Come here.'	and he said to the man who had the withered hand, 'Come and stand here.' And he rose and stood there.
11 He said to them, 'What man of you, if he has one sheep and it falls into a pit on the sabbath, will not lay hold of it and lift it out? 12 Of how much more value is a man than a sheep! So it is lawful to do good on the sabbath.'	4 And he said to them, 'Is it lawful on the sabbath to do good or to do harm, to save life or to kill?'	9 And Jesus said to them, 'I ask you, is it lawful on the sabbath to do good or to do harm, to save life or to destroy it?'

	But they were silent.	
	5 And he looked around at them with anger, grieved at their hardness of heart,	10 And he looked around on them all,
13 Then he said to the man,	and he said to the man,	and he said to him,
'Stretch out your hand.' And the man stretched it out, and it was restored, whole like the other.	'Stretch out your hand.' He stretched it out, and his hand was restored.	'Stretch out your hand.' And he did so, and his hand was restored.
14 But the Pharisees went out and took counsel against him how to destroy him.	6 The Pharisees went out and immediately held counsel with the Herodians against him, how to destroy him.	11 But they were filled with fury and discussed with one another what they might do to Jesus.

Mark 3:1–6

The context

Mk 3:1–6 is the last pericope of a collection of five which we find in Mk 2:1 – 3:6. For a discussion of its context we refer to our comments on the context of Mk 2:1–12 in the preceding chapter.

The text proper

Analysis of the text

> **Verse 1:** Again he entered the synagogue, and a man was there who had a withered hand.

Verse 1a, 'again he entered the synagogue', is a redactional transition. As such the expression is found only here and in the undoubtedly redactional Mk 1:21. The use of 'synagogue' elsewhere in the gospel of Mark may be compared: it is redactional in Mk 1:21, 29, 39; 6:2; possibly traditional in Mk 1:23 and 13:9, and certainly in Mk 12:39. 'Again' (*palin*) is a typically Marcan link formula.[91] While Mk 2:1–12 dealt with making firm the feeble knees (Isa 35:3b), this story deals with strengthening the weak hands (Isa 35:3a).

While Mk 3:1a is composed by Mark, verse 1b is edited at least by the addition of 'there' (*ekei*). A more extensive redactional activity may be suspected but it can no longer be exactly described. So much is clear: the original exposition spoke of a man whose hand was withered. The original text may have been as follows: And (Jesus) saw a man who had a withered hand.

Verse 2: And they watched him, to see whether he would heal him on the sabbath, so that they might accuse him.

Verse 2a shows little sign of redactional activity. The unique appearance of the verb *paratēreō*, 'to watch', in the gospel of Mark indicates the traditional character of verse 2a. The verb *therapeuō*, 'to heal', may be traced to Mark. It is certainly redactional in Mk 1:34; 3:10; possibly redactional in Mk 6:13, and possibly traditional in Mk 6:5. Here, however, it belongs unquestionably to the pre-Marcan tradition.

As discussed below in connection with verse 6, verse 2b is almost certainly redactional.

Verses 3–4: And he said to the man who had the withered hand, 'Come here.' (4) And he said to them, 'Is it lawful on the sabbath to do good or to do harm, to save life or to kill?' But they were silent.

Verses 3–4 show signs of tradition: *xēros*, 'dry' (RSV: 'withered') is found only here in Mark. Verse 3b, 'Come here', is literally 'rise in the midst'. 'Rise' (*egeirein*) is traditional in Mk 1:31; 2:9, 11, 12; 4:27, 38; 5:41; 6:14, 16; 9:27; 10:49; 12:26; 13:8, 22; 14:42; 16:7; redactional only in Mk 14:28, but there in the sense of 'to rise (= resurrection)', not in the sense of 'to get up'. 'In the midst' (*eis to meson*) is not found elsewhere in Mark; typical for Mark is the expression *en mesōi*, 'in the midst' (redactional in Mk 6:47; 9:36). The expressions 'to do good' (*agathon poiein*) and 'to do harm' (*kakopoiein*) are not found elsewhere in Mark. There is no middle, there are no neutral acts. For Jesus failure to do good is the same as to do evil. 'To save life' (*psuchēn sōsai*) is found only here and in Mk 8:35 where it is traditional. Only the reaction of Jesus' opponents, 'but they were silent', has been inserted by Mark himself. Compare the redactional beginning of Mk 9:34, 'but they were silent'.

Verse 4 is almost certainly an authentic saying of Jesus, but may at first have existed in the tradition as an independent saying or in another context.

Verse 5: And he looked around at them with anger, grieved at their hardness of heart, and said to the man, 'Stretch out your hand.' He stretched it out, and his hand was restored.

Although 3:5 does not present the syntactical difficulties of 2:10, it does present the same shift from opponents to sick man.[92]

Word-use statistics support the largely traditional character of the verse: *orgē*, 'anger', is found only here in Mark; *sullupeomai*, 'to be grieved', occurs only here in the New Testament; *pōrōsis*, 'hardness', is found only here in this gospel, and *ekteinō*, 'to stretch', outside this pericope only in the traditional Mk 1:41; *apokathistēmi*, 'to be restored', occurs in Mk 8:25 and 9:12, in both cases probably from the tradition. But the clause 'grieved at their hardness of heart' reveals a psychological concern of Mark's (compare Mk 6:52 and 8:17, where the same is said in similar words of the disciples). Like the redactional clause 'and looking around', it must therefore be attributed to the activity of the second evangelist.

> **Verse 6:** The Pharisees went out, and immediately held counsel with the Herodians against him, how to destroy him.

The assessment of verse 6 constitutes the most important and most disputed literary problem of the whole pericope. There are two diametrically opposed positions: one that the verse is entirely redactional, the other that it is certainly traditional.

For its pre-Marcan origin, the following arguments are presented: Firstly, the fact that with the words 'that they might accuse him' verse 2 almost demands the decision to kill him in verse 6. Without verse 6—according to this opinion—verse 2 would remain a meaningless part of the introduction. Moreover, verse 4 with the catchword 'kill' and verse 5 with the reference to 'hardness of heart' also lead to verse 6.

Secondly, according to some scholars, the pericope escapes any precise form-critical classification because we have here an account based on biographical recollection which has as its central theme the confrontation between Jesus and his opponents. Once this is established there are no serious objections to affiliating verse 6 to the pericope. The mention of a group of 'Herodians' reinforces the impression of historicity of this scene, since it is not in agreement with the customary typical description of Jesus' opponents.

Thirdly, two not specifically Marcan terms argue against Mark as author of the verse: 'held counsel' (*sumboulion edidoun*) and the final *hopōs*, 'that', are found only here in Mark.

A critical consideration of these arguments shows, however, that they cannot bear the burden of proof for the pre-Marcan origin of Mk 3:6.

To the first argument it must be conceded that verse 2b indeed does prepare for verse 6 and that to that extent the two verses require each other; but it is possible that verse 2b too is a redactional insertion. Only verse 2a, 'and they watched him, to see whether he would heal him on the sabbath', is an essential part of the pericope; verse 2b is altogether dispensable. If reasonable grounds can be found for the redactional character of verse 6, verse 2b should not stand in the way. That verses 4 and 5 prepare for verse 6 is not very significant for the decision whether verse 6 should be attributed to Mark or not: neither verse 4 nor 5a requires verse 6; both of them fulfil a meaningful role in Mk 3:1–5 without verse 6. Moreover, we shall see that verse 5a is also largely redactional.

Secondly, the opinion that Mk 3:1–6 escapes exact form-critical classification applies only to the version which we find now in the gospel of Mark. We will show below how different the picture becomes once the Marcan insertion has been identified and removed. Besides, it has been pointed out that what is reported in Mk 3:1–5 in its present form sounds very improbable and resists an easy interpretation as history. Concerning the mention of the 'Herodians', it is highly questionable whether the existence of such a group can be verified in the time of Jesus. If they really did exist, it must still be considered improbable that the Herodians would have been in agreement with the Pharisees in urging a strict observance of the sabbath. '*The* Pharisees' is certainly a Christian expression.

Thirdly, the few un-Marcan features are completely submerged by the typically Marcan ones, and so should not be given too much weight.

So we can now look at the features which make the redactional character of verse 6 very probable.

Firstly, the expression '(And) they went out' is almost certainly Marcan. 'Immediately' (*euthus*) is certainly redactional. The addition of personal names by means of *meta*, 'with', and a genitive is also to be attributed to Mark in Mk 1:29; 15:1, 31. The 'Herodians' in Mk 12:13 are likewise certainly redactional. In verse 6b the positioning of *auton*, 'him', just before the verb 'to destroy' is in typical redactional style. Furthermore, this part of the verse has an almost word-for-word redactional parallel in Mk 11:18: in Mk 3:6 we read 'how to destroy him', and in Mk 11:18, '(how) to destroy him'.

Secondly, with regard to content, a reason for accepting the secondary attachment of verse 6 is found in the unusually late mention of Jesus' actual opponents. The observers, until then anonymous, appear only in verse 6 and are identified as the Pharisees and the Herodians. For a narration of an incident from Jesus' life it would have been more appropriate to have mentioned Jesus' opponents by name already in verse 2a. The tendency of verse 6 with its negative perspective somewhat contradicts verses 1–5, the intention of which is to present Jesus as the victor over his opponents.

Thirdly, despite some scholars' counter-arguments, the two

arguments developed in the time of Bultmann against verse 6 originally belonging to Mk 3:1–5 remain valid: verse 6 shows a generally unusual biographical interest and goes beyond the stylistic conclusion of the narrative unit in verse 5.

Fourthly, verse 6 expresses the Marcan interest, found in the whole of the gospel, in Jesus' passion, in that from the beginning Mark places the powerful activity of the Son of God in the perspective of the cross.

'Moreover, 3:6, as it is expressed, is not complete in itself; it raises the question of the further progress and outcome of the plot against Jesus.'[93] Therefore, Mk 3:6 does not round off a pre-Marcan collection, nor is it a pre-Marcan isolated pericope, but it needs the continuation provided by the Marcan passion narrative.

Summing up, verse 6 must be considered an addition composed by Mark. It may therefore be left aside in the further analysis of the prehistory of the tradition here under discussion. Since verse 2b—as we saw—presupposes verse 6, it is also to be considered an insertion by the evangelist.

The pre-Marcan form of the story, then, will have been as follows:

1 And (Jesus) saw a man who had a withered hand.
2 And they watched him, to see whether he would heal him on the sabbath.
3 And he said to the man who had the withered hand, 'Come here.'
4 And he said to them, 'Is it lawful on the sabbath to do good or to do harm, to save life or to kill?'
5 And with anger, he said to the man, 'Stretch out your hand.'
  He stretched it out, and his hand was restored.

Most probably the evangelist knew this pericope, not in the context of a pre-Marcan collection, but as an isolated unit. Mark himself attached this pericope to Mk 2:23–28 on the grounds of the suitability of its content (sabbath conflict; motif of killing in verse 4), and by inserting verses 2b, 5a and 6 made it into a first culminating point of Jesus' debate with the representatives of Judaism.[94]

Mark 3:1–5: a composite story?

Unlike Mk 2:1–12, in Mk 3:1–5 the healing and the controversy, i.e., Jesus' question, seem to be closely related, so that the central verses of Mk 3:1–5 could not be considered an insertion. And yet they are not inseparable.

The pre-Marcan text contains the following features of a miracle story:

(1) An exposition with presentation of the sick person and indication of his illness. Most probably in the original exposition the healer himself was also explicitly or implicitly mentioned (verse 1b): 'and he (Jesus) saw a man who had a withered hand'.
(2) Mention of the agitation of spirit of the miracle worker (verse 5a): 'with anger'.
(3) A healing word (verse 5ab): 'He said to the man, "Stretch out your hand"'.
(4) Statement of the execution of the command (verse 5c): 'he stretched it out'.
(4) Explicit establishment of the healing (verse 5d): 'and his hand was restored'.

Some scholars would add to this the setting of the scene in verse 3, 'And he said to the man who had the withered hand, "Come here"'. But this is not necessary since the motif does not occur in other miracle stories, but can be found in apophthegms, that is, lapidary sayings of Jesus set in a brief narrative context (Mk 9:36; Jn 8:3). The motif, then, is not typical of miracle stories. Probably Mk 3:3 did not belong to the pre-Marcan miracle story (see also above).

The miracle story presented above is admittedly brief, but it is in accordance with the style of miracle stories, and complete. The healing of Peter's mother-in-law (Mk 1:29–31) furnishes evidence that there were very short miracle stories in the synoptic tradition. If the Marcan additions in Mk 1:29 are omitted, that miracle story consists of about the same number of words as the story presented above. Besides, in adding Mk 3:6, the evangelist may have omitted a concluding proclamation or a demonstration with the withered hand. In that case, the healing of Peter's mother-in-law would be shorter than the pre-Marcan miracle story found in Mk 3:1–5. Thus the possibility of this 'pure' miracle story cannot be rejected.

Concerning the close interlocking often maintained between controversy elements and miracle story, the findings are that controversy and miracle stories do not alternate and are not organically interwoven, but rather that the miracle story constitutes the beginning and the end of the pre-Marcan story and that the 'controversy' is found in the middle, in verses 2–4. As in Mk 2:1–12, the controversy interrupts the miracle story; again in analogy with Mk 2:1–12, the controversy elements alone form a unit which cannot have existed by itself, but is viable only in the context of the surrounding miracle story. It presupposes the mention of the sick person and the miracle-worker, and is dependent on the fulfilment of the healing. So it may be concluded that Mk 3:1–5 was possibly a traditional miracle story which was secondarily, but still in the pre-Marcan tradition, expanded by means of a 'controversy'.

Such a secondary compilation of controversy elements and a miracle story may be supported by the following.

Firstly, verse 2a, 'and they watched him, to see whether he would heal him on the sabbath', constitutes a second exposition which makes possible the 'controversy' and is awkwardly attached to verse 1. On the one hand, an explicit reference to the subject of the action is lacking, so that it is not clear who was watching Jesus. On the other hand, the simple description of the object by *auton*, 'him', is ambiguous. Strictly speaking, *auton* should mean the man with the withered hand, but, as the continuation in verse 2a indicates, it undoubtedly refers to Jesus. These two awkward features indicate a 'seam' between verse 1b and 2a.

Secondly, verse 3a constitutes a combination of two linguistic features which both appear once more by themselves elsewhere in the story: 'and he said to the man' should be compared with verse 5a, and 'who had a withered hand' repeats verse 1b. This repetition in verse 3, combining verses 1b and 5a, is easily explained if, before the insertion of verses 2–4, verses 1b and 5a followed each other immediately.

Thirdly, in the elements of a miracle story indicated above, any reference to a healing *on the sabbath* is lacking. Conversely, the central statement of verse 4 lacks any reference to the healing story. Both observations are easily explained by means of the hypothesis that the 'controversy' saying and the miracle were only secondarily combined.

Fourthly, verse 4 has tradition-historical parallels (compare Mt 12:11 and parallel Lk 14:5/Lk 13:15) which were originally handed on without their present context. The observation favours the acceptance of an originally isolated tradition of Mk 3:4.

Fifthly and finally, linguistic accords with the healing found in I Kgs 13:4–6 in the Septuagint version suggest the supposition that in the course of the composition of the healing of the man with the withered hand in Mk 3, an Old Testament tradition, if it was not the model for, influenced at least the terminology of the pre-Marcan story. It is striking that the parallels with I Kgs 13:4–6 are found only in the miracle, except for verse 3 which, as seen above, is composed by means of elements borrowed from the miracle story. This seems to indicate that at the time of the composition of the miracle story, the 'controversy' did not yet figure in the picture.

These considerations support not only the possibility but even the probability of a secondary combination of miracle and controversy elements.

The origin of this story in the Gentile Christian community, the fact that it seems to be directed against Jewish Christians in connection with the legitimacy, if not the necessity, of healing non-perilous illnesses on the sabbath, and the kind and manner of its tradition-historical genesis, i.e., the secondary incorporation of a controversy marked by a divine-man Christology into a healing miracle, all indicate that Mk 3:1–5 can be placed in the context of early Christian practice, and reflects a controversy between Gentile Christian miracle-workers and strict Jewish Christians on the question whether someone not dangerously ill may be subjected to healing ministry on the sabbath or not. (We therefore disagree with those who think we have here a controversy between the Palestinian Christian community and orthodox Judaism.) The Gentile Christians defended their practice by means of this story, especially Mk 3:4 which identifies (Jesus') healing as saving activity. In Jesus, whom the Jews persecuted as a violator of the sabbath, God himself was present and working salvation. That in this they remained faithful to the historical Jesus can be seen from authentic sayings of Jesus on this theme (Mt 12:11 and parallel; Mk 2:27).[95]

The early Christian community composed and used this account to defend and justify its own conduct by appealing to Jesus' practice of 'doing good' on the sabbath. This is supported by the multiple attestation of Jesus' healings on the sabbath found in various levels of the tradition. Evidently the early Church did not appeal to Jesus simply as teacher and interpreter of the law, but especially to his acts of 'doing good' on the sabbath which were understood as the authoritative acts of the Messiah. The early Christians agreed that 'doing good' on the sabbath is God's will, not only on account of the argument 'from minor to major' (cf. Mt 12:11–12, 'What man of you, if he has one sheep … of how much more value is a man than a sheep!'), but especially because the argument is put forward and exemplarily acted upon by the Messiah.[96]

The Marcan redaction

Mark has repeatedly intervened in the formulation of the story. To begin with, he has rewritten the introduction so as to link the story closely to the preceding context, to produce not only a material but also a historical connection. Mk 3:1–6 now appears as the immediate continuation of Mk 2:23–28. At the same time the evangelist deliberately concluded the series of controversy stories which started with Mk 2:1. This conclusion results, however, in an orientation of all the preceding stories towards the cross. Thus in the Marcan context they are no longer primarily concerned with the justification of early Christian Christology (Mk 2:1–12) or community practice (Mk 2:15–18) by the Son of man, but in a real sense establish 'biographically' that paradoxically, and notwithstanding his divine activity and authority, Jesus' end was the cross. His activity and authority did not lead to recognition of his 'divinity', but to callousness and hardness of heart among his listeners and witnesses. Mark emphasized this by his redactional intervention in verse 5. The hardness of heart, as appears from verse 6, concerns the leaders of the people, but also the people themselves (see Mk 4:11), and even the disciples (Mk 6:52; 8:17). Except for Mk 4:11 the motif of hardness of heart in Mark is always related to miracles. According to Mark, then, even Jesus' miracles could not overcome hardness of heart.

In Mk 3:6 the evangelist adds the names of the opponents. He thus personifies the conflict and continues in Mk 3:6 the tendency, already observed in Mk 2:6, 2:16 and 2:18, to connect the different groups of opponents with each other. In all conflicts the Pharisees are the chief opponents, since according to Mk 2:16 they can be identified with the scribes. The evangelist thereby historicizes the conflicts presented in Mk 2:1 – 3:6. Jesus' mission failed because of the opposition and the hardness of heart of the leaders of the Jewish people.

Almost all scholars admit that the reference to the 'Herodians' in Mk 3:6, not reproduced in the parallels Mt 12:14 and Lk 6:11, is a problem. This group of people is mentioned once more in the New Testament, in Mk 12:13 (parallel Mt 22:16), again in the context of a series of controversy sayings. A good number of commentators identify them as friends and supporters of Herod Antipas, and Mk 3:6 is then interpreted as saying that the Pharisees and the Herodians, that is, the religious and political leaders, held counsel against Jesus. It has been argued that the Herodians 'were at one with the Sadducees religiously, but generally speaking, were more pro-Herodian than they'.[97] It has also been suggested that Mk 3:6 refers not to Herod Antipas, king of Galilee from 4 B.C. to A.D. 40, but to Herod Agrippa I who became king of Galilee in A.D. 40 and of Judea in A.D. 41, who was known for his pro-Pharisaic policies, and of whom Epiphanius said that a group of 'Herodians' considered him the Messiah. After his death in A.D. 44 this group most probably disbanded. Thus in the early part of the fifth decade A.D. Pharisees and 'Herodians' could have conspired in persecuting Christians, and Mark traced this opposition back 'to the beginning'.[98] Others think that 'Herodians' refers to a rather amorphous group of pro-Herod aristocrats; while again others have looked for an explanation in the fact that Mark takes pains to link the fates of John the Baptist and Jesus. Since John the Baptist met his fate at the hands of Herod Antipas, it would have been natural for Mark to link the two figures in this respect too by mentioning among Jesus' enemies a group of 'Herodians'. It is not clear from other literary sources that a group of 'Herodians' existed in Jesus' time; neither can evidence be produced that 'Herodians' existed at the time of the writing of Mark's gospel. The 'Herodians', then, 'may be a product of Mark's theological interests rather than an actual, functioning group of people'.[99] Some, however, consider the phrase pre-Marcan.

The evangelist's purpose in Mk 2:1 – 3:6, however, should not be limited to pragmatically preparing the readers for Jesus' end. If it is taken into account that in Mk 3:1–6, as in Mk 2:1–12, Jesus' miraculous activity is obviously interpreted by the community Christologically, in the sense that the miracles refer to Jesus' divinity and his divine power, it can be understood that the Marcan redaction opposes this interpretation. If, according to the historical presentation of the evangelist, Jesus' 'divine' actions did not lead to the acknowledgement of his true nature, but to his cross, according to Mark the miracles do not have the decisive revelatory character which the community attributed to them. No doubt, Mark too would agree that the miracles reveal aspects of the Lord and his mission, that the Lord has authority which appears in his miracles. However, by referring to the cross, Mark emphasized that Jesus is more than a miracle-worker, that his true divine being is shown on the cross, where his mission was fulfilled.[100]

Matthew 12:9–14

The context

Unlike Mark (and Luke) where the present healing story is the last in a series of five 'controversy' stories (Mk 2:1 – 3:6; Lk 5:17 – 6:11), in Mt 12 we find only two of these controversy stories together (Mt 12:1–8 and 9–13) in a chapter which reveals a striking variety of material.

The first two pericopes are apophthegms or pronouncement stories (Mt 12:1–8 and 12:9–13) dealing with Jesus' attitude towards sabbath regulations. They are followed by mention of the Pharisees' plotting against Jesus (Mt 12:14) and Jesus' corresponding decision to 'withdraw' from there (Mt 12:15–16). At this point Matthew places the formula quotation of Isa 42:1–4. The connection for this quotation should be found in the immediate context. Jesus deliberately withdrew from public view because of the Pharisees' plot. Matthew saw Jesus' action as fulfilment of the prophet's words, as expressed especially in Mt 12:19 = Isa 42:2, 'He will not cry or lift up his voice, or make it heard in the street'. The connection between Isa 42:1–4 and its Matthean context is therefore Jesus' refusal to put himself forward.

The next section of Mt 12 is introduced by a healing story (Mt 12:22–23) which leads to a debate between Jesus and the Pharisees about the source of Jesus' healings and exorcisms (Mt 12:24–37). Verses 27–32, which deal with the Holy Spirit, may be related to Mt 12:18 = Isa 42:1, 'Behold my servant, whom I uphold, my chosen, in whom my soul delights; I have put my Spirit upon him, he will bring forth justice to the nations' (see Mt 3:17, at Jesus' baptism: 'This is my beloved Son, with whom I am well pleased'). Isaiah's text

> makes two promises about the servant who has been chosen by God. 1) He will have the Spirit of God, and 2) he will proclaim justice to the Gentiles. If anyone makes a claim to fulfilling this prophecy, he must show that these promises are fulfilled. This is the background of Matthew's construction of the rest of the chapter.[101]

The Beelzebul controversy (Mt 12:24–37) establishes that Jesus is the Messiah on whom the Spirit rests. In Mt 25:31–46 Jesus as the messianic king announces justice to the Gentiles or nations.

The next section begins with the request for a sign performed by Jesus. Jesus justifies his refusal by citing the example of Jonah (Mt 12:38–41). Mt 12:38–41 refers to Jonah who announced judgement and justice to the Ninevites. Jesus, who is greater than Jonah, will announce justice to the Gentiles, thus fulfilling the second promise expressed in Isa 42:1–4. This is followed by the passage dealing with the queen of the South which has the same comparative form (Mt 12:42), although there is no discernible pattern of Matthean logic connecting the verses dealing with Jonah and the queen of the South. This is again followed by an unusual story which relates the fate of a man with an unclean spirit to that of the present generation (Mt 12:43–45).

The chapter ends with the story of Jesus' relatives who come to see him and Jesus' refusal to go with them (Mt 12:46–50). Is this final pericope in any way related to Isa 42:1–4?

The opening phrase of the quotation from Isa 42:1 in Mt 12:18 was adjusted to the words spoken by the voice from heaven at Jesus' baptism (Mt 3:17) except in one important respect. At Jesus' baptism the voice from heaven refers to Jesus as 'son' (*huios*), while in Mt 12:18 the word used can mean either 'son' or 'servant' (*pais*). The fact that Matthew adapted the Isaiah quotation in the baptism account indicates that *pais* in Mt 12:18 is a deliberate choice. Isa 42:1 in the Septuagint has *pais*, but its treatment in Mt 3:17 is a reminder that *pais* can also mean 'son'. Mt 12:46–50 deals with a son and his family. As such, this does not constitute a convincing link with Isa 42:1–4, in which the important element is 'my', that is, God's servant or son. Matthew has edited the tradition in such a way that it conveys that Jesus is God's son. He achieves this by editing Jesus' answer to his family's request: 'And stretching out his hand toward his disciples, he said, "Here are my mother and my brothers! For whoever does the will of my Father in heaven is my brother, and sister, and mother"' (Mt 12:49–50).[102]

Thus it appears that Isa 42:1–4 played a decisive role in the redactional organization of Mt 12. Jesus' withdrawal led to the citation, and then Matthew took separate words or ideas from that citation and illustrated them in the different sections of Mt 12:22–50.

The text proper

Verse 9: And he went on from there, and entered their synagogue.

Matthew links this pericope closely to the preceding one by situating it clearly during the same day. Thus Hosea's saying added by Matthew in Mt 12:7, 'I desire mercy, and not sacrifice', fulfilled by the Son of man, also underlies the statement of Mt 12:11–12.

The verb 'went' (*metabainō*: five times in Matthew; once in Luke, not in Mark) and the phrase 'from there', 'thence' (*ekeithen*: twelve times in Matthew; three in Luke, five in Mark) are Matthean terms. Only Matthew speaks of 'their synagogue(s)' (compare Mt 9:35; 10:17; 13:54; 23:34). Because of the general tone of Mt 12 and the constant presence of the Pharisees as opponents (Mt 12:2, 14, 24, 38) it has been considered probable that Matthew intends to refer to the synagogues frequented by Pharisees only.

Verse 10: And behold, there was a man with a withered hand. And they asked him, 'Is it lawful to heal on the sabbath?' so that they might accuse him.

'Behold' (*idou*) is used very often by Matthew (sixty-two uses) and Luke (fifty-six) in comparison with Mark (eight). The attention of the listener/reader is directed towards the person in need. Verse 10bc is a considerably modified version of Mk 3:2. The Pharisees are not mentioned by name but they are presumably present as suggested by 'their synagogue' in verse 9 (see also Mt 12:14). The Marcan phrases 'they watched him' and 'to see whether' are omitted. The opponents here formulate a direct question. 'Is it lawful?' is an anticipation of Jesus' answer in Mt 12:12b/Mk 3:4a (a question). Since Matthew omits the Marcan motif of 'watching', the change of the Marcan subordinate clause into a question is understandable. Jesus' answer is thus prepared. But generally speaking, Mt 12:9–10 is closely parallel to Mk 3:1–2.

In Matthew we have a 'purer' form of controversy than in Mark. While the latter portrays Jesus' enemies as watching him to see whether he will violate the sabbath, Matthew presents them as raising a question about the sabbath law with him.

> **Verses 11–12:** He said to them, 'What man of you, if he has one sheep and it falls into a pit on the sabbath, will not lay hold of it and lift it out? (12) Of how much more value is a man than a sheep! So it is lawful to do good on the sabbath.'

Verses 11–12a are redactionally inserted. To the theoretical question of the Pharisees Jesus opposes a concrete example. Verse 11 can be traced back to the same logion or saying of Jesus as Lk 14:5, where, however, instead of a sheep, the evangelist speaks of 'an ass or an ox'. By its choice of image the saying qualifies Jesus' healing activity as the saving of life. The emphasis on *one* is to be attributed to Matthew. Verse 12a is constructed in analogy to the formulation in Mt 6:26b, 'are you not of more value than they?' and accentuates the legitimate activity of Jesus. Verse 12b is borrowed from Mk 3:4a. 'So' links the latter clause to the redactional insertion. The omission of the rest of Mk 3:4 and of Mk 3:5ab, 'and he looked around at them with anger, grieved at their hardness of heart', by Matthew can be explained by the preceding Matthean insertion as well as by the fact that Matthew, as already noted at the beginning of the pericope, says little about the opponents themselves and concentrates on the dialogue.

Jesus adopts the rabbinical method of solving a disputed question by appealing to a similar but clearer case, on which an argument *a minori ad maius* can be constructed (if it is done for an animal, then *a fortiori* it can be done for a human being). The introduction of the comparison too is typically rabbinic: 'what man of you'.

Matthew's abbreviation and rewriting of Mk 3:4 in Mt 12:12b entirely removes the point of the former as well as a good deal of its radical edge. Instead, a positive guideline for the community's conduct on the sabbath is introduced with 'So it is lawful', an expression prepared for by the question 'Is it lawful ...?' in Mt 12:10 (unlike Mk 3:2). Since Matthew's version cannot be explained from the one he received, it should be considered the result of a deliberate alteration. In this connection Matthew's insertion of Mt 12:11–12a can be readily understood. If he intended in Mt 12:12b to state a positive guideline for the community's conduct on the sabbath, he needed a basis for it. This basis is provided by Mt 12:11–12a. Two things are clear from the guideline of Mt 12:12b; firstly, it assumes that the Matthean community still kept the sabbath; secondly, love of neighbour was placed above the sabbath commandment.[103] As a result of all this, Matthew's account leads on to the description of the healing which follows in a way quite different from that of Mark and Luke.[104]

'Good' is not just good, but is concerned with salvation and wholeness. People are brought to salvation, people are made whole. The sabbath, the day of the Lord, is the time *par excellence* 'to do good'.

> **Verse 13:** Then he said to the man, 'Stretch out your hand.' And the man stretched it out, and it was restored, whole like the other.

Matthew adds the clause 'whole like the other'. As in Mt 15:31, 'whole', 'healthy' (*hugiēs*) is redactional. All three synoptics use here the verb *apokathisthēmi* which means 'to return to its right condition', while it is also a medical term meaning 'to restore physically'.

> **Verse 14:** But the Pharisees went out and took counsel against him, how to destroy him.

The omission of the 'Herodians' may be because this group had long ceased to exist by the time Matthew wrote, but may also be in accordance with his tendency to declare the Pharisees chiefly responsible for Jesus' death (compare Mt 22:15).

It has been pointed out that Mt 12:9–14 has a structure following the *inclusio* pattern and consists of exactly two hundred syllables. The pattern is as follows:
(1) Introductory narrative part (verses 9–10 = sixty-two syllables).
(2) Argumentative part, ending with the decisive principle rule (verses 11–12a, 12b = sixty-one + thirteen syllables).
(3) Concluding narrative part (verses 13–14 = sixty-four syllables).
The main point is found in verse 12b, 'So it is lawful to do good on the sabbath'. The pericope is primarily a controversy, and the healing, which is not in the foreground in this pericope, fulfils the function of a 'norm' miracle or 'rule' miracle, that is, a miracle which seeks to reinforce sacred prescriptions.

While Matthew had parted company with 'their synagogues', he was nevertheless intent on proving his church's adherence to true

Judaism. It can hardly be denied, however, that there had been a final separation between Matthew's church and Judaism in the light of his references to 'their synagogues' (Mt 4:23; 9:35; 10:17; 12:9; 13:54), 'your synagogues' (Mt 23:34), 'their scribes' (Mt 7:29), and 'the Jews' (Mt 28:15). Moreover, Matthew manifests an awareness of distinction from the synagogue in his use of the term *ekklēsia* in Mt 16:18 and 18:17 (not found in Mark and Luke).

Summing up, we may say that Matthew somewhat weakened the traditional statements about Jesus' healing on the sabbath. While it is not entirely excluded that these editorial changes were motivated by apologetic considerations, the main reason was undoubtedly positive in nature. The Matthean community and the evangelist himself remained faithful to the sabbath commandment and were deeply reluctant to undermine its importance. Hence it was their conviction that Jesus had upheld the sabbath commandment while, however, revealing its original intention. He stated by word and deed that the sabbath commandment did not constitute a hindrance to 'doing good' and hence was no obstacle to healings.[105]

Luke 6:6–11

The context

Lk 5:17 – 6:11 is parallel to Mk 2:1 – 3:6. The present story is parallel to the last of Mark's 'Galilean controversies', Mk 3:1–6. But it should be understood in the context of Luke's overall redactional purpose. The material following the programmatic statement of Jesus' ministry in Lk 4:16–30 was designed to interpret the theme of 'release' found in the quotation from Isaiah in Lk 4:18–19. First, release from the power of Satan (Lk 4:31–44); then release from sin (Lk 5:1–32); and finally release from cultic tradition (Lk 5:33 – 6:11). The third section contains a pericope about fasting (Lk 5:33–35), two illustrations, of the old patch on a new garment and new wine in old wineskins (Lk 5:35–39), and two sabbath pericopes (Lk 6:1–11). This section shows how Jesus brought release to people burdened and oppressed by human restrictions, and how he freed them for a proper and meaningful relationship with God. For a further discussion of the context, see our comments on the context of Lk 5:17–26 in the previous chapter.

The text proper

Verse 6: On another sabbath, when he entered the synagogue and taught, a man was there whose right hand was withered.

The observation about Jesus' repeated entrance into the synagogue on the sabbath ('another sabbath') serves the purpose of inserting the pericope into the course of Jesus' mission in the cities (cf. Lk 4:43). Besides that, the phrase refers to the preceding pericope, Lk 6:1–5, which already dealt with an aspect which dominates both pericopes, namely Jesus' attitude towards the sabbath. Compared to Mk 2:23–28, we see that Lk 6:5 omits the reference to the eschatological freedom of man (compare Mk 2:27) and instead emphasizes the lordship of the Son of man over the sabbath. However, in Luke, Jesus' answer is heard by only 'some of the Pharisees' (compare Lk 6:2 and Mk 2:24). Through this 'correction' the question remains acute and allows for a further demonstration.

The note on Jesus' teaching results in making the following story part of Jesus' teaching activity (see also Lk 13:10). According to Luke, the man's *right* hand is withered. This may be intended to underline the necessity of Jesus' intervention on the sabbath by heightening the condition of the person concerned. Compare Lk 22:50, where the servant's *right* ear is cut off, unlike Mark and Matthew.

> **Verse 7:** And the scribes and the Pharisees watched him, to see whether he would heal on the sabbath, so that they might find an accusation against him.

For clarity's sake, Luke introduces Jesus' opponents here as 'the scribes and the Pharisees', since in the previous pericope he mentioned as Jesus' opponents only '*some* of the Pharisees'. He then goes on to say, like Mark, that Jesus' enemies were seeking evidence for an accusation against Jesus.

> **Verse 8:** But he knew their thoughts, and he said to the man who had the withered hand, 'Come and stand here.' And he rose and stood there.

Luke adds the clause 'but he knew their thoughts', thus presenting Jesus as knowing his enemies' plans. Luke thereby adjusts this statement to Lk 5:17f., and also initiates the event and presents it as a demonstration of Jesus' will to save human life. Mark's command 'come here' is transformed into 'come and stand here'. Luke adds again 'and he rose and stood there' (compare 'and he did so' in verse 10) to emphasize the obedience of the sick person. Lk 6:8b–10 is closely parallel to Mk 3:3–5a.

Verse 9: And Jesus said to them, 'I ask you, is it lawful on the sabbath to do good or to do harm, to save life or to destroy it?'

Luke substitutes 'Jesus' for Mark's 'he', and adds at the beginning of Jesus' address, 'I ask you'. The rest of the verse is practically identical with Mark's except for the conclusion, 'or to destroy it' instead of Mark's 'or to kill'. The question, which shows its ancient character in the parallelism of its two parts, is edited by Luke only by the use of 'to destroy' (compare Mk 3:4, 'to kill') and adjusted to the formulation of Lk 9:24, 'For whoever would save his life will lose it; and whoever loses his life for my sake, he will save it'. In Luke's context, the pericope states that Jesus' act of liberation cancels the sabbath command.

Verse 10: And he looked around on them all, and he said to him, 'Stretch out your hand.' And he did so, and his hand was restored.

Like Matthew, Luke does not include the reference to Jesus' anger and grief. He changes Mark's 'he stretched it out' into 'and he did so'.

ἄνοιας

Verse 11: But they were filled with fury and discussed with one another what they might do to Jesus.

Verse 11 is independently formulated. An intention to kill Jesus can be deduced only indirectly. Unlike 'to destroy him' in Mark, the Lucan opponents of Jesus gather 'points of accusation against Jesus for later use before the court' (see Lk 6:7). The announcement of Jesus' death, which is necessary in the history of salvation, remains reserved for Jesus himself (compare Lk 9:21f., 44; 18:31–33). The term *anoia* (compare Lk 5:26), which is rendered by 'fury' (RSV) or 'frenzied' (NAB), may, based on Philo, be better translated as 'lack of understanding' or 'folly'.

Luke has edited Mk 3:1–6 into something approaching a demonstration miracle. This raises two questions. Following Lk 6:1–5, it still remains to be clarified why the opponents react with 'anger' (or, better, 'lack of understanding') to Jesus' activity. It also needs to be asked how Jesus legitimates what he actually does.

In contrast to Mark, Lk 5:5 restricts the eschatological freedom of man over the sabbath command, while Luke brings to the fore the lordship of the Son of man. Jesus' opponents, who must acknowledge that he not only saves himself and his disciples from a precarious situation (see Lk 6:1–5), but also heals sick people on the sabbath, react with lack of understanding (compare Lk 6:7 and 11). They consider the keeping of Torah more important than a healing favour. Although, unlike Mark, Luke does not mention an early decision of the Pharisees and Herodians, he already indicates here the violent fate of Jesus. In their lack of insight Jesus' opponents fail to see God's will that the sick should be cured and saved. Nevertheless, since in Luke's view of salvation history the Messiah must suffer (Lk 24:46), Luke cannot take over Mark's decision of the Pharisees to kill Jesus (Mk 3:6). They will kill Jesus in ignorance (*agnoia*; see Acts 3:17).

Luke therefore uses here the appropriate term *anoia* which corresponds in many ways to *agnoia* in Acts 3:17, 'I know that you acted in ignorance, as did also your rulers'. The negative reaction of the opponents is directed in the first place against Jesus' claim to lordship (Lk 6:5).

In the preceding pericope Jesus legitimates the attitude of his disciples by means of a reference to David (Lk 6:1–5), the normative Biblical model. In the present pericope the legitimation should be evident from the content itself. Jesus' activity centres on the twofold ethical question (verse 9). According to Luke, Jesus' readiness to help is based on the ethical principle of 'doing good'. The evangelist emphasizes this by twice repeating the same word later in this chapter (Lk 6:33, 35) where he interprets it in competition with Hellenistic popular ethics. According to his view it is Jesus' mission to spread the message of the kingdom and to heal all the sick (see Lk 9:1). To fail to help because of a prescription of the law is to betray the mission as well as the message which proclaims the liberation and salvation of the sick (Lk 4:18). To fail to heal is to do evil. The negative attitude of Jesus' opponents is directed against his claiming to set aside the sabbath command in the name of the mercy of the kingdom.[106]

7 The Stilling of the storm

Mt 8:23–27	Mk 4:35–41	Lk 8:22–25
(8:18 Now when Jesus saw great crowds around him,		
	35 On that day, when evening had come,	22 One day he got into a boat with his disciples, and he said to them,
he gave orders to go over to the other side.)	he said to them, 'Let us go across to the other side.'	'Let us go across to the other side of the lake.'
	36 And leaving the crowd,	
23 And when he got into the boat, his disciples followed him.	they took him with them, just as he was, in the boat. And other boats were with him.	So they set out,
		23 and as they sailed he fell asleep.
24 And behold, there arose a great storm on the sea, so that the boat was being swamped by the waves;	37 And a great storm of wind arose, and the waves beat into the boat, so that the boat was already filling.	And a storm of wind came down on the lake, and they were filling with water, and were in danger.
but he was asleep.	38 But he was in the stern, asleep on the cushion;	
25 And they went and woke him, saying, 'Save, Lord; we are perishing.'	and they woke him and said to him, 'Teacher, do you not care if we perish?'	24 And they went and woke him, saying, 'Master, Master, we are perishing!'
26 And he said to them 'Why are you afraid, O men of little faith?'	39 And he awoke	And he awoke

168

Then he rose and rebuked the winds and the sea;	and rebuked the wind, and said to the sea, 'Peace! Be still!' And the wind ceased, and there was a great calm.	and rebuked the wind and the raging waves; and they ceased, and there was a calm.
and there was a great calm.		
	40 He said to them, 'Why are you afraid? Have you no faith?'	25 He said to them, 'Where is your faith?'
27 And the men marvelled, saying,	41 And they were filled with awe, and they said to one another,	And they were afraid, and they marvelled, saying to one another,
'What sort of man is this, that even winds and sea obey him?'	'Who then is this, that even wind and sea obey him?'	'Who then is this, that he commands even wind and water, and they obey him?'

Mark 4:35–41

The context

The gospel of Mark is divided into two principal parts (Mk 1:14 – 8:26 and 8:27 – 16:8), each of which contains three main sections. The three main sections of the first half are contained in Mk 1:14 – 3:6, 3:7 – 6.6a, and 6:6b – 8:26. The second part is likewise divided into three main sections contained in Mk 8:27 – 10:52, 11:1 – 13:37, and 14:1 – 16:8. In the context of the first part, Mark's parable chapter (Mk 4:1–34) constitutes a culminating point in the proclamation of the kingdom of God (see Mk 1:14–15). After the 'controversies' concerning the sabbath (Mk 2:1 – 3:6), the persecution of Jesus by relatives and scribes (Mk 3:20–21, 22–30), and the instructive account on the true relatives of Jesus (Mk 3:31–35), Mark unfolds Jesus' teaching in parables (Mk 4:1–34).

The immediately following story of the stilling of the storm (Mk 4:35–41) is situated in the middle of the second main section of this part of the gospel, Mk 3:7 – 6:6a. In the introduction of this section, Mk 3:7–12, there is already a certain preparation for the stilling of the storm. When great crowds came to Jesus (Mk 3:7–8), so that those who were sick might touch him and be cured (Mk 3:10), Jesus 'told his *disciples* to have a *boat* ready for him because of the *crowd*, lest they should crush him' (Mk 3:9). Mk 3:9 initiates a whole series of statements which illustrate Jesus' gradual withdrawal from the crowd by means of a boat, in preparation for a revelation of his true personality to his disciples in the storm-stilling epiphany. The second statement occurs at the beginning of the parable discourse, Mk 4:1, 'a very large *crowd* gathered about him, so that he got into a *boat* and sat in it on the sea; and the whole *crowd* was beside the sea on the land'. The actual withdrawal from the crowd takes place in the introduction of the stilling of the storm: 'And leaving the *crowd*, they took him with them, just as he was, in the *boat*. And other boats were with him' (Mk 4:36). Thus the pattern formed by these three verses progresses as follows:

Mk 3:9   And he told his *disciples* to have a *boat* ready for him because of the *crowd*, lest they should crush him.

Mk 4:1b   And a very large *crowd* gathered about him, so that he got into a *boat* and sat in it on the sea; and the whole *crowd* was beside the sea on the land.

Mk 4:36   And leaving the *crowd*, they took him with them, just as he was, in the *boat*. And other boats were with him.

So Jesus prepares for his withdrawal from the crowds who flock to him as a healer, and forbids the unclean spirits to make him known as the exorcistic 'Son of God' (Mk 3:11f.), thereby refusing to be identified as *only* a healer-exorcist. This implies that he will show himself to be *more* than a healer-exorcist. This will begin to appear in the stilling of the storm, and continue to be revealed throughout the rest of the gospel.

The confession of Jesus as 'Son of God' by the unclean spirits (Mk 3:11) is the first of a series of positions taken by various groups to Jesus' identity in Mk 3:7 – 6:6a. The pattern progresses as follows:

Mk 3:11b   ...cried out, 'You are the Son of God.'

Mk 3:21b   ...saying, 'He is beside himself.'

Mk 3:22b   ...said, 'He is possessed by Beelzebul, and by the prince of demons he casts out the demons.'

Mk 4:41b   ...said to one another, 'Who then is this, that even wind and sea obey him?'

Mk 6:2b–3a   ...saying, 'Where did this man get all this? What is the wisdom given to him? What mighty works are wrought by his hands! Is not this the carpenter, the son of Mary...'

After Jesus had silenced the unclean spirits (Mk 3:12), he went up into the hills and appointed the Twelve 'to be with him, and to be sent out to preach and have authority to cast out demons' (Mk 3:14–15). The significance of this privilege 'to be with him' (Mk 3:14) becomes clear when 'those who were about him with the twelve' (Mk 4:10) are separated from 'those outside' (Mk 4:11) and designated as those to whom 'has been given the secret of the kingdom of God' (Mk 4:11). This privilege, expressed in Mk 3:14 and 4:11, is then illustrated when

Jesus explains the parable of the sower (Mk 4:3–8) privately to his disciples (Mk 4:13–20) and reveals the deeper mystery of his person again privately to his disciples in the storm-stilling epiphany (Mk 4:35–41), which immediately follows the statement of the disciples' privileged position: 'but privately to his own disciples he explained everything' (Mk 4:34b).

After appointing the Twelve (Mk 3:13–19), Jesus unfolds more and more of his character by reacting to the negative attitudes adopted toward him (Mk 3:20–35). This unfolding of the mystery of his person continues in the parable discourse (Mk 4:1–34). To the disciples 'has been given the secret of the kingdom of God' (Mk 4:11) which concerns the identity of Jesus' person.[107] The concluding statement on Jesus' use of parables in Mk 4:33–34 links the revelation of his person in the parables (Mk 4:1–32) to his revelation in the epiphany of the stilling of the storm (Mk 4:35–41). The statement about the 'secret of the kingdom of God' (Mk 4:11) is further developed in Mk 4:33–34, as can be seen in the following:

Mk 4:11a   To you has been given the secret...
Mk 4:11b   but for those outside everything is in parables.
Mk 4:33a   With many such parables he spoke the word to them...
Mk 4:34b   but privately to his own disciples he explained everything.

Just as 'secret' and 'everything' in Mk 4:11 are concerned with the identity of Jesus' person, so too are 'the word' and 'everything' in Mk 4:33–34. The latter summary statement not only concludes the parable discourse, but also serves as a transition between that discourse and the story of the stilling of the storm (Mk 4:35–41).

Mk 3:7 – 4:34 gradually progresses towards Mk 4:35–41 by developing the revelation of Jesus' character through his teaching, healing and exorcizing. So far, the disciples have not yet reacted to the private instruction they received in Mk 4:13–25. This sets the stage for the stilling of the storm which fulfils the expectation that the disciples would receive a manifestation of Jesus on a level deeper than that given by his teaching and healing-exorcizing (Mk 4:11–34).

The unfolding of Jesus' character through his teaching, healing and exorcizing never provoked the disciples to wonder about Jesus' significance. It was only when they experienced Jesus' power to rescue them by the stilling of the storm that they finally reacted and raised the question about Jesus' identity which went beyond his significance as healer and exorcist: 'Who then is this, that *even* wind and sea obey him?' (Mk 4:41).

Clearly, for Mark, Jesus' power manifested in the stilling of the storm surpassed his power to heal and to exorcize, as can be gathered from a comparison of the stilling of the storm with Jesus' first exorcism (Mk 1:21–28; see Chapter 2 above). Jesus' rebuke of the unclean spirit and of the storm are recorded in very similar terms:

Mk 1:25   But Jesus rebuked him, saying, 'Be silent, and come out
          of him!'
Mk 4:39a And he awoke and rebuked the wind, and said to the sea,
          'Peace (*siōpa* = 'keep silent')! Be still!'

The surpassing character of the stilling of the storm becomes even
clearer when we compare the reactions of the witnesses of these
events. Firstly, the respective expressions of amazement:

Mk 1:27a And they were all amazed...
Mk 4:41a And they feared a great fear (RSV: filled with awe).

Secondly, the repetition of the verb 'obey' (*hupakouō*; in Mark only
in 1:27 and 4:41), the second time with the addition of 'even':

Mk 1:27b ...he commands even the unclean spirits, and they obey
          him.
Mk 4:41b Who then is this, that *even* wind and sea obey him?

Over and above the fact that the unclean spirits obey Jesus (Mk
1:21–28), *even* the wind and the sea obey him (Mk 4:35–41). But the
latter story also constitutes a highlight of the revelation of Jesus'
deeper significance in Mk 3:7 – 6:6a. It unfolds an aspect of his
character and importance which goes beyond his activities of healing
and exorcizing. But at the same time it raises a question concerning
this deeper level of Jesus' person which remains somehow
unanswered and unresolved even at the end of this section. Thus at
the opening of the next section, Mk 6:6b – 8:26, the reader is still
awaiting an answer to the question 'Who then is this, that *even* wind
and sea obey him?'[108]
    So far we have been dealing with the preceding context. As for
the following context, several attempts have been made to show that
the stilling of the storm and the miracles following it, Mk 4:35 – 5:43,
belong to a pre-Marcan catena or linked account of miracles.[109] Some
also include the multiplication of the loaves (Mk 6:32–44) and the
walking on the water (Mk 6:45–51) in this collection,[110] so that all the
miracle stories found between the two summary statements of Mk
3:7–12 and Mk 6:53–56 would be part of it. It has even been
suggested that this miracle catena exhibited a concentric arrangement
and a continuous intensification.[111]
    Others have posited two parallel sets of miracle catenae, either
beginning with the accounts of the feedings and together forming the

'section of the loaves',[112] or else two parallel catenae beginning with two sea-miracles, Mk 4:35 – 6:44 and Mk 6:45 – 8:26.[113] We do not intend to go into the question of these pre-Marcan miracle catenae here, but it seems clear that there was certainly some kind of link between the stilling of the storm and (some of) the succeeding miracle stories. If these catenae really existed, Mark edited them, but much of the connection between these miracle stories remained true for Mark. It is clear therefore that in the Marcan redaction too, the stilling of the storm is related to some, if not all, of the miracle stories in Mk 4:35 – 6:6a, and even Mk 4:35 – 8:26.

The text proper

The original account

Reconstructing the original account

> **Verse 35:** On that day, when evening had come, he said to them, 'Let us go across to the other side.'

In Greek, the pericope begins with the clause 'and he said to them', which is generally considered redactional. The phrase 'on that day' is found only here in the gospel of Mark. 'In those days' is found twice (Mk 1:9; 8:1), but this phrase is different from Mk 4:35, not only because of the plural, but also because of its meaning which remains very general, while in Mk 4:35, 'on that day' intends to situate the story which follows on the day which is further defined by its Marcan context. The indication of the day links the stilling of the storm with Mk 4:1 (and possibly also with Mk 3:7) and is therefore certainly redactional. 'When evening had come' is a second indication of time which occurs four more times in the gospel, mostly redactional (compare Mk 1:32; 6:47; 14:17; 15:42). This could indicate Marcan redaction, since Mark likes double indications of time (compare Mk 1:32, 35; 10:30; 13:24; 14:30, 43; 15:42, 16:2). It is at any rate not impossible that Mark created the two indications of time found in verse 35. 'When evening had come' indicates that the crossing took place in the dark and thus underlines its dangerous character.

Some authors support the traditional character of the expression 'when evening had come' by saying that it provides a motivation for Jesus' sleeping (Mk 4:38), but it could also be argued that Mark added 'when evening had come' in order to account for Jesus' sleeping, which he found in the tradition. Moreover, the original story of the stilling of the storm was not determined by psychological, but rather by Christological motifs. Jesus' sleeping indicated not a state of exhaustion, but his superiority over the rising winds and waves. It was therefore significant even without any indication of time in the story's introduction.

Others have considered 'when evening had come' traditional, because it stands in tension with Mk 5:1f., which immediately follows Mk 4:35–41 and apparently presupposes daytime. Since Mark combined the two pericopes, thus shaping Mk 4:1 – 5:43 into a unity, it would be difficult to explain why he would have disturbed the seamless combination of Mk 4:35–41 and Mk 5:1–20 by creating the expression 'when evening had come'. Therefore it would be better to accept that Mark found the expression already in the tradition.

However, this is far from certain. Some consideration of the background to the theme of the story could be helpful here. It has often been remarked that in Mk 4:39 Jesus addresses the wind and the waves as demonic powers (compare Mk 1:25). The story should therefore be understood against the background of late Jewish and Hellenistic beliefs in demons. 'When evening had come' can be related to this context, since it was a general belief that darkness was the field of operation of demons. It is therefore not improbable that 'when evening had come' in verse 35 belongs to the original tradition.

In Jesus' commission to his disciples, 'Let us go across to the other side', the expression 'to the other side' (*eis to peran*; compare Mk 5:21; 6:45; 8:13) is considered Marcan. The other side is not reached in Mk 4:35–41 and is mentioned only in the next story in Mk 5:1 which is redactional. Within Mk 4:35–41, the order to 'go across to the other side' has no meaning. It gets its meaning only from the redactional context. 'Let us go across to the other side' must therefore be redactional. So the only part of verse 35 that is possibly traditional is 'when evening had come'.

Verse 36: And leaving the crowd, they took him with them, just as he was, in the boat. And other boats were with him.

Verse 36 is closely connected with verse 35 by means of the participle construction, 'and leaving the crowd'. It describes the execution of Jesus' order. At the same time the expression also shows that Mk 4:35f. still presupposes the situation depicted in Mk 4:1, 33f. Both features underline the probability of Marcan redaction, which is further supported by the fact that time and again the evangelist stresses that Jesus with his disciples withdrew from the crowd (compare Mk 1:35, 36; 1:45; 3:9, 13; 4:1, 10ff., 34). The phrase 'and leaving the crowd' shows a concentration on Jesus and his disciples that appears already in the parable discourse (Mk 4:1–34). The phrase cannot be traditional in Mk 4:35–41, since the story still indicates that originally a larger circle of witnesses was present at the stilling of the storm (compare Mk 4:36b and 41). By means of verse 36a, therefore, what was originally a 'general' miracle becomes a miracle reserved for the disciples. We perceive here already a special interest of the evangelist's which becomes entirely clear in verse 40. The phrase 'and leaving the crowd' should therefore be considered redactional.

The tensions which exist in the continuation of the verse between 'they took him with them' and 'just as he was, in the boat' seem to indicate that we have here at least some features of the introduction of the original story, which must have said that some people took Jesus into a boat and started the crossing. Together with other parts of verses 35–36, the clause 'just as he was in the boat' (in the Greek text there is no comma) establishes a close connection with Mk 4:1. At least the expression 'just as he was' is certainly Marcan. It says that 'without delay', that is, without going ashore, the crossing begins. Originally, 'in the boat' may have belonged to the verb 'took', so that the original may have been: 'they took him into the boat'.

Verse 36b, 'and other boats were with him', causes difficulty in the present context. It contradicts Mk 4:1, to which verses 35–36a are closely related. Mk 4:1 speaks of only one boat in which Jesus sat, while the crowd stood on the shore. The boats now mentioned in verse 36b are apparently manned by some of the crowd who listened to Jesus along the shore. But this contradicts verse 36a, in which Jesus and the disciples left the crowd. The mention of the other boats also stands in tension with the story as a whole, in which the 'other boats' are never mentioned again. This is also true of the redactional link with Mk 5:1f., where the other boats are again forgotten. All these contradictions and tensions allow only one conclusion: verse 36b must be a remnant of the old introduction of the original story. This means, then, that the original tradition contained a wider circle of eyewitnesses of the miracle than the disciples who were with Jesus in the boat. To the mention of this wider circle here in verse 36 there corresponds the 'chorus-ending' in verse 41. In the original story verse 36b prepared for verse 41. Verse 36b, then, will have belonged to the original introduction of the story.

Summing up, we may say that verses 35–36 should to a considerable extent be ascribed to the evangelist. The only part which is certainly traditional is verse 36b. But 'when evening had come' (verse 35) and 'they took him (Jesus) into the boat' may also be considered formulations of the old tradition. What remains after removing the redactional features must also have more or less sufficed as the original introduction, since it is improbable that Mark omitted a considerable part of this introduction, because in that case it would become incomprehensible why, of all things, Mark retained verse 36b. The original introduction must then have read more or less as follows:

> When evening had come, they took him (Jesus) into the boat, and other boats were with him.

Verse 37: And a great storm of wind arose, and the waves beat into the boat, so that the boat was already filling.

The opening clause, literally, 'and occurs a great storm of wind', emphasizes the strength and the suddenness of the storm. The main clause describes its effects which are distinguished as the storm and the unrest of the lake (see verse 39). The description as a whole characterizes the great danger for the seafarers.

Lailaps, 'great storm', is also found in Lk 8:23 (and II Pet 2:17), while Mt 8:24 has *seismos megas*, 'great storm', literally, 'great quake'. The descriptive genitive 'of wind' is a usage in popular speech. The verb *epiballein*, 'to throw upon' (compare Mk 11:7; 14:46, 72) is here used intransitively with the meaning 'to go straight towards'. With *eis* and accusative it suggests waves breaking into the boat.[114] Sudden storms are still feared today on the lake of Galilee. They were dangerous even for experienced fishermen. That there was grave danger in this case is clear from the fact that 'the boat was already filling'. A similar feature is found in *Testament of Naphtali* 6:5. We do not find any clear sign of redactional activity in this verse.

Verse 38: But he was in the stern, asleep on the cushion; and they woke him and said to him, 'Teacher, do you not care if we perish?'

Verse 38 is contrasted with verse 37. The periphrastic construction 'he was...asleep' (*ēn katheudōn*, 'he was sleeping'), a special expression of the durative imperfect, stresses the contrasting character of this statement.

Jesus is depicted as being 'in the stern', a term found only here and in the account of the storm in Acts 27:29, 41, and 'asleep on the cushion' (*proskephalion* is found only here in the New Testament). We note the striking contrast between Jesus asleep (compare Jon 1:5) and the raging waters. The whole scene leads to the call for help by the disciples. As a whole, the verse turns the attention of the listener/reader from the storm to Jesus and the occupants of the boat.

The reaction of the disciples is expressed in two short parallel main clauses, 'they woke him' and 'they said to him'. These clauses fulfil an introductory function with regard to the following call for help.

Since verse 40 which, as will be shown below, is to be attributed to the evangelist, refers back to verse 38, 'Teacher, do you not care if we perish?', it has been thought possible that verse 38c and verse 40 originated on the same level of the tradition, especially since verse 39 with 'he awoke' (*diegertheis*) fits in very well with 'they woke him' (*egeirousin auton*) in verse 38b. But this view has been rejected for several reasons, especially that the present place of verse 40 would become totally incomprehensible if together with verse 38c it belonged to the same editorial reworking of the account.

Others have tried to eliminate verse 38c, 'Teacher, do you not care if we perish?', as being the result of 'catechetical redaction', but this attempt too is not convincing. We should conclude, therefore, that there are neither literary-critical nor stylistic grounds to declare verse 38c secondary.

Verse 39: And he awoke and rebuked the wind, and said to the sea, 'Peace! Be still!' And the wind ceased, and there was a great calm.

Verse 39 contains the narrative answer to the situation prepared in verses 37–38. Jesus' intervention is described by means of a participle (*diegertheis*; literally, 'being roused'), and again two parallel main clauses, 'he rebuked' and 'he said'. Jesus' command is expressed in two imperatives, 'peace!' (*siōpa*; literally, 'be quiet') and 'be still!' followed by the effect of Jesus' words in two short clauses, 'the wind ceased' and 'there was a great calm'.

Diegertheis (RSV: 'awoke') does not so much state the mere fact of Jesus' awakening as depict an impressive scene: the Lord arises as the ruler of the wind and the sea. Related to this is the verb 'rebuked' (*epetimēsen*) which in the Septuagint is often used for God's reprimanding the ungodly powers (Pss 9:5; 68:30; 106:9; 119:21). The Hebrew equivalent occurs quite often in the Old Testament and the Qumran writings, but *epitiman* belongs to the fixed traditional vocabulary of the Hellenistic pagan exorcism stories. In Mark's gospel *epitiman* is a technical term for Jesus' rebuking demons (Mk 1:25; 3:12; 4:39; 9:25; compare Mk 8:33, where Peter is addressed as 'Satan': cf. Zech 3:2). It is clear, then, that in the present story the wind and the sea are presented as demonic powers. This is confirmed by Jesus' command, 'Peace! Be still!' which should not be understood as if 'Peace!' were addressed to the wind and 'be still!' to the sea. The whole expression is addressed to the demon who manifests himself in both. The phrase 'be still' especially belongs to the traditional exorcism vocabulary and is found as such in Mk 1:25 and the magical formulas of the Hellenistic world. This should be understood against the background of the general ancient belief that the natural elements too, are controlled by demonic powers and can be influenced by exorcism.

The effect is introduced by means of the lapidary 'and' which probably suggests that Jesus' word took effect immediately: 'and the wind dropped' (RSV: 'and there was a great calm'). This formulation is traditional, as appears from the literal parallel in Mk 6:51 (RSV: 'and the wind ceased'). Verse 39 is formulated in an effective contrast to verse 37: as the wind was followed by the raging waves, so the ceasing of the storm is followed by a great calm. Again, we do not find any clear signs of redactional activity in this verse.

> **Verse 40:** He said to them, 'Why are you afraid? Have you no faith?'

It has often been remarked that Mk 4:35–41, which relates the story of the stilling of the storm in a concise way, has a double and tension-rich conclusion. At first glance it may seem that the tensions are caused by verse 41, which seems different in tone from the rest of the story, and would therefore be secondary. But this first impression is contradicted by several features. As seen above, the concentration of the event on Jesus and the disciples is not original, but due to the evangelist. Verse 41 can therefore be an original feature of the tradition. Verse 40, however, stands in tension with many features of the pericope.

Firstly, it stands in tension with verse 41. Verse 41 cannot be understood as a reaction to Jesus' question in verse 40, which thus remains without answer, but in the present context refers to the description of the miracle in verse 39. In its present location verse 40 disturbs the natural flow of verses 39 and 41, which is indicative of a secondary intervention.

Secondly, the awkward position of Jesus' question *after* the miracle is also remarkable. Verse 40 would be expected to follow verse 38, but then again no break can be discovered between verses 38 and 39. The present location of verse 40 reinforces the impression that we are dealing here with a redactional intervention.

Thirdly, the relation of verse 40 to verse 38 is also strained since the former speaks of the disciples' (absolute) lack of faith, which does not seem to agree with verse 38. It must be concluded, then, that at least the motif of lack of faith in verse 40 is secondary. Its present position *after* verse 39 seems to indicate that the motif is intended as a secondary interpretation of the whole story in a particular direction.

Verse 40a, however, could originally have followed verse 38. But the whole of verse 40 plays an important part in the interpretation of the pericope by the redactor. So one can say with certainty that verse 40 is not original and that no break can be detected between verses 38 and 39.

Fourthly, in their present context there is tension between verse 40 and verse 36b. While in verse 40 Jesus addresses the occupants of only one boat, verse 36b speaks of several boats, which again indicates a definite concentration of the present account, and specifically verse 40, on the one boat with the disciples. This contradicts the original story which presupposes a wider circle of witnesses.

Fifthly, verse 40 also stands in tension with the pericope as a whole, which now has two emphases, one Christological, and another concentrating on the disciples and their lack of faith. Both cannot be equally original. This double emphasis suggests that verse 40 is an addition; it falls outside the narrative framework.[115]

Sixthly, there is also a tension between the word *oupō*, 'not yet', in verse 40 (RSV: 'not') and the story taken by itself, since 'not yet' suggests a wider context in which the disciples had had previous opportunities to attain faith, which goes against the finding that the stilling of the storm was originally an isolated story. Again this argues against the originality of verse 40.

Seventhly, if by way of a counter-check verse 40 is omitted, it is found that the remaining story displays a clear unity of form and contents: verse 41 links up easily with verse 39.

Finally, all these observations lead to the conclusion that verse 40b is certainly a secondary addition; verse 40a may be original, but must then originally have occurred after verse 38. The latter remains, however, a conjecture.[116]

As to the question when and by whom verse 40 in its present form and location was inserted into the story, it has been shown that both betray Marcan redaction and should therefore be attributed to the evangelist.

The clause 'have you no faith (yet)' refers to a wider context into which Mark himself inserted the pericope.

There is agreement between the Marcan redaction in verses 35–36a and verse 40 in which the initial concentration on the disciples receives its true meaning.

Verse 40 expresses a typical motif of the Marcan redaction, namely, the *failure* or *faltering* (rather than the lack of understanding, or misunderstanding) of the disciples which, in the context of the 'messianic secret', has been recognized as redactional. Throughout the gospel the disciples are presented as incapable of understanding and following Jesus' real mission. Verse 40 is to be seen in this light. In particular, Mk 6:52 and 8:17ff., which speak of the disciples' lack of insight and hardness of heart, and Mk 9:19, where they are described as a 'faithless generation', are closely related to our present verse. Verse 40, then, must be attributed to the evangelist.

The adjective 'afraid' (*deilos*) is very strong; it suggests a violent confusion. The noun occurs in II Tim 1:7, 'for God did not give us a spirit of timidity (*deilias* = 'cowardice')': to the person who reacts in the face of danger as if God does not exist, the author opposes 'a spirit of power and love and self-control'. According to Jn 14:27, during the last supper, Jesus adjured his disciples, worried by the approaching departure of their Master, neither to let their hearts be troubled, nor to let them be afraid (*deiliatō*). In Rev 21:8, the cowardly (*deiloi*) and faithless are mentioned side by side. Those delivered from this anxiety can enter into the deep calm which Jesus expects (Mt 6:25–33). Paul testifies to a similar assurance in the middle of a storm which shook the ship bringing him to Rome (Acts 27:23–25).[117]

By means of verse 40 Mark has redactionally widened the perspective of the original tradition. This is confirmed by the verse's vocabulary, especially verse 40b. The evangelist is also responsible for the present emphatic position of verse 40 after verse 39. Mark, then, has not just added a few *details* to the original story, but also definitely intervened in the *structure* of the account and thus made his interpretation of the account unmistakably clear.[118]

Verse 41: And they were filled with awe, and said to one another, 'Who then is this, that even wind and sea obey him?'

In agreement with other New Testament miracle stories of Hellenistic origin, the present account concludes with the reaction of the witnesses and a 'chorus-ending'. First, the effect of the miracle on the witnesses is described with the Semiticizing formula 'they were filled with awe' (*ephobēthēsan phobon megan*, literally, 'they feared a great fear'; see Jon 1:10, 16). 'To fear' is already in the Septuagint a technical term for the presentation of the human reaction to a divine epiphany (Gen 15:1; 18:5; 21:17, etc.), and expresses not only the elementary existential fear of a person before the numinous, but also the awe and submissive acknowledgement of the person of God. In the New Testament the term is mostly found in miracle and epiphany stories (Mk 5:15; 5:33, 36; 6:50; 9:6; 16:8), in which it has a Christological meaning. This is especially clear in Mk 4:41 in which the crowd asks '*Who* then is this', and not '*What* then is this?', emphasizing not the greatness of the miracle, but the greatness of the miracle-worker.

Some scholars consider the last part of verse 41, 'that even wind and sea obey him', secondary, but the important form-critical parallel, Mk 1:27, 'What is this? (or perhaps: 'Who is this?'; see Chapter 2 above). With authority he commands even the unclean spirits, and they obey him', argues against this opinion.

The formulation of the 'chorus-ending' is traditional, as can be seen from the parallel, Mk 1:27. The concluding question should not be interpreted simply in terms of the faith or unbelief of the witnesses. Rather, it prolongs the story into the present of the listeners/readers. On the basis of the story, they should answer the question 'Who then is this?' This question is not to be taken as a catechism question, but rather as a question that should lead to a decision, that can be answered only by the faithful acknowledgement of Jesus as the Lord. The narrator's intention is to set in motion a faith process by means of this concluding question.

The original account will have been more or less as follows:

35 When evening had come,
36 they took him with them in the boat,
    and other boats were with him.
37 And a great storm of wind arose,
    and the waves beat into the boat,
    so that the boat was already filling.
38 But he was in the stern,
    asleep on the cushion;
    and they awoke him,
    and said to him,
    'Teacher, do you not care if we perish?'
39 And he awoke and rebuked the wind,
    and he said to the sea, 'Peace! Be still!'
    And the wind ceased,
    and there was a great calm.
41 And they were filled with awe,
    and said to one another,
    'Who then is this,
    that even wind and sea obey him?'

This account has a threefold structure:
The first part contains:
    (a) The reconstructed introduction depicting the situation on
        the lake.

    (b) The description of the rising storm and the threat to the boat.

    (c) The description of Jesus' attitude, the disciples' call for help (and, if verse 40a was originally attached to verse 38c [see above], the rejoinder of Jesus).

The second part (verse 39) depicts:

    (a) Jesus' miraculous intervention,

    (b) and the consequent calm.

The third part (verse 41) deals with:

    (a) The reaction of the witnesses, and

    (b) concludes the account with a 'chorus-ending'.

A similar threefold structure is found in many miracle stories in Mark, especially in Mk 1:21–27, but also in Mk 1:40–45; 2:1–12, etc. The style of the account also agrees with that of other miracle stories. The account is intended as a story surpassing its Old Testament precedent and to some extent an epiphany story along the lines of the motif 'something greater than Jonah is here' (Mt 12:41; Lk 11:32: Jesus acts in the power of God himself). The story is an attempt to surpass the story of Jonah (1:4–15) with allusion to Ps 107:23ff. (see below). The concluding question 'Who then is this?' (compare Mk 1:27) aims at the confession: Jesus is more than a prophet.

Literary genre

According to Bultmann, the stilling of the storm cannot properly be called a *miracle* story, since, firstly, the story shows no knowledge of a modern concept of 'nature', as its construction according to the schema of an exorcism shows, and, secondly, the story is only secondarily interested in the miracle. It is the miracle-*worker* who stands at the centre of the story. It is a Christ story intended to make people recognize who is the One whom the wind and the sea obey. Therefore, the story should rather be called an 'epiphany story' (Dibelius). But even this designation needs modification. Epiphany stories may be told with very different intentions. The intention of the stilling of the storm, however, becomes clear in verse 41: it intends to bring the listener/reader to a Christological decision. It should, therefore, be designated as primarily a 'recruiting epiphany story'.[119]

Jesus is not the first or the only person of whom a rescue from a storm is narrated in the literature of that time.

The Old Testament already narrated miracle stories about Moses (Ex 14:15ff.), Joshua (Jos 3:10ff.), and Elijah (II Kgs 2:8) which illustrated their power over the natural element water. The beginning of the story of Jonah (Jon 1:4–16) is directly related to Mk

4:35–41. The correspondence of contents and vocabulary is such that time and again it has been concluded that there is a direct literary dependence of the stilling of the storm on the story of Jonah. Indeed, the Christian narrator must have known the Jonah story, and he also seems to have used some of its particular features in the formulation of his story. It should be noted, however, that the real core of Mk 4:35–41, the powerful exorcizing activity of Jesus, is altogether lacking in the Jonah story. Moreover, the opposition between pagan and Jew which underlies Jon 1 plays no part in Mk 4:35–41, and the Old Testament miracle happens in response to prayer, unlike Mk 4:35–41 where Jesus commands the demonic powers of nature by his own power. In this sense one simply cannot speak of a 'transfer' of Jon 1 to Jesus. The obvious verbal correspondences remain superficial and relatively irrelevant. They have some minor importance only on the level of verbal borrowing and are almost without any influence on the form and the proper theological content of the New Testament passage.[120]

In late Judaism too there occur water miracles performed by rabbis and stories which relate the stilling of a storm. There is the famous story of a Jewish boy who made a sea voyage amongst pagan passengers. The ship was caught in a storm and after the pagans had invoked their gods, the boy prayed to Yahweh and the storm subsided. The point of the story is found in the acclamation of the pagans who praise Israel because of the powerful help of their God. The story definitely has a late date and is possibly a *midrash* on Deut 4:7, 'For what great nation is there that has a god so near to it as the Lord our God is to us, whenever we call upon him?' It has strongly edifying and proselytizing features. But its correspondences with Mk 4:35–41 are only of an external nature. The stilling of a storm by Rabbi Gamaliel may also be cited, again as the result of prayer.

An interesting, symbolically interpreted rescue from an eschatological storm which contains surprising parallels to Mk 4:35–41 is found in the *Testament of Naphtali* 6:29:

> And behold a ship came sailing past,
> full of dried fish, without sailor or pilot.
> Inscribed on it was 'The Ship of Jacob'.
> So our father said to us, 'Get into our boat'.
> As we boarded it, *a violent tempest arose,*
> *a great windstorm,*
> and our father, who had been holding us on course,
> was snatched away from us.
> After being tossed by the storm,
> *the boat was filled with water*

and *carried along on the waves* until it broke apart....
Levi, putting on sackcloth,
prayed to the Lord in behalf of all of us.
When the storm ceased,
the ship reached the land, as though at peace.[121]

The correspondences of vocabulary and content of this text with Mk 4:35–41 lead to the conclusion that the Christian narrator also knew this story and used it in the formulation of the stilling of the storm. But a 'transfer' of the story as a whole to Jesus is clearly excluded.

In the Hellenistic world the power to rescue people from storm was attributed to Asclepius and Serapis, as well as to emperors and kings, philosophers and 'divine men' (see Chapter 1 above). II Mac 9:8 mentions that Antiochus Epiphanes thought 'he could command the waves of the sea'. Caesar and Caligula made similar claims. But Mk 4:35–41 shows no dependence on any of the stories narrated about these great men. The Hellenistic stories, however, indicate the atmosphere and the general background in which Mk 4:35–41 originated and which may have influenced the story. Mk 4:35–41 has one characteristic in common with the Hellenistic stories: unlike the Old Testament and late Jewish stories, in which God himself performs the miracle in response to the prayer of a prophet or a rabbi, it ascribes the calming of the wind and the sea directly to the miracle-worker. This constitutes the chief difference between Mk 4:35–41 and the Old Testament and late Jewish stories.

The Old Testament often asserts that God has power over the sea and the sea-demon. In particular, the remembrance of the creation in the Psalms and the prophets presents Yahweh as the victor in the struggle with the chaotic powers (Pss 74:13f.; 89:9–10; 104:6–9; Job 26:12f.; 38:8ff.; Prov 8:27ff.; Isa 27:1; 51:9; Jer 5:22). The dominant way in which the Old Testament understood creation was in terms of God's conquest of chaos. Likewise, the remembrance of the rescue of Israel at the Red Sea is a constant occasion for praise of God's power over the sea (Ex 15:10; Ps 77:16ff.; Isa 51:10).

Closely related to the story of the stilling of the storm are those psalm texts in which somebody appeals to Yahweh to save him from the danger of hostile waters, and expresses his certainty that the floods cannot harm him because Yahweh is with him (Pss 69:13–15; 18:16f.; 32:6; 46:2f.; 65:7). A typical example is the following passage from the great thanksgiving psalm 107:23–31:

Some went down to the sea in ships,
doing business on the great waters;
they saw the deeds of the Lord,
his wondrous works in the deep.

For he commanded, and raised the stormy wind,
which lifted up the waves of the sea.
They mounted up to heaven, they went down to the depths;
their courage melted away in their evil plight;
they reeled and staggered like drunken men,
and were at their wits' end.
Then they cried to the Lord in their trouble,
and he delivered them from their distress;
he made the storm be still,
and the waves of the sea were hushed.
Then they were glad because they had quiet,
and he brought them to their desired haven.
Let them thank the Lord for his steadfast love,
for his wonderful works to the sons of men!
Let them extol him in the congregation of the people,
and praise him in the assembly of the elders.

Undoubtedly the Old Testament had a definite influence on the formulation of the story of the stilling of the storm. The real intention of this tradition should be further identified against the background of the Old Testament texts mentioned above.[122]

It has already been stated that by means of the Christologically decisive question in verse 41 the story is prolonged into the present situation of the readers/listeners. Their answer to that question is the real aim of the story. To that extent the story has no instructive or catechetical intention. Its intention is rather to raise the decisive Christological question and at the same time to enable the listeners/readers to give the answer. On the one hand, the early Church utilizes the familiar theme of rescue from distress at sea by gods and divine men, while, on the other hand, it constructs the story in such a way that the uniqueness of the One who performs the rescue in this particular case becomes clear. He does not need magic to control the natural elements. Thus in Jesus God's power manifests itself. In him the liberation from the demonic powers of chaos is present in a way in which the worshippers of the Old Testament found it only in God. Who then is he? Only one answer is acceptable: Jesus is the Lord. However, he does not compete with God, but acts on his behalf, as his 'Son' who is equipped with his divine power. By its shape and numerous Old Testament reminiscences the story intends to mediate for its listeners/readers the answer to verse 41.

The *Sitz im Leben*

(a) The story is not intended as documentation of the great miracles the earthly Jesus did during his ministry, for listeners or readers already assuming and believing in Jesus' divine quality. Rather, it is intended to lead its listeners/readers from the miracle to the miracle-worker, from Jesus' action to faith in Jesus himself. The story, then, seems to presuppose listeners who do not yet believe. In order to determine its 'situation in life', one should therefore start from the question in verse 41 and situate it in the early Christian missionary proclamation. The story was developed for the mission in which it may also have originated.

In favour of an origin in the Christian mission to the Jews is the fact that the Jewish-Christian communities of Palestine undoubtedly knew of Jesus' miracles, as appears from sayings transmitted by the Q source (Mt 12:27f. and parallel), and also from some miracle stories with undeniable Palestinian colouring (Mk 1:29–31; 1:40–45; 2:1–12; 3:1–5). Mk 4:35–41 could likewise have originated in a Palestinian environment. The expression 'they feared a great fear' (Mk 4:41; RSV: 'they were filled with awe') is a Semitism, and the address 'teacher' refers to the Aramaic address 'rabbi'. But especially the many allusions to the Old Testament and at times verbatim parallels to Jon 1 and the *Testament of Naphtali* 6 are fully understandable only to Jewish listeners. But this could also be true of Hellenistic Jews of the diaspora, especially since the established verbal parallels occur between Mk 4:35–41 and the *Greek* version of the texts adduced for comparison. In favour of a Greek-speaking Jewish-Christian origin of Mk 4:35–41 is, in particular, the 'epiphany' character of the story, which distinguishes it from its Old Testament and late Jewish parallels. At its centre stands the miracle-worker and his divine power. He does not just call on divine power by prayer and incantation, but is himself the bearer of that power. Similarly, Hellenistic diaspora Judaism presented the great men of Israel's history in line with the Hellenistic concept of 'divine men' for the purpose of propaganda and mission.

It is important to note that Mk 4:35–41 is also understandable for Gentiles, to whom the missionary efforts of both Hellenistic Judaism and Christianity were directed. The decisive Christological question of verse 41 may therefore also have been addressed to Gentiles. This is supported by the fact that the story does not deal with Jesus' Messiahship in the Old Testament sense, but with his 'divinity'. In the context of the ancient pagan concept of 'divine men', the story intends to demonstrate Jesus' superiority over Asclepius and Serapis. This miracle story (and others) thereby entered into competition with the various messages of salvation proclaimed in the Hellenistic world. By narrating great miracles performed by Jesus, the early Church witnesses to Jesus as the Saviour *par excellence*. The absolute character of this faith affirmation is discernible in Mk

4:35–41; verse 41 demands from the listeners/readers the confession that Jesus is also their Lord.

(b) The 'situation in life' of the original story of the stilling of the storm was the early Christian mission of Hellenistic Jewish Christianity. But this constitutes a relatively short phase in the history of the early Church, especially when we consider the different local churches. The mission situation soon gave way to a new situation of consolidation of the Church's life. In this context a 'recruiting epiphany story' like Mk 4:35–41, and especially verse 41, would lose some of its relevance. And yet the story remained part of the living tradition which developed further in the situation of the community. The story, therefore, must have switched to a second 'situation in life', as is often observed in Old as well as New Testament tradition-history.

This may have happened in one of two ways, either by a radical new interpretation and actualization affecting the formulation of the text, or because its verbal and theological fullness enabled it to continue to function after the end of the initial 'situation in life' described above. The first possibility prevailed if verse 38 is considered a secondary insertion. As seen above, not only the outcry of the disciples, but also the note concerning Jesus' sleeping do not entirely fit in a concise story entirely aimed at verse 41. But, again as seen above, in that case one would have expected the simultaneous omission of verse 41, which would then have become incomprehensible. Therefore, the second possibility is the more probable.

Indeed the story as such has enough points of departure for a new interpretation in a new 'situation in life' of the Christian community. In particular, verse 38 could be understood in a new way by the Christian community, and related to its own situation, and even interpreted as a presentation of that situation, more specifically of one of the chief problems of the early Christian community, the delay of the parousia or (second) glorious coming of Christ. The Lord seems to linger, to sleep, and to have left the community in danger. The community recognizes itself in the occupants of the boat and expresses its being at a loss in the words 'Teacher, do you not care if we perish?' Such an allegorical interpretation is not only possible, but even probable in the early pre-Marcan Church.

Water, sea, storm, wind and waves are symbols generally known in the ancient world, in the Old Testament as well as in Greek literature, for instance, in the works of Homer. Moreover, the boat and its journey through the storms of the world-sea is a favourite image of the vicissitudes of the life of an individual. In the *Testament of Naphtali* 6, the boat is a symbol of Israel. Tertullian, Clement of

Alexandria and other Church Fathers interpret the boat in Mk 4:35–41 as the Church.[123] But this interpretation can already be discerned in Matthew's version (Mt 8:18–27; see below). This and the generally known and widely attested metaphorical use of the boat make it probable that the pre-Marcan Hellenistic community could already identify itself with the boat and its situation, as well as with the occupants of the boat.

The new 'situation in life' of Mk 4:35–41 must have been a situation of extreme opposition or challenge, probably associated with persecution. Indeed, 'there are numerous indications that Mk was written with an eye to a situation of persecution. The meaning of the passage in question in Mk comes fully to light only against this background'.[124] This situation was aggravated by the experience of the delay of the parousia. In such a situation the story of the stilling of the storm, interpreted symbolically and eschatologically oriented, must have been experienced as a consolation and an exhortation to expect with firm faith the speedy and marvellous intervention of the Lord, who had already miraculously demonstrated his help on a particular occasion.

While the original account aimed at the believers' confession of Jesus as Lord, the new interpretation seeks to strengthen the faith and hope of believers in the imminent and wonderful action of Jesus, the Son of God. While the original account was entirely Christological, the new interpretation is rather soteriological and ecclesiological.[125]

(c) But this hypothetical distinction between first and second 'situation in life' has recently been questioned. If a new understanding of the story cannot be supported by verifiable alterations in the text, the claimed change to a new 'situation in life' remains hypothetical and elusive. Why should the original redactor of the story himself not have wanted to express the faithful understanding allegedly read into his words only at a later stage? Old Testament religiosity and theology must have decisively influenced the way and the intention of narrating stories.[126]

A detailed study of the parallels between Ps 107:23–32 and Mk 4:35–41 shows that the latter, while certainly not to be considered a literary paraphrase of the former, is indeed a story which speaks in strikingly intellectual closeness and from similar theological angles of a miracle of Jesus, in order to manifest him as a divinely empowered Saviour.[127] This is confirmed by a study of separate motifs, like Jesus' sleeping, the disciples waking him, their outcry 'Teacher, do you not care if we perish?' (e.g., Ps 44:23–26), Jesus' rebuking the wind and saying to the sea: 'Peace! Be still!' (Pss 9:5; 68:30; 106:9; 119:21), the miraculously effected calm and the reaction of the witnesses (Pss 65:7f.; 77:13–20; 89:5–10).[128] As in the psalms the cultic community of Israel proclaimed its belief and trust in the surpassing greatness of God, so here one of Jesus' great deeds is actualized in narrative to restate and revive trust in him as the powerful Redeemer and Saviour of his community.

The story therefore does not in this view seem to presuppose listeners who are not yet believers. The fact that in the earliest synoptic version in Mark, the disciples address the question concerning Jesus' greatness 'to one another' (Mk 4:41) also points in this direction.

In the light of the prayer experience of the psalms, the story tells in an exemplary way how people can get into difficulties with Jesus. Jesus' 'sleep' causes them fear and doubt, but notwithstanding their lack of faith they are saved and thus regain trust in him. The story does not provide new information about Jesus but presupposes in the narrator as well as the listener a consciousness of faith which is marked by a prayerful worship of God and Jesus.[129]

The Marcan redaction

One should start from the consideration that Mark was acquainted with the life situation in which the original story was re-interpreted, and that his redaction consciously refers to it. On the other hand, it is less probable that he would still have been aware of the original 'situation in life' of the account in the mission.

Firstly, the evangelist has changed the introduction so thoroughly that the remnant of the original introduction, verse 36b, has become pointless and unintelligible. On the one hand, the changes are intended to link Mk 4:35–41 immediately with the preceding parable passage, Mk 4:1–34. This is the purpose of the phrases 'on that day' and 'just as he was in the boat'. On the other hand, the introductory verses also prepare the connection with the following miracle stories, Mk 5:1–20, 21–43. This is the function of 'let us go across to the other side', for the expression 'to the other side' is also found in Mk 5:1 and 5:21, and clarifies the immediate sequence of the four miracle stories in Mk 4:35 – 5:43. The insertion of the story, which was originally handed down in isolated form, into the context of the gospel, is a first important interpretation by the evangelist. As an isolated tradition, the story sought to proclaim Jesus' being and significance as concentrated in one focal point. Now it becomes only one of several, and should be understood as an episode of 'Jesus' way' which will end in Jerusalem on the cross. Thereby the story loses (part of) its original relevance; the person or significance of Jesus can no longer be determined on its basis alone.

Behind the redactional literary connection established by Mk 4:35f., a wider redactional perspective can be recognized. Thus the phrases 'on that day' and 'as he was in the boat' link the pericope closely with a context which, in its final redactional formulation, is dominated by the thought of Jesus' separation from the crowd and the concentration of his teaching activity on the disciples (compare the redactional activity Mk 4:1, 10ff., 13, 34). This tendency continues in Mk 4:35f. It is also recognizable in the clause 'let us go across to the other side' and the boat journey thus introduced and motivated. Already in Mk 3:9 and 4:1 the boat is a redactional instrument whereby Jesus is presented as evading the rush of the crowd. Mk 4:40; 6:30ff.; 6:45f.; 8:10–21 indicate that this withdrawal from the crowd means at the same time a concentration on the disciples. In the first part of the gospel (Mk 1:14 – 8:26) there is an indication of what, starting with Mk 8:27, will be a constant situation: Jesus progressively reduces the public character of his activity and concerns himself more and more with the understanding of his disciples; admittedly, as Mk 1:35ff.; 4:40; 6:52; 8:14ff. and 9:19 show, without success.

That the reformulation of Mk 4:35f. by the evangelist situates the stilling of the storm in the redactional context indicated above is finally made clear by the phrase 'and leaving the crowd' (compare Mk 6:45, 'while he dismissed the crowd'; Mk 8:13, 'and he left them'). This remark contradicts verse 36b, which presupposes that Jesus was accompanied by a (great) crowd. Mark thus limits the circle of eye-witnesses of the miracle that follows to the disciples. The miracle is thus no longer to be understood as a *public* sign, but as a *secret* event for the chosen circle of the 'Twelve' (compare Mk 3:13–19; 4:10; 5:37; 9:2f.). This reveals a particular Marcan understanding of the traditional miracle story.

Secondly, irrespective of whether Mark completely composed verse 40 or is responsible only for the formulation 'have you no faith (yet)', he is certainly responsible for placing the verse in its present position after the miracle, where it disturbs the structure of the pericope. By this awkward and conspicuous place in the story, the verse and its basic affirmation receive a special emphasis which is clearly important to the evangelist. He has given the pericope a new redactional climax which consists in Jesus' establishment of the disciples' unbelief. The evangelist, then, is no longer interested in the demonstration of Jesus' power, but in establishing the disciples' attitude as unbelief. What already appeared in the redactional treatment of Mk 4:35–36 is now clear: by the removal of the crowd, not only is the circle of characters reduced to Jesus and the Twelve, but by means of verse 40 the attitude of the Twelve towards Jesus has become the new assertion of the account. The story now deals with the unbelief of the disciples, i.e., their failure in discipleship and following of Jesus. Mark thus has changed a Christ story into a disciple story.

What exactly does the Marcan denunciation of the disciples' unbelief consist in? The disciples' unbelief appears in their fearful attitude towards the storm (verse 38). While the Lord sleeps, they cry out 'Teacher, do you not care if we perish?' They want a visible, miraculous rescue. The question arises, of course, why Mark can interpret this outcry of the disciples as a sign of unbelief. Does it not rather express a certain measure of faith, and is it not, in its pre-Marcan formulation too, an expression of faith, though worried and reproachful, that only the Lord can help in this situation, and that rescue can be expected from him alone?

A possible answer to this question is that the unbelief of the disciples is manifested precisely in the fact that, worried and reproachful, they wake up the Lord, for they should have known that while he was with them in the boat, he would not desert them, but would certainly intervene before it was too late. With him in the boat the disciples could not perish.

But this answer is not sufficient since, on the one hand, after the description of verse 37 it seems that things cannot get any worse, and, on the other hand, the disciples could be said to be exhibiting a simple lack of patience, instead of an absolute failure of faith. Moreover, this answer is proven wrong in that in his gospel Mark describes the way of Jesus as his undoing on the cross. Already in Mk 3:6, and again in Mk 11:18, it is said in redactional statements that Jesus' opponents took counsel and discussed 'how to destroy him' (*hopōs auton apolesōsin*). This fate also threatens the disciples in Mk 4:38 (*hoti apollumetha*, 'if we perish'). In a Marcan context, the statement that where Jesus is, no 'undoing' is possible would therefore be highly problematic. To reckon with 'undoing' is for Mark part of discipleship, following the example of Jesus' fate (Mk 8:34f.).

What, according to the evangelist, was the attitude in the given situation which could have been called faith? The disciples should have trustfully endured the storm, ready to perish with Jesus. They should have believed that Jesus could also save them from ruin through death. For the task of the disciples consists in maintaining their faith in Jesus as sole Saviour even in their undoing. Verse 38 shows, however, that the disciples did not count on perishing with Jesus. They were not prepared for unconditional faith in Jesus, the

Son of God, but requested the manifestation of his saving power. They called for the epiphany of his divine sonship, although Jesus' sonship really shows itself only on the cross, and can be understood only from there (compare Mk 8:27ff.; 9:9ff.; 15:39).

The redactional statement about the unbelief of the disciples in verse 40 must be read against the background of a whole series of statements concerning the failure of the disciples which are either compositions of the evangelist or at least statements employed redactionally.

While in some texts the disciples are closely associated with Jesus from the beginning, that is, the time of their calling (Mk 1:16–20; 3:13–19; 6:30f.), many other statements show the disciples completely failing to understand the person, and especially the mission of Jesus.[130] Since they fail to understand that the way of the cross is Jesus' true mission, and that the cross is *the* epiphany of the Son of God (Mk 15:39), they cannot fathom the mystery of his person. For the cross is the true reference point for the failure of the disciples. From the beginning of the gospel the question can be raised, 'have you no faith (yet)?' (Mk 4:40); 'Do you not yet understand?' (Mk 8:21). This 'not yet' refers to the understanding of Jesus' cross and taking up one's cross, and is overcome only by the Risen One (Mk 9:19; 14:28; 16:7).[131]

Mk 4:40 also expresses the disciples' wrong attitude towards the cross. In verse 38 they ask Jesus, in order to save them, to give a proof of his divine power and his epiphany as the Son of God, while they do not understand that Jesus is truly manifested as Son of God only in the event of the cross. The cross, not miracles, is the true sign of his divine sonship.

The evangelist's redactional activity does not have the character of a theoretical, theological statement or thesis, but is to be understood in the actual faith situation of a particular early Christian community.

The reduction of the circle of characters to Jesus and his disciples in verses 35f. already suggests an actualization for the Christian community, since for Mark the disciples are not just historical figures, but representatives of the Christian community. The continually critical treatment of the disciples should not be understood as a general polemic against the 'Twelve'. If the evangelist presents them as misunderstanding and failing disciples, he does not do so just on historical grounds, but he is addressing himself paraenetically, that is, both in a warning and an encouraging way, to the community.

To be a disciple means to follow Jesus also in failure and death. Even Christians shrink from this risk time and again, and so Mark exemplarily reprimands them in the persons of the disciples.[132]

Matthew 8:23–27

The context

In Matthew the story of the stilling of the storm is found in a context very different from that of Mark and Luke. In the latter two the miracle story is found after the parable discourse. If it were to occupy the same place in Matthew, it would occur after Mt 13:1–52. Matthew, however, includes the stilling of the storm in the miracle-cycle of Mt 8 – 9 which follows the Sermon on the Mount (Mt 5 – 7). For a more detailed discussion of Mt 8 – 9 as context we refer to Chapter 3 of this book. There we saw that the scripture quotation which concludes the group of the first three miracles (Mt 8:1–17) gives a deeper sense to the healing of Peter's mother-in-law. The second group of miracles, Mt 8:18 – 9:17, contains not only miracle stories but also calls to follow Jesus. After Jesus' words about following (Mt 8:18–22; parallel in Lk 9:57–60 and therefore a Q-text),[133] Matthew narrates the stilling of the storm without any transition (Mt 8:23–27). A (redactional) geographical point of contact with the previous context is, however, found in the story of the healing of Peter's mother-in-law and many other people in Capernaum (Mt 8:14–17). As in Mark, the stilling of the storm is followed by the exorcism 'in the country of the Gadarenes' (Mt 8:28–34). Since, despite their very different context, the Marcan and Matthean versions of the stilling of the storm and the exorcism in Gerasa are connected with each other, this connection may have originated on the level of the apostolic tradition.

A study of the wider context, Mt 5 – 11, shows that Matthew is speaking of Jesus as the Lord of the community and of the situation of the community after Easter. Jesus' disciples, sharing his power of teaching and miracle-working, encounter the same reactions as Jesus did during his public ministry, and consequently also share his fate. It is in this perspective that Matthew has arranged the traditional material under consideration.

After Mt 8:1–17, the first group of miracle stories capped by the quotation from Isa 53:4, Matthew writes: 'Now when Jesus saw great crowds around him, he gave orders to go to the other side' (Mt 8:18). Then comes Mt 8:19–22 about following, clearly inserted here by Matthew, since these verses obviously interrupt the normal sequence of the account and the parallel text in Luke is found in a totally different context, namely the beginning of the Travel Narrative (Lk 9:57–60). This addition of Mt 8:19–22 is connected with a number of revisions in Mt 8:23–27 itself. In contrast to Mark's and Luke's 'Let us go across to the other side' (Mk 4:35; Lk 8:22), Matthew writes: 'he gave orders (= he commanded) to go to the other side' (Mt 8:18).

Now, the command Jesus often gives is 'Follow me'. The answer to this command is in fact found in Mt 8:19, 'I will follow you wherever you go', and in Mt 8:22 the command 'follow me' is explicitly mentioned. Besides, Mt 8:18 says literally 'he commanded to go away (*apelthein*)'. The expression 'to go away' indicates an aspect of following Jesus, namely, the aspect of giving up something in order to follow, as is illustrated in Mt 8:19–22. Unlike Lk 9:57–60, the command 'follow me' in Mt 8:18 dominates the whole passage, Mt 8:18–22. It should also be noted that, unlike Lk 9:59–60, in Mt 8:21–22 the command 'follow me' is addressed to a 'disciple'. In fact, we are dealing here with a *renewed* command, since it is addressed to a disciple, that is, to somebody who is already a follower. But now he faces the consequences of his initial following, as he hesitates, and therefore needs a renewed command.

It is obvious from the insertion of Mt 8:19–22 that, on the level of the redaction of the gospel, the following narrative is going to be told in the situation of the Christian community to which Matthew addresses himself. This is perfectly in accordance with the Matthean perspective of the context as established above. From this insertion it appears that in Matthew's view the miracle story deals with the perseverance in discipleship of those who are already disciples, and particularly with the perseverance of the Twelve who are sent with his message and his powers (Mt 10:1), and experience the implications and consequences of this discipleship.

The pericope proper

Verse 23: And when he got into the boat, his disciples followed him.

Verse 23 should be read in close association with Mt 8:18, 'Now when Jesus saw great crowds around him, he gave orders to go over to the other side' (compare Mk 4:35, 36a). In fact, Mt 8:18–27 'must be considered per se as a unit'.[134] The proposal to go across is changed into an order. The verb 'go across' (Mk 4:35) is changed into 'go (away)' to link up with the same word in Mt 8:19, 'I will follow you wherever you go (away)'. Mt 8:21–22 contains the terms 'disciple' and 'follow' which link up with 'the disciples followed him' in verse 23. Thus it is clear that the story of the stilling of the storm is really dealing with the following of the disciples. Unlike in Mark, where the disciples 'took him with them', Matthew says that Jesus 'got into the boat' and describes the boarding of the boat as 'the disciples followed him'. Jesus embarks first and his disciples follow. The voyage called 'going away' (Mt 8:18–19) represents discipleship as a response to

Jesus' command to follow him (Mt 8:18–22). Neither the sending away of the crowds nor the presence of other boats (Mk 4:36) is mentioned. All attention is focused on the one boat into which the disciples follow Jesus.

> **Verse 24:** And behold, there arose a great storm on the sea, so that the boat was being swamped by the waves; but he was asleep.

The phrase 'and behold' imitates the language of the Old Testament and suggests that God's history is being narrated here. Matthew often uses it to emphasize what seems important to him. Instead of 'a great gale of wind' (Mark, literally), Matthew uses the unusual expression *seismos* which normally means 'earthquake', and is only very rarely used for a storm at sea. Matthew therefore adds the phrase 'in the sea' (RSV: 'on the sea'). The same word occurs in Mt 24:7 designating earthquakes as part of the events which will precede the close of the age. It is also found to indicate the earthquake at Jesus' crucifixion (Mt 27:51: *eseisthē*), and in Mt 28:2 for the earthquake at Jesus' resurrection. In the Book of Revelation it occurs as a designation of apocalyptic horrors (Rev 6:12; 8:5; 11:13, 19; 16:18). The storm in which the disciples find themselves may therefore have connotations of eschatological distress as well as of a theophany (see Ex 19:18; I Kgs 19:11; Job 38:1; 40:6).

Instead of Mark's 'and the waves beat into the boat, so that the boat was already filling', Matthew writes 'so that the boat was being swamped by the waves'. It may be wondered whether this stylistic change has something to do with the symbolism of the boat, which is more pronounced in Matthew than in Mark. Matthew again omits the concrete details of Mk 4:38 and says briefly: 'but he was asleep'. The omission of 'on the cushion' (Mk 4:38) may be due to the presence of 'the Son of man has nowhere to lay his head' in Mt 8:20. The contrast between the raging of the storm and Jesus' attitude already present in Mark is here expressed in a terser, more impressive way.

> **Verse 25:** And they went and woke him, saying, 'Save, Lord, we are perishing.'

The disciples 'went and woke him, saying' (literally, 'and approaching they woke him saying'). Matthew uses the verb *proserchesthai* forty-one times to describe the respectful approach of people to Jesus. In many instances it is combined with the verb 'to say'. Matthew thus emphasizes the dialogue part of many miracle stories for didactic purposes. The disciples' plea is drastically changed (compare Mk 4:38). We may have an allusion here to Ps 44:23, 'Rouse yourself! Why do you sleep, O Lord? Do not cast us off for ever!' or even more Ps 107:28–29: 'Then they cried to the Lord in their trouble, and he delivered them from their distress; he made the storm be still, and the waves of the sea were hushed'.

All connotation of reproach or irritation disappears, and the disciples' words almost sound like an ejaculatory prayer, 'Lord, save, we are perishing'. It has been suggested that the cry 'Lord, save (us)' (*kurie, sōson*) 'may have been a ritual form in Matthew's church, like the later *kurie eleison*, "Lord, have mercy" ',[135] 'reminiscent of the cry with which the community calls on its Lord to save'.[136] The same prayer is found in Mt 14:30, 'Lord, save me'. Other related prayers are found in Mt 20:31, 'Lord, have mercy on us, Son of David!' and in Mt 9:27; 20:30, 'Have mercy on us, Son of David'. The title 'Lord' expresses a Christological confession of faith in the risen, glorified Christ (compare Mt 8:2). The prayer clearly reaches out beyond the miracle story itself to a wider application in the life situation of the Christian community.

Verse 26a: And he said to them, 'Why are you afraid, O men of little faith?'

At this point Matthew effects a striking transposition of narrative features. In Mark the disciples' dramatic cry for help (Mk 4:38b) is immediately followed by Jesus' miraculous intervention (Mk 4:39; compare Lk 8:24), expressed in the terse command, 'Peace! Be still!' Then follows the description of the effect of Jesus' intervention: 'And the wind ceased, and there was a great calm'. In Mk 4:39 we are clearly in the centre of the miracle story. Jesus' words about the disciples' failure of faith only follow afterwards.

Matthew places Jesus' words in the centre of the story. They immediately follow the disciples' cry for help and are therefore expressed before the storm calms down, as it were, in the midst of the turmoil. This 'dialogue' is already prepared for by the stereotyped participle 'approaching' at the beginning of verse 25. 'Here, too, the dialogue is more important than the miracle performed, which is much more an illustration of what Jesus says in the dialogue.'[137] The structure of the Matthean pericope clearly points to Jesus' words as the core of the story. This structure can be presented as follows:

The storm (24)
  Jesus asleep (24b)
    Lord, save (25)
      reproach to the disciples: little faith (26a)
    threat to the sea (26b)
  sea is calm (26c)
amazement of people (27)

It is important, therefore, to have a closer look at Jesus' words, which mean literally: 'Why are you cowardly (*deiloi*), little-faiths (*oligopistoi*)?' Mk 4:40 suggests that the disciples have no faith at all. In Matthew they are blamed for not having much faith. *Oligopistoi*, 'men of little faith', is a favourite expression of Matthew's. Except for Lk 12:28 (parallel Mt 6:30; therefore Q), it is found only in Matthew, namely Mt 6:30; 8:26; 14:31; 16:8 (compare Mt 17:20: *oligopistia*). In Mark the disciples have no faith (yet). This Marcan theme is considerably softened in the gospel of Matthew, and many Marcan passages are changed in the same direction: Mt 8:26 (Mk 4:40); Mt 13:18 (Mk 4:13); Mt 14:33 (Mk 6:52); Mt 16:8f. (Mk 8:17); Mt 17:4 (Mk 9:6), etc. This is often explained as a tendency to spare the disciples, especially the apostles who, by the time of the writing of the gospel, were already the leaders of Christian communities. Mark, indeed, often speaks in embarrassingly harsh terms of the disciples' lack of understanding. We doubt, however, whether this is a fully satisfactory explanation, because in some instances Matthew maintains this theme, and even inserts it where it is not found in the tradition (Mt 13:36). So, it is obvious that Matthew does not drop this Marcan theme altogether, but rather interprets it. There is faith and comprehension, but they are still subject to doubts and temptations. The disciples are in a situation of 'already' and 'not yet'. And it is exactly to express this that Matthew develops the theme of 'little faith'. This theme was undoubtedly already found in the tradition (Lk 12:28 = Mt 6:30 = Q). In fact, the idea was also known among the rabbis. 'Of little faith' is applied to people who belong to the people of God, who have proved their faith before, but who now seem to succumb to temptations and doubts.[138] This is exactly the situation of those of little faith in the gospel of Matthew. There is faith, but there is also a problem of perseverance. A very relevant text in this connection is the pericope of Jesus' walking on the water (Mk 6:45–52; Mt 14:22–33).

The idea of 'little faith' introduced by Matthew into the account of the stilling of the storm is in harmony with the perspective of the wider context. In Mt 8:19–22, Matthew speaks of a *renewed* command to follow Jesus addressed to disciples who experience the implications of their discipleship and therefore begin to waver. As to the miracle story itself, Matthew edits it in such a way that it becomes a lesson for his readers who are already disciples. Indeed, 'Matthew characteristically introduces Jesus' speaking to the disciples—and through them to the church—with the historical present *legei*'.[139] Here, as elsewhere, the phrase 'men of little faith' is obviously addressed to Matthew's readers who believe in the risen Christ, the Lord, but whose faith begins to waver when they face the consequences of this faith when lived in the world, when the Church seems to be about to perish and to go down in the turbulent sea of persecution and oppression.

> **Verse 26b:** Then he rose and rebuked the winds and the sea; and there was a great calm.

What in Mark was still the centre of the miracle story becomes here, as it were, secondary, following Jesus' words to the disciples (Christians of Matthew's community) which now dominate the account. This does not mean that Matthew's account altogether loses its character as miracle story, but the didactic purpose becomes predominant and influences the literary form. The words which, in Mark, Jesus addressed to the wind and the sea are no longer quoted, and nothing is said explicitly about the abating of the wind and the waves. However, the contrast with Mt 8:24 (Mk 4:37), and consequently the implication of the extraordinary character of the miracle is still present. 'Matthew's brevity accentuates the authority of Jesus; the calm comes suddenly just as the storm did (vs. 24).'[140]

> **Verse 27:** And the men marvelled, saying, 'What sort of man is this, that even winds and sea obey him?'

According to Mark, 'they (= disciples) were filled with awe', literally, 'they feared a great fear'. In Matthew, the final reaction of amazement is attributed to 'the men', which is highly surprising in a pericope and a context in which the evangelist draws special attention to the disciples (Mt 8:21, compare Lk 9:59; Mt 8:23).

Some interpreters suggest that Matthew uses 'the men' thinking of the disciples who, although they somehow know who Jesus is, remain (mere) 'men' with (too) little faith. But most probably Matthew really intends to shift subjects and to refer to outsiders who do not yet believe (see Mt 4:19; 5:13, 16, etc.) and do not know who Jesus is. They would represent 'the men', that is, the people to whom this story is addressed in the Christian proclamation.[141] The disciples who, according to Matthew, already know who Jesus is, would no longer ask the question 'What sort of man is this?' In Mt 9:33, which is part of the conclusion of the miracle-cycle (Mt 8 – 9), 'the crowds (= outsiders) marvelled, saying, "Never was anything like this seen in Israel" '. In Mt 12:23, 'All the people were amazed, and said, "Can this be the Son of David?" '. But in Mt 14:33, the disciples 'worshipped him, saying, "Truly you are the Son of God" ' (contrast Mk 6:52). In Mt 8:27 the evangelist maintains the content of the reaction, but preserves the theme of the faith and comprehension of the disciples (= Christians) by ascribing the guessing question to outsiders.

From the connection of the stilling of the storm with the general context mentioned above, from the insertion of the verses about following Jesus (Mt 8:19–22), and from a number of editorial changes introduced in the text of the miracle story itself, it appears that the scene receives an exemplary, paradigmatic meaning for the Christians of Matthew's community whose faith faced great difficulties in the world in which they lived. Matthew has made the story 'an illustrative picture of what following Jesus means.... The story of the stilling of the storm has become in Matthew a paradigm of discipleship. The church sees herself and what is happening to her in the disciples in the boat'.[142] The boat which is almost covered by the waves (Mt 8:24: 'swamped by the waves') but miraculously saved by Jesus is for Matthew indeed the *navis ecclesiae*, the ship of the Church. The faith of the Christians is strengthened. If they get the impression that the Lord sleeps while the Church seems to be about to perish, they are greatly mistaken. The Lord stays in perfect control at any time. He can also demonstrate this perfect control by a powerful intervention. Such intervention cannot but be of great kerygmatic value and instil the beginning of faith in those who are still outside the community of the believers (see the question of the outsiders in Mt 8:27).

Luke 8:22–25

The context

The beginning of Lk 8 marks a new development in Jesus' public ministry. The disciples are deliberately integrated into Jesus' missionary activity; summoned by Jesus to bear fruit with steadfast faith, they know about the secrets of the kingdom of God. Since, unlike Mark, Luke speaks in the plural of 'secrets', Jesus' statement (Lk 8:10) remains relevant beyond the instruction of the disciples proper (Lk 8:11–18).

For Mark's scene at the lake (Mk 4:1ff.) Luke has substituted an instruction in a rural environment (see Lk 8:4) which is better attuned to the contents of the parable of the sower (Lk 8:5–8). Luke must therefore provide a new transition to the stilling of the storm. By means of a very general indication of time, 'one day' (Lk 8:22; literally, 'and it came to pass on one of the days'), he achieves a temporal sequence of events and integrates the stilling of the storm in the narrative context described in Lk 8:1–3: 'Soon afterward (literally: and it came to pass afterwards) he went on through cities and villages, preaching and bringing the good news of the kingdom of God. And the twelve were with him, and also some women who had been healed of evil spirits and infirmities: Mary, called Magdalene, from whom seven demons had gone out, and Joanna, the wife of Chuza, Herod's steward, and Susanna, and many others who provided for them out of their means'. Beyond that, the evangelist motivates the crossing by Jesus' intention of missionary activity on 'the other side of the lake'. By so doing, Luke loosens the pericope from the preceding parable scene (Lk 8:4ff.), although 'one day' also anchors the story in the framework of Lk 8:1–3, and links it more closely to the following healing of the Gerasene demoniac (Lk 8:26–39). In the miracle trilogy (Lk 8:22–56), which Luke narrates in the same order as Mark, the lake becomes the determining, local framing factor which links the three individual pericopes together.

In Lk 8:4 (compare Mk 4:1–2), there was no mention of the lake or a boat. The lake of Galilee which in Mark remains for a long time the centre of Jesus' teaching has, together with Capernaum, already been out of sight and 'left behind' by Luke (the lake has last been mentioned in Lk 5:1f. and Capernaum in Lk 7:1; although Capernaum is mentioned once more in Lk 10:15, Jesus never returns there after Lk 7:1). In Luke, the lake is not simply the place of Jesus' teaching. Together with 'the mountain', the lake which, as it were, lies on the very frontier of Jesus' ministry, becomes the place of Jesus' manifestation for the benefit of the closed circle of disciples. All this is in keeping with the geographical-theological development of Luke's gospel.[143]

The pericope proper

> **Verse 22:** One day he got into the boat with his disciples, and he said to them, 'Let us go across to the other side of the lake.' So they set out,

Mark's double indication of time, according to which Jesus requested his disciples to cross the lake 'when evening had come', is omitted. In Luke, the account does not follow immediately after the parable discourse as in Mark, but is separated from it by Lk 8:19–21. With its emphasis on hearing and doing the word of God (Lk 8:21b, different from Mk 3:35), Lk 8:19–21 is an additional instruction on the meaning of Jesus' proclamation. Because of Luke's different setting, the note 'and leaving the crowd, they took him with them, just as he was, in the boat' (Mk 4:36a) can be omitted. Luke concentrates on Jesus and the disciples. According to him they all find room in one boat. Therefore, Mark's remark that 'other boats were with him' is passed over. Moreover, the preceding omission of Jesus' preaching 'beside the sea' in 'a boat' (Mk 4:1) explains why in Lk 8:22 Jesus first 'got into a boat' before going 'across to the other side of the lake'. As in Mark, but unlike Matthew (see Mt 8:18), Jesus' command/ exhortation is presented in direct speech. For clarity's sake Luke adds 'of the lake' (*limnē*; in the New Testament only in Lk 5:1, 2; 8:22, 23, 33 and five times in Revelation). Luke briefly mentions the execution of the command: 'so they set out' (*anagein*; except for Mt 4:1; Rom 10:7 and Heb 13:20, only in Luke-Acts: twenty times). In connection with Luke's journey theme attention should be called to the peculiar clause 'let us go across (*dielthōmen*) to the other side of the lake'. *Dierchomai*, 'to go through', is normally used of a journey by land. In Acts it implies missionary travel (Acts 8:40; 18:23, etc.), an indication which is not to be lost sight of, because of the close connection with the missionary character of the exorcism in the country of the Gerasenes. Luke's addition, 'So they set out' (*anēchthēsan*), also seems to reveal a missionary interest, as the same verb is used in the miraculous catch of fish: 'Put out (*ep-anagage*) into the deep and let down your nets for the catch' (Lk 5:4). Verse 22 is undoubtedly redactional.

> **Verse 23:** and as they sailed he fell asleep. And a storm of wind came down on the lake, and they were filling with water, and were in danger.

Verse 23 introduces the main part of the account. Because of the omission of the clause 'when evening had come', Luke anticipates Mark's later mention that Jesus 'fell asleep' before the arrival of the storm. Thus he achieves a clear sequence of events, and also creates a contrast between Jesus' present sleeping, which indicates that he is subject to human fatigue, and the power he will soon manifest.

In vivid manner the author describes the 'descent' of the storm. The verb *katabainein*, 'to come down', suggests that the forces of nature come from heaven. The effects of the storm are expressed by two predicative clauses in the imperfect tense, 'they were filling with water' (*sumplēroun*, only in Lk 8:23; 9:51; Acts 2:1 in the New Testament, the latter two instances with a theological meaning), and 'were in danger' (*kinduneuein*, only in Lk 8:23; Acts 19:27, 40; I Cor 15:30 in the New Testament). The disciples are the subject of both verbs, unlike Mk 4:37.

> **Verse 24:** And they went and woke him, saying, 'Master, Master, we are perishing!' And he awoke and rebuked the

wind and the raging waves; and they ceased; and there was a calm.

The expression 'they went and woke' (*di-ēgeiran*, an intensification of Mark's *egeirousin* by means of the prefix *dia*) describes the urgency of the disciples' action. They address Jesus by the repeated 'Master, Master' (*epistata*, in the New Testament only in Luke, and only as an address to Jesus, mainly by the disciples; Lk 5:5; 8:24, 45; 9:33, 49; 17:13). The address expresses the relationship between Jesus and the disciples as distinguished from that of Jesus and other people. The repetition of 'Master' suggests the urgency of the request.

Luke omits Mark's 'do you not care if', which may seem to have a derogatory undertone, and merely retains 'we are perishing'. In the light of its repeated use later in the gospel, *apollumai*, 'to perish', may have a wider meaning than merely physical perishing, and may signify both spiritual and physical danger (e.g., Lk 13:3, 5; 15:24, 32; 19:10). This leads in due course to a wider interpretation of the miracle story in terms of the spiritual needs of the Christian community and its members.

Instead of Mark's 'he rebuked the wind and said to the sea', Luke writes 'he rebuked the wind and the raging waves', but omits the direct address. So, unlike Mark, the verb 'rebuked' has here two objects: the 'wind' and the 'waves' (*kludōn* in the New Testament only here and in Jas 1:6). Jesus rebuked the spirit(s) believed to have caused the sudden storm and this thwarts the danger described in verse 23. Two short clauses state the effect of Jesus' intervention: the wind and the waves 'ceased' (*pauomai*; three times in Luke, six times in Acts), 'and there was a great calm' (*galēnē*, only here and in the parallel texts of Mark and Matthew).

Verse 25: He said to them, 'Where is your faith?' And they were afraid, and they marvelled, saying to one another, 'Who then is this, that he commands even wind and water, and they obey him?'

In agreement with his editing of the disciples' outcry, Luke now also edits Jesus' question about their faith. He eliminates the reproachful undertone found in Mark, and concentrates the question on the faith of the disciples. 'The Lucan form does not say outright that the disciples lack all faith; Jesus merely asks where it is. At first sight the query of Jesus could refer to the disciples' lack of faith in God or his providence; but the following comment of the evangelist makes it clear that some form of faith in him is meant.'[144]

Luke edited verse 25 under the influence of Lk 4:36 and Lk 8:24.

In Lk 4:31–37, Jesus had not yet called any disciples in Capernaum—the calling of the first disciples occurs in Lk 5:1–11—so that the disciples' question here does not appear as a repetition. In adapting the acclamation to verse 24b Luke adds the verb 'command' (parallel Lk 4:36, but different Mk 4:41), thereby indirectly alluding to the *dunamis*, 'power', of Lk 4:36. Luke omitted *hupakouein*, 'to obey', in Lk 4:36 (different Mk 1:27), but retains it here, because in Lk 4:35f. the evangelist emphasizes the salutary liberation of a possessed person from the power of the demons, while here he is interested in Jesus' extraordinary demonstration of power over the raging elements in the presence of the disciples.

The disciples' reaction is marked by the event experienced: 'and they were afraid, and they marvelled', literally, 'fearing, they expressed surprise'. This, like their talking to one another, expresses their inner disturbance and uncertainty, illustrated by their question, 'Who then is this?' The grounds for this question are formulated in two clauses which are connected by means of 'and': 'he commands even wind (literally: the winds) and water *and* they obey him'. The reaction of the disciples repeats the distinction between the demonic elements already found in verse 24: 'wind and water', 'wind and waves'. 'He commands' refers back to 'he rebuked' in verse 24 and prepares the formulation of the second clause, 'and they obey him' (*hupakouein*; Mk 1:27; 4:41; Mt 8:27; Lk 8:25; 17:6). The verb 'obey' here expresses the complete submission of the powers of nature to Jesus' authority. Luke concludes his account by this reflection on Jesus' powerful intervention.

Luke somewhat corrects Mark and presents a clearer account: the reference to Jesus' sleep (Mk 4:38) is now mentioned before the storm (Lk 8:23). 'Luke clearly attaches importance to an orderly narrative sequence.'[145] By not mentioning the crowd (see Mk 4:36) Luke concentrates the action on Jesus and his disciples and brings to the fore Jesus' initiative: while in Mark the disciples took Jesus with them, in Luke Jesus 'got into the boat with his disciples'. Jesus' sleep and the storm are mentioned only briefly, and the disciples' cry for help has a rhetorical character. All this seems to be only a presupposition for the decisive question 'Where is your faith?' (Lk 8:25), which is formulated in a terser and more direct way. The storm is only an occasion for this question and the succeeding reaction of the disciples, in order to take up again the perplexed surprise and questioning already encountered in Capernaum (Lk 4:31–37).

In such a text which receives a clearly Christological emphasis by means of Jesus' decisive intervention and the concluding unanswered question, there is no room for a reproach on the part of the disciples.

Jesus is designated as 'Master', who is above all dangers and banishes them by his powerful word. Jesus' miraculous power is thereby highlighted. Consequently, Luke mentions as objects of the verb 'rebuke' both the previously mentioned sources of danger (Lk 8:23; different Mk 4:39) and omits the order to be silent expressed in direct speech in Mk 4:38f. While a demonic understanding of the events as it is found in Mark is not excluded, Luke certainly does not emphasize it. The emphasis is not on the interpretation of the storm, but on the perception which Jesus formulates in the form of a question to his disciples, 'Where is your faith?' For Luke, the failing faith in the face of threatening danger, here expressed by storm and water, is the peak of the text, along with the absence of trust in Jesus' power which is once more impressively and exemplarily demonstrated by his word. The concluding question which, as in Lk 4:37, summarizes the event and the power and authority of Jesus, is a didactic repetition which keeps alive the basic question concerning Jesus, the Christological interest of the evangelist, and creates a transition to the next miracle story. By his redactional activity Luke makes it clear that he understands the story of the stilling of the storm as a 'didactic saving act'. It gives a specific instance of Jesus' power and the faith in it required from Luke's community.[146]

We are therefore dealing with a story with two peaks. On the one hand, the story focuses on Jesus' demonstration of power over the raging elements which provokes the question concerning his identity. With his power over the natural elements Jesus exercises a divine prerogative (Ps 89:9f.). Luke edits the traditional story of the stilling of the storm in order to state at the beginning of the section Lk 8:22 – 9:17 the Christological question which is its theme, by means of a theophanic demonstration of power.[147]

On the other hand, the story deals with the question of faith. Jesus' sleep should have given the disciples an opportunity to demonstrate the strength of their faith according to the instruction of Lk 8:11–18. In the Lucan perspective, Jesus' question reminds them of the admonition to endure all situations with steadfastness. For a moment the disciples fail. Since, according to Luke, Jesus presumes faith in the disciples, their failure is only momentary. The miracle becomes an instruction for the disciples in the future to hold on to their faith, even in extraordinary situations. Luke, then, gives to Jesus' demonstration of power a strongly didactic, paraenetic trait. The disciples should recognize in it Jesus' identity as the one who realizes God's saving will, and at the same time take seriously Jesus' teaching that a strong faith by itself means salvation. By a minimum of editorial interventions in the text Luke has fitted the pericope into the narrative context of Lk 8:1 – 9:50 in which didactic word and demonstrative deed are closely related.[148]

8 The raising of a widow's only son

Lk 7:11–17

11 Soon afterward he went to a city called Nain,
   and his disciples and a great crowd went with him.
12 As he drew near to the gate of the city,
   behold, a man who had died was being carried out,
   the only son of his mother, and she was a widow;
   and a large crowd from the city was with her.
13 And when the Lord saw her, he had compassion on her
   and said to her, 'Do not weep.'
14 And he came and touched the bier,
   and the bearers stood still.
   And he said, 'Young man, I say to you, arise.'
15 And the dead man sat up, and began to speak.
   And he gave him to his mother.
16 Fear seized them all; and they glorified God, saying,
   'A great prophet has arisen among us!' and
   'God has visited his people!'
17 And this report concerning him spread
   through the whole of Judea and all the surrounding country.

The context

The account of the raising of the only son of the widow of Nain is
found in Luke alone. Lk 7:1 – 8:3 constitutes a section which
illustrates the reception Jesus received from various persons or
groups of persons as his ministry continued, beginning with the
healing of the centurion's servant (Lk 7:1–10) and ending with the
special Lucan pericope about the women who followed Jesus (Lk
8:1–3). Lk 7 contains a considerable amount of material in common
with Matthew (Lk 7:1–10 = Mt 8:5–13; Lk 7:18–35 = Mt 11:2–19),
but Luke carefully shapes the pericopes into a unity which is
thematically closely related to the programmatic Nazareth pericope
(Lk 4:16–30). In fact, taken together, Lk 7:1–10 and 7:11–17 form a
rough correspondence to the examples of Elijah and Elisha cited in
the Nazareth pericope (Lk 4:25–27). As Elisha cured the Gentile

officer Naaman through the intervention of a Jewish girl and instructed Naaman through delegates (II Kgs 5:1–14), so Jesus cured the servant of a Gentile centurion through the intervention of some Jews and communicated with the centurion through delegates. As Elijah raised the son of the widow of Zarephath (I Kgs 17:17–24), so Jesus raised the son of the widow of Nain. If, especially in the first story, the details do not match up, this is because Luke was working with a story he received from the tradition (Lk 7:1–10 = Mt 8:5–13 = Q). The literary relationship between I Kgs 17:17–24 and Lk 7:11–17 is, however, obvious, as will be shown below. This is further supported by the obvious reference of Lk 7:22 to Lk 4:16–30.[149]

The resuscitation of a dead man deliberately follows the healing of a critically ill person (Lk 7:1–10), thus leading to a climax, and serving as evidence for the message addressed to John the Baptist that 'the dead are raised up' (Lk 7:22; Mt 11:5). There is a certain gradation as well as a unity between the two narratives. Jesus shows compassion to a man and a woman afflicted by what has happened to a person dear to them, but the first is a servant while the second is an only child, the first is 'at the point of death' (Lk 7:2) while the second is already dead. Jesus cures the one and raises the other by a mere word.[150] After the servant of a centurion, the only son of a widow is saved. Luke pointedly contrasts the woman with the centurion: she is not just a woman, but a mother of an only son and a widow. Moreover, unlike the previous story, Jesus himself takes the initiative, consoles the woman and raises her son. These features clearly indicate that Luke deliberately intends to surpass the preceding healing at Capernaum without interrupting the narrative context. Without the story of the centurion's servant, the present pericope could not have been fitted in so well.[151]

The new theme of the narrative unity is indicated by the catchword 'prophet' (Lk 7:16; see Lk 7:26, 39). The theme is thus literarily reflected in several pericopes from three distinct perspectives.

The story is not only successfully linked to the preceding context of Jesus' urban ministry by the mention of 'a city called Nain', but is also closely related to the following question of John the Baptist (Lk 7:18–23). The transition between Lk 7:11–17 and Lk 7:18–23 is achieved by the notice 'and this report concerning him spread through the whole of Judea and all the surrounding country' (Lk 7:17), which prepares for the following verse. In Lk 7:18, 'all these things' refers explicitly to the preceding pericope or pericopes (Lk 7:1–10, 11–17). But Lk 7:22 ends with the words, 'the poor have good news preached to them', which refers to Lk 4:18, 'to preach good news to the poor', but also to Lk 6:20, 'Blessed are you poor, for yours is the kingdom of God', and indirectly to the whole Sermon on the Plain (Lk 6:20–49). Therefore, 'all these things' may refer to the whole section, Lk 6:20 – 7:17, containing 'what you have seen and heard' (Lk 7:22). In any case, the Nain story gains special importance for the interpretation of John's question. Jesus refers to the fulfilment of the scripture, 'the dead are raised up' (Lk 7:22; Isa 26:19; for the rest of Lk 7:22 see Isa 35:5–6). In the Lucan context these words clearly refer to the raising of the young man. The account is therefore to be interpreted in the context of Lk 7:21 where Luke calls special attention to the actual realization in Jesus' activity of Isaian themes referring to the last days, admittedly without explicit mention of the fulfilment of scripture, as in Lk 4:18–21.

The insertion of an account from Luke's special material (L) in this context is very successful. The pericope is the literary transition to a thematic cycle of the redactor's: the elucidation of the concept 'prophet'.

The section beginning with the Baptist's question (Lk 7:18–35) combines two very important aspects of Jesus' ministry which Luke relates to his prophetic role: on the one hand, a demonstration of the mighty works of the one who is to come (Lk 7:21) and, on the other hand, a note of the people's rejection (Lk 7:31–35). The first is associated with Galilee, while the second, the destination for violent rejection, underlies the Lucan 'journey' to Jerusalem. These two Christological phases belong to the prophetic role which Luke attributes to Jesus.

The acclamation of the crowd in Lk 7:16, confirmed by Jesus' declaration in Lk 7:22–23, also constitutes a distant preparation for the account of the forgiven sinner (Lk 7:36–50). The sceptical remark by the Pharisee, 'If this man were a prophet, he would have known who and what sort of woman this is who is touching him, for she is a sinner' (Lk 7:39), contradicts the popular ovation in verse 16, but justifies Jesus' severe judgement on Israel's ruling class (Lk 7:29–35).

The Nain pericope, therefore, occupies an important place in the structure of Lk 7 whose cornerstone is the cry of the crowd, 'God has visited his people', and Jesus' declaration in Lk 7:22–23. God shows himself favourable to the Gentiles, to the little ones in need, and to sinners, but he resists the Pharisees and the lawyers who refuse to enter into salvation history and God's purpose (Lk 7:30).[152]

Analysis of the text

Verse 11: Soon afterward he went to a city called Nain, and his disciples and a great crowd went with him.

The expression 'soon afterward' may be a rewording of 'after this' in I Kgs 17:17. The formula is almost the same as Lk 8:1, also translated by RSV as 'soon afterward'. The phrase is probably Lucan. Instead of the foreign 'Zarephath', Luke has 'Nain', a location which fits the flow of his narrative. Nain is about ten kilometres southeast of Nazareth, not far from Shunem where Elisha resuscitated a young boy (II Kgs 4:32–37). It is mentioned only here in the Bible. The expression 'a city called Nain' makes one think of Lk 9:10, 'a city called Bethsaida'. The expression 'called' (*kaloumenos*) is typically Lucan. The mention of 'a city called Nain' makes the pericope fit into the context of Jesus' urban mission.

The distinction between 'his disciples' and 'a great crowd' is reminiscent of Lk 6:17, 'with a great crowd of his disciples and a great multitude of people' (compare Lk 9:16; 20:45, as against Mk 12:37b). Although Lk 7:9 presumes that Jesus was accompanied by a crowd when he entered Capernaum in Lk 7:1, 2, it was not mentioned there. Here in Lk 7:11, however, it is emphatically stated. The 'disciples and a great crowd' mentioned here have no counterpart whatsoever in I Kgs 17.

There is no tension between verse 11 and verse 12a, as is assumed by those who say that according to verse 11 Jesus entered Nain, while verse 12a says that he arrived at the gate. In reality, verse 11 indicates the goal of the journey, while verse 12a describes the actual arrival (compare Lk 24:15, 28).

The analysis seems to indicate that Luke's source contained: 'He went to Nain'.[153]

> **Verse 12:** As he drew near to the gate of the city, behold, a man who had died was being carried out, the only son of his mother, and she was a widow; and a large crowd from the city was with her.

The expression 'as he drew near' may be Lucan (Lk 15:25; 19:29, 41; compare Acts 7:17). It has been noted that when used of Jesus the expression 'to draw near' (*engizein*) or 'to approach' (*proserchesthai*) may refer to a first step in a messianic activity (cf. Mk 1:31; Mt 17:7; 28:18). The meeting at the gate of Nain has no counterpart in I Kgs 17:17–24, but seems to be modelled on the meeting at the gate of Zarephath in the preceding pericope (I Kgs 17:10). In a single word, 'having died' (*tethnēkōs*), Luke 'summarizes' the Old Testament counterpart 'the son of the woman...became ill, and his illness was so severe that there was no breath left in him' (I Kgs 17:17). While in the Old Testament story Elijah 'carried him up...and laid him upon his own bed' (I Kgs 17:19), and after he was revived, 'took the child...and brought him down' (I Kgs 17:23), in Luke the man 'was being carried out' on the road to the burial place. The verb 'to be carried out' (*ekkomizesthai*) is found only here in the New Testament. But in the continuation of the story we are told that this movement towards burial was arrested by Jesus, 'and the bearers stood still' (Lk 7:14).

The second part of the verse shifts attention from the dead man to his mother and her plight, a trend which will be continued in the next verse. She was a widow and had lost her only son. Since Luke several times introduces the motif 'only son' (*monogenēs*) into the miracle tradition (see Lk 8:42; 9:38), it may be redactional here too. But it could also be traditional if it is explained as derived from the Hebrew text of I Kgs 17:12, 'for myself and my son' (the Septuagint has: 'for myself and my children'). The expression 'and she was a widow' is almost identical with that in Lk 2:37. The fate of widows was very hard. 'Widows' or 'widows and orphans' are the typical defenceless figures in the Old Testament. They had practically no legal protection, and could hardly defend themselves against unjust claims (Lk 18:3; compare Job 24:3; Isa 1:23). Since Old Testament times there had been a tradition in Israel that God protects and defends widows and orphans against injustice (Deut 24:17; 27:19; Isa 1:17; Ps 146:9). A widow who had lost her only son was the embodiment of those who had no hope and no future left. The death of her only son meant the end of her line.

Next to Jesus, the woman is the most important person in the story. The dead man is identified in terms of his relation to her ('the only son of his mother'), and the large crowd from the city—which has no counterpart in I Kgs 17—accompanied her (not the dead man or the bier). The word *hikanos* used for 'enough and to spare' (RSV: 'large') occurs frequently in Luke (Lk 8:27, 32; 20:9; 22:38; 23:8, 9; Acts 8:11; 9:23, 43; 11:24, 26, etc.). It is variously translated by RSV as: 'long', 'large', 'enough', etc. The large crowd is on its way to the site of the funeral outside the gate. Attending a funeral was considered a work of charity.

Luke's source probably contained: 'a man who had died was being carried out (the only son of a widow)'.[154]

The analysis suggests that the primitive tradition was formed in a Jewish milieu, because this part of the tradition which is a pastiche of I Kgs 17:10 seems to be closer to the Hebrew text than to the Septuagint.[155] But the motif of the encounter of the miracle-worker and the funeral procession at the gate of the city, while possibly derived from I Kgs 17:10, may come from a Hellenistic milieu. The mention of the disciples and a great crowd who accompanied Jesus undoubtedly does not belong to the original tradition, but is a characteristic feature of New Testament miracle stories.

Verse 13: And when the Lord saw her, he had compassion on her and said to her, 'Do not weep.'

Luke uses the title 'Lord' (*kurios*) nineteen times to designate Jesus. In the present text it is probably to be attributed to Luke, who may have substituted it for 'Jesus' found in his source. He used the title here for the first time in the narrative sections of the gospel and gave it a transcendent messianic meaning. In the Septuagint, *kurios* is the Greek translation for the divine name Yahweh. In New Testament literature it is a post-Easter Christian title implying Jesus' exaltation by God (Rom 1:4; 10:9; Phil 2:9). Here the Lord of life meets sorrow and death.

In the Old Testament Elijah addressed the Lord God as 'the witness of the widow' (*ho martus tēs chēras*; not translated in RSV). Luke expressed the same idea, 'when the Lord saw her', i.e., when the Lord witnessed her plight, thus expressing himself more vividly. While Elijah cried out in a way which implied compassion (I Kgs 17:20a), and his sympathy for the widow is sensed from his having stayed with her for some time (I Kgs 17:20b), Luke expresses Jesus' attitude with a brief 'he had compassion' (*esplanchnistē*; Lk 7:13; 10:33; 15:20). Jesus' first action was to console and reassure the widow, thus immediately taking the initiative. The clause 'do not weep' is also found in Lk 8:52, where the evangelist softens down Jesus' words to the mourners, 'Why do you make a tumult and weep?' (Mk 5:39), and in Lk 23:28.

Jesus' whole life is at the service of people in need. His raising of people from the dead reveals how he confronts the need caused by death. By his action which leads from death to life, Jesus confronts the 'law' that what has died is irrevocably dead. In Lk 7:11–17 this is illustrated in the person of the widow who with the death of her son had lost all hope for the future. The 'Author of life' (Acts 3:15) counteracts the grip of death.

While some scholars consider this verse a 'contribution of Luke, the evangelist who depicts feelings and who readily mentions women',[156] others consider it on linguistic grounds probably pre-Lucan.[157] Summing up, we would say that verse 13 may have been redactionally rephrased. 'He had compassion (on her)' is certainly traditional, while 'when he saw her' is doubtful.

Verse 14: And he came and touched the bier, and the bearers stood still. And he said, 'Young man, I say to you, arise.'

The expression 'and coming (*proselthōn*) he touched the bier' is Lucan (compare Lk 8:44; literally, 'and coming up [*proselthousa*] behind him she touched the fringe of his garment'), although it is not altogether his creation since in Lk 8:44 he derives it from Mk 5:27. The word 'bier' (*soros*) is used only here in the New Testament. But see Gen 50:26 in the Septuagint, 'So Joseph died...and he was put in a coffin (*soros*) in Egypt'. Contact with the dead was supposed to defile a person (Sir 34:25–26).

While Elijah 'stretched himself upon the child three times' (I Kgs 17:21; more literally, 'he breathed into the boy three times'), Luke writes that 'approaching/coming he touched the bier, and the bearers stood still', thereby giving a hint of Jesus' majestic authority. The same hint is found in the continuation of the account. The expression 'I say to you' (compare Lk 5:24) underlines the authority of Jesus and strongly contrasts with Elijah's invocation of God and his repeated efforts to reanimate the corpse of the child. Unlike Elijah who called on the Lord to restore the child's life (I Kgs 17:21), Jesus utters a sovereign command, 'Young man, I say to you, arise'. For the use of 'I say' (*legō*) in the sense of 'I command', compare Lk 11:9; 12:4; 16:9. Just as in Lk 7:12 Luke's 'having died' abbreviated the much longer description of I Kgs 17:17, so here Luke's single word 'arise' abbreviates 'and the soul of the child came into him again, and he revived' (I Kgs 17:22). Luke confines himself to the stark language of death and resurrection. The aorist imperative passive *egerthēti*, 'be raised up', indicates that we are dealing here with an instance of veritable raising from the dead (compare Lk 9:7, 22; 20:37; 24:6, 34).

The touching of the bier and Jesus' raising word are traditional.

Verse 15: And the dead man sat up, and began to speak. And he gave him to his mother.

The verb 'to sit up' (*anakathizein*) occurs in the New Testament only here and in Acts 9:40, the resuscitation of Tabitha. In the Septuagint I Kgs 17:22 reads literally: 'And it was so, and the child cried out'. Similarly, 'the dead man sat up, and began to speak'. Just as there is a precise correspondence between Elijah's request that 'the child's soul come into him again' (I Kgs 17:21) and the matter-of-fact statement 'and it was so' (I Kgs 17:22; explicitated by RSV: 'and the soul of the child came into him again'), so there is between Jesus' words, 'Young man, I say to you, arise' (Lk 7:14) and 'the dead man sat up'. Moreover, both the child and the young man break out in utterance.

The paradoxical expression 'and the dead man sat up' is found in analogous manner in Lk 11:14, 'the dumb man spoke' (parallel Mt 12:22 = Q). The word *nekros*, 'dead (man)', may have come naturally to Luke since it fits in his general conception, referring to Lk 7:22, 'the dead (*nekroi*) are raised up'.

In the first part of the verse only *ērxato* (*lalein*), 'he began (to speak)', is redactional (compare Acts 2:4; 11:15). Luke's source may have stated simply: 'and the child cried out', as in the Septuagint and the story by Philostratus (see below). That he 'began to speak' proves the young man's restoration to life. Unlike the sceptical Philostratus, Luke does not admit of any doubt that the young man was really dead and, therefore, really brought back to life.

The clause 'and he gave him to his mother' is in the Greek text identical with I Kgs 17:23 (RSV: 'and delivered him to his mother'), and corresponds to Lk 9:42, 'and gave him back to his father', which is added by Luke to the tradition (compare Mk 9:27; Mt 17:18). Jesus restores the relationship destroyed by death. He returns the son, and thereby life, to the widow. The story, which had left the woman after the invitation not to cry, now returns to her. This part of the verse is probably redactionally inserted.

The resurrection, which itself cannot be perceived, is visualized by the reactions it brings about.

Summing up our findings concerning verses 12–15, we may say that literary analysis indicates that, generally speaking, Luke has faithfully followed his source. The only theologically important change is the probable substitution of 'Lord' for 'Jesus'. The author of Luke's source has used I Kgs 17 and combines what he derives from this model with motifs inspired by accounts of healings or raisings-on-the-way (see below). Jesus' order to the dead person is not derived from either the Old Testament or pagan tradition. Its only equivalents are found in the miracle stories of the New Testament.

> **Verse 16:** Fear seized them all; and they glorified God, saying, 'A great prophet has arisen among us!' and 'God has visited his people!'

The expression 'fear seized them all' (*elabon de phobos pantas*) occurs only here in the New Testament. Luke refers here to religious awe in the presence of the Lord of life and death. God alone is master of life. 'For you have power over life and death; you do lead men down to the gates of Hades and back again' (Wisd 16:13). The first part of verse 16 is very close to Lk 5:26, 'and amazement seized them all, and they glorified God' (parallel Mk 2:12). Opinions are divided as to whether these first two clauses of verse 16 are traditional or redactional. The expression 'to glorify God' is certainly typical of Luke (Lk 2:20; 5:25, 26; 13:13, etc.).

I Kgs 17:24 reads: 'And the woman said to Elijah, "Now I know that you are a man of God, and that the word of the Lord in your mouth is truth" '. While I Kgs 17 speaks of the reaction of only one person, the woman, Luke records the reaction of 'all', which is, as it were, a synthesis of the two crowds mentioned in Lk 7:11–12. 'Luke often emphasizes the universal reaction of people to Jesus' activity (Lk 5:25; 7:16; 9:43; 18:43; 19:37).'[158]

The response of the people is praise of God expressed in two statements which complement each other. The first reads literally: 'a great prophet has been raised among us', the passive mood indicating divine action: 'God has raised up a great prophet among us'. The crowd's reaction is in keeping with biblical notions of expressing God's intervention.

The title 'great prophet' is found only here in the New Testament. The term 'prophet' applied to Jesus by the crowd is also found in Lk 9:8 (parallel Mk 6:15) and 9:19 (parallel Mk 8:28). Jesus refers to himself as a prophet in Lk 4:24f. and in Lk 13:33. In Lk 24:19, the disciples on the road to Emmaus describe Jesus as 'a prophet mighty in deed and word before God and all the people'. This may be a formula of the early Christian proclamation in which, with reference to Deut 18:15, Jesus is presented as the other prophet like Moses whom God would raise up (Acts 3:22f.; 7:22). But in the present verse Jesus is presented not as an ordinary prophet, nor as the prophet awaited for the last days, or a new Moses, but as the 'great prophet' comparable to but at the same time also surpassing Elijah.

The theme of God's visitation, which occurs frequently in the Old Testament (e.g., Ruth 1:6; I Sam 2:21) and intertestamental Judaism, is found relatively rarely in the New Testament. The second part of the people's praise, 'God has visited his people (in and through the prophet)', recalls Lk 1:68, 'Blessed be the Lord God of Israel, for he has visited and redeemed his people', and Lk 19:44, '...because you did not know the time of your visitation'. In consideration of Acts 15:14, 'how God first visited the Gentiles', some think the phrase redactional, while others think that Luke derived this theme from his source. By the mention of God's visitation Luke develops the eschatological aspect of Jesus' activity. He interprets the raising of the young man as a fulfilment of the prophetic words of Zechariah (Lk 1:78–79) and Lk 7:22. The latter 'corrects' the overwhelming statement of the crowd. Although expressly informed about 'all these things', John the Baptist is not freed from all his doubts; he sends two disciples to ask whether Jesus is 'he who is to come' or not. Jesus' powerful deeds as such do not remove all doubts concerning his person. Rather, as a manifestation of God's visitation the miracle presupposes a decision of faith (compare Lk 16:31) in order for the event to be recognized as *kairos*, the hour of salvation.[159]

ὁ λόγος οὗτος

Verse 17: And this report concerning him spread through the whole of Judea and all the surrounding country.

The report (*logos*) went forth to two distinct geographic entities, 'the whole of Judea' and 'all the surrounding country'. The phrase 'concerning him' is intended to specify the meaning of 'this report'. Some authors conclude from this that it is the confession of faith in Jesus expressed in verse 16 that spreads, not the news of the event itself. But most scholars hold that it is the news of the raising of the dead man which is reported. If *logos* is the Greek rendition of the Hebrew *dabar* it can mean both '(this) word' and '(this) event'. Faith in Jesus and the reputation of the Master expand more and more. At the beginning of Jesus' activity his fame did not reach beyond the region in which he was at work (Lk 4:14b, 37). Then it expanded to the whole of Galilee, Judea and Jerusalem (Lk 5:17), soon afterwards to the cities of Tyre and Sidon (Lk 6:17), and now to Judea and the neighbouring pagan regions. It is almost certain that to achieve this effect Luke added to his source 'the whole of Judea concerning him and' (the word-order of the Greek text).

The expression 'the whole of Judea' is also found in Lk 23:5 (RSV: 'throughout all Judea') and Acts 10:37 (RSV: 'throughout all Judea'). 'Judea' here would mean 'the land of the Jews', that is, the whole of Palestine, not just the province of Judea. This extended meaning of Judea is found regularly in Luke (Lk 1:5; 4:44; 6:17; 23:5; Acts 10:37).

'All the surrounding country', then, does not mean the region around Nain, but the territory beyond Palestine. Some would even see here a subtle reference to the future Gentile mission.[160] May there not be a similar reference in the mention of the 'great crowd' which followed Jesus and the 'large crowd from the city' of Nain which, according to some, may have been thought of as outside Judea? The report spread beyond Palestine into the surrounding Gentile country. Luke would thus be pointedly concluding the note of expansion begun in Lk 4:14.

The original account

Literary genre

The analysis of Lk 7:11–17 has shown that, though closely related to the raising of the child of the widow of Zarephath (I Kgs 17:17–24), the pericope does not entirely follow its literary model. As far as form is concerned, the Nain pericope is related to the accounts of healings or raisings-on-the-way, the oldest example of which is an inscription of Epidaurus relating the raising by Asclepius of a young woman carried on a bier. By the third century A.D. this account had been transferred to Apollonius of Tyana, as evidenced in Flavius Philostratus' *The Life of Apollonius of Tyana* IV, 45:

> Here also is a miracle (*thauma*) of Apollonios. A young girl seemed to have died in the very hour of her marriage and the bridegroom was following the bier weeping over his unfulfilled marriage. Rome mourned also, for it happened that the dead girl was from one of the best families. Apollonios, happening to be present where they were mourning, said, 'Put down the bier, for I will end your weeping for this girl', and at the same time he asked what her name was. The bystanders thought that he was going to give a speech like those which people give at burials to heighten everyone's sorrow. But he didn't; instead he touched her and saying something no one could hear, awakened the girl who seemed dead. And the girl spoke and went back to her father's house, just like Alcestis who was brought back to her life by Herakles. And when the relatives of the girl offered Apollonios 150,000 silver pieces as a reward, he replied that he would return it to the child as a gift for her dowry. Now whether he found a spark of life in her which had escaped the notice of the doctors—for it is said her breath could be seen above her face as it rained—or whether, her life actually being completely extinguished, she grew warm again and received it back, no one knows. A grasp of this mystery has not been gained either by me or by those who chanced to be there.[161]

The contacts between Lk 7 and the other accounts are thematic rather than literary. We deal here apparently with an oral tradition which, according to the time, was reported of a god like Asclepius, or of a 'divine man', like Apollonius of Tyana. This tradition followed a rather fixed literary schema: It begins with the accidental encounter of the healer and the sick or dead person somewhere along the road. Then the order to put down the bier is given (Epidaurus, Philostratus). In Lk 7, Jesus touches the bier and the bearers stop. Thirdly, follows the order not to weep; in the stories of Philostratus and Luke a few words suffice to bring the dead person back to life. Finally, in the story of Philostratus the reanimated person cries out; in Luke's story the young man begins to speak. The story ends with the amazement and doubt of the witnesses in the story by Philostratus, corresponding to the fear and the glorification of God by the bystanders in Luke's account.

The tradition of a healing or raising-on-the-way is attested in writings earlier than, contemporary with, and later than the redaction of the New Testament. The discovery of this literary genre would invite one to search for the origin of the Lucan story in the Hellenistic world. For apologetic reasons, the first Christian preachers would have been led in a Hellenistic milieu to align themselves with Greek legends and to develop similar stories. But the theology and language of Luke, as well as the obvious dependence on I Kgs 17 where Elijah raises the son of the widow of Zarephath, invite us to turn our attention to a Judeo-(Hellenistic)-Christian milieu. The similarity of literary genre does not as such allow a decision on the origin or the historicity of the account.[162]

Origin of the account

The probability is clearly in favour of an account of Judeo-Christian origin, Palestinian or Syrian. The Semitizing tone of the text, the Christology implied in it, and the literary genre make us look for the origin and life-situation of the account in Syria where the Judeo-Christian Church was in close contact with Greek thought. Luke's source has several points in common with I Kgs 17, while other features are not found in I Kgs 17 but occur in popular traditions about healings or raisings-on-the-way. However, all these analogies should not obscure the original features of Luke's source: its localization in Nain, Jesus accompanied by his disciples and a large crowd, the insistence on the suffering of the widow, and Jesus' compassion on her. The last two features make some scholars think that the narrative may have belonged to a section centred on Jesus and the women (Lk 7:11–17; 7:36–50; 8:1–3). Other features are Jesus' order to the dead man, the Christology of verse 16, and finally the notice that the news of the event spread throughout the surrounding country. Do these specific features find their explanation in an underlying historical event?

In view of the rather extensive borrowings from I Kgs 17:17–24 and the literary genre of 'raising-on-the-way', the historical character of this particular account cannot be categorically affirmed or denied. Since absolute certainty seems to be excluded, we can speak only in terms of the more or less probable. Without categorically excluding that there may be a historical event at the basis of this account, a recent study has concluded that it seems nevertheless more probable that this raising story, while following the literary genre of 'raising-on-the-way', is in fact a Christological re-elaboration of the raising performed by Elijah at Zarephath.[163]

Two reasons prompt the author to take this option. Firstly, none of the specific features of the story of the raising at Nain guarantees its historicity. Secondly, it is practically certain that after the resurrection of Jesus the early Church considered and preached Jesus as the new Elijah who would return at the end of time. It can then easily be understood that in order to express this conviction specifically the first Christian preachers and popular religiosity 'Christologized' several episodes of the life of Elijah.

To return to the first reason: the localization of the miracle at Nain is one of the most important arguments in favour of the historicity of the miracle. But it has been shown that Lk 7:11–12 is a pastiche of I Kgs 17:10. This called for substituting the name of another city for Zarephath. Nain was chosen. Arguing from the texts, we can only affirm that the localization can be evidence for imitation as much as for historicity.

The other features of the account which have no parallel in I Kgs 17 or the accounts of 'resurrection-on-the-way' are most of them quite common in New Testament miracle stories, like, e.g., Jesus' authoritative word (compare Mk 1:41; 2:11; 3:5; 10:52; Lk 8:54; 13:12; 17:14), and do not constitute a decisive argument in favour of the historicity of the account.[164]

Very recently, in a study which considers Lk 7:11–17 an example of imitation (*mimēsis*), a literary exercise quite common in the Greco-Roman world, it has been stated that, apart from its undeniable dependence on I Kgs 17:17–24, Lk 7:11–17 is also the result of the 'interweaving of a specifically New Testament theme—the glorious union of Jews and Gentiles around the death-defeating word of Christ'.[165] This theme, which is clearly expressed in Eph 1:15 – 2:22, for instance, was incorporated by Luke into the narrative framework of I Kgs 17:17–24. Luke thus attests to a tradition about the life-giving power of Christ, drawn from Christian preaching and writing rather than from an original single event in Jesus' ministry. 'Hence, a major proportion of the *theological content* of Luke 7.11–17 may be from the New Testament period, but the *narrative shape* is drawn very largely from the Old Testament.'[166]

The Lucan redaction

Although Luke's theological intention can already be perceived from the place the account occupies in his gospel, his editorial intervention does not just serve the purpose of inserting the originally independent account into its new narrative context. Not only the 'frame' of the account—that is, its beginning and conclusion—but the whole story is edited. It is also highly significant that Luke, who repeatedly describes Jesus with the features of Elijah, is the only evangelist to relate this miracle story.

The revision of the original account interprets it anew. Its insertion in this particular context and the explicit reference to it in Lk 7:18 ('all these things') make the composition into a means of interpretation. The readers' attention is drawn to the distressed widow whose miserable condition is emphasized. By the formal construction of the exposition Luke succeeds in balancing the sympathy with the fate of the widow and his presentation of Jesus' sovereign appearance. The shift of accent from the original powerful act to Jesus' mercy on the widow serves the purpose of enlarging the image of Jesus by another aspect. Jesus is not only a powerful miracle-worker who through his commanding word demonstrates his Lordship (*kuriotēs*), but he is also the merciful benefactor (*euergetēs*). The demonstration of power and the theme of mercy are closely related. Jesus' miracle demonstrates both his power and his loving mercy.[167]

Jesus, the new Elijah

Elijah was one of the most popular figures of post-biblical Judaism. In Jesus' time the expectation of his return was very common (Mk 6:15; 8:28; 9:4, 11–13), but he was seen through the prism of Jewish messianic expectation and thought of either as the Messiah, or the predecessor of the Messiah, high priest of the last days, or the prophet of the last days. But whatever his title, Elijah would play an important role in the last days.

By his proclamation and life Jesus announced the coming of the kingdom of God. It should not be surprising then that the crowds, and later the first Christian community, took him to be the new Elijah (Mk 6:15; 8:28). In the early Christian preaching the universal restoration which Judaism reserved for Elijah during the last days (Mal 3:23 Hebrew; 4:5 Greek) is referred to 'the Christ appointed for you, Jesus, whom heaven must receive until the time for establishing all that God spoke by the mouth of his holy prophets from of old' (Acts 3:20–21). We may be in touch here with the earliest Christology.

It is remarkable that Luke, sometimes relying on ancient sources or particular traditions, sometimes changing the text of Mark or the Q-source, is the only one who has conserved and amplified this ancient Christology in which Jesus is regarded as the new Elijah. In this connection Luke avoids all identification of John the Baptist with Elijah. It is Jesus who in Luke 'wears the mantle of Elijah'.[168] This image is not created by Luke but derived from the tradition and enhanced by a number of additions as well as omissions.

Seen in this context the Nain account is but one episode of the Jesus–Elijah typology, and here too the typology rather than underlying historical facts is food for reflection.[169]

The title 'Lord' in verse 13

Some scholars think that Luke substituted 'Lord' for 'Jesus' found in the source because he thus wanted to *correct* the primitive Christology of verse 16 ('prophet'). But this is doubtful. As a messianic sign, the miracle illustrates also Jesus' response to John the Baptist, 'Go and tell John what you have seen and heard: ...the dead are raised up, the poor have good news preached to them' (Lk 7:22). In a word, the messianic era is here! Jesus, then, is called 'Lord' because he accomplishes the works of mercy God was going to perform either by himself or through his anointed one, at the beginning of the messianic era. The title 'Lord' therefore has here a messianic connotation. For Luke, the two terms 'Christ/Messiah' and 'Lord' are closely related to each other. In Lk 2:11 the angel announces to the shepherds 'a Saviour, who is Christ the Lord'. In Acts 2:36, Peter says to his Jewish audience: 'God has made him both Lord and Christ, this Jesus whom you crucified'. Unlike Matthew, who refers to Jesus' works as 'the deeds of the Christ' (Mt 11:2), Luke qualifies them as those of the Lord (Lk 7:13, 19) who is the transcendent Messiah. They reveal his mission rather than authenticate it. The title 'Lord' which Luke substitutes for 'Jesus' therefore underlines the transcendent messianic quality of Jesus.[170]

God's visitation

The manifold interventions of God in the history of humanity, of Israel and of some privileged people are called in the Bible 'God's visitation'. The God of history intervened in the life of his people to punish or to show his favour, but always to save. The prophets were the heralds of these divine visitations. However, the term 'visitation' is never used in the Bible to indicate the final and decisive (eschatological) intervention of God at the end of time. But starting with the second century A.D., the word 'visit/visitation' and the verb 'to visit' often have an eschatological connotation.

The crowd's acclamation 'God has visited his people' could simply be understood as referring to a particular favourable manifestation of God. This would be a parallel to Ex 4:30–31: 'and [Aaron] did the signs in the sight of the people. And the people believed; and when they heard that the Lord had visited the people of

Israel and that he had seen their affliction, they bowed their heads and worshipped'.

But Luke has certainly understood this acclamation in an eschatological sense; it deals with the definite and salvific visitation of God (Lk 1:68, 78; 19:44). It is also probable that the author of Luke's source and the early Christian tradition already intended to express by the crowd's exclamation the eschatological significance of Jesus' coming.

A text of the Damascus Document,[171] Manuscript B, presents some analogy with the text of Luke:

> Awake, O Sword, against my shepherd, against my companion,
> says God. Strike the shepherd that the flock may be scattered
> and I will stretch my hand over the little ones (Zech 13:7).
> The humble of the flock are those who watch for Him.
> They shall be saved at the time of the Visitation
> whereas the others shall be delivered up to the sword
> when the Anointed of Aaron and Israel shall come,
> as it came to pass at the time of the former Visitation
> concerning which God said by the hand of Ezekiel:
> They shall put a mark on the foreheads of those who sigh and
> groan (Ezek 9:4).
> But the others were delivered up to the avenging sword of the
> Covenant.[172]

This is most probably the only contemporary text which fuses the 'visitation of God' and the coming of the Messiah. It is the little ones who are saved on the occasion of this visitation, which is in perfect agreement with Lk 7. There is, on the other hand, also a certain analogy between the eschatological expectation of the community of Qumran and that of the first Christian community.

The predominantly eschatological connotation of the term 'visitation' in the first century and the comparison between Jesus and Elijah incline us to understand the acclamation of the crowd as an eschatological and messianic confession of faith. In Jesus God has inaugurated the messianic and eschatological era.[173]

Concluding, we may say that Luke presents Jesus as reproducing in a more majestic fashion the miracle once accomplished by Elijah at Zarephath. The account is therefore a proclamation that, in imitation of Elijah, Jesus is a great prophet in whom God has visited his people, the new Elijah who inaugurates the messianic era.

This account fits well in the framework of Luke's gospel, which aims at presenting Jesus with the features of Elijah. Nevertheless, Luke has accentuated the messianic character of the account by placing it just before Jesus' statement to the disciples sent by John the Baptist (Lk 7:18–23). The change of the name 'Jesus' into 'Lord' underlines the transcendent character of this messianism.

The account which brings to the fore Jesus' compassion for the afflicted widow also fits very well in the totality of chapter 7 in which Luke describes the gracious visitation to those who are broken-hearted because of suffering or sin, and Jesus' severe judgement addressed to the haughty who have 'rejected the purpose of God for themselves' (Lk 7:30).[174]

9 The healing of ten lepers

Lk 17:11–19

11 On the way to Jerusalem he was passing along
   between Samaria and Galilee.
12 And as he entered a village, he was met by ten lepers,
   who stood at a distance
13 and lifted up their voices and said,
   'Jesus, Master, have mercy on us.'
14 When he saw them he said to them,
   'Go and show yourselves to the priests.'
   And as they went they were cleansed.
15 Then one of them, when he saw that he was healed,
   turned back, praising God with a loud voice;
16 and he fell on his face at Jesus' feet, giving him thanks.
   Now he was a Samaritan.
17 Then said Jesus, 'Were not ten cleansed? Where are the nine?
18 Was no one found to return and give praise to God
   except this foreigner?'
19 And he said to him, 'Rise and go your way;
   your faith has made you well.'

The context

The account occurs in the Travel Narrative (Lk 9:51 – 19:44) in which
the journey to Jerusalem is explicitly mentioned in Lk 9:51, 53; 13:22,
(33); 17:11; 18:31; 19:11, while the journey motif is also found in Lk
9:57; 10:1, 38; 14:25; 18:35. Within the Travel Narrative, the
references to the journey to Jerusalem serve the literary purpose of
giving this section its structure: (1) Lk 9:51 – 13:21; (2) Lk 13:22 –
17:10; (3) Lk 17:11 – 19:44. Before Lk 17:11 where Luke takes up
again the motif of the journey to Jerusalem—which has last been
mentioned in Lk 13:22—thereby marking the beginning of a new
section, he has placed three groups of sayings (Lk 17:1–2, 3–4, 5–6)
which he concludes with a parable (Lk 17:7–10). Lk 17:11–19 is
clearly distinguished from the preceding and following texts from a

literary point of view. This is indicated in verse 11 by a threefold indication of situation, by the introduction of a group of characters, ten lepers, not previously mentioned, and formal phrases in verse 19 which are also found in other conclusions of Lucan miracle stories. Lk 17:11–19 is followed by several sayings-passages which begin in Lk 17:20 with a question about the coming of the kingdom of God. How important Lk 17:11–19 is for the Pharisees' question and Jesus' answer will still have to be determined. The sayings which begin with Lk 17:20ff. are concluded by the parable of the Pharisee and the tax collector (Lk 18:9–14). After that Luke returns to the Marcan order with the pericope of the blessing of the children (Lk 18:15–17 = Mk 10:13–16).[175]

The immediate context

While it may be said that Lk '17:1–19 is organized around the question: "What is faith" (it forgives, vss. 1–4; it can do all things, vss. 5–6; it is humble, vss. 7–10, and grateful, vss. 11–19)', and that 'the point of the "miracle-story", therefore, is faith',[176] the immediate context of Lk 17:11–19 is, on the one hand, the request of the apostles for more faith and Jesus' answer which ends with a parable (Lk 17:5–10) and, on the other hand, the Pharisees' question concerning the kingdom of God and Jesus' answer (Lk 17:20–21).

Lk 17:11–19 in relation to Lk 17:5–10

The connection is established in particular by means of the key word 'faith'. The apostles request Jesus to increase their faith (Lk 17:5); Lk 17:19 speaks of the faith of the returning Samaritan. The saying about miracle-working faith is found in Lk 17:6 and Mt 17:20 and is therefore derived from Q. But it is used in different combinations: while Luke speaks of the presence of faith, Matthew speaks of its absence. Luke's framework is redactional: he himself has formulated the apostles' request. But it is believed that compared with Mt 17:20, Jesus' answer in Luke is closer to the original.

The similitude about the power of faith makes the question of the quantity of faith—great or small—recede into the background. Faith cannot be measured—even the smallest faith has an unexpected power. The saying, therefore, is not really about great or small faith, but about faith or unbelief. Lk 17:11–19 also deals with faith, as verse 19 explicitly states. The Samaritan's return to Jesus and his praise of God express the faith which, as Jesus tells him, has saving power. Both Lk 17:5–6 and 17:11–19 deal with the power of faith.

Jesus' instruction ends with a parable, Lk 17:7–10, which shows several indications of Lucan redaction. Luke stylistically revised a parable which he found in his special material. Its affirmation is clear: in the context of Luke it is directed against all self-righteousness and all considerations of reward on grounds of one's own performance. It is addressed to the apostles (and Luke's community); even where they have done everything that is expected from them, they should not think that they have special merit; there can be no question of gratitude (cf. Lk 17:9). Here again there may be a connection with Lk 17:11–19, in which verse 16 speaks of the gratitude which the returning Samaritan shows to Jesus. In the corresponding rhetorical questions, especially verse 18, this thanksgiving is not repeated, but only the praise given to God. This may suggest that Jesus did not claim any thanks for what he had done and thus displayed the attitude he expected from his disciples.[177]

Lk 17:11–19 in relation to Lk 17:20–21

There are good grounds for thinking that with Lk 17:11–19 the evangelist begins the last great section in the Travel Narrative under the unifying theme of 'the coming of the kingdom of God', and the consequences people should draw from it. In this context Lk 17:11–19 expresses a basic idea which will be further developed in the following pericopes. In this context the healing of the ten lepers of itself raises the question about the 'when' of the coming of the kingdom of God (verse 20a), which serves again as introduction to the following eschatological instruction (Lk 17:20b–37).[178] The healing of the ten lepers is about the right kind of faith in him who has received from God the power to cleanse people from leprosy. Returning to Jesus and giving God praise, the Samaritan acknowledges faithfully that in the person of Jesus and his activity God's kingdom is present. The question of the Pharisees, therefore, only confirms what has already been made clear in Lk 17:11–19.

With good reason it has been stated that Lk 17:20–21 was composed by Luke, possibly partly from traditional material, as a product of his redactional work, which thus goes beyond Lk 17:11–19. If Luke composed Lk 17:20–21, one should not over-interpret the question of the Pharisees. Its literary function is to make Jesus' answer possible. This answer is addressed not only to the Pharisees of Jesus' time, but also to a Pharisaic tendency in Luke's community. The 'new Pharisees' are warned because of their wrong attitude towards the kingdom of God and its coming and, therefore, ultimately towards Jesus himself.

Jesus' answer contains three parts, two negative (Lk 17:20b–21a) and one positive (Lk 17:21b). The two negative statements can be considered as practically synonymous. The positive statement, 'the kingdom of God is in the midst of you', is Jesus' answer to the Pharisees' 'when'. They fail to see that in the person and the activity of Jesus the kingdom of God is present among them. The returning Samaritan saw what the Pharisees fail to see: the presence of the kingdom in Jesus. The Pharisees, therefore, stand on the same level as the nine lepers.

This state of things is illustrated in the dramatic episode, Lk 17:11–19, in order clearly and intelligibly to represent Jesus' word concerning the kingdom of God 'in your midst'. The miracle constitutes an ideal setting for the question about the kingdom and Jesus' answer that it is in their midst, in that it relates how the lepers are granted restoration to a state of wholeness. Therefore, Luke is not starting an altogether new theme in Lk 17:20. Rather, Lk 17:11–19 and 17:20–21 complement each other. The latter may be understood as 'exemplary word' (German: *Deutewort*) to the miracle story, while the question concerning the kingdom of God is already forcibly posed by the cleansing of the ten lepers. The kingdom of God, present in the person of Jesus, experienced in his miraculous activity—faith or unbelief as possible human responses to the kingdom of God present in Jesus as the endtime prophet—these are the basic theological lines which connect Lk 17:11–19 with its context, and find a visible presentation in the account.[179]

The wider context

Apart from Lk 17:11–19 Luke refers in three passages to the cleansing of lepers. Two of these are found in the sayings tradition, Lk 4:27 and Lk 7:22 (Q). The third text deals with another cleansing of a leper, which Luke derives from Mark (Lk 5:12–16 = Mk 1:40–45). (See above, Chapter 4.)

Mention of Naaman's cleansing in Lk 4:27

With Lk 4:25f., Lk 4:27 forms a double saying reminding the reader of two episodes from the Elijah- and Elisha-tradition: I Kgs 17 and II Kgs 5. The importance of the 'programmatic sermon' of Lk 4:16–30 which 'as a whole is a product of Lukan editorial activity',[180] has often been emphasized. The double saying occurs in the second part of the pericope, the theme of which is the rejection of Jesus by his compatriots. In this rejection Jesus shares the fate of the prophets, as is stated in verse 24, in which the key word 'prophet' carries the principal weight, and prepares for verses 25–27, which are again in a sense the basis for verses 28–30.

Verses 25–27, which were introduced at a later stage into the Nazareth pericope, have a parallel structure. Scholars do not agree on whether the combination of the Elijah- and Elisha-sayings is pre-Lucan or Lucan. A good number of grounds favour the second opinion. With reference to the missions of Elijah and Elisha, Jesus announces the hour of the Gentiles and the rejection of Israel. This prophetic claim of Jesus explains his complete rejection by the multitude. The reference to Elijah and Elisha is also a reference to the proclamation of salvation to the Gentiles.

The Elisha–Naaman story provides in part the structure/pattern for the healing of the ten lepers. Moreover, Lk 17:11–19 makes clear what was announced in Nazareth: the gift of salvation to the Gentiles, since they acknowledge Jesus' powerful deeds as the beginning of the time of salvation. All ten are cleansed of leprosy. But only for the Samaritan, the foreigner, does this healing mean salvation, because he recognizes it as an act of him who by order of God brings the kingdom (compare Lk 17:21). By returning to Jesus and giving praise to God, the Samaritan shows the faith which Jesus has not found in Israel (compare Lk 7:9). It is the belief that through Jesus, the eschatological prophet who is greater than Elisha, the kingdom is already present. Like the people of Nazareth, the nine in Lk 17:11–19 and the Pharisees do not accept this. But these obvious parallels do not necessarily mean that Lk 4:27 is the basis in tradition-history for Lk 17:11–19. There are good reasons to believe that Luke himself shaped Lk 4:27, possibly in anticipation of the Samaritan pericope in Lk 17.[181]

Reference to the cleansing of lepers in Lk 7:22

Lk 7:22 (parallel Mt 11:4–5) occurs in the context of Jesus' answer to John the Baptist's question in Lk 7:19–20 (parallel Mt 11:2–3). A comparison with Matthew suggests that Luke found the whole pericope in the Q-source, but this did not prevent him from placing it in a new context and redactionally altering the indications of its situation. Verses 20–21, which have no parallel in Matthew, may be attributed to Luke. Verse 21 has been called 'an illustration of the programme set out in IV, 18ff.'.[182] In Lk 7:22 we have a saying which was already connected in Q with John the Baptist's question. This does not necessarily mean that both can be traced to the historical Jesus and John the Baptist.[183]

Jesus' answer is composed of three parts. First, Jesus' commission to the disciples of John to go and tell him what they see and hear. Second, an enumeration of several miracles and a reference to the proclamation of the gospel to the poor. And finally, a macarism, 'blessed is he...'. The second part consists of six elements, all taken from Isaiah:
— the blind receive their sight (Isa 29:18; 35:5; 42:18; 61:1).
— the lame walk (Isa 35:6).
— lepers are cleansed (Isa 35:8; compare II Kgs 5).
— the deaf hear (Isa 29:18; 35:5; 42:18).
— the dead are raised up (Isa 26:19; compare I Kgs 17; II Kgs 4).
— the poor have the good news preached to them (Isa 29:19; 61:1).
Isa 61:1 seems to have determined the framework, that is the basic text, and Isa 35:5-6 the order of the enumeration. The references to the cleansing of lepers and the raising of the dead are especially remarkable. They are, however, two miracles attributed to Elijah (I Kgs 17:17-24) and Elisha (II Kgs 4:18-37; II Kgs 5). Since these prophet-traditions have influenced several synoptic texts (Mk 5:22-24, 35-42 and parallels; Lk 7:11-17), it is not impossible that the Elisha-tradition played a role in the addition of 'lepers are cleansed'. The inclusion of the cleansing of lepers and the raising of the dead as prophetic miracles suggests that Jesus' miracles are understood as the powerful deeds of the endtime prophet. While the first five elements refer to Jesus as the miracle-working prophet of the endtime, the last (compare Lk 6:20ff.) designates him as the messenger of good news (Isa 61:1).

Luke has heightened the motif of miracle-working by inserting a summary of Jesus' miraculous activity (Lk 7:21). Moreover, he places the pericope of John's question (Lk 7:18-23) right after the healing of the centurion's servant (Lk 7:1-10) and the raising of the young man of Nain (Lk 7:11-17). Luke, then, emphasizes Jesus' powerful deeds in which the kingdom of God manifests itself. But since in Lk 7:23 Luke refers also to the possibility of taking offence, the meaning of faith becomes clearer. We thus find ourselves again close to the train of thought developed in Lk 17:11-19 and its context.[184]

The cleansing of the leper (Lk 5:12-16 and parallels)

Luke sticks essentially to Mk 1:40-45 (see Chapter 2 above). Unique in this account is the leper's request, 'If you *will*, you can make me clean' (Lk 5:12 and parallels), in which Jesus' will is directly characterized as God's will, and Jesus' power as God's power. The leper expresses in his request his faith in Jesus, by asking him something which according to current beliefs only God could do: the cleansing of a leper was considered equal to the raising of a dead person. However, already in the Elisha–Naaman story it appeared that God could use a prophet to do this. By addressing himself so explicitly to Jesus' will, the leper credits him with more than the Old Testament prophets. Jesus' answer confirms the leper's confidence. In Luke's redaction the cleansing seems to be a specific illustration of Lk 5:15b, 'and great multitudes gathered to hear and to be healed of their infirmities', in a way reminiscent of the relationship between Lk 17:11–19 and 17:20–21. Lk 5:12–16 and 17:11–19 share the description of Jesus' activity as greater than that of the prophets. Both also agree in presenting Jesus as the one in whom God's saving intervention manifests itself to whoever approaches him in faith. Although not in exactly the same way as the Samaritan, the leper of Lk 5:12–16 also clearly shows signs of faith.[185]

Analysis of the text

> **Verse 11:** On the way to Jerusalem he was passing along between Samaria and Galilee.

The expression *kai egeneto*, 'and it happened', usually not translated in English, but Luke's 'favourite form of preface', indicates the beginning of an altogether new act. The whole expression, literally, 'and it happened in the going', is a favourite Lucan formula which clearly shows the influence of the Septuagint. The clause 'he was passing...' is also dependent on the Septuagint. The verb *poreuesthai*, 'to go, to travel', is characteristic of Luke (about fifty-one times in the gospel and thirty-seven times in Acts). Used in connection with Jerusalem, it has a special meaning for Luke (Lk 9:51, 53; Acts 19:21). Even when Jerusalem is not explicitly mentioned *poreuesthai* is a reminder of Jesus' journey to Jerusalem (Lk 9:57; 10:38; 13:33; 19:28).

For Luke, Jerusalem is a 'theological' place.[186] But it is not only the place of Jesus' suffering. Also in Jerusalem, the risen Christ meets the disciples (Lk 24:34, 36ff.); by his word they must stay there 'until you are clothed with power from on high' (Lk 24:49; compare Acts 1:4). In Jerusalem too the mission begins (compare Acts 2:1ff.), and from there it expands (Lk 24:47; Acts 1:8). Not only the solemn Old Testament style, but also the notice that Jesus was on his way to *Jerusalem* gives weight to this introductory verse of a pericope which by its mention of Jerusalem forms the beginning of a larger section of several literary units, beyond Lk 17:11–19.

The verb *dierchesthai*, 'to pass along', is often used by Luke after the example of the Septuagint (ten times in Luke; twenty-one times in Acts, against twice in Mark and once in Matthew). He uses it to say that Jesus 'went about doing good and healing all that were oppressed by the devil' (Acts 10:38), as well as to describe the journeys of early Christian missionaries.[187] The clearest verbal parallel to Lk 17:11c is Lk 4:30, 'but passing through the midst of them he went away' (*autos de dielthōn dia mesou autōn eporeueto*), the conclusion of the programmatic scene at the beginning of Jesus' 'Galilean' ministry.

Like Lk 17:11, 'Galilee and Samaria', some passages in Acts also mention two regions (Acts 15:3, 41; 16:6; 18:23; 19:21). Except for Lk 17:11, Samaria is mentioned in the New Testament only in Acts (seven times) and John (three times). Luke's repeated mention of and positive attitude to Samaria is characteristic of him. Jesus' prohibition, 'enter no town of the Samaritans' (Mt 10:5), is not found in Luke. In the Acts of the Apostles Samaria is mission country and constitutes the next stage of the mission after Jerusalem and Judea (Acts 1:8). Luke's three Samaritan pericopes (Lk 9:51–56; 10:30–37; 17:11–19) show a special interest in the Samaritans. Jesus' contact with them, as is clear from Lk 9:51–56 and 17:11–19, originates apparently from Luke's intention to anchor the Samaritan mission of Acts in Jesus' life and mission.

Unlike Samaria, Galilee is often mentioned in the New Testament (sixty-one times). Compared with Mark, Luke has a very personal way of using Galilee. Only in Lk 4:14 does he take the term over from Mk 1:14, while he introduces it in five texts where it is not found in Mark (Lk 4:31; 5:17; 8:26; 23:49, 55), and it occurs four times in special Lucan material (Lk 1:26; 2:4, 39; 3:1). Galilee is not just a region of Palestine, but rather the place that marks the beginning of Jesus' ministry, 'teaching throughout all Judea, from Galilee even to this place' (Lk 23:5; compare Acts 10:37). Luke also specially mentions those who have followed Jesus from Galilee to Jerusalem (Lk 23:49, 55).

The association of Samaria and Galilee is also found in Acts 9:31 (together with Judea). In both cases the order 'Samaria and Galilee' is the same, and is therefore probably from Luke's hand. As to the topographical reference which underlies Lk 17:11, many opinions have been expressed. Most interpreters understand it to mean 'in between Samaria and Galilee', i.e., along the border of Samaria and Galilee, but often disagree on the direction from which Jesus approached this border. It is especially intriguing that Samaria is mentioned before Galilee. Most probably, Samaria is mentioned first simply because of the important part played by the Samaritan in the account, and no deep explanation is called for. 'The geographical statement is totally obscure...But Luke's only purpose is to account for the presence of a Samaritan...among the Jews.'[188] The whole expression is definitely Lucan and reveals a typically Lucan topographical reference in which this indication does not contradict the previous indication 'on the way to Jerusalem'.[189]

When in his solemn Old Testament style Luke begins an account by saying that Jesus went up to Jerusalem, this is not just an indication of the goal of his journey. Jerusalem is the place of Jesus' death and resurrection, of his appearances to his disciples, and his ascension. In Jerusalem the disciples receive the Spirit and the mission begins. It is the place where Jesus experiences acceptance and rejection; faith and unbelief is also the reaction there to the preaching of the disciples (Acts 2:13, 37ff.). Jerusalem is the place of the beginning of the mission which from there reaches out beyond Judea and Samaria to the end of the earth (Acts 1:8; 9:31), and in the mission of *Samaria* (Acts 8:5ff.) goes beyond the circle of the Jews and includes for the first time 'foreigners' (heathen). Among them the message is accepted with a faith which was not found among the Jews. The Samaritan and the nine in Lk 17:11–19 represent the two poles of this tension. Also in Galilee (Lk 4:15, 28–30) and in Samaria (Lk 9:52; 10:1, 17) Jesus and his disciples experience acceptance and rejection. In the context of Luke-Acts, then, and alongside Jerusalem, 'Samaria and Galilee' suggest the basic tension of the account: faith and unbelief.[190]

Verse 11 is probably a Lucan creation, similar to other introductions in Lk 9:51, 52, 56; 13:22; 19:11, which can be explained by the evangelist's tendency to superimpose his own geographical framework upon the material which he incorporates in his work.[191]

Verse 12: And as he entered a village, he was met by ten lepers, who stood at a distance

λεπροι ἄνδρες

In verse 12a we have a third indication of situation: 'as he entered a village' (after 'on the way to Jerusalem' and 'between Samaria and Galilee' in verse 11). The verb *eiserchesthai*, 'to enter', is used about fifty times in Luke and thirty-two times in Acts and is often redactional. Apart from Lk 17:12, it is used in combination with *eis kōmēn*, '(into) a village', in Lk 9:52 and 10:38. The vague indication 'a village' is typical of Luke, and it has been maintained that Luke's geographical and topographical material 'is a purely literary device...employed...to heighten the effect of his account, not because they actually meant anything concrete to him'.[192] All attempts to locate the village should therefore be considered futile.

The real action begins in verse 12b, 'he was met by ten lepers'. Apart from Lk 17:12 the verb *apantaō*, 'to meet', is found in the New Testament only in Mk 14:13 (different in Luke), but it is used more often in the Septuagint. The number 'ten' is used nine times in Luke against once in Mark and three times in Matthew. Since Luke has the tendency to omit numbers mentioned in Mark (e.g., Lk 5:18 compared with Mk 2:3), the use of 'ten' here may be considered the result of deliberate choice. This is confirmed by the further use of the numbers 'nine' and 'one'. The contrast between these numbers belongs to the essence of the account. Unlike the New Testament where outside Luke and the Apocalypse the number 'ten' does not play an important part, in the Old Testament it is found in important contexts (Ex 34:28; Deut 4:13; 10:4) and is there the symbol of a rounded-off whole; ten representatives can legitimately represent the whole community (Ruth 4:2). It is, however, difficult to establish whether Luke would have been aware of this background. Four lepers are mentioned as a group in II Kgs 7:3.

The adjective *lepros*, 'leprous', is found only here in the New Testament, but often occurs in the Septuagint (Lev 13:44; II Sam 3:29; II Kgs 7:3, etc.). The word *anēr*, 'man', is a favourite word of Luke's (twenty-seven times in Luke; a hundred times in Acts; four times in Mark; eight times in Matthew). The expression *deka andres*, 'ten men', is found only here in the New Testament, but seven times in the Septuagint. Only in II Kgs 7:3, which is not too far from the story of Naaman (II Kgs 5), do we find another text dealing with *several* (four) lepers. The question exactly which kind of leprosy the story talks about must be left open. More important is that any kind of leprosy made the leper cultically unclean and thus excluded him from the community. Leprosy was considered a severe punishment from heaven (Num 12:10–15; II Chron 26:19).

The lepers stood 'at a distance', in Greek *porrōthen*, which occurs only here and in Heb 11:13 in the New Testament, but sixteen times in the Septuagint. The phrase is based on Num 5:2–3; Lev 13:46. The author of verse 12, who may be Luke, as several indications suggest, continues to use the vocabulary of the Septuagint.[193]

The clause 'who stood at a distance' is usually understood as referring to the prohibition to lepers against approaching healthy people. But no trace of this prohibition is found in the other cleansing of a leper (Mk 1:40–45 parallel Lk 5:12–16), and besides, Luke's special material contains several references to 'far' and 'at a distance' (Lk 15:13, 20; 16:23, followed in 16:24 by 'Father Abraham, have mercy upon me'!; 18:13). In the same context Acts 2:39 should be mentioned: 'For the promise is to you and to your children and to all that are far off, every one whom the Lord our God calls to him'. The text may refer to the Gentile mission by which God calls to himself those who were far (Isa 57:19; Eph 2:13, 17). Thus 'at a distance' in

Lk 17:12 may also have a deeper, theological meaning. This is supported by the observation that many Psalms speak in similar terms about being far from God: 'Why do you stand afar off, O Lord?' (Ps 10:1); 'Why are you so far from helping me, from the words of my groaning?' (Ps 22:1b); 'Be not far from me, for trouble is near and there is none to help' (Ps 22:11); 'But you, O Lord, be not far off! O you my help, hasten to my aid!' (Ps 22:19). Guilt, suffering and persecution cause not only religious isolation, but also cultic uncleanness. A sick person is not fit to perform worship. He calls on God 'from afar' and waits for the saving word (Ps 130:5). His condition also causes social isolation: 'My friends and companions stand aloof from my plague, and my kinsmen stand afar off' (Ps 38:11). Unlike Lk 17:12, in the Psalms it is always the sufferer who looks towards God; it is God who is 'far off', while in Lk 17:12 the narrator stands with Jesus, and the lepers 'stood at a distance'. But despite this difference, the same experience is expressed in both instances: their existence is characterized by 'being at a distance'—from Jesus, or from their fellow human beings.[194]

On his way to the city in which he will experience acceptance and rejection, while travelling through regions in which he encounters faith and unbelief, Jesus is met by ten lepers. Unlike the leper of Lk 5:12–16, they remain at a distance, which in Luke's account has less to do with existing regulations than with the fundamental distance between Jesus and the ten which—at least for nine of them—even the miracle of their cleansing does not bridge.[195]

Verse 13: and lifted up their voices and said, 'Jesus, Master, have mercy on us.'

The expression *ēran phōnēn*, 'they lifted up their voices', continues the biblical style of the previous verses. In the New Testament the expression is found only here and in Acts 4:24, where it introduces a solemn prayer of the early Christian community: 'And when they heard it, they lifted their voices together to God and said, "Sovereign Lord..." '. In the Old Testament the expression 'to lift up one's voice' is almost always combined with the verb 'to weep' (Judg 2:4; 21:2f.; I Sam 24:16; 30:4, etc.), the utterance of a shaken soul. While the expression 'to lift up one's voice' is not found in the Psalms (but see Ps 93:3, 'the floods have lifted up their voice'), they contain several expressions in which people, in a way similar to Lk 17:13, address themselves to God with a loud voice (Ps 28:1–2, etc.). When in Lk 17:12 the lepers 'lifted up their voices and said', the formulation shows a close relationship with the vocabulary and the motifs of Old

Testament prayer language. It expresses their situation of special distance as well as their cultic-social isolation and the anguish of soul at being far from God.[196] The clause is again patterned in imitation of the Septuagint (e.g., Judg 2:4; 9:7; 21:2).

The address 'Jesus' does not often occur in the New Testament (five times in Luke; once in Acts; three times in Mark; none in Matthew). Apart from Lk 23:42, it is never found alone but always combined with a title or another designation; 'Jesus of Nazareth' (Lk 4:34), 'Jesus, Son of the Most High God' (Lk 8:28), 'Jesus, Son of David' (Lk 18:38), and here in Lk 17:13, 'Jesus, Master'.

The word *epistatēs*, 'master', occurs in the New Testament only in Luke (seven times), and twelve times in the Septuagint. Luke uses it four times where his source has *didaskale*, 'teacher'. Apart from Lk 17:13, *epistatēs* always serves as an address by people who belong to the circle of disciples, whereas *didaskale*, 'teacher', is attributed to people who are not disciples, or opponents. We also find *kurie*, 'lord', as an address by disciples and people in need. In Lk 17:13 *kurie* would be expected rather than *epistata*. So, in this verse Luke may have found *epistata* in his source.

The use of 'master' seems to suggest that the lepers were already on friendly terms with Jesus. It has been pointed out that in all instances where people use *epistata*, 'master', they misunderstand Jesus' *exousia*, 'authority/power', and their faith can be considered only preliminary. This interpretation also seems to fit Lk 17:13. Nine of the lepers who address Jesus as 'master' have only a 'preliminary' faith. They ask Jesus for mercy, obey his order, but do not understand the real meaning of their cleansing.

In Luke, the formula 'have mercy on us' occurs only four times (Lk 16:24; 17:13; 18:38, 39). In the tradition it had its fixed place in the healings of the blind (Mk 10:47, 48 parallel Lk 18:38, 39). Luke may have introduced the expression in Lk 17:13 from Lk 18:38, 39. In fact, the present verse is reminiscent of Lk 18:38f., 'And he cried, "Jesus, Son of David, have mercy on me"...but he cried out all the more, "Son of David, have mercy on me!" ' It has even been suggested that the whole of Lk 17:11–19 has been influenced by Lk 18:35–43. At any rate, the address bears several marks of Lucan composition.[197]

The lepers try to bridge the distance by their loud cries for mercy (compare Pss 27:7; 86:6). They approach Jesus with the prayer which in the Old Testament is addressed to God especially in the Psalms. The supplication 'Jesus, Master, have mercy on us' is closely related to Ps 123:3, 'Have mercy upon us, O Lord, have mercy upon us'. The ten lepers turn to Jesus in the same way as the afflicted of the Old Testament turn to God.

Verse 14: When he saw them he said to them, 'Go and show yourselves to the priests'. And as they went they were cleansed.

The beginning of verse 14, literally, 'and seeing he said to them', should not be understood as if Jesus first *saw* the lepers and then *spoke* to them (should one not rather expect *heard* in that case?), but as an example of biblical style where *idōn*, 'seeing', is often used pleonastically (e.g., Gen 18:2; 38:15; 49:15). There is a definite connection between 'seeing' and 'saving' in the Old Testament as well as in the gospel of Luke (e.g., Lk 13:12). The situation described in Lk 17:13–14 corresponds closely to that presented in Lk 15:20. Just as 'while he was yet at a distance, his father saw him', and ran to him to bring about reconciliation, so Jesus 'saw' the lepers who called out to him for mercy from 'a distance', and healed them.[198]

Jesus' order, 'go and show', should again be understood in a pleonastic way. The expression may have been influenced by Lk 5:14, 'go and show', and II Kgs 5:10, 'go and wash'. The beginning of verse 14b (*kai egeneto en tōi hupagein*) constitutes a clear parallel with the beginning of verse 11 (*kai egeneto en tōi poreuesthai*) which forms a syntactic framework around verses 11–14. Luke uses different verbs for the lepers' going (*hupagein*) and for Jesus' going to Jerusalem (*poreuesthai*—but see Lk 17:19, *poreuou*, 'go your way'!) which has for him a highly theological meaning. The verb 'to cleanse' is often used in the Septuagint to refer to the cure of a leper (Lev 13:6, 7, 13, 17, 28, etc.). Luke uses it seven times in his gospel and three times in Acts. The passive 'were cleansed' presents the healing as a divine act (II Kgs 5:10; compare 5:14). The description of the action is here clearly more influenced by II Kgs 5:8–19 than by Lk 5:12–16 (as can also be shown by a comparison of the structure of the different accounts).

The healing of the lepers happened while they were on their way to the priests. Indeed the account leaves no doubt that all ten lepers were healed. That Jesus does not heal them right away, as in Lk 5:12–16, but sends them off unhealed is, in comparison with II Kgs 5:10–12, interpreted by a number of scholars as a test of faith. But this certainly remains in the background. The account stresses not that the nine *did* pass the faith test, but that after their cleansing they *did not* praise God and thank Jesus. The feature of the sending creates the necessary distance between Jesus and the lepers which makes it possible for one of them to *return*.[199] For Luke faith appears only in the return to Jesus *after* the cleansing. He therefore avoids speaking of faith in the first part of the account. The feature of the sending and return may be dependent on the Naaman story. Elisha sent Naaman to the Jordan; surpassing the Naaman story, the ten lepers are cleansed along the way. Their obedience results in a healing at a distance (compare Lk 7:7–10).

Without doubt, verse 14 concludes the miracle story proper, which is framed by the expression *kai egeneto*, 'and it happened' (not translated in English) in verses 11 and 14. The account reached a first peak in the request for Jesus' mercy (verse 13). However, with 'they were cleansed' the deliverance from leprosy is established. Here the first scene reaches its climax: the fulfilment of the request, the removal of the distress. As such, nothing indicates a continuation of the account. However, with 'then one of them' a second scene begins which likewise reaches its climax in a 'healing', which with the words 'has saved' takes on a more comprehensive meaning than 'they were cleansed'.[200]

Verse 15: Then one of them, when he saw that he was healed, turned back, praising God with a loud voice;

The beginning of verse 15 constitutes a clear break with the previous. Not only does the subject change, but with 'one', which is emphasized by 'then' (*de* could be translated 'but') and placed at the beginning of the clause, a totally new subject appears, which is further specified by the partitive genitive 'of them', thus assuring the logical connection with the previous subject. The phrases 'praising God' and 'giving him thanks' (verse 16b) are parallel. The former seems to be the more important phrase since it is referred to once more in verse 18, 'to return and give praise to God', while the actions of verse 16 are not mentioned a second time.

As introduction to a sentence, the expression '(then) one of them' is found only here in the New Testament. Since Luke has the tendency to omit numbers, it is almost certain that here where it is placed at the beginning of a sentence, 'one' receives a special emphasis, and may be read as 'only one!' This one leper becomes 'a leading actor...the others become secondary actors'.[201]

The expression *idōn hoti*, 'seeing that', occurs in Luke only here and in Lk 8:47, but several times in Acts and may be attributed to Luke. The phrase *iathē*, 'he was healed', is found eleven times in Luke and four times in Acts, against once in Mark, four times in Matthew, and four in John. In New Testament cures of *lepers*, however, what is found is usually not 'healed' but 'cleansed'. In the Septuagint 'to heal' is used of lepers in Lev 14:3, 48; Num 12:13. It seems that the use of 'he was healed' should here be attributed to Luke. It is possible that he used it for stylistic purposes, i.e., to avoid the repetition of 'cleansed' (verses 14 and 17), but it is remarkable that the latter word is used twice for the *ten*, while the *one* who returns is 'healed'. Luke may be using this 'neutral' term here as a transition from the technical term 'they were cleansed' to the highly significant 'saved' (verse 19).

That Jesus uttered his promise of healing 'when he saw (*idōn*) them' corresponds to the present note that 'one of them, when he saw (*idōn*) that he was healed, turned back'. To Jesus' merciful, saving 'seeing' there corresponds the insightful 'seeing' of the Samaritan. The correspondence between the two is not accidental and plays a part in the structure of the account. A similar agreement is found in Lk 5:1–11. The calling of the first disciples begins with the note that Jesus 'saw two boats by the lake' (Lk 5:2), and selected Peter's boat, which led on to the miraculous catch of fish. Peter's conversion and following is introduced by the words 'But when Simon Peter saw it, he fell at Jesus' feet...'. The Samaritan who returned 'saw that he was healed'. The nine others must also have noticed that they were cured, but this one man's seeing was different, meaning that he had understood what happened to him. For this Samaritan the very concept of healing received a deeper meaning: the realization 'that he was healed' became the realization that he was 'saved' (*sesōken*; RSV: 'has made (you) well').[202]

In Luke-Acts the connection between the experience of salvation in 'seeing' and the faithful, praising response of the person concerned has special importance. In Lk 2:15, 17, after the appearance of the angels, the shepherds go to Bethlehem to 'see this thing that has happened'. Afterwards they 'returned, glorifying God for all they had heard and seen, as it had been told them' (Lk 2:20). Simeon was promised that 'he should not see death before he had seen the Lord's Christ' (Lk 2:26). At the presentation of Jesus in the Temple Simeon 'blessed God...for my eyes have seen your salvation' (Lk 2:28, 30). Acts 9:32–35, the healing of Aeneas by Peter, ends with the remark: 'And all the residents of Lydda and Sharon saw him, and they turned to the Lord'. In the healing of the paralytic we are told: 'And all the people saw him walking and praising God' (Acts 3:9). At the end of the healing of Bartimaeus, Lk 18:43 considerably reformulates Mk 10:52. While Mark says only that the blind man saw again and followed Jesus, Luke adds the motif of 'praising God', and again, 'and all the people, when they saw it, gave praise to God'. Lk 18:43 particularly indicates that the connection between 'seeing' and 'praising' betrays to some extent a literary preference of the evangelist's, but since most of the instances are found in Luke's special material and in Acts it is difficult to determine exactly to what extent Luke has edited his sources.[203]

The verb *hupostrephein*, 'to return', is used twenty-one times in Luke and twelve times in Acts, while it does not occur in the other gospels. It may be said, therefore, that Luke has a special predilection for the motif of 'return'. Just as after his cleansing Naaman returned to Elisha, so one of the cleansed men returned to Jesus. That one out of ten returned is emphasized so strongly as to recall the one sheep out of a hundred (Lk 15:3–7) or the one drachma out of ten (Lk 15:8–10). Since these parables deal among other things with conversion, *metanoia*, return, it is not excluded that Lk 17:11–19 also alludes to it.

The participle-construction 'praising God' is found only in Luke in the New Testament (Lk 2:20; 5:25; 17:15; 18:43). The object of this praise in Luke-Acts is most of the time God, twice Jesus (Lk 4:15; Acts 3:13), and once 'the word of the Lord' (Acts 13:48). Praise of God in Luke is always the reaction of people who receive or are witnesses of a marvellous event. In three instances Jesus' deeds are the occasion for praising God (Lk 7:16; 8:39; 23:47; cf. Lk 17:18). The phrase 'with a loud voice' recalls 'lifted up their voices' of verse 13. This may suggest that the 'praise of God' of the one is 'louder' than the request of the ten.[204]

The Samaritan praises God with a loud voice. This reminds us of the multitude of disciples who at the descent of the Mount of Olives 'began to rejoice and praise God with a loud voice for all the mighty works that they had seen' (Lk 19:37; in particular, the last part of the verse constitutes an interesting parallel with Lk 17:15). Elsewhere in the gospel too, the powerful deeds of Jesus draw praise to God from the people (Lk 7:16: Jesus himself is referred to as a prophet; Lk 23:47: Jesus himself is called 'innocent' or 'just'). In parallel with II Kgs 5:15 the praise of God precedes the thanks given to Jesus, which, moreover, is not repeated in verse 18. But Jesus is not dissociated from the praise given to God.

Verse 16: and he fell on his face at Jesus' feet, giving him thanks. Now he was a Samaritan.

While the expressions 'to fall on one's face' and '(to fall) at somebody's feet' (Mk 5:22; 7:25) are both found in the tradition, the combination of the two occurs only in Lk 17:16. The expression 'to fall on one's face' occurs in Luke only here and in Lk 5:12 (different Mk 1:40; Mt 8:2), in both cases most probably influenced by the Septuagint, where it occurs forty-four times (e.g., Gen 17:3, 17; Lev 9:24). In more than half the Septuagint passages the expression refers to God or to a messenger of God, but it is also applied to other persons (Ruth 2:10; II Sam 9:6, etc.). In the New Testament people fall on their faces before Jesus and God. In contrast to other New Testament writings, Luke uses it only with regard to Jesus. It may here be attributed to Luke.

Whereas Mark and Matthew use the verb *eucharistein*, 'to thank', only in a eucharistic or quasi-eucharistic sense, in Lk 18:11 we find it used in the sense of 'to thank' (see also Acts 27:35; 28:15). In these instances the thanks are addressed to God, except in Lk 17:16 where 'him' clearly refers to Jesus. This is in fact the only place in the New Testament where thanks are explicitly expressed in a healing story, presumably under the influence of the Naaman story (II Kgs 5:15). The action of giving thanks is secondary to that of glorifying God. It has been noted that verses 15–16 are arranged in a chiastic structure:

then one of them
    praising *God* with a loud voice
  turned back;
  and he fell
    on his face at *Jesus'* feet, giving him thanks;
now he was a Samaritan.

The phrases 'praising God' and 'fell (falling) on his face at Jesus' feet' are clearly parallel. In this way Luke places Jesus in parallel with God and in God's immediate vicinity. Whereas Luke, unlike Mark and Matthew, avoids the use of *proskunein*, 'to prostrate', in reference to Jesus until after the resurrection (Lk 24:52), he does refer to worship of Jesus during his ministry, though in a veiled way and in close relation to God's activity through Jesus. From now on the only place where one can properly give thanks to God is at Jesus' feet.

One of the centres of gravity of Lk 17:11–19 is situated in the affirmation that the right place for praising God is Jesus himself. As God's representative, Jesus is the locus where God is to be praised.[205] This is already presupposed in the return of the Samaritan. Exactly what place Jesus occupies in this connection is expressed in the conduct of the returned man: 'he fell on his face at Jesus' feet, giving him thanks'. Luke has given the whole scene a 'liturgical' character. Even though before the ascension the evangelist does not use the verb *proskunein*, 'to prostrate', there cannot be any doubt about the place which Jesus occupies. In the light of II Kgs 5:15 where Naaman 'returned to the man of God...and came and stood before him', it becomes clear that Jesus' dignity far exceeds that of the prophet Elisha, who would not have allowed Naaman to fall down before him, and who actually refused the thanks of the Syrian. But see also II Kgs 4:37, 'She came and fell at his feet, bowing to the ground'.

'One of them' is now emphatically (*kai autos*; compare Lk 1:22; 3:23; 5:14; 6:20; 22:41; 24:25, 31) identified as a Samaritan. Apart from Lk 17:16, *a* Samaritan is mentioned only in Lk 10:33 (both in Luke's special material). If it is true that this indicates a particular interest of Luke's special source(s), Acts 1:8; 8:1, 5, 9, 14, 25; 9:31; 15:3 show that Luke's interest goes beyond that of his source(s). The clause 'now he was a Samaritan' is probably redactional.[206]

Like Naaman the Syrian, the returnee of Lk 17:11–19 is not a Jew; he is a Samaritan, and therefore in the eyes of the Jews a pagan. In his return and subsequent behaviour this non-Jew acts as the Jews should have acted. The Samaritan represents the pagan nations who turn to the Lord, whereby Luke expresses that the time of salvation has come. The contrast between the Samaritan and the nine others may be compared to that between the Samaritan and the priest and Levite in Lk 10:30–37. But by his return to Jesus and his praising God in Jesus' presence the Samaritan of Lk 17:11–19 surpasses the Samaritan of the parable. He recognizes that in Jesus he receives much more than the cleansing from leprosy. The miracle has for him the character of a sign which refers to Jesus. Therefore, within the journey towards Jerusalem, the Samaritan of Lk 17:11–19 occupies a place comparable to that of the centurion of Capernaum during Jesus' travels in Galilee (Lk 7:1–10). Both are contrasted with Israel, for they show the only attitude which truly responds to Jesus: faith.[207]

Verses 17–18: Then said Jesus, 'Were not ten cleansed? Where are the nine? (18) Was no one found to return and give praise to God except this foreigner?'

Verses 17–18 may well have been composed in imitation of original sayings of Jesus. One may also wonder whether the three questions constituted an original unity. Some scholars believe that the first two questions formed a double question expressing Jesus' astonishment that the nine others did not come back. It has also been pointed out that this double question is formally parallel to that found in Lk 13:15–16. The third question was probably added at a later stage, together with the secondary development in verse 16, 'now he was a Samaritan'.[208]

The phrase 'then he said', literally, 'then answering/taking the floor Jesus said', which constitutes another caesura or break in the account, introduces three rhetorical questions. A literal parallel to this solemn introduction is found in Lk 22:51 (and Mt 20:22). The name Jesus occurs about ninety times in Luke and sixty-eight times in Acts. In Luke almost half the occurrences are found in connection with a verb of speaking.

As is quite often the case in the Septuagint (e.g., Gen 18:9, 27; 24:50), it is not mentioned to whom the statements/questions are addressed. They do not immediately concern the Samaritan, but rather the disciples (Lk 17:5) and the Pharisees (Lk 17:20). They constitute a reflection which ultimately aims at the (real) addressees: Luke's community.

The subject of the first question, 'ten', refers back to the 'ten lepers' of verse 12. 'Were cleansed' is a traditional term which Luke last used in verse 14. The second question has as subject 'the nine', an entity logically implied by the expression 'one of them' in verse 15.

The subject of the third question is not explicitly mentioned, but it is clear that the 'nine' are meant who are the subject of the previous clause. Luke often uses the verb *heuriskein*,[209] 'to find', but apart from Lk 17:18, the passive 'to be found' occurs in Luke-Acts only in Lk 9:36; 15:24, 32; Acts 5:39; 8:40. As already mentioned under verse 15, *hupostrephein*, 'to return', is a favourite Lucan verb. Together with 'ten' and 'were cleansed', 'return' is repeated and constitutes a solid link with the earlier part of the story. The motif of the 'return' gives a paraenetic character to the account.

The expression 'to give praise (*doxa*, 'glory') to God' is obviously biblical. Apart from Lk 4:6 (different in Mt 4:9), the New Testament always says that glory is given to God. Luke speaks of Jesus' glory only in connection with the resurrection and exaltation (Lk 9:26; 21:27; 24:26; Acts 22:1: RSV, 'brightness'). Since there are hardly any abstract nouns in the account, one may suspect that the only two that are found in it—*doxa*, 'praise, glory' (verse 18) and *pistis*, 'faith' (verse 19)—have a special importance. Moreover, 'praise' is emphasized since it constitutes a resumption of 'praising God' in verse 15. In both cases it is God who is praised.

'This foreigner' stands in contrast with 'the nine' (adversative *ei mē*, rather than exceptive) and refers to the 'Samaritan' of verse 16. This part of the verse is apparently influenced by Lk 4:27, 'none of them was cleansed, but only (*ei mē*) Naaman the Syrian'. The word *allogenēs*, 'foreigner', occurs only here in the New Testament, but is found quite often in the Septuagint (e.g., Ex 12:43; 29:33; 30:33; Lev 22:10, 12, 13, 25). By calling the Samaritan a 'foreigner', Luke makes him a representative of all aliens[210] who were excluded from the Temple worship and therefore could not give glory to God where, according to the Jews, it should be done. But here a foreigner is said to give glory to God without having to break through the barriers of the Temple. He has found a new locus of worship (cf. Jn 4:21). 'The Samaritan returns to give thanks vis-a-vis the new temple, namely Jesus. This pericope, therefore, shows some affinity to John 4.'[211] For Luke, the Samaritan is one of the true worshippers mentioned in Jn 4:23. If Lk 17:11–19 is to be considered a transformation of Mk 1:40–45 parallel Lk 5:12–16, 'the detailed reshaping of the story...[is due to]...the switch to a mission to the Gentiles and inner dissociation from the Temple. If one wishes to thank God, one no longer uses the mediation of the Temple, but the mediation of Jesus'.[212] Lk 17:11–19 'presupposes the definite breach between Judaism and Christianity' and 'the success of the Christian mission to the Samaritans'.[213]

The three questions were developed from the story itself. Of course, Jesus 'knows' that all ten were cleansed. The question 'where are the nine?' can be answered only by 'with the priests'. That too Jesus must know since he sent them there himself. What is unusual is the behaviour not of the nine, but of the one who does not stick to Jesus' instructions. The third question is likewise rhetorical, since the fact that none but this foreigner has returned to give praise to God is obvious. No answer is expected to any of these questions. Moreover, who should give the answers? The Samaritan? This is definitely ruled out by the third question. Or the disciples mentioned in Lk 17:5? The account clearly leaves the question about the addressees open. The questions thereby acquire a meaning which goes beyond the immediate setting. The readers are drawn into the account and have to take a stand.

By these questions Luke intends to clarify what the account is all about. They are superfluous for the course of the action and add no new elements. Verse 19 could easily follow right after verse 16 and the introduction to Jesus' reply, 'and answering Jesus said' (verse 17a). Verses 17–18 are a commentary which Luke places on the lips of Jesus. By way of key words he repeats once more the whole account: 'the ten'—'were cleansed'—'no...to return and give praise to God'—'foreigner', thus letting us know what he emphasizes and which words are the real bearers of the message. 'The ten' and 'the foreigner' act like brackets at the beginning and the end of the three questions. In these questions, but especially in the third, Luke makes clear what theological message he intends to convey. The third question already shows what the faith of the Samaritan consists in: in his return to Jesus to give glory to God! The third question thus has, unlike the other two, the character of a real answer. Both vocabulary and style suggest that these verses may have been composed by Luke.[214]

It is a 'pagan' who praises God in Jesus' presence; the nine fail to come. That the Samaritan represents the pagans is clear from the fact that at the end of verse 18 Luke lets Jesus speak of 'this foreigner'. The return of the Samaritan seems here to be concerned only with 'praising God'. In the Old Testament, Israel was requested to proclaim the glory (*doxa*) of God and his miraculous deeds (Ps 96:2–3). But the pagan nations are also called to do this (Ps 96:7–9; Isa 42:12). In the New Testament, apart from Luke, the Book of

Revelation speaks especially of giving praise to God (Rev 14:6f.; 16:9; 19:7).

In the context of a miracle, the expression 'give God the praise' is also found in Jn 9:24. The cured man there designates Jesus as a prophet (Jn 9:17) and confesses him as being 'from God' (Jn 9:33). Finally he reaches faith in Jesus and worships him (Jn 9:38). Here too we find a close connection between 'giving praise to God' and faithful recognition of Jesus. Not simply praising God as such, but the combination of return to Jesus and praise given to God constitutes faith in the understanding of Lk 17:11–19. This is so because in Jesus God's salvation comes to people or, as Lk 17:21 expresses it, '(in him) the kingdom of God is in the midst of you' (compare Lk 11:20; 10:9, 11). The kingdom of God which has come near in Jesus is the real ground for returning to him and giving praise to God in his presence. This is the Christological affirmation of the account.[215]

> **Verse 19:** And he said to him, 'Rise and go your way; your faith has made you well.'

Jesus now addresses the Samaritan. The expression 'rise and go' presupposes that the Samaritan is still at Jesus' feet. Luke uses the verb *anistēmi*, 'to rise', twenty-six times in the gospel and forty-five times in Acts, and it is a favourite word of Luke's. The particular form of the verb used here, *anastas* (strong aorist participle), is found about thirty-five times in Luke-Acts. The verb also occurs often in the Septuagint. Luke apparently uses the expression 'rise and go' in imitation of the Septuagint. He uses the same combination of verbs also in Lk 1:39; 15:18; Acts 8:27; 22:10 (compare Acts 8:26; 9:11).

The verb *poreuesthai*, 'to go, to travel', occurs several times in Lucan miracle stories: Lk 5:24 and 8:48; see also Lk 7:8. In Lk 5:24 and 8:48 it is found in Jesus' final address to the healed person. The imperative 'go' in Luke is used almost exclusively by Jesus. It has therefore a special importance. In the Septuagint, the imperative 'go' is often combined with 'in peace' (e.g., II Kgs 5:19). In Lk 17:19 'in peace' does not occur, most probably because the decisive statement follows in the enunciation about faith.

The clause 'your faith has made you well/has saved you' occurs four times in Luke (Lk 7:50; 8:48; 17:19; 18:42). In Lk 8:48 and 18:42 it is derived from Mark (Mk 5:34; 10:52). Elsewhere in the gospels the expression does not occur in exactly this form. It is a fixed motif of the literary genre of miracle stories. In Lk 17:19 it constitutes an inclusion with Lk 17:5, 'Increase our faith!'

Luke likes to emphasize that faith saves (compare, e.g., Lk 8:50 and Mk 5:36). Besides Lk 17:19 Luke also speaks of 'saving' in connection with healing and liberation from bodily defects and demons in Lk 6:9; 8:36, 48, 50; 18:42 (compare Acts 4:9; 14:9). Among the synoptics Luke is the only one to use the title Saviour (Lk 1:47; 2:11; see also Acts 5:31; 13:23). Summing up, one may say that, more than Mark and Matthew, Luke has a special interest in 'saving faith'. See Acts 16:31, 'Believe in the Lord Jesus and you will be saved', where 'believe' (*pisteuein*) and 'to be saved' (*sōthēnai*) are almost identical. Salvific faith presupposes God's salvific activity in and through Jesus, but equally includes thankful praise of God as well as turning to Jesus.[216]

Some scholars have said that verse 19 does not entirely fit the account and would, therefore, be secondary. But these scholars are not consistent, since the caesura of the account is found at the end of verse 14, and so they should query not only verse 19, but the whole of verses 15–19. From verse 15 the account becomes a story about faith. As already said, Luke distinguishes between 'were cleansed'—'was healed'—'has made you well/saved you', and uses them to indicate a progression. All ten lepers were cleansed, but only one understood the meaning of this sign, returned to Jesus and praised God. Together with verses 15–18, verse 19 does therefore essentially belong to the account and fits it perfectly.[217]

Jesus dismisses the healed man with the formal assurance, 'your faith has made you well/saved you'. Thus Luke places the emphasis on the second part of the account.

> The final stress is produced by the fact that expositional motifs of approach (hindrance and faith) appear only after the miracle. Here the first outward approach is followed by a second, and it is only in this that the healed man breaks through the real barrier between himself and the miracle-worker.[218]

In line with the train of thought developed in the previous verses, verse 19 speaks of the faith of the Samaritan. Obviously the promise of faith and salvation, while surpassing it, stands in parallel to the statement that the ten 'were cleansed'. In the tension between bodily healing ('they were cleansed') and the healing which encompasses the whole person ('saved you'), it becomes once more clear what Luke intends to say by means of this account. Those who do not understand the cleansing as a sign of the dawning kingdom of God in Jesus may regain their physical health, but they pass by the real meaning of the miraculous event. Although, unlike II Kgs 5:19–27, no punishing miracle follows, nevertheless the nine fail to experience salvation. Luke likes to speak of saving faith, especially in connection with Jesus' powerful deeds (Lk 8:48, 50; Acts 3:16;

4:5–12). Nevertheless faith, and through it salvation, are given only to those who open themselves to God's saving action in Jesus and understand Jesus' powerful deeds as signs of the kingdom of God, which has come near in him. In the Samaritan, therefore, there is already fulfilled what Paul says to the Jews in Rome: 'Let it be known to you then that this salvation of God has been sent to the Gentiles; they will listen' (Acts 28:28). In a dramatic episode, Lk 17:11–19 exemplarily anticipates this idea in Jesus' ministry. In reference to the Old Testament prophetic story in II Kgs 5, from which it derives its structure, Luke brings together past, present and future. The promise contained in the Elisha–Naaman story, that God offers salvation to all people, has become reality in Jesus and finds ever new fulfilment in the Church's preaching on Jesus.[219]

Literary genre

Lk 17:11–19 can be tentatively classified under the broad literary genre of miracle stories, more precisely in the group of the cleansing of lepers. But this classification is too general and too abstract and the structural pattern of miracle stories is too wide-meshed to do justice to the specific character of the pericope under study. Moreover, the emphasis of the literary unit as a whole is not on the cleansing from leprosy, but on what happens and what is said in the second part of the account, starting with the return of the Samaritan.

Lk 17:11–19 seems to have been composed in dependence on the cleansing of the Syrian Naaman by the prophet Elisha. In II Kgs 5:1–19, too, we have an account which clearly has two peaks: the cleansing of Naaman, and the acknowledgement by Naaman of the God of Israel as the only true God at his return to the prophet; the centre of gravity is thus situated in the second part, for which the miraculous cleansing is a presupposition.

In Lk 17 Jesus occupies the central place in the account; he performs the cleansing miracle and promises the Samaritan salvation because of his faith. Likewise in II Kgs 5 the prophet Elisha who 'serves the Lord' (II Kgs 5:16) and mediates the miracle stands at the centre of the event. Since II Kgs 5 is a prophetic story which stresses the importance of Elisha who is, however, completely at the service of the Lord, and the author of Lk 17:11–19 composes his literary unit according to this prophetic story, the pericope may be characterized as 'imitation prophetic story'.[220] In a particular situation of need Jesus acts as the prophet Elisha did before. He cleanses the leper and thus manifests his prophetic power. However, the New Testament author leaves no doubt that Jesus is greater than Elisha. What Elisha did in the service of Yahweh, Jesus can perform out of his own fullness. The Christian author thereby transfers prophetic character-istics to Jesus and interprets his person by means of an 'imitation prophetic story'. But by means of skilful changes in structure as well as by the choice of and emphasis on particular elements of the story he goes beyond mere imitation. In so doing he reveals his intention to use the given prophetic story as his pattern as well as to surpass it.[221]

But it cannot be overlooked that in the second part of the pericope the emphasis ultimately lies on Jesus' pronouncement concerning the response of the Samaritan (Lk 17:17–18 and 19). Lk 17:11–19 can therefore also be called a pronouncement story. But while a pronouncement story usually develops from a single saying of Jesus for which the tradition has provided a narrative setting, here we are dealing with 'a miracle-story that has become a pronouncement-story either under Luke's pen or—more likely—in the pre-Lucan tradition'.[222]

The Lucan redaction

The insertion of the account at its present point in the Travel Narrative (Lk 9:51 – 19:44) presents Jesus as once more using his power (Lk 4:14, 36; 5:17) to save people from an evil which ostracized them from the human community and to restore them to their rightful place in that community. This liberating action of Jesus manifests that 'the kingdom of God is in the midst of you' (Lk 17:21).

After the cleansing only the Samaritan returns praising God and giving thanks to Jesus, who emphasizes that the Samaritan is the only one to do so (Lk 17:17–18) and declares 'your faith has made you well/saved you' (Lk 17:19). The latter statement may be a Lucan addition, since it 'surcharges' the point of verses 17–18 by pointing to a second statement of Jesus and introducing another theme. As in Lk 7:48–50 and elsewhere, here too salvation is not the healing, since healing is also granted to the nine others. Only the one who returned to Jesus in faith, the one who understood his healing as a gift of God through Jesus, is called 'saved'.[223] Faith which is translated into unlimited service (Lk 17:7–10) can do the 'impossible' (Lk 17:5–6), and makes people whole, thus allowing them to go their way and follow the 'Master' (*poreuomai* in Lk 17:11 and 19).

The account refers 'prophetically' to the future Gentile mission in which, in contrast to the hardened Jews, the positive reaction of 'foreigners' to the gospel manifests itself. All ten lepers, Jews as well as the Samaritan, are cured (verse 17). But only one, the Samaritan, returns to give praise to God (verse 18). The thought which is reflected in other Lucan miracle stories is modified in two respects.

Firstly, the account clearly presupposes a Gentile missionary situation in which God can henceforth be praised only 'at Jesus' feet', since God has finally and decisively linked salvation to his person (Acts 10:36, 42). Secondly, through the motif of return the account acquires a paraenetic character. Jesus is the sole mediator of divine salvation; one should hold on to him.

The twofold structure of the account with its emphasis on the statement of verses 17–18, in which Jesus himself raises the open questions derived from the preceding action, turns the account into a kind of paraenetic example story which questions the attitude of the public, i.e., also that of the reader, and tries to correct it. Thereby Luke intends to establish his community (see Lk 17:13, 'Master') in the belief that God is praised only by turning to Jesus and thanking him. In so doing he starts from the assumption that his community identifies itself with the attitude of the Samaritan who, although he is a 'foreigner', is nevertheless close to Judaism (compare Lk 7:3–6).[224]

10 Preaching the miracle stories

General considerations

Since fifteen to twenty Sunday gospels in our Lectionary for the years
A-B-C consist of miracle stories, the homilist can hardly avoid them.
While the informed preacher will no longer treat these miracle stories
simply as so many proofs of Jesus' divinity and miraculous power or
as humanitarian acts, he will have to do justice to the fact that they
are an integral part of Jesus' message in words and deeds and,
therefore, of the Church's proclamation as well.

Is it possible in a homily based on a miracle story to expound 'the
mysteries of the faith and the guiding principles of the Christian life'
(*Constitution on the Sacred Liturgy*, art. 52)? Yes, it is, if the place of
the miracle stories in the overall context of the gospels and the
intentions of the evangelists are properly understood by the homilist
and consequently by his audience. The evangelists did not record
factual, 'objective', methodical reports of events, similar to
newspaper accounts, but rather the catechetical instructions, or
affirmations of faith appealing for assent, of the early Christian
communities. Thus these stories proclaim the good news and were
edited to fit the needs and outlook of the community within which
and for which they were composed. They seek to make Christ known
and to elicit faith in him. If the homilist isolates the miracle stories
from the overall context of the gospel in order to demonstrate certain
truths like, e.g., the divinity of Christ, he goes contrary to the
intention of the evangelists, who want to proclaim the *person* of
Christ and his place in our life today, leading to a total commitment
to Christ.

In approaching the miracles of Jesus the homilist, making a clear
distinction between these *miracles* as performed during Jesus'
ministry and the *miracle stories* largely developed after and in the
light of the resurrection event, should not so much ask the question
'Did they really happen?' as develop the question 'What did they
mean to Jesus and his contemporaries?', and hence 'What should
they mean to us now?' Nevertheless, it may be helpful occasionally to

247

establish the general or global historicity of Jesus' miracles (see Chapter 1), since it would be no use speaking of Jesus' miracles if he never performed any.[225] Yet it should not be overlooked that homiletics is not primarily concerned with the possibility and nature of miracles in general, or with a theology of miracles. The homilist should concern himself rather with the message of the specific miracle stories embedded in specific gospels.

Here too apply the words addressed by Pope John Paul II to the members of the Executive Committee of the World Catholic Federation for the Biblical Apostolate on 7 April 1986: 'Ministers of God's word—priests, deacons, catechists and other lay people—should be immersed in the Scriptures through constant reading and diligent study, accompanied by prayer. As far as possible, *they should be acquainted with the insights of modern biblical scholarship.* Attention must be given to the *literary forms* of the various biblical books in order to determine the intention of the sacred writers. And it is most helpful, at times crucial, to be aware of the personal situation of the biblical writer, to the *circumstances of culture, time, language* and so forth which influenced the way the message was presented' (italics mine).

These 'insights of modern biblical scholarship' tell the informed homilist that in the miracle stories as they now appear in the gospels we are *not immediately* in touch with the miraculous events themselves, as if recorded by eyewitnesses right there and then, but that, like all gospel pericopes, they have come to us through 'three stages of tradition'.[226] These stages are, firstly, Jesus during his ministry in Palestine, living in a particular time and culture and speaking a particular language with its own particular characteristics; secondly, the early Christian communities passing on the words and deeds of Jesus mainly by word of mouth from the time of Jesus' death and resurrection until the writing of the gospels; and thirdly, the recording of this (oral) tradition by the evangelists whose presentation was influenced by their 'personal situation' as well as that of the community or communities which they addressed, and by 'circumstances of culture, time, language and so forth'. It is important that the homilist clearly decide which stage or layer of the tradition he will deal with in his homily, since each of them has its own identity and salient point(s).

While it is true that genuine historical memory underlies the miracle stories, as can be seen from authentic sayings in which Jesus spoke of his exorcisms and healings, and it is quite generally accepted that Jesus did perform such acts as part of his earthly ministry, it will nevertheless most of the time be very difficult if not altogether impossible to trace the actual stories back to the first stage. But exegetes often succeed in detecting and presenting the second stage, which may at times consist of several sub-levels, and thus the homilist will most of the time have to choose between the second stage, the form in which the miracle story was handed on in the oral tradition, or the third stage, the evangelist's presentation of the story.

In his address quoted above, the Holy Father also drew attention to 'the literary forms of the various biblical books in order to determine the intention of the sacred writers'. It has long been accepted that even within one and the same writing different literary forms can be and are often found. Miracle stories constitute such a literary form. As indicated in Chapter 1, a more or less general agreement has been reached regarding the structure of the miracle stories, and since there is undoubtedly a close relationship between the structure of a text and its function, it is advisable to keep the structure of the homily close to the structure of the pericope under consideration. Therefore, 'let every text have, if possible, its maximum exposure. Get as much of the form of the sermon as you can from the form of the text'.[227] 'The structure of the text is not merely a topcoat which can be left on the coatrack while the sermon enters the sanctuary. The *way* in which the text unfolds is a part of the *meaning* of the text.'[228]

In addressing his audience the homilist should take a number of things into account. Firstly, he should remember that the word 'miracle' may make his listeners think of an extraordinary, inexplicable, if not bizarre, event which interrupts the natural laws prevailing in the world, an idea somewhat supported by the way 'miracles' are treated in Lourdes and elsewhere, creating the impression that miracles can be measured by purely objective (medical and other) standards. Theology and preaching, which, in their controversy with positivism, allowed themselves to be imprisoned in the very system they were supposed to fight, by accepting as a common starting-point that a chain of natural causality governs the cosmos, share the responsibility for the unbiblical concept of miracle prevailing among the faithful, as explained in Chapter 1. Attempts to explain Jesus' miracles in terms of the laws of nature are not supported by the gospels. The kerygmatic dimension of the miracle stories indicates that the miracles belong to the realm of personal decision in which they operate *as signs* indicating that in the events of Jesus' ministry people have seen God at work, and *not as proofs* that natural laws have been suspended or interrupted. The miracles belong to the realm of faith, and the faith which Jesus demands is not achieved by proofs. To be sure, external events can bring people to the threshold of faith, but they do not dispense with the need for personal decision.

Secondly, a homilist should do his part in creating the conditions in which the message of the miracles as expressed in the miracle stories can be properly understood. They are to be presented not at the level of 'objective' demonstrations of God's power, but at the level of personal encounter, as can be derived from the kerygmatic character of the miracle stories. Miracles should 'be thought of as signs of personal encounter between God and man'.[229] The homilist must try to help his listeners overcome the attitude of mind which fails to see that truth has other and deeper levels of meaning than mere factual exactitude. The truth of the gospels is not purely factual, but a personal event: God addressing us in and through Jesus. All miracle stories ultimately bear witness to the miracle of God's presence in Jesus and invite us to encounter him. The audience should be invited not to belief in the miracles themselves, but to belief in Jesus who has shown by word and deed that he is the Christ. The miracle stories are an integral part of the gospels, which were written after and in the light of the Easter experience and therefore bear witness to the early Church's understanding of and belief in the risen Christ. The miracle stories were none of them recorded for the sake of the miracle itself, but for what they say about Christ. Relating the healing of a blind man by Jesus, the evangelist affirms that the risen Christ opens people's eyes and enables them to see the light. The healing of a deaf person means that the risen Christ opens people's ears, making it possible for them to listen to the word. A healed paralytic can walk again and thus is enabled to follow Christ, etc. This does not mean that we intend to 'spiritualize' the miracle stories and understand, e.g., the healing of the blind merely as a liberation from spiritual blindness. The Bible always envisages the whole person, which it represents as a unity. The miracle stories in particular emphasize that God addresses the whole person, also in his or her existence as a physical being. We want to stress, however, that the miracle stories are not merely dealing with physical processes and that the evangelists record them first of all for that 'more' which the miracle stories convey after and in the light of the Easter events.

If the homilist were to insist too much on 'what happened' and on the miraculous character of the event during Jesus' ministry, he would make it harder for his listeners to encounter the risen Christ who overcomes evil *now*, heals *now*, gives life *now*.

A look at particular miracle stories

Mark 1:21–28 (4th Sunday in Ordinary Time, Year B)

Our interpretation of Mk 1:21–28 and its context in Chapter 2 has revealed that a clear distinction can be made between the meaning of the account as it was formulated in the pre-Marcan community and the present pericope as edited by the evangelist. While the former apparently focused on the *person* of Jesus as 'the Holy One of God', and the question found in the 'chorus-ending' was most probably 'Who is this?' (compare Mk 4:41), Mark emphasized Jesus' *teaching* and correspondingly reformulated the original question as 'What is this?' This is in keeping with the fact that Mark's gospel as a whole presents Jesus' teaching activity as the central thrust of his ministry as the One who proclaimed that 'the kingdom of God is at hand' (Mk 1:15).[230]

While in theory the homilist could choose to focus on the earlier form of the account and what it said about the person of Jesus and his authority/power (*exousia*; Mk 1:27), the intention of the Lectionary, with its three cycles focusing on the theology of Mark, Matthew and Luke, suggests making the most of the third level of tradition, and coupled with the fact that on this Sunday, Mk 1:21–28 is combined with a first reading from Deut 18:15–20, referring to 'the prophet' whose coming Moses predicted and whom the people should heed since he speaks the words God puts in his mouth, seems to indicate that the homilist should focus on the Marcan version of the account and deal with Jesus' teaching with authority.

One effect of this approach is to counteract a possible one-sided emphasis on the miracles which may very well have existed among Mark's addressees, and certainly exists among a good number of Christians today.

Mark calls this teaching with authority 'new', that is, not just 'what was not there before', but 'superior in quality, different'. Jesus does not teach like other teachers; he teaches and works by the Spirit of God (Mk 1:11; 3:11; 5:7; 9:7, 'listen to him'; cf. Deut 18:15!). It is 'new' because it touches people's whole existence and frees them from 'demons' (Mk 1:21–28; 5:1–20), sin (Mk 2:1–12), and false burdens (Mk 7:1–16).

As we saw in Chapter 2, Mk 1:21–28 is part of a unit referred to as 'a day at Capernaum' (Mk 1:21–34) which in its turn belongs to a larger ensemble (Mk 1:14–39) in which Jesus manifests himself in Galilee, which shows that Jesus does everywhere what he did in the synagogue at Capernaum: teaching and exorcism. Mk 1:21–28, then, is the core of a 'movement of concentration and extension' and, as such, typical. It represents a significant condensation of Jesus' activity. What Jesus did in the synagogue of Capernaum—the liberation from a demon that he achieved there—is destined to spread throughout the whole of Galilee which, after Easter, will be the locus of the universal mission.

Considering the situation prevailing today in society, the Church, the parish, the homilist could try to point out in what way and how far Jesus' teaching is 'with authority' as well as 'new'. He could particularly try to identify today's demons and false burdens—while resisting the temptation to bias and one-sidedness which might lead us to locate all the demons and burdens in just one area or sector of society—and give examples of how Jesus' word can and does liberate people from these demons and burdens. Do the Christian community and individual Christians speak and enact this liberating word of Jesus in today's world?

Mark 1:29–31 (5th Sunday in Ordinary Time, Year B)

Mk 1:29–31 is the first part of this Sunday's gospel reading (Mk 1:29–39). The gospel accounts of the healing of Peter's mother-in-law do not allow us to determine exactly what was Jesus' intention in performing this healing nor what precise meaning the first witnesses attributed to it. We do know, however, that the Jews considered fever a divine punishment associated with consumption (Deut 28:22) or pestilence (Hab 3:5). In a later period fever was commonly attributed to a demon. In this perspective the healing at Capernaum will have meant for the first witnesses that Jesus was God's envoy promised by Isaiah who would come and save people from their afflictions (Isa 26:19; 29:18f.; 35:5, etc.).

Mark made this healing one of the features of his 'day at Capernaum', a typical day in the first period of Jesus' ministry. It illustrates by means of an example the 'summaries' of the healings performed by Jesus, just as Mk 1:21–28 is an illustration of the 'summaries' of exorcisms (Mk 1:32–34, 39). Hence the miracle is a sign of the dawning of the eschatological or messianic times in the person of Jesus: he acts with God's own power. But at present it is only a sign. It will take people a long time to discover and accept its true significance (cf. Mt 11:4–6). Mark's own intention appears from a closer examination of verse 31 (and its parallel, Mt 8:15).

As mentioned in Chapter 3, verse 31 contains an anomaly which calls for some explanation. Mark writes literally: 'and approaching, Jesus raised her (made her stand up), taking her by the hand; and the fever left her'. One would expect him to write: 'Jesus took her by the hand and the fever left her; she stood up...'. Furthermore, the verb *egeirein* used here by Mark became a technical term for the resurrection. The phrase 'he raised her up' seems to have been inserted by Mark at the centre of a simpler narrative, especially since it is found in Mark only. The deliberate choice of the verb *egeirein* reveals his symbolic intention. Just as Jesus freed Peter's mother-in-law from the fever that immobilized her, he makes us stand up, he raises us up, so that we too can serve.

In the context of the miracle, more precisely in the context of the reception Jesus received in the house, 'to serve' means first of all to serve at table, to serve a meal (cf. Mk 1:13). But it also has a wider meaning: 'For the Son of man also came not to be served but to serve' (Mk 10:45). To serve, then, does not consist only in serving at table but, if need be, also in giving 'his life as a ransom for many' (Mk 10:45). Such is the ideal proposed by Christ to those whom he raises from the death of sin (an allusion to baptism?). In the shorter and more catechetical version of Matthew, Jesus enters the house alone. The singular object 'and she served *him*' widens the meaning of the verb. Clearly, we are no longer dealing with serving a meal to Jesus (and his disciples) but with a more general reality. The previous condition of the sick woman symbolizes the condition of sin which paralyses the unredeemed, the non-liberated person, and her healing signifies the raising liberation performed by Jesus, thus enabling that person to serve Christ and people.[231]

The homilist will most probably choose to develop his homily on the basis of the Marcan redaction of the account. Relating it to the specific situation of his audience, he will try to show how today, too, many people suffer from all kinds of fever, 'gold fever' and others, which tie them down to the bed of their self-centredness, or other obstacles which prevent them from serving others. He should be able to give his audience concrete examples of how some people have experienced being raised by Christ, thus becoming capable of serving him and people. Thus he may kindle hope in the hearts of his listeners that they too can be set free for the service of the community, even to the extent of 'giving their life' for others.

Mark 1:40–45 (6th Sunday in Ordinary Time, Year B)

The homilist may like to base his homily on the pre-Marcan form of the account which follows the usual pattern of a healing story, made more specific, however, by the fact that we are dealing here with the healing of a *leper*. The homilist should try to point out the Christological and missionary aspects of the story, following the interpretation of the account on this level presented in Chapter 4 above (pp. 84–90).

But again it may seem preferable to turn to the Marcan redaction of the account, which is now found in between Mk 1:21–39, presenting Jesus' authority over evil powers, and Mk 2:1 – 3:6, highlighting the opposition of the Jewish authorities. Compared with Mk 1:21–39, Mk 1:40–45 refers to a new entity indicated by 'the priest' and '(for a proof to) them'. This should make us aware of the fact that the healing concerns not only Jesus and the leper, but also a third party.

The leper is a paradigm of the isolated, ostracized person, victim of an almost entirely negative relationship with others, with individuals as well as society as a whole. More serious than the illness itself are the consequences it entails. The leper is practically cut off from society. The plea to make him clean addressed to Jesus is a request for a liberation which goes well beyond cleansing from leprosy as such. He asks for reintegration into the human community, to which Jesus responds, besides healing him, by *touching* him, a gesture of personal intimacy which prefigures a total reintegration. People who have experienced isolation and loneliness will understand the importance to the leper of Jesus' gesture.

But Jesus also sends him away lest, having been liberated by Jesus, the man should now attach himself to Jesus in a way which would make him miss the chance of once more taking his rightful place in the community. The relationship with Jesus is not sufficient to liberate him totally. Therefore, in an extension of his liberating gesture, Jesus sends him away. By extending his 'healing' gesture beyond the removal of physical leprosy, he liberates the man from his isolation and returns him to the network of human relations and encounters. Jesus sets the man free; he does not just comfort him. He challenges him and sends him forth. He does not want the man to cling to him. Neither does he want us to do so.

The former leper regains his social relations and, in fact, begins to proclaim the salvation he has experienced. His experience of salvation and liberation is translated into words and draws people to come and see Jesus. Thus the man who initially lived in isolation and alienation becomes instrumental in gathering people around Jesus. The testimony of the former victim of ostracism is creative of the community and constitutive of the people of God. Thus it also becomes clear that Jesus does not save people in isolation from the texture of their social life. In the same way, he sends us forth to our family, our community, our professional and political responsibilities. [232]

The homilist could challenge his audience, asking them if they do not ostracize the poor and the oppressed, that is, treat them as lepers, and what would happen if they did touch them. Would not their testimony too be creative of community and constitutive of the people of God? Would not that make us experience the joyful spirit of community and the renewed and deepened life of worship which results from the Church's identification with the poor of which, e.g., Cardinal Paulo Arns of São Paulo, Brazil, speaks so convincingly?

But we do not have to limit our reflections to reaching out, or touching the 'leprous' person(s). What if we extend the perspective to 'leprous' features of today's society, today's economic systems and political structures? Do they not somehow pose a challenge to Christians: 'if you will, you can make me clean'? If as a Church we show by our reaching out, by our touching them that we really care, then people who thought we did not may come again 'from every quarter'.

Mark 2:1–12 (7th Sunday in Ordinary Time, Year B)

As seen in Chapter 5, Mk 2:1–12 is a composite text consisting of a miracle story (Mk 2:1–5a, 11–12) in between the two parts of which has been inserted an apophthegm, a saying of Jesus set in a short narrative context (Mk 2:5b–10). We distinguished three stages in the tradition history of this pericope. Firstly, the pre-Marcan (but already post-Easter) miracle story, the unique feature of which was the explicit mention of faith. Secondly, the miracle story expanded by the apophthegm dealing with forgiveness of sins, still on the pre-Marcan level, reducing the original miracle story to the status of framework and resulting in an instruction account in which Jesus' answer to faith is no longer the expected healing, but the forgiveness of sins. Thirdly, Mk 2:1–12 on the level of the Marcan redaction. All three levels seem to provide interesting material for a homily.

The first level gives the homilist an opportunity to speak about faith, not in general, but specifically of the kind of faith manifested in *this* miracle story, which is certainly more than initial faith in a miracle-worker. The narrator has in mind faith in the post-Easter kerygma and, therefore, a truly Christian faith, faith in Jesus dead and risen, faith in Christ present and active here and now in his community and in the world. This faith should not be held back by any obstacles. The homilist could refer here to what may possibly be obstacles to living out faith in the situation of his audience, and challenge them to overcome these obstacles and thus to experience how Jesus encounters those who come to him with such Christian faith. Jesus can and will heal them of the paralysis of their inaction and complacency, and orders them to walk in the practice of justice and peace. Again the homilist should try to specify what this means for his particular audience in practical terms.

If the homilist decides to focus his attention on the second level, the combination of the miracle story and the apophthegm on forgiveness of sins, he will have to treat the miracle as radically subordinate to the apophthegm about the power of the Son of man to forgive sins as perceived by the Christian community after Easter.

The result of enshrining the apophthegm about forgiveness within the healing miracle story is a powerful demonstration of what the kingdom is all about. Moved by the faith of those who lower the paralytic into his presence, Jesus speaks the word of forgiveness, thus announcing the breaking-in of the kingdom into the twisted frame of the paralytic's existence, and assuring him of God's acceptance. The encounter with God in Jesus is now understood to take place in forgiveness rather than in a healing miracle. But Jesus' approach did not so much consist in *talking* about forgiveness as in *manifesting* God's forgiveness in socializing with marginals and outcasts. Jesus who during his ministry received sinners and ate with them, and by his death and resurrection gained forgiveness, is now the Lord who actually forgives sins. Do today's Christian community and the wider society concretely experience this, and if so, how? If the sacrament of reconciliation has lost so much of its credibility among the faithful, is it not to some extent because while still saying the words 'your sins are forgiven' in sacramental context, the institutional Church often shows so little of God's compassion which Jesus manifested in the face of weakness and failure? Instead the institutional Church adopts legalistic and therefore rigid, even harsh and inhuman, attitudes outside that sacramental context. Only when the Church manifests God's compassion and mercy at all times will the sacramental celebration of this reality regain credibility.

Forgiveness should certainly not be seen only as a remission of past failures but rather as a starting-point for a commitment to society, especially to the little ones, the least of our brothers and sisters. Jesus' *word* of forgiveness is uttered in the framework of an *act* of healing, the two illuminating each other. The paralytic's physical helplessness implies other limitations: he cannot work, he cannot participate in the political, social and religious life of society. It may also refer to another disability, another fundamental need and condition of poverty, that is, his need for God, his poverty of being. It is the latter Jesus comes to transform and turns his attention to in the first place. But the effectiveness and effect of his word addresses the whole person, as illustrated by the ensuing physical cure.

Finally, if the homilist chooses to develop his homily from the level of the Marcan redaction, he should give due attention to the way Mark integrated this instruction about forgiveness into the totality of Jesus' ministry. By saying in the expanded introduction that Jesus was preaching the word, Mark implies that the event which follows is a demonstration of the content of his preaching. It is not by chance that Mark (or the tradition before him?) placed the call of Levi (Mk 2:13–17) immediately after the pericope under consideration. Mark proclaims the enduring meaning of the Christ event to the disciples of his community and, through them, to the disciples and people of all times. In and through Jesus God touches our lives. We too, like Levi, are offered love, acceptance and forgiveness, and invited to enter into the experience of the kingdom. In one way or other we are paralytics: fearful, weary, disillusioned, cynical, feeling inadequate and helpless—so many forms of paralysis revealing our sinful situation as well as expressing our need for God's healing and forgiving touch. Mark wants us to enjoy the integral experience of the kingdom, like the paralytic. But he may be still asking us who in the Church today are given a contemporary label similar to 'publicans and sinners' in Jesus' time. Who are the outcasts, the oppressed in our society, the voiceless marginals of our community? Do we, sinners who have been forgiven, touch their lives and proclaim in a language which they understand today the word of Jesus, 'stand up...and walk', the message of God's kingdom of justice and love?

Mark 3:1–6 (9th Sunday in Ordinary Time, Year B)

Mk 3:1–6 is the last part of this Sunday's gospel reading (Mk 2:23–3:6). Again we can distinguish three levels in its tradition history.

Originally it was a healing miracle. Some indications suggest that the setting on a sabbath does not belong to the oldest layer of the account. It is not mentioned in the parts of the text which are parallel in Mark and Matthew, which as such form a very coherent narrative: 'And he entered in a synagogue and a man was there who had a withered hand. And he said to the man, "Stretch out your hand". He stretched it out, and his hand was restored'.

Still within the pre-Marcan tradition, this healing miracle was developed into a controversy in the context of a sabbath. In it the healing proper is reduced to a minimum while all attention is focused on the confrontation between Jesus and his adversaries: the healing takes place at the *synagogue* on the *sabbath* in full view of everybody. The context of this confrontation could hardly be more 'sacred': in Galilee; it prefigures the final confrontation in the Temple of Jerusalem, just before the passion (cf. Mk 3:6!). This last point may, however, belong to the Marcan redaction.

Mark's presentation throws into relief the 'violence' of this confrontation. The whole account is based on a scene from which the secondary characters, the multitude and the disciples, are eliminated so that only Jesus and his adversaries remain. The latter, who are identified only at the end of the account, spy on Jesus in silence, hoping that he will perform a healing on the sabbath so that they can accuse him, without the slightest concern for the afflicted person.

They do not say a word throughout the encounter. Jesus, on the other hand, acts and speaks openly in an effort to avoid all ambiguity. He makes the sick person stand in full view of everybody, and poses a difficult 'theological question' to his adversaries in the classical style of controversy, 'Is it lawful...?' The question is equivocal: certainly, it is permitted to violate the sabbath law to save life, and in this sense the question calls for a positive answer. But, according to the rabbis, this was true only in immediate danger of death, which is not the case here. But Jesus does not allow himself to be enclosed by the subtleties of casuistry. For him the sabbath is *par excellence* the time of salvation; not to heal would amount to killing. Jesus therefore completely changes the perspective usually prevailing in discussions on this subject. It is no longer a question of subtle scholastic distinctions but a radical choice between 'to do good or to do harm (evil; *kakopoiein*)...to save life or to kill'. But his adversaries are insensitive to the plight of this afflicted man, as they are to the plight of so many poor and oppressed. Therefore, Jesus 'looked around at them *with anger*, grieved at their hardness of heart' (Mk 3:5), that is, a total incapacity to perceive the reality of God and to share his compassion with all forms of human suffering, 'blindness toward the liberating will of God being made manifest in his [Jesus'] praxis...Jesus reveals the true will of God. He heals on the sabbath in order to demonstrate that nothing can separate God's cause from the struggle against the suffering of poor and marginalized human beings'.[233] The homilist should experience no difficulty in illustrating this hardness of heart in today's society.

The usual conclusion of miracle stories, expressing the admiration of the multitudes, is here changed into a 'death sentence' in which both religious and political powers participate (Mk 3:6; *sumboulion*, 'council'). This sentence seems premature and much more justified in Mk 11:18 after Jesus' entry into Jerusalem. In Mk 15:1 the evangelist mentions the same 'council' once more gathering to decide on Jesus' death. In Mk 3:6 the evangelist does not intend to narrate a carefully dated historical reaction, but to point out that the radical opposition between Jesus and the powers of his time was present from the very beginning of his ministry. Mk 3:6 orients the whole of Mk 2:1 – 3:6 towards the cross. Again, the homilist should experience no difficulty in coming up with contemporary parallels which challenge his audience here and now.

In the gospel of Mark, as in the reading for this Sunday, Mk 3:1–6 is closely related to Jesus' statement, 'The sabbath was made for man, not man for the sabbath' (Mk 2:27). Nobody ever pronounced a more liberating statement with regards to the law. Radical in its simplicity, it could be heard by all people. The sabbath, sign of God's love for his people, necessarily consists in service to people, not the opposite. This kind of simple and straightforward liberation and the ensuing freedom cannot be tolerated by the powers that be, religious and political. Deciding to 'uphold the law' of the sabbath, they prefer to kill the one who proclaims this freedom, rather than to heal the afflicted and oppressed.[234]

Mark 4:35–41 (12th Sunday in Ordinary Time, Year B)

The study of Mk 4:35–41 and its context in Chapter 7 showed that we can distinguish three phases in the tradition of the account.

Firstly, in its original form, that is, stripped of all its redactional and secondary features, the account was formulated in the Gentile-oriented preaching of Judaism in the Diaspora, where it functioned not so much as a miracle story highlighting a miraculous event, but as the account of an epiphany or manifestation which focused on the person of Jesus. He was presented as the one in whom is made manifest the awesome power of God who stills the storm (cf. Job 26:12, etc.) and who rescues the just person from threatening waters (cf. Ps 18:16, etc.). The account thus presented Jesus to the Gentile world as one superior to all their wonder-working 'divine men', and summoned them to a Christological decision. This was evidenced in the concluding question 'Who then is this?', which was not meant to be a catechetical question testing the knowledge of believers, but a kerygmatic question inviting unbelievers to faith.

Secondly, with the addition of verse 38a, 'but he was in the stern, asleep on the cushion', a secondary but pre-Marcan insertion, the account was given a new meaning in response to a new situation in the early Church. With the Church as an already established but persecuted community, living in imminent expectation of the parousia, concern for mission gave way to need for consolidation. The account now serves internal community exhortation rather than missionary preaching. It invites the community, tossed by the storms of persecution (cf. Mk 4:17) and waiting, apparently in vain, for the appearance of the saving Lord who never seems to come, to an unconditional trust in Jesus who can and will save them even though 'sleeping'.

Thirdly, Marcan redaction, and in particular the addition of the rebuke, 'Why are you afraid? Have you no faith (yet)?' (Mk 4:40), gave the account a new point. Unconditional trust in Jesus could lead to a 'divine man' soteriology which would expect the risen Lord to save his persecuted community through a miraculous intervention. Mark's redactional intervention corrected this view. The disciples were rebuked not because they were not reassured by the presence of

Jesus even though he was sleeping, but because they were not willing to perish with him. They were not willing, that is, to follow him on the way to the cross as true disciples should (Mk 8:34), but expected to be delivered by him through a miracle. Along with the whole of Mark's gospel, the account teaches that salvation comes not through miracles but through the cross. For it is the cross rather than his miracles which constitutes the true epiphany of Jesus.

The original form of the story could serve as material for a homily in a missionary or quasi-missionary situation where people in some way cling to 'divine men' or their contemporary counterparts, be they people, structures, or regimes from which they expect 'wonders'. In this context the homilist may try to challenge his audience to a Christological decision by asking the question 'Who then is this?' and present Christ as the one who, more than anybody or anything else, has the power to save those who believe in him from all 'storms'.

If the homilist is confronted by the task of consolidation rather than missionary preaching, he will try to start his homily from the second phase of the account's tradition history. He must then ask himself what in the context of the life of his community makes its members feel helpless, as if overcome by forces which are stronger than they. In other words, what in the world of his community functions in a way analogous to the storm at sea in the setting of the early Christian community? He must try to specify what situations or conditions at times give his community, or part of it, a feeling of sinking, and how their relationship to Jesus, who today too may seem 'asleep' to many, can help them overcome that experience. In other words, how they can feel the storm subside.

On the level of the Marcan redaction, the account deals with the disciples' reluctance to follow Jesus on the way to the cross, and their expectation of deliverance by miracles. The homily may start from this redactional level to tell his audience that salvation and liberation from whatever oppresses and burdens people is achieved not through 'miracles' but through suffering and the cross. Mark is no longer interested in Jesus' demonstration of power as such, but in establishing the disciples' attitude as unbelief. Similarly, the homilist should address himself to the unbelief of today's disciples who cannot face the sinking of the boat of a bourgeois Church, of a community whose highest value is 'law and order', no matter what the cost. He should challenge them to undergo the storm trustfully, ready to 'perish with Jesus', believing that he can save them from ruin even through 'death'. They should be ready to let the boat of a (crypto-)triumphalistic Church perish so that the real community of Christ may emerge from the waves. They should be prepared to die to a smug, institutionalized Church so that the Church of the little ones, the least of my brothers and sisters, may live. Jesus' words, 'Why are you afraid? Have you no faith (yet)', are also addressed to today's disciples who time and again shrink from the risk of following Jesus in failure and death. Accordingly, they too are challenged and reprimanded by Mark's Jesus.

Luke 7:11–17 (10th Sunday in Ordinary Time, Year C)

Because of Luke's intense redactional activity, it is difficult to get a clear picture of the pre-Lucan account. But it probably presented Jesus as the 'great prophet', greater than Elijah and greater than the 'divine men' of the Greco-Roman world.

On the level of the Lucan redaction the homilist should try to read the account in the context of Lk 7, which highlights the messianic power of Jesus who heals (Lk 7:1–10) and raises from the dead (Lk 7:11–17), thus realizing the wonders prophesied by Isaiah (Lk 7:18–35), and who forgives sins (Lk 7:36–50). While the whole of Lk 7 sheds light on the raising at Nain, it appears that its meaning can be more precisely grasped from its immediate link with the pericope of the disciples sent by John the Baptist (Lk 7:18–35). Did Luke not insert the account at this very place to prepare and justify Jesus' words addressed to John's disciples, especially 'the dead are raised up' (Lk 7:22)? But, doing justice to the fact that Lk 7:11–17 emphasizes Jesus' compassion for the *widow* rather than for the dead man, should we not say that the account also underscores the next statement of Lk 7:22, 'the poor have good news preached to them'? Should this raising of the son of a widow not be understood as a proclamation of the good news to the poor in action? Therefore, at least an important part of the meaning of the raising at Nain will have to be found in the answer sent to John the Baptist. Apparently John and his disciples were disconcerted by Jesus' 'style' to the extent of wondering whether he was really the one they were expecting. By means of the present miracle linked to the response to John the Baptist, Luke completes and illustrates the picture of Jesus' messianic mission given in the inaugural scene at Nazareth (Lk 4:16–30): the long citation of Isaiah about the anointed one sent to bring good news to the poor, to give sight to the blind, and freedom to the oppressed (Isa 61:1–2 = Lk 4:18–19) is now justified. The raising of the young man constitutes a major sign of the advent of the messianic times and the identity of Jesus as 'he who is to come' (Lk 7:19). But this will be fully understood only after and in the light of Easter, as Luke seems to suggest by calling Jesus 'the Lord' (Lk 7:13).

Jesus intervenes on behalf of a widow, victim of social and affective deprivation. Luke pays special attention to widows (mentioned nine times) presented as exemplary figures of the vindication of justice (Lk 18:3) or the scandalously exploited defenceless (Lk 20:47; 21:2). Jesus' response to this particular widow, a paradigm of the poor and the oppressed, does not concern this individual person only, but is a manifestation of God's visiting his people. Jesus' compassion for the widow is the instrument of God's compassion for the whole people (*laos*). In and through Jesus God manifests that he is on the side of the poor *for* the whole people, for the sake of the whole of humanity, *not against* the rest of society.

The hope generated by the resurrection of Christ, proclaimed in Lk 7:11–17, contradicts suffering and death experienced in so many ways in everyday life. Suffering, evil, injustice, death are experienced by people as abandonment by God, remoteness of God. The hope of the resurrection, founded on God's fidelity to his promise, announces the proximity of God, the victory of life over death. To the Christian death remains real, but it loses its fatal character. God has raised Jesus, and in his victory over death ours is included as the promise of our faithful God who has visited his people in and through Jesus.

Luke 17:11–19 (28th Sunday in Ordinary Time, Year C)

The immediate context of the account provides the homilist with two possibilities.

The preceding pericopes allow him to develop a homily on different aspects of faith. Real faith can do what is otherwise impossible (Lk 17:5–6); but this is true only of faith that has been translated into unlimited service (Lk 17:7–10). This faith which makes one return time and again to God 'at Jesus' feet', can make the person whole, that is, transform the whole person in a manner which goes far beyond the healing of the nine lepers. Although all ten are cured of their leprosy, only one, the Samaritan, is assured 'your faith has made you well'. While the other nine may still be on their way to the priests (Lk 17:14), the Samaritan is told to go his way which is also the way of Jesus (cf. *poreuesthai*, 'to go, to journey' in Lk 17:11 and 19).

In conjunction with the succeeding pericope (Lk 17:20–21), the cleansing of the ten lepers raises the question about the 'when' of the kingdom of God (Lk 17:20a), and is both illustration and demonstration of Jesus' answer, 'the kingdom of God is in the midst of you' (Lk 17:21b). And yet in the everyday reality of Jesus' ministry the kingdom of God was not more visible than it is in our day. The homilist could ask his audience what may be the signs of God's kingdom in our midst, pointing out that, like the Samaritan in Luke's account, the most unlikely persons may be the ones to recognize the signs of God's saving presence and respond appropriately.

Turning to the account itself, the homilist could have recourse to a number of observations made in connection with Mk 1:40–45 and parallels, without however overlooking the distinctive character of Lk 17:11–19. As pointed out in the analysis of the text, the emphasis of the pericope is on the second part which starts with verse 15, 'Then one of them, when he saw that he was healed, turned back'. The other nine must also have noticed that they were cured, but this one man's seeing was different; he had a deeper understanding of what had happened to him. Luke does not intend merely to relate an event in Jesus' ministry, but by means of the three rhetorical questions of verses 17–18 he draws the listeners/readers into the event and challenges them to take a stand. Today too there are different ways of seeing, and it takes seeing like that of the Samaritan to recognize that the kingdom of God is in our midst. It takes a faith-full way of seeing to discover God's saving hand at work in the midst of so much sinfulness, suffering, injustice, violence and oppression. It takes this particular seeing to turn to Jesus and to praise God, the same seeing that recognizes the presence of the risen Christ. But today too many eyes are kept from recognizing him (Lk 24:16), and Jesus has to reach out when we are 'yet at a distance' (cf. Lk 15:20) so that our eyes may be opened and we may recognize him (Lk 24:31) in our midst. In other words, the seeing which eventually results in the words 'your faith has made you well' is a gift; not a gift received once and for all and hence a constant possession, but one that is offered time and again and has to be likewise received time and again in thanksgiving. The homilist could also ask himself and his audience who the 'foreigner(s)' would be today.

Notes

1 M. Smith, 'Prolegomena to a Discussion of Aretalogies, Divine Men, the Gospels and Jesus', *Journal of Biblical Literature* 90 (1971), 179.

2 P. J. Achtemeier, 'Gospel Miracle Tradition and the Divine Man', *Interpretation* 26 (1978), 185.

3 C. K. Barrett, *The Holy Spirit and the Gospel Tradition* (London: SPCK, 1966), pp. 71–77, distinguishes six special uses of the term *dunamis* in the synoptic gospels: (1) *dunamis* as miracle; (2) *dunamis* as a periphrasis for God; (3) *dunamis* as a doxology; (4) *dunameis* as heavenly beings; (5) *dunamis* as eschatological power; (6) *dunamis* as miraculous power.

4 W. D. Dennison, 'Miracles as "Signs": Their Significance for Apologetics', *Biblical Theology Bulletin* 6 (1976), 194–202, distinguishes the judicial, messianic and eschatological character of *sēmeion*, *terata* and *erga*.

5 H. Remus, 'Does Terminology Distinguish Early Christian from Pagan Miracles?', *Journal of Biblical Literature* 101 (1982), 535, 550–551. See Rev 13:13–14; 16:14; 19:20 for pagan 'signs'.

6 The parallel text, Mt 12:28, 'But if it is by the Spirit of God...', is apparently thinking of the new creation.

7 P. J. Achtemeier, 'Gospel Miracle Tradition', 185.

8 T. M. Suriano, 'Christian Faith and the Miracles of Jesus', *The Bible Today* no. 92 (November 1977), 1361.

9 R. J. Allen, *Our Eyes Can Be Opened. Preaching the Miracle Stories of the Synoptic Gospels Today* (Washington, D.C.: University Press of America, 1982), pp. 23–24.

10 A. C. Wire, 'The Structure of the Gospel Miracle Stories and Their Tellers', *Semeia* 11 (1978), 109.

11 R. E. Brown, 'The Gospel Miracles' in *New Testament Essays* (Milwaukee: Bruce/London and Dublin: Geoffrey Chapman, 1965), p. 169. For a summary of the apologetic use of miracles, see J. A. Hardon, 'The Concept of Miracles from St Augustine to Modern Apologetics', *Theological Studies* 15 (1954), 229–257.

12 G. Theissen, *Urchristliche Wundergeschichten* (Gütersloh; G. Mohn, 1974); Eng. trans.: *The Miracle Stories of the Early Christian Tradition* (Edinburgh: T. & T. Clark/Philadelphia; Fortress Press, 1983).

13 X. Léon-Dufour, *Les miracles de Jésus selon le Nouveau Testament* (Parole de Dieu; Paris: Éditions du Seuil, 1977).

14   The verb *erchesthai*, 'to come', 'to go', and its compounds occur seventeen times in Mk 1:21–45.

15   Note the seven words derived from the root *kathar-* ('(un)clean', 'to cleanse') in Mk 1:23, 26, 27 and in 1:40, 41, 42, 44.

16   The verb *erchesthai* applied to Jesus is used in Mk 1:21, 45; 2:1; 3:1.

17   Cf. D. Dideberg and P. Mourlon Beernaert, '"Jésus vint en Galilée." Essai sur la structure de Marc 1,21–45', *Nouvelle Revue Théologique* 98 (1976), 306–323, especially 318–320; *idem*, '"Jesus Came into Galilee": the Structure of Mark 1:21–45', *Theology Digest* 25 (1977), 111–116.

18   R. Pesch, '"Eine neue Lehre aus Macht." Eine Studie zu Mk 1,21–28' in *Evangelienforschung. Ausgewählte Aufsätze deutscher Exegeten* (ed. J. B. Bauer; Graz/Vienna/Cologne: Styria, 1968), pp. 241–276, especially p. 245. The pages which follow are dependent on this study.

19   Cf. B. Robinson, 'The Challenge of the Gospel Miracle Stories', *New Blackfriars* 60 (710–711; July-August 1979), 326–327.

20   J. M. Robinson, *The Problem of History in Mark* (Studies in Biblical Theology 21; London: SCM Press/Naperville, Ill.: A. R. Allenson, 1957), p. 37.

21   Cf. H. C. Kee, 'The Terminology of Mark's Exorcism Stories', *New Testament Studies* 14 (1967–68), 242–243.

22   Cf. E. Schweizer, *The Good News According to Mark* (Richmond, Va.: John Knox Press, 1970/London: SPCK, 1971), p. 50.

23   E. Schweizer, *ibid*.

24   H. C. Kee, 'Terminology', 242.

25   The pages that follow are based in particular on U. Busse, *Die Wunder des Propheten Jesus* (Stuttgart: Verlag Katholisches Bibelwerk, 1977), pp. 66–90. See also W. Kirchenschläger, *Jesu exorzistisches Wirken aus der Sicht des Lukas* (Klosterneuburg: Österreichisches Katholisches Bibelwerk, 1981), pp. 27–41; C. P. März, *Das Wort Gottes bei Lukas* (Leipzig: St. Benno Verlag, 1974), pp. 38–41.

26   For an explanation which holds that in this pericope Mark depends on and is derived from Luke, see D. Flusser, *Die rabbinische Gleichnisse und der Gleichniserzähler Jesus* (Berne/Frankfurt am Main: P. Lang, 1981), pp. 209–215.

27   K. Lake and F. J. Foakes-Jackson (eds), *The Beginnings of Christianity* (London: Macmillan, 1920–33), IV, p. 203.

28   While aware of the difficulties raised against the 'two-source theory' which holds that Matthew and Luke depend on Mark for their narrative sections, while they derive their 'sayings' or discourses of Jesus mainly from a (hypothetical) source known as Q (the initial letter of the German word *Quelle*, 'source'), and of alternative solutions, like that of a deutero-Mark (A. Fuchs), and prepared to give a more important role to oral tradition than the original proponents of the 'two-source theory', the present author nevertheless accepts the basic tenets of this theory.

29   D. E. Nineham, *The Gospel of St Mark* (Pelican Gospel Commentaries; Harmondsworth, Middx/Baltimore: Penguin, 1963), p. 81.

30   H. Van der Loos, *The Miracles of Jesus* (Leiden: E. J. Brill, 1965), p. 554.
31   X. Léon-Dufour, 'La guérison de la belle-mère de Simon Pierre' in *Études d'Évangile* (Paris: Éditions du Seuil, 1965), p. 138.
32   Cf. J. M. Robinson, *The Problem of History in Mark* (above, note 20), p. 41.
33   P. Lamarche, 'La guérison de la belle-mère de Pierre', *Nouvelle Revue Théologique* 87 (1965), 520–521.
34   Cf. S. M. Praeder, 'Acts 27:1 – 28:16: Sea Voyages in Ancient Literature and the Theology of Luke-Acts', *The Catholic Biblical Quarterly* 46 (1984), 702–703.
35   J. A. Fitzmyer, *The Gospel According to Luke I – IX* (The Anchor Bible 28; Garden City, N.Y.: Doubleday, 1981), p. 550.
36   H. J. Held, 'Matthew as Interpreter of the Miracle Stories' in *Tradition and Interpretation in Matthew* (ed. G. Bornkamm, G. Barth and H. J. Held; Philadelphia: The Westminster Press/London: SCM Press, 1963), pp. 165–299.
37   C. Burger, 'Jesu Taten nach Matthäus 8 und 9', *Zeitschrift für Theologie und Kirche* 70 (1973), 272–287, especially 284–287.
38   Cf. J. D. Kingsbury, 'Observations on the "Miracle Chapters" of Matthew 8 – 9', *The Catholic Biblical Quarterly* 40 (1978), 567–568.
39   H. J. Held, 'Matthew as Interpreter', p. 245.
40   R. Pesch, *Jesu ureigene Taten?* (Freiburg: Herder, 1970), pp. 56–59; L. Schenke, *Die Wundererzählungen des Markusevangeliums* (Stuttgart: Verlag Katholisches Bibelwerk, 1974), pp. 130–134; K. Kertelge, *Die Wunder Jesu im Markusevangelium* (Munich: Kösel Verlag, 1970), pp. 62–64.
41   E. Schweizer, *The Good News According to Mark* (above, note 22), p. 57.
42   R. Pesch, *Jesu ureigene Taten?*, pp. 60–76; L. Schenke, *Die Wundererzählungen*, pp. 135–141; K. Kertelge, *Die Wunder Jesu*, pp. 64–70.
43   R. H. Fuller, *Interpreting the Miracles* (London: SCM Press/Philadelphia: The Westminster Press, 1963), p. 49, note 1.
44   R. Pesch, *Jesu ureigene Taten?*, p. 58; L. Schenke, *Die Wundererzählungen*, p. 138.
45   Cf. F. W. Danker, 'Mark 1:45 and the Secrecy Motif', *Concordia Theological Monthly* 37 (1966), 493, note 7.
46   R. Pesch, *Jesu ureigene Taten?*, pp. 76–80; L. Schenke, *Die Wundererzählungen*, pp. 139–141.
47   B. Standaert, *L'Évangile selon Marc. Composition et genre littéraire* (Nijmegen: Stichting Studentenpers, 1978), pp. 126–134.
48   R. Pesch, *Jesu ureigene Taten?*, pp. 84–87; L. Schenke, *Die Wundererzählungen*, pp. 141–145; K. Kertelge, *Die Wunder Jesu*, pp. 70–75.
49   G. Minette de Tillesse, *Le secret messianique dans l'Évangile de Marc* (Paris: Éditions du Cerf, 1968), p. 68.
50   H. J. Held, 'Matthew as Interpreter' (above, note 36), p. 214.
51   Cf. H. J. Held, *ibid.*, p. 229.

52 Cf. B. Gerhardsson, *The Mighty Acts of Jesus According to Matthew* (Lund: Gleerup, 1979), p. 86.

53 Cf. F. Neirynck, 'Papyrus Egerton 2 and the Healing of the Leper', *Ephemerides Theologicae Lovanienses* 61 (1985), 158.

54 Cf. H. J. Held, 'Matthew as Interpreter', pp. 239–240.

55 R. Pesch, *Jesu ureigene Taten?*, pp. 98–107; U. Busse, *Die Wunder des Propheten Jesus* (above, note 25), pp. 115–134; W. Bruners, *Die Reinigung der zehn Aussätzigen und die Heilung des Samariters, Lk 17, 11–19* (Stuttgart: Verlag Katholisches Bibelwerk, 1977), pp. 370–380.

56 P. J. Achtemeier, 'The Lucan Perspective on the Miracles of Jesus: A Preliminary Sketch', *Journal of Biblical Literature* 94 (1975), 552.

57 L. Feldkämper, *Der betende Jesus als Heilsmittler nach Lukas* (St. Augustin: Steyler Verlag, 1978), pp. 51–83.

58 Cf. J. Dewey, *Markan Public Debate. Literary Technique, Concentric Structure, and Theology in Mark 2:1 – 3:6* (Chico, Cal.: Scholars Press, 1980), pp. 42, 54–55.

59 J. Dewey, 'The Literary Structure of the Controversy Stories in Mark 2:1 – 3:6', *Journal of Biblical Literature* 92 (1973), 397–398.

60 See W. Thissen, *Erzählung der Befreiung. Eine exegetische Untersuchung zu Mk 2,1 – 3,6* (Würzburg: Echter Verlag, 1976), pp. 151–186.

61 See R. Pesch, *Das Markus-evangelium* (Herders theologischer Kommentar zum Neuen Testament II.1; Freiburg/Basel/Vienna: Herder, 1976), p. 156.

62 Cf. J. Dewey, *Markan Public Debate*, p. 72.

63 Cf. E. Schweizer, *The Good News According to Mark* (above, note 22), p. 62.

64 Cf. W. L. Lane, *Commentary on the Gospel of Mark* (The New International Commentary on the New Testament; Grand Rapids: Eerdmans, 1974), p. 96.

65 Cf. J. Dewey, *Markan Public Debate*, pp. 72–73.

66 J. Dewey, *ibid.*, pp. 78–79.

67 Cf. J. Dewey, *ibid.*, p. 72.

68 See I. Maisch, *Die Heilung des Gelähmten. Eine exegetisch-traditionsgeschichtliche Untersuchung zu Mk 2,1–12* (Stuttgart: Verlag Katholisches Bibelwerk, 1971), pp. 29–39.

69 See M. Trautmann, *Zeichenhafte Handlungen Jesu* (Würzburg: Echter Verlag, 1980), pp. 240–243.

70 See H.-J. Klauck, 'Die Frage der Sündenvergebung in der Perikope von der Heilung des Gelähmten (Mk 2,1–12 parr)', *Biblische Zeitschrift* N.S. 25 (1981), 235–236, 241–242.

71 G. Theissen, *The Miracle Stories* (above, note 12), p. 278.

72 'Original' means here, of course, as far as we can reach back into the tradition, and does not imply that on that level we would have found an eyewitness report. Even on the oldest level we can reach, we are dealing with a post-resurrection interpretative story.

73 See I. Maisch, *Die Heilung des Gelähmten*, pp. 57–71.

74 I. Maisch, *ibid.*, pp. 77–101.

75 G. Minette de Tillesse, *Le secret messianique* (above, note 49), p. 121.

76 See I. Maisch, *Die Heilung des Gelähmten*, pp. 105–125.
77 E. Schweizer, *The Good News According to Matthew* (Atlanta: John Knox Press, 1975/London: SPCK, 1976), p. 224.
78 Cf. R. H. Gundry, *Matthew. A Commentary on His Literary and Theological Art* (Grand Rapids: Eerdmans, 1982), p. 164.
79 Cf. D. Hill, *The Gospel of Matthew* (The New Century Bible Commentary; London: Marshall, Morgan & Scott, 1972), p. 171.
80 Cf. F. W. Beare, *The Gospel According to Matthew* (San Francisco: Harper & Row/Oxford: Blackwell, 1981), p. 223.
81 Cf. R. H. Gundry, *Matthew*, p. 165.
82 Cf. D. Senior, *Invitation to Matthew* (An Image Book; Garden City, N.Y.: Doubleday, 1977), p. 96.
83 C. H. Talbert, *Reading Luke. A Literary and Theological Commentary on the Third Gospel* (New York: Crossroad, 1984), p. 63.
84 J. A. Fitzmyer, *The Gospel According to Luke I – IX* (above, note 35), p. 580.
85 Cf. J. A. Fitzmyer, *ibid.*, p. 581.
86 Cf. J. A. Fitzmyer, *ibid.*, p. 548.
87 Cf. J. A. Fitzmyer, *ibid.*, p. 584.
88 S. Brown, *Apostasy and Perseverance in the Theology of Luke* (Analecta Biblica 36; Rome: Pontifical Biblical Institute, 1969), p. 82.
89 E. Schweizer, *The Good News According to Luke* (Atlanta: John Knox Press/London: SPCK, 1984), pp. 110–111.
90 U. Busse, *Die Wunder des Propheten Jesus* (above, note 25), p. 134.
91 Depending on the variant readings followed, it occurs between twenty-three and twenty-eight times in Mark, as against sixteen or seventeen times in Matthew, three times in Luke.
92 J. Dewey, *Markan Public Debate* (above, note 58), p. 103.
93 J. Dewey, *ibid.*, p. 47.
94 J. Sauer, 'Traditionsgeschichtliche Überlegungen zu Mk 3.1–6', *Zeitschrift für die neutestamentliche Wissenschaft* 73 (1982), 185–196.
95 J. Sauer, *ibid.*, 196–203.
96 Cf. A. J. Hultgren, *Jesus and His Adversaries* (Minneapolis: Augsburg, 1979), p. 84.
97 H. W. Hoehner, *Herod Antipas* (SNTS Monograph Series 17; Cambridge: Cambridge University Press, 1972), p. 339.
98 A. J. Hultgren, *Jesus and His Adversaries*, pp. 154–157.
99 W. J. Bennett, Jr, 'The Herodians of Mark's Gospel', *Novum Testamentum* 17 (1975), 13.
100 L. Schenke, *Die Wundererzählungen* (above, note 40), pp. 171–172.
101 O. L. Cope, *Matthew: A Scribe Trained for the Kingdom of Heaven* (CBQ Monograph Series 5; Washington, D.C.: Catholic Biblical Association of America, 1976), p. 36.
102 Cf. O. L. Cope, *ibid.*, p. 45.
103 Cf. G. Bornkamm *et al.*, *Tradition and Interpretation in Matthew* (above, note 36), p. 79.
104 Cf. T. R. W. Longstaff, *Evidence of Conflation in Mark? A Study in the Synoptic Problem* (Missoula, Mont.: Scholars Press, 1977), p. 159.

105 Cf. B. Gerhardsson, *The Mighty Acts of Jesus* (above, note 52), p. 81.
106 Cf. U. Busse, *Die Wunder des Propheten Jesus* (above, note 25), pp. 139–140.
107 K. Stock, *Boten aus dem Mit-Ihm-Sein* (Analecta Biblica 75; Rome: Biblical Institute Press, 1975), p. 75.
108 J. P. Heil, *Jesus Walking on the Sea* (Analecta Biblica 87; Rome: Biblical Institute Press, 1981), pp. 118–127.
109 W. Schmithals, *Wunder und Glaube. Eine Auslegung von Markus 4:35 – 6:6a* (Neukirchen-Vluyn: Neukirchener Verlag, 1970).
110 W. Schmithals, *ibid.*, p. 7.
111 R. Pesch, *Das Markus-evangelium* I (above, note 61), pp. 277–280.
112 L. Cerfaux, 'La section des pains' in *Recueil Lucien Cerfaux* I (Gembloux: Éditions J. Duculot, 1954), pp. 471–485.
113 P. J. Achtemeier, 'Toward the Isolation of Pre-Markan Miracle-Catenae', *Journal of Biblical Literature* 89 (1970), 265–291.
114 V. Taylor, *The Gospel According to St Mark* (London: Macmillan/New York: St Martin's Press, 1957), p. 274.
115 H. J. Klauck, *Allegorie und Allegorese in synoptischen Gleichnistexten* (Münster: Aschendorff, 1978), p. 345.
116 L. Schenke, *Die Wundererzählungen* (above, note 40), pp. 33–41. Compare X. Léon-Dufour, *Études d'Évangile* (above, note 51), pp. 159–161.
117 X. Léon-Dufour, *ibid.*, p. 162.
118 L. Schenke, *Die Wundererzählungen*, pp. 41–44.
119 L. Schenke, *ibid.*, p. 59.
120 R. Glöckner, *Neutestamentliche Wundergeschichten und das Lob der Wundertaten Gottes in den Psalmen* (Mainz: Matthias-Grünewald Verlag, 1983), pp. 60–61. Compare *idem*, *Biblischer Glaube ohne Wunder?* (Einsiedeln: Johannes Verlag, 1979), pp. 55, 129f.
121 J. H. Charlesworth (ed.), *The Old Testament Pseudepigrapha* I: *Apocalyptic Literature and Testaments* (Garden City, N.Y.: Doubleday/London: Darton, Longman and Todd, 1983), p. 813.
122 L. Schenke, *Die Wundererzählungen*, pp. 59–60.
123 E. Best, *Following Jesus. Discipleship in the Gospel of Mark* (Sheffield: JSOT Press, 1981). On Mk 4:35–41, see pp. 230–234.
124 B. M. F. van Iersel and A. J. M. Linmans, 'The Storm on the Lake. Mk 4:35–41 and Mt 8:18–27 in the Light of Form-Criticism, "Redaktionsgeschichte" and Structural Analysis' in *Miscellanea Neotestamentica* II (ed. T. Baarda *et al.*; Leiden: E. J. Brill, 1978), p. 23. See T. J. Weeden, *Mark. Traditions in Conflict* (Philadelphia: Fortress Press, 1971), pp. 81–90.
125 L. Schenke, *Die Wundererzählungen*, pp. 71–79.
126 R. Glöckner, *Neutestamentliche Wundergeschichten*, p. 62.
127 R. Glöckner, *ibid.*, pp. 63–67.
128 R. Glöckner, *ibid.*, pp. 67–76.
129 R. Glöckner, *ibid.*, pp. 76–79.
130 W. Wrede, *The Messianic Secret* (trans. J. C. G. Greig; London: James Clarke, 1971), especially pp. 102ff.
131 W. Wrede, *ibid.*, pp. 108, 113–114.

132   L. Schenke, *Die Wundererzählungen*, pp. 80–93; H. J. Klauck, *Allegorie und Allegorese* (above, note 115), p. 347.

133   A. Polag, *Fragmenta Q. Textheft zur Logienquelle* (Neukirchen: Neukirchener Verlag, 1979), p. 42.

134   B. M. F. van Iersel and A. J. M. Linmans, 'The Storm on the Lake', p. 24.

135   F. W. Beare, *The Gospel According to Matthew* (above, note 80), p. 215.

136   E. Schweizer, *The Good News According to Matthew* (above, note 77), p. 221.

137   B. M. F. van Iersel and A. J. M. Linmans, 'The Storm on the Lake', p. 26.

138   H. L. Strack and P. Billerbeck, *Kommentar zum Neuen Testament aus Talmud und Midrasch* I (Munich: Beck, 1922), pp. 438–439.

139   R. H. Gundry, *Matthew* (above, note 78), p. 156.

140   E. Schweizer, *The Good News According to Matthew*, p. 221.

141   G. Bornkamm *et al.*, *Tradition and Interpretation in Matthew* (above, note 36), p. 56; G. Theissen, *The Miracle Stories* (above, note 12), pp. 165–167.

142   G. Bornkamm *et al.*, *Tradition and Interpretation in Matthew*, pp. 30, 100.

143   H. Conzelmann, *The Theology of St Luke* (London: Faber and Faber, 1960/New York: Harper & Row, 1961), pp. 49–50.

144   J. A. Fitzmyer, *The Gospel According to Luke I – IX* (above, note 35), p. 730.

145   G. Theissen, *The Miracle Stories*, p. 181.

146   W. Kirchenschläger, *Jesu exorzistisches Wirken* (above, note 25), pp. 85–89.

147   H. J. Klauck, *Allegorie und Allegorese* (above, note 115), p. 346.

148   U. Busse, *Die Wunder des Propheten Jesus* (above, note 25), pp. 202–204.

149   Cf. L. T. Johnson, *The Literary Function of Possessions in Luke-Acts* (SBL Dissertation Series 39; Missoula, Mont.: Scholars Press, 1977), pp. 96–98.

150   G. Rochais, *Les récits de résurrection des morts dans le Nouveau Testament* (Cambridge: Cambridge University Press, 1981), p. 18.

151   U. Busse, *Die Wunder des Propheten Jesus*, p. 161.

152   G. Rochais, *Les récits*, p. 19.

153   U. Busse, *Die Wunder des Propheten Jesus*, pp. 165–166; G. Rochais, *Les récits*, pp. 22–23; J. Fitzmyer, *The Gospel According to Luke I – IX* (above, note 35), p. 656.

154   U. Busse, *Die Wunder des Propheten Jesus*, p. 167.

155   G. Rochais, *Les récits*, p. 24.

156   M. Dibelius, *From Tradition to Gospel* (New York: Charles Scribner's Sons, n.d.; reprinted Edinburgh and London: James Clarke, 1971), p. 75.

157   H. Schürmann, *Das Lukas-evangelium* (Herders theologischer Kommentar zum Neuen Testament III.1; Freiburg: Herder, 1969), p. 401.

158 J. Fitzmyer, *The Gospel According to Luke I – IX*, p. 524.

159 U. Busse, *Die Wunder des Propheten Jesus*, pp. 174–175.

160 H. Schürmann, *Das Lukas-evangelium*, pp. 29 note 12, 404; W. Grundmann, *Das Evangelium nach Lukas* (Theologischer Kommentar zum Neuen Testament; Berlin: Evangelische Verlagsanstalt, 1966), p. 161.

161 D. R. Cartlidge and D. L. Dungan, *Documents for the Study of the Gospels* (Philadelphia: Fortress Press/London: Collins, 1980), p. 231.

162 G. Rochais, *Les récits*, pp. 19–21.

163 G. Rochais, *ibid.*, p. 30.

164 G. Rochais, *ibid.*, pp. 30–32.

165 T. L. Brodie, 'Towards Unravelling Luke's Use of the Old Testament: Luke 7.11–17 as an *imitatio* of 1 Kings 17.17–24', *New Testament Studies* 32 (1986), 247–267; quotation: 263.

166 T. L. Brodie, *ibid.*, 263.

167 U. Busse, *Die Wunder des Propheten Jesus*, p. 173.

168 P. Dabeck, 'Siehe es erschienen Moses und Elia', *Biblica* 23 (1942), 181.

169 G. Rochais, *Les récits*, pp. 32–35.

170 G. Rochais, *ibid.*, pp. 35–36.

171 Two medieval manuscripts (A and B) of a work called the Damascus Covenant or Damascus Document were found in the Geniza (repository for old synagogue manuscripts) of Cairo in 1896–97. Fragments of several manuscripts of the same work were found at Qumran. The original work may have been written around 100 B.C. Some think that 'Damascus' was a figurative name for Qumran.

172 G. Vermes, *The Dead Sea Scrolls in English* (A Pelican Original; Harmondsworth, Middx: Penguin, 1962), p. 104.

173 G. Rochais, *Les récits*, pp. 36–37.

174 G. Rochais, *ibid.*, pp. 37–38.

175 W. Bruners, *Die Reinigung der zehn Aussätzigen* (above, note 55), pp. 44–47.

176 P. Achtemeier, 'The Lucan Perspective on the Miracles' (above, note 56), 554.

177 W. Bruners, *Die Reinigung der zehn Aussätzigen*, pp. 308–319.

178 J. Zmijewski, *Die Eschatologiereden des Lukas-Evangeliums. Eine traditions- und redaktionsgeschichtliche Untersuchung zu Lk 21,5–36 und Lk 17,20–37* (Bonner Biblische Beiträge 40; Bonn: Hanstein, 1972), p. 331.

179 W. Bruners, *Die Reinigung der zehn Aussätzigen*, pp. 319–336.

180 R. C. Tannehill, 'The Mission of Jesus According to Luke IV, 16–30' in *Jesus in Nazareth* (ed. W. Eltester; Beihefte zur ZNW 40; Berlin: Walter de Gruyter, 1972), p. 58.

181 W. Bruners, *Die Reinigung der zehn Aussätzigen*, pp. 336–354.

182 H. Conzelmann, *The Theology of St Luke* (above, note 143), p. 191.

183 See A. Vögtle, 'Wunder und Wort in urchristlicher Glaubenswerbung (Mt 11,2–5/Lk 7,18–23' in *Das Evangelium und die Evangelien. Beiträge zur Evangelienforschung* (Düsseldorf: Patmos, 1971), pp. 219–252, especially pp. 222–236.

184   W. Bruners, *Die Reinigung der zehn Aussätzigen*, pp. 334–369.
185   W. Bruners, *ibid.*, pp. 370–382.
186   See Lk 2:22, 41, 43, 45; 9:31, 51, 53; 13:32f.; 18:31. It is 'the place of suffering required doctrinally': H. Conzelmann, *The Theology of St Luke*, p. 65.
187   Acts 8:4, 40; 9:32, 38; 11:19; 13:6, 14; 14:24; 15:3, 41; 16:6; 18:23, 27; 19:1, 21; 20:2, 25.
188   E. Schweizer, *The Good News According to Luke* (above, note 89), p. 267.
189   W. Bruners, *Die Reinigung der zehn Aussätzigen*, pp. 124–163.
190   W. Bruners, *ibid.*, pp. 383–386.
191   H. D. Betz, 'The Cleansing of the Ten Lepers (Luke 17:11–19)', *Journal of Biblical Literature* 90 (1971), 314; W. Bruners, *Die Reinigung der zehn Aussätzigen*, p. 163.
192   C. C. McCown, 'Gospel Geography: Fiction, Fact and Truth. IV. Geography in the Third Gospel', *Journal of Biblical Literature* 60 (1941), 15–17.
193   W. Bruners, *Die Reinigung der zehn Aussätzigen*, pp. 164–180.
194   R. Glöckner, *Neutestamentliche Wundergeschichten* (above, note 120), pp. 141–142.
195   W. Bruners, *Die Reinigung der zehn Aussätzigen*, pp. 386–388.
196   R. Glöckner, *Neutestamentliche Wundergeschichten*, pp. 142–144.
197   W. Bruners, *Die Reinigung der zehn Aussätzigen*, pp. 180–193, 321.
198   R. Glöckner, *Neutestamentliche Wundergeschichten*, pp. 108, 115–117, 144.
199   H. D. Betz, 'The Cleansing of the Ten Lepers', 317–318.
200   W. Bruners, *Die Reinigung der zehn Aussätzigen*, pp. 194–214.
201   G. Theissen, *The Miracle Stories* (above, note 12), p. 44.
202   H. D. Betz, 'The Cleansing of the Ten Lepers', 325.
203   R. Glöckner, *Neutestamentliche Wundergeschichten*, pp. 145–146.
204   W. Bruners, *Die Reinigung der zehn Aussätzigen*, pp. 215–228.
205   R. Pesch, *Jesu ureigene Taten?* (above, note 40), p. 133.
206   W. Bruners, *Die Reinigung der zehn Aussätzigen*, pp. 229–245.
207   W. Bruners, *ibid.*, pp. 395–397.
208   U. Busse, *Die Wunder des Propheten Jesus* (above, note 25), pp. 321–322; H. D. Betz, 'The Cleansing of the Ten Lepers', 320–321.
209   Forty-five times in the gospel and thirty-five times in Acts, against eleven times in Mark, twenty-seven times in Matthew, and nineteen times in John.
210   Against J. Jervell, 'The Lost Sheep of the House of Israel' in *Luke and the People of God* (Minneapolis: Augsburg, 1972), pp. 117–123.
211   J. M. Ford, 'Reconciliation and Forgiveness in Luke's Gospel' in *Political Issues in Luke-Acts* (ed. R. J. Cassidy and P. J. Scharper; Maryknoll, N.Y.: Orbis Books, 1983), p. 93.
212   G. Theissen, *The Miracle Stories* (above, note 12), p. 187.
213   H. D. Betz, 'The Cleansing of the Ten Lepers', 321.
214   W. Bruners, *Die Reinigung der zehn Aussätzigen*, pp. 246–280.
215   W. Bruners, *ibid.*, pp. 397–401.

216 G. Schneider, *Das Evangelium nach Lukas* (Ökumenischer Taschen-
      buch-Kommentar 3.2; Würzburg: Echter Verlag, 1977), p. 252.
217 W. Bruners, *Die Reinigung der zehn Aussätzigen*, pp. 280–295.
218 G. Theissen, *The Miracle Stories*, pp. 113–114.
219 W. Bruners, *Die Reinigung der zehn Aussätzigen*, pp. 401–403.
220 W. Bruners, *ibid.*, p. 119.
221 W. Bruners, *ibid.*, pp. 118–122.
222 J. A. Fitzmyer, *The Gospel According to St Luke I – IX* (above, note
      35), p. 1150.
223 A. George, *Études sur l'oeuvre de Luc* (Sources Bibliques; Paris;
      Éditions Gabalda, 1978), p. 313.
224 U. Busse, *Die Wunder des Propheten Jesus* (above, note 25), pp.
      325–326.
225 R. H. Fuller, *Interpreting the Miracles* (above, note 43), pp. 110–113.
226 *The Instruction on the Historical Truth of the Gospels*, VI, 2. See J. A.
      Fitzmyer, 'The Biblical Commission's Instruction on the Historical
      Truth of the Gospels', *Theological Studies* 25 (1964), 386–408; revised
      reprint in *A Christological Catechism: New Testament Answers*
      (Ramsey, N.J.: Paulist Press, 1982), pp. 97–140.
227 J. W. Cox, *A Guide to Biblical Preaching* (Nashville: Abingdon Press,
      1976), p. 22.
228 R. J. Allen, *Our Eyes Can Be Opened* (above, note 9), p. 23.
229 F. Kamphaus, *The Gospels for Preacher and Teachers* (London: Sheed
      and Ward, 1974), p. 169.
230 Cf. P. J. Achtemeier, *Mark* (Proclamation Commentaries; Phi-
      ladelphia; Fortress Press, 1975), pp. 60–70.
231 Cf. G. Gaide, 'De l'admiration à la foi. Mc 1,29–39', *Assemblées du
      Seigneur* 36 (1974), 41–43.
232 Cf. A. Fossion, 'From the Bible Text to the Homily. Cure of a Leper
      (Mk 1,40–45)', *Lumen Vitae* 35 (1980), 284–287.
233 J. Cárdenas Pallares, *A Poor Man Called Jesus. Reflections on the
      Gospel of Mark* (Maryknoll, N.Y.: Orbis Books, 1986), p. 25.
234 Cf. A. Duprez, 'Deux affrontements un jour de sabbat. Mc 2,23 – 3,6',
      Assemblées du Seigneur 40 (1972), 41–53.

Further Reading

Bailey, J. H., *The Miracles of Jesus for Today* (Nashville: Abingdon Press, 1977).

Fuller, R. H., *Interpreting the Miracles* (London: SCM Press/ Philadelphia: The Westminster Press, 1963).

Groot, P. de, *The Bible on Miracles* (De Pere, Wisc.: St Norbert Abbey Press, 1966).

Kallas, J., *The Significance of the Synoptic Miracles* (London: SPCK, 1961).

Keller, E. and M.-L., *Miracles in Dispute: a Continuing Debate* (London: SCM Press/Philadelphia: Fortress Press, 1969).

Lewis, C. S., *Miracles: a Preliminary Study* (London: Geoffrey Bles/New York: Macmillan, 1947).

Lynch, J. E., *Miracles, Signs and Wonders* (Doctrinal Pamphlet Series; New York: Paulist Press, 1967).

Monden, L., *Signs and Wonders: A Study of the Miraculous Element in Religion* (New York: Desclee, 1966).

Mussner, F., *The Miracles of Jesus: An Introduction* (Notre Dame, Ind.: University of Notre Dame Press/Shannon: Ecclesia Press, 1970).

Richards, H. J., *The Miracles of Jesus: What Really Happened?* (London: Collins, 1975; reissued Oxford: A. R. Mowbray & Co. Ltd, 1983).

Richardson, A., *The Miracle-Stories of the Gospels* (London: SCM Press, 1941/New York: Harper, 1942).

Weiser, A., *The Miracles of Jesus Then and Now* (Herald Biblical Booklets; Chicago: Franciscan Herald Press, 1972).

Bibliography

I. On the miracles in general

Achtemeier, P. J., 'Person and Deed. Jesus and the Storm-Tossed Sea', *Interpretation* 16 (1962), 169–176.

Achtemeier, P. J., 'Toward the Isolation of Pre-Markan Miracle Catenae', *Journal of Biblical Literature* 89 (1970), 265–291.

Achtemeier, P. J., 'The Origin and Function of the Pre-Markan Miracle Catenae', *Journal of Biblical Literature* 91 (1972), 198–221.

Achtemeier, P. J., 'Miracles and the Historical Jesus: Mark 9:14–29', *The Catholic Biblical Quarterly* 37 (1975), 471–491.

Achtemeier, P. J., 'The Lucan Perspective on the Miracles of Jesus: A Preliminary Sketch', *Journal of Biblical Literature* 94 (1975), 547–562.

Achtemeier, P. J., 'Jesus and the Disciples as Miracle Workers in the Apocryphal New Testament' in *Aspects of Religious Propaganda in Judaism and Early Christianity* (ed. E. Schüssler-Fiorenza; Notre Dame, Ind.: Notre Dame University Press, 1976), pp. 149–184.

Achtemeier, P. J., 'An Imperfect Union: Reflections on Gerd Theissen, *Urchristliche Wundergeschichten*', *Semeia* 11 (1978), 49–68.

Achtemeier, P. J., 'The Ministry of Jesus in the Synoptic Gospels', *Interpretation* 35 (1981), 157–169.

Allen, D., 'Miracles Old and New', *Interpretation* 28 (1974), 298–306.

Allen, R. J., *Our Eyes Can Be Opened. Preaching the Miracle Stories of the Synoptic Gospels* (Washington, D.C.: University of America Press, 1982).

Annen, F., 'Die Dämonenaustreibungen Jesu in den synoptischen Evangelien', *Theologische Berichte* 5 (1976), 107–146.

Antona, G., 'I miracoli di guarigione di Gesù: un' ipotesi esplicativa', *Studia Patavina* 32 (1985), 23–41.

Arendt, R. P., 'Der Begriff des Wunders, besonders im Hinblick auf Bultmann und Kierkegaard', *Neue Zeitschrift für systematische Theologie und Religionsphilosophie* 12 (1970), 298–306.

Arowele, P. J., 'This Generation Seeks Signs. The Miracles of Jesus with Reference to the African Situation', *Africa Theological Journal* 10 (1981), 17–28.

Ashe, G., *Miracles* (London: Routledge and Kegan Paul, 1978).

Aune, D. E., 'Magic in Early Christianity' in *Aufstieg und Niedergang der Römischen Welt* II.23/2 (Berlin: W. de Gruyter, 1980), pp. 1507–1557.

Bailey, J. H., *The Miracles of Jesus for Today* (Nashville: Abingdon Press, 1977).

Baltensweiler, H., 'Wunder und Glaube im Neuen Testament', *Theologische Zeitschrift* 23 (1967), 241–256.

Barclay, W., *And He Had Compassion* (Edinburgh: The Saint Andrew Press, 1975/Valley Forge, Pa.: Judson Press, 1976).

Barr, J., 'The Miracles' in *Jesus and Man's Hope* II (ed. D. G. Miller and D. Y. Hadidian; A Perspective Book; Pittsburgh: Pittsburgh Theological Seminary, 1971), pp. 305–310.

Barrett, C. K., *The Holy Spirit and the Gospel Tradition* (London: SPCK, 1966), pp. 69–93.

Barton, S., 'Jesus and Health', *Theology* 87 (718; 1984), 266–272.

Basinger, D., 'Miracles and apologetics: a response', *Christian Scholar's Review* 9 (1980), 348–354.

Bastin, M., 'Jesus Worked Miracles (Texts from Mt 8)', *Lumen Vitae* 39 (1984), 131–139.

Baur, A., and Kogel, H., *Die Wunder Jesu—Von der Exegese zur Katechese (Handreichungen des Religionspädagogischen Seminars Augsburg* Band 2; Donauwörth: Auer, 1970).

Becker, J., 'Wunder und Christologie. Zum literar-kritischen und christologischen Problem der Wunder im Johannesevangelium', *New Testament Studies* 16 (1970), 130–148.

Becker, U., and Wibbing, S., *Wundergeschichten*, 5th ed. (Gütersloh: Gerd Mohn, 1972).

Beinert, W., 'Das Heil der Welt: Befreiung von Mächten und Gewalten', *Lebendiges Zeugnis* 31 (1976), 42–61.

Belle, G. van, *Jezus: een 'wonder-man'. Over bijbelse wonderverhalen* (Katechetische unit; Antwerp: Patmos, 1976).

Berends, W., 'The Biblical Criteria for Demon-Possession', *Westminster Theological Journal* 37 (1975), 342–365.

Berghe, P. Van den, 'De wonderverhalen uit de evangelien. Een handreiking', *Collationes* 19 (1973), 433–458.

Best, E., 'Exorcism in the New Testament and Today', *Biblical Theology* 27 (1977), 1–9.

Best, E., 'The Miracles in Mark', *Review and Expositor* 75 (1978), 539–554.

Best, E., 'Healing and the New Testament', *Irish Biblical Studies* 5 (1983), 65–72.

Best, T. F., 'St Paul and the Decline of the Miraculous', *Encounter* 44 (1983), 231–243.

Best, T. F., 'St Paul and the Decline of the Miraculous', *East Asia Journal of Theology* 4 (1986), 68–76.

Betz, H. D., 'Jesus as Divine Man' in *Jesus and the Historian. Festschrift E. C. Colwell* (ed. F. T. Trotter; Philadelphia: The Westminster Press, 1968), pp. 114–133.

Betz, H. D., 'The Early Christian Miracle Story: Some Observations on the Form Critical Problem', *Semeia* 11 (1978), 69–81.

Betz, O., 'Wie können wir heute die Wunderberichte im Neuen Testament verstehen?', *Katechetische Blätter* 91 (1966), 443–453.

Betz, O., 'The Concept of the So-Called "Divine Man" in Mark's Christology' in *Studies in New Testament and Early Christian Literature* (ed. D. E. Aune; Leiden: E. J. Brill, 1972), pp. 229–240.

Betz, O., 'Das Problem des Wunders bei Flavius Josephus im Vergleich zum Wunderproblem bei den Rabbinen und im Johannesevangelium' in *Josephus Studien...Festschrift O. Michel* (ed. O. Betz, K. Haacker and M. Hengel; Göttingen: Vandenhoeck & Ruprecht, 1974), pp. 23–44.

Betz, O., and Grimm, W., *Wesen und Wirklichkeit der Wunder Jesu...* (Arbeiten zum Neuen Testament und Judentum 2; Frankfurt am Main/Berne: P. Lang, 1977).

Blandino, G., 'Miracolo e leggi della natura', *Civiltà Cattolica* 133 (3159; 1982), 224–238.

Blank, J., 'Zur Christologie ausgewählter Wunderberichte' in *Schriftauslegung in Theorie und Praxis* (Munich: Kösel Verlag, 1969), pp. 104–128.

Blank, J., 'Die biblische Wunderberichte als Kerygma und als Glaubensgeschichten' in *Verändert Interpretation den Glauben?* (Freiburg: Herder, 1972), pp. 138–159.

Bligh, J., 'Signs and Wonders: Contemplating the Miracles of the Gospels', *The Way* 11 (1971), 44–53.

Blomberg, C. L., 'New Testament Miracles and Higher Criticism: Climbing Up the Slippery Slope', *Journal of the Evangelical Theological Society* 27 (1984), 425–438.

Böcher, O., *Das Neue Testament und die dämonischen Mächte* (SBS 58; Stuttgart: Verlag Katholisches Bibelwerk, 1972).

Böcher, O., 'Exorzismus. I. Neues Testament', *Theologische Realenzyclopädie* 10 (1982), 747–750.

Böhles, M., 'Von der Macht und Ohnmacht des Bösen', *Ordens-Korrespondenz* 18 (1977), 129–146.

Böhm, H., *Des Glaubens liebstes Kind? Der heutige Mensch vor der neutestamentlichen Wunderfrage* (Moers: Brendow-Verlag, 1981).

Boers, H., 'Sisyphus and His Rock. Concerning Gerd Theissen, *Urchristliche Wundergeschichten*', *Semeia* 11 (1978), 1–48.

Boespflug, F.-D., 'Jésus le toucha...', *Vie Spirituelle* 133 (634; 1979), 651–678.

Boismard, M.-E., 'Rapports entre foi et miracles dans l'évangile de Jean', *Ephemerides Theologicae Lovanienses* 58 (1982), 357–364.

Boobyer, G. H., 'The Gospel Miracles: Views Past and Present' in *The Miracles and the Resurrection* (ed. I. T. Ramsey; London: SPCK, 1964), pp. 31–49.

Borgen, P., 'Miracles of Healing in the New Testament: Some Observations', *Studia Theologica* 35 (1981), 91–106.

Borsch, F. H., *Power in Weakness. New Hearing for Gospel Stories of Healing and Discipleship* (Philadelphia: Fortress Press, 1983).

Bostock, D. G., 'Jesus as the New Elisha', *Expository Times* 92 (1980–81), 39–41.

Bourke, M. M., 'The Miracle Stories of the Gospels', *Dunwoodie Review* 12 (1972), 21–34.

Braude, W. G., 'Jesus and His Miracles', *The Bible Today* no. 58 (February 1972), 627–631.

Brodie, T. L., 'Jesus as the New Elisha. Cracking the Code', *Expository Times* 93 (1981–82), 39–42.

Brown, C., *Miracles and the Critical Mind* (Grand Rapids: Eerdmans/Exeter: Paternoster, 1984).

Brown, C., *That You May Believe. Miracles and Faith Then and Now* (Grand Rapids: Eerdmans, 1985).

Brown, P., 'The Rise and Function of the Holy Man in Late Antiquity', *Journal of Roman Studies* 61 (1971), 80–101.

Brown, R. E., 'The Gospel Miracles' in *New Testament Essays* (Milwaukee: The Bruce Publishing Company/London and Dublin: Geoffrey Chapman, 1965), pp. 168–191.

Brown, R. E., 'Jesus and Elisha', *Perspective* 12 (1971), 85–104.

Brox, N., 'Magie und Aberglaube an den Anfangen des Christentums', *Trierer Theologische Zeitschrift* 83 (1974), 157–180.

Bultmann, R., 'Zur Frage des Wunders' in *Glaube und Verstehen* I, 4th ed. (Tubingen: J. C. B. Mohr, 1961), pp. 214–228.

Bultmann, R., *The History of the Synoptic Tradition* (Oxford: Basil Blackwell, 1972), pp. 209–244.

Burger, C., 'Jesu Taten nach Matthäus 8 und 9', *Zeitschrift für Theologie und Kirche* 70 (1973), 272–287.

Burkill, T. A., 'The Notion of Miracle with Special Reference to St Mark's Gospel', *Zeitschrift für die neutestamentliche Wissenschaft* 50 (1959), 33–48.

Burkill, T. A., *Mysterious Revelation* (Ithaca, N.Y.: Cornell University Press, 1963), pp. 41–61.

Burkill, T. A., 'Mark 3,7–12 and the Alleged Dualism in the Evangelist's Miracle Material', *Journal of Biblical Literature* 87 (1968), 409–417.

Busse, U., *Die Wunder des Propheten Jesus. Die Rezeption, Komposition und Interpretation der Wundertradition im Evangelium des Lukas* (Forschung zur Bibel 24; Stuttgart: Verlag Katholisches Bibelwerk, 1977).

Cangh, J.-M. van, 'Les sources de l'Évangile: les collections pré-marciennes de miracles', *Revue Théologique de Louvain* 3 (1972), 76–85.

Cangh, J.-M. van, 'Santé et salut dans les miracles d'Epidaure, d'Apollonius de Tyane et du Nouveau Testament. Gnosticisme et Monde Hellénistique', *Publications de l'Institut Orientaliste de Louvain* 27 (1982), 263–277.

Cangh, J.-M. van, 'Miracles des rabbins et de Jésus. La tradition sur Honi et Hanina', *Revue Théologique de Louvain* 15 (1984), 28–53.

Carlston, C. E., 'The Question of Miracles', *Andover Newton Quarterly* 12 (1971), 99–107.

Carrez, M., 'L'Héritage de l'Ancien Testament' in *Les Miracles de Jésus* (ed. X. Léon-Dufour; Parole de Dieu; Paris: Éditions du Seuil, 1977), pp. 45–58.

Carter, J., 'Theological Recognition of Miracles', *Theological Studies* 20 (1959), 175–197.

Cavnar, N., 'Miracles: do they really happen? Fr René Laurentin knows they do—he has seen the evidence', *New Covenant* 12 (1982), 4–7.

Clark, D. K., 'Signs in Wisdom and John', *Catholic Biblical Quarterly* 45 (1983), 201–209.

Collins, R. F., 'Jesus' Ministry to the Deaf and the Dumb', *Melita Theologica* 35 (1984), 12–36.

Comber, J., 'Critical Notes: The Verb *Therapeuō* in Matthew's Gospel', *Journal of Biblical Literature* 97 (1978), 431–434.

Connolly, D., 'Ad miracula sanationum apud Mt', *Verbum Domini* 45 (1967), 306–327.

Corsani, B., *I miracoli di Gesù nel quarto vangelo. L'ipotesi della fonte dei segni* (Studi biblici 65; Brescia: Paideia, 1983).

Countryman, L. W., 'How Many Baskets Full? Mark 8:14–21 and the Value of Miracles in Mark', *Catholic Biblical Quarterly* 47 (1985), 643–655.

Court, J. M., 'The Philosophy of the Synoptic Miracles', *Journal of Theological Studies* 23 (1972), 1–15.

Craghan, J. F., 'Biblical Images of Healing', *The Bible Today* no. 81 (December 1975), 566–572.

Craig, W. L., 'Colin Brown, *Miracles and the Critical Mind:* A Review Article', *Journal of the Evangelical Theological Society* 27 (1984), 473–485.

Crane, T. E., 'The Marvellous Element in the Gospel' in *Studies in Faith and Culture* IV, 3 (ed. N. Brown; Sydney: Manly, 1980), pp. 68–78.

Crespy, G., 'Maladie et guérison dans le Nouveau Testament', *Lumière et Vie* 17 (1968), 45–68.

Crossan, J., 'The Presence of God's Love in the Power of Jesus' Works', *Concilium* 50 (10.5; 1969), 65–79.

Davey, F. M., 'Healing in the New Testament' in *The Miracles and the Resurrection* (ed. I. T. Ramsey; London: SPCK, 1964), pp. 50–63.

Davies, W., 'The Arrangement of Ten Miracles in Matt. VIII.1 – IX.34' in *The Setting of the Sermon on the Mount* (Cambridge: Cambridge University Press, 1964), pp. 86–93.

Delling, G., 'Das Verständnis des Wunders im Neuen Testament', *Zeitschrift für systematische Theologie* 24 (1955), 265–280.

Delling, G., 'Josephus und das Wunderbare', *Novum Testamentum* 2 (1958), 291–309.

Delling, G., 'Botschaft und Wunder im Wirken Jesu' in *Der historische Jesus und der kerygmatische Christus* (ed. H. Ristow and K. Matthiae: Berlin: Evangelische Verlagsanstalt, 1964), pp. 389–402.

Delling, G., 'Zur Bedeutung des Wunders durch die Antike (1955)' in *Studien zum Neuen Testament und zum hellenistischen Judentum* (Göttingen: Vandenhoeck & Ruprecht, 1970), pp. 53–71.

Denaux, A., 'Het wonder bij Lucas' in *Ziende blind? Bijbelse Wonderverhalen exegetisch en catechetisch toegelicht* (Antwerp: Patmos, 1976), pp. 117–126.

Dennison, W. D., 'Miracles as "Signs": Their Significance for Apologetics', *Biblical Theology Bulletin* 6 (1976), 190–202.

Dhanis, M., 'Qu'est-ce qu'un miracle?', *Gregorianum* 40 (1959), 201–241.

Dibelius, M., 'Tales—Legends' in *From Tradition to Gospel* (New York: Charles Scribner's Sons, n.d.; reprinted Edinburgh and London: James Clarke, 1971), pp. 70–132.

Dietl, P. J., 'On Miracles' in *Contemporary Philosophy of Religion* (ed. S. M. Cahn; Oxford: Oxford University Press, 1982), pp. 146–153.

Dietzfelbinger, C, 'Vom Sinn der Sabbatheilungen Jesu', *Evangelische Theologie* 38 (1978), 281–298.

Dignath, W., 'Die Wundergeschichten des Neuen Testaments und die Redlichkeit ihrer unterrichtliche Behandlung', *Der evangelische Erzieher* 15 (1963), 197–213.

Donahue, J. R., 'Miracle, Mystery and Parable', *The Way* 18 (1978), 252–262.

Doyle, J. P., 'Healing Means the Presence of the Healer', *Chicago Studies* 23 (1984), 273–284.

Duling, D. C., 'Solomon, Exorcism, and the Son of David', *Harvard Theological Review* 68 (1975), 235–252.

Dumas, B. A., *Los milagros de Jesús. Los signos mesiánicos y la teología de la liberación* (Cristianismo y sociedad 4; Bilbao: Desclée de Brouwer, 1984).

Dunn, J. D. G., *Jesus and the Spirit* (New Testament Library; London: SCM Press/Philadelphia: The Westminster Press, 1975), pp. 69–76.

Duprez, A., 'Guérisons païennes et guérisons évangéliques', *Foi et Vie. Cahiers Bibliques* 69 (May-June 1970), 3–28.

Duprez, A., *Jésus et les dieux guérisseurs. A propos de Jean V* (Paris: Gabalda, 1970).

Duprez, A., 'Les miracles évangéliques peuvent-ils avoir un sens aujourd'hui?', *Assemblées du Seigneur* 54 (1972), 45–50.

Duprez, A., 'Le fait des miracles', *Journal de la vie. Aujourd-hui la Bible* 130 (March 1973), 6–9.

Duprez, A., 'Le sens des miracles', *Journal de la vie. Aujourd'hui la Bible* 130 (March 1973), 12–13.

Duprez, A., 'Les récits évangéliques de miracle', *Lumière et Vie* 23 (119; 1974), 49–69.

Eckert, J., 'Zeichen und Wunder in der Sicht des Paulus und der Apostelgeschichte', *Trierer Theologische Zeitschrift* 88 (1979), 19–33.

Edgar, T. R., *Miraculous Gifts: Are They for Today?* (Neptune, N.J.: Loizeaux Brothers, 1983).

Elmar Wilms, F., *Wunder im Alten Testament* (Regensburg: Pustet Verlag, 1979).

Entrevernes Group, *Signs and Parables. Semiotics and Gospel Texts* (Pittsburgh Theological Monograph Series 23; Pittsburgh: Pickwick Press, 1978).

Éparvier, J., and Hérisse, M., *Le dossier des miracles* (Paris: Hachette, 1967).

Erlandson, D. K., 'A New Look at Miracles', *Religious Studies* 13 (1977), 417–428.

Evely, L., *The Gospels Without Myth* (Garden City, N.Y.: Doubleday, 1971).

Farmer, H. H., *Are Miracles Possible?* (London: SPCK, 1960).

Farrer, A., *A Study in St Mark* (Westminster: Dacre Press, 1951/New York: Oxford University Press, 1952), pp. 30–52.

Farrer, A., 'Loaves and Thousands', *Journal of Theological Studies* 4 (1953), 1–14.

Fascher, E., *Kritik und Wunder. Eine geschichtliche Skizze* (Aufsätze und Vorträge zur Theologie und Religionswissenschaft; Berlin: Evangelische Verlagsanstalt, 1960).

Feuillet, A., 'Le règne de Dieu et les miracles de Jèsus d'après les Évangiles synoptiques', *Esprit et Vie* 87 (49; 1977), 655–669.

Feuillet, R., 'Les miracles de Jésus en saint Marc', *Prêtre et Pasteur* 76 (1973), 525–532.

Feuillet, R., 'L'activité miraculeuse de Jésus en saint Marc', *Prêtre et Pasteur* 76 (1973), 597–604.

Freyne, S., 'Query: Did Jesus Really Work Miracles?', *The Furrow* 26 (1975), 283–286.

Fridrichsen, A., *The Problem of Miracle in Primitive Christianity* (Minneapolis: Augsburg Publishing House, 1972).

Funk, R. W. (ed.), *The Early Christian Miracle Story: Reviews and Essays* (*Semeia* 11; Missoula, Mont.: Scholars Press, 1978).

Funk, R. W., 'The Form of the New Testament Miracle Story', *Semeia* 12 (1978), 57–96.

Fusco, V., 'Dall' esegesi all' ermeneutica: i miracoli in Marco', *Rassegna di Teologia* 25 (1984), 481–491.

Gallagher, E, *Divine Man or Magician. Celsus and Origen on Jesus* (SBL Dissertation Series 64; Chico, Cal.: Scholars Press, 1982).

Galot, J., 'Il miracolo, segno di Cristo', *Civiltà Cattolica* 125 (2972; 1974), 131–142.

Gatzweiler, K., 'La conception paulinienne du miracle', *Ephemerides Theologicae Lovanienses* 37 (1961), 813–846.

Gatzweiler, K., 'Les miracles évangéliques', *La Foi et le Temps* 1 (1971), 115–129.

Gatzweiler, K., 'Réflexions sur le miracle', *La Foi et le Temps* 1 (1971), 581–599.

Gatzweiler, K., 'L'exégèse historico-critique. Une guérison à Capharnaüm', *La Foi et le Temps* 9 (1979), 297–315.

Geisler, N. L., *Miracles and Modern Thought* (Exeter: Paternoster, 1982).

Geller, M. J., 'Jesus' Therapeutic Powers—Parallels in the Talmud and Incantation Bowls', *Journal of Jewish Studies* 28 (1977), 141–155.

George, A., 'Les miracles de Jésus dans les évangiles synoptiques', *Lumière et Vie* no. 33 (1957), 7–24.

George, A., 'Les miracles de Jésus. Les données de l'exégèse actuelle pour l'apologétique', *Bulletin du Comité des Études* no. 35 (1961), 387–403.

George, A., 'Paroles de Jésus sur ses miracles (Mt 11,5.21; 12,27.28 et par.)' in *Jésus aux Origines de la Christologie* (ed. J. Dupont; Louvain: Leuven University Press, 1975), pp. 283–301.

George, A., 'Miracles dans le monde hellénistique' in *Les miracles de Jésus* (ed. X. Léon-Dufour; Parole de Dieu; Paris: Éditions du Seuil, 1977), pp. 95–108.

Georgi, D., 'Socioeconomic Reasons for the "Divine Man" as a Propagandistic Pattern' in *Aspects of Religious Propaganda in Judaism and Early Christianity* (ed. E. Schüssler-Fiorenza; Notre Dame: Notre Dame University Press, 1976), pp. 27–42.

Gerhardsson, B., *The Mighty Acts of Jesus According to Matthew* (Lund: Gleerup, 1979).

Glasswell, M. E., 'The Use of Miracles in the Markan Gospel' in *Miracles. Cambridge Studies in Their Philosophy and History* (ed. C. F. D. Moule; London: A. R. Mowbray & Co. Ltd, 1965), pp. 149–162.

Gleason, R. W., 'Miracles and Contemporary Thought', *Thought* 37 (1962), 12–34.

Glöckner, R., *Biblischer Glaube ohne Wunder?* (Sammlung Horizonte, N.F. 14; Einsiedeln: Johannes Verlag, 1979).

Glöckner, R., *Neutestamentliche Wundergeschichten und das Lob der Wundertaten Gottes in den Psalmen* (Walberger Studien, Theologische Reihe 13; Mainz: Matthias-Grünewald Verlag, 1983).

Gonzáles Faus, J. I., '¿Qué pensar de los milagros de Jesús?', *Razón y Fe* 205 (1008; 1982), 479–494.

Gonzáles Faus, J. I., *Clamor del Reino. Estudio sobre los milagros de Jesús* (Verdad e Imagen 79; Salamanca: Sígueme, 1982).

Goodwin, J., *Why Miracles?* (Simeon Booklets no. 10; London: SPCK, 1964).

Grant, R. M., *Miracle and Natural Law in Graeco-Roman and Early Christian Thought* (Amsterdam: North-Holland Publishing Company, 1952).

Grant, R. M., 'The Problem of Miraculous Feedings in the Greco-Roman Period', *Center for Hermeneutical Studies Protocol Series* 42 (1982), 1–15.

Grassi, J. A., 'Miracles—Magic or Teaching?' in *Jesus as Teacher. A New Testament Guide to Learning 'The Way'* (Winona, Minn.: St Mary's College Press, 1978), pp. 55–59.

Gravel, P., 'Hume et le miracle', *Études Philosophiques* 28 (1973), 19–41.

Guillemette, P., 'La forme des récits d'exorcisme de Bultmann. Un dogme à reconsidérer', *Église et Théologie* 11 (1980), 177–193.

Gutbrod, V., *Die Wundergeschichten des Neuen Testament dargestellt nach den drei ersten Evangelien* (Stuttgart: Calwer Verlag, 1967).

Gutwenger, E., 'Die Machterweise Jesu im formgeschichtlicher Sicht', *Zeitschrift für Katholische Theologie* 89 (1967), 176–190.

Hamblin, R. L., 'Miracles in the Book of Acts', *Southwestern Journal of Theology* 17 (1974), 19–34.

Hamp, V., 'Genus litterarium in Wunderberichten', *Estudios Eclesiásticos* 34 (1960), 361–366.

Harrisville, R. A., *The Miracles of Mark. A Study in the Gospel* (Minneapolis: Augsburg Publishing House, 1967).

Havener, I., 'Jesus, the Wonder Child', *The Bible Today* 22 (November 1984), 368–372.

Hay, E., 'A Contranatural View of Miracles', *Canadian Journal of Theology* 13 (1967), 266–280.

Hay, E., 'Bultmann's View of Miracles', *Lutheran Quarterly* 24 (1972), 286–300.

Heidrich, W., *Die Wunder der Evangelien in der Sicht der Gegenwart* (St. Michael: Blaschke, 1981).

Heil, J. P., 'Significant Aspects of the Healing Miracles in Matthew', *Catholic Biblical Quarterly* 41 (1979), 274–287.

Heinemeyer, K., *Synoptische Wunder als Problem der Religionspädagogik. Eine kritische Analyse aus didaktischer Sicht und Aufweis neuer Konsequenzen* (Berlin: Die Spur, 1975).

Heising, A., 'Exegese und Theologie der alt- und neutestamentlichen Speisewunder', *Zeitschrift für Katholische Theologie* 86 (1964), 80–96.

Held, H. J., 'Matthew as Interpreter of the Miracle Stories' in *Tradition and Interpretation in Matthew* (ed. G. Bornkamm, G. Barth and H. J. Held; Philadelphia: The Westminster Press/London: SCM Press, 1963), pp. 165–299.

Hengel, R. and M., 'Die Heilungen Jesu und medizinisches Denken (1959)' in *Der Wunderbegriff im Neuen Testament* (ed. E. Suhl; Wege der Forschung; Darmstadt: Wissenschaftliche Buchgesellschaft, 1980), 338–373.

Hermann, W., *Das Wunder in der evangelischen Botschaft. Zur Interpretation der Begriff 'blind' und 'taub' im Alten und Neuen Testament* (Berlin: Evangelische Verlagsanstalt, 1961).

Hesse, M., 'Miracles and the Laws of Nature' in *Miracles. Cambridge Studies in Their Philosophy and History* (ed. C. F. D. Moule; London: A. R. Mowbray & Co., Ltd, 1965), pp. 33–42.

Hiers, R. H., 'Satan, Demons and the Kingdom of God', *Scottish Journal of Theology* 27 (1974), 35–47.

Hislop, I., 'Miracles and the Gospels', *Blackfriars* 39 (1958), 57–60.

Hobbs, E. C., 'Gospel Miracle Story and Modern Miracle Stories', *Anglican Theological Review* Suppl. Series 3 (March 1974), 117–126.

Hobbs, H. H., 'The Miraculous Element in Matthew', *Southwestern Journal of Theology* 5 (1962), 41–54.

Holladay, C. H., *Theios Aner in Hellenistic Judaism. A Critique of the Use of This Category in New Testament Christology* (Missoula, Mont.: Scholars Press, 1977).

Hollenbach, P., 'Jesus, Demoniacs, and Public Authorities: A Socio-Historical Study', *Journal of the American Academy of Religion* 49 (1981), 567–588.

Hollenbach, P., 'The Conversion of Jesus: From Jesus the Baptizer to Jesus the Healer' in *Aufstieg und Niedergang der Römischen Welt* II.25/1 (ed. W. Haase; Berlin/New York: W. de Gruyter, 1982), pp. 196–219.

Holstein, H., 'Le miracle, signe de présence', *Bible et Vie Chrétienne* 38 (1961), 49–58.

Hooker, M. D., *The Message of Mark* (London: Epworth Press, 1983), pp. 34–50.

Hoskyns, E., and Davey, N., *The Riddle of the New Testament* (London: Faber and Faber Ltd, 1958), pp. 117–126.

Howard, J. K., 'New Testament Exorcism and its Significance Today', *Expository Times* 96 (4; 1985), 105–109.

Hruby, K., 'Perspectives rabbiniques sur le miracle' in *Les miracles de Jésus* (ed. X. Léon-Dufour; Parole de Dieu; Paris: Éditions du Seuil, 1977), pp. 73–94.

Hull, J. M., *Hellenistic Magic and the Synoptic Tradition* (Studies in Biblical Theology, 2nd ser., 28; London: SCM Press/Naperville, Ill.: A. R. Allenson, 1974).

Jeremias, J., *New Testament Theology* I: *The Proclamation of Jesus* (London: SCM Press/New York: Scribner, 1971), pp. 86–92.

Jervell, J., 'Die Zeichen des Apostels. Die Wunder beim lukanischen und paulinischen Paulus', *Studien zum Neuen Testament und seiner Umwelt* 4 (1979), 54–75.

Johnston, W., 'The Concept of Miracle for Today', *Theology* 63 (1960), 143–150.

Jonge, M. de, 'Signs and Works in the Fourth Gospel' in *Jesus, Stranger from Heaven and Son of God* (Missoula, Mont.: Scholars Press, 1977), pp. 117–140.

Käsemann, E., 'Is the Gospel Objective?' in *Essays on New Testament Themes* (Studies in Biblical Theology 41; London: SCM Press/Naperville, Ill.: A. R. Allenson, 1964), pp. 48–62.

Käsemann, E., 'La guérison des démoniaques', *Études Théologiques et Religieuses* 54 (1979), 231–241.

Käsemann, E., 'Die Heilung der Besessenen' in *Kirchliche Konflikte* I (Göttingen: Vandenhoeck & Ruprecht, 1982), pp. 189–200.

Kahlefeld, H., 'Jesus as a Therapist', *Concilium* 99 (1974), 111–117.

Kamphaus, F., 'Die Wunderberichte der Evangelien', *Bibel und Leben* 6 (1965), 122–135.

Kamphaus, F., *The Gospels for Preachers and Teachers* (London: Sheed and Ward, 1974), pp. 114–223.

Karris, R. J., 'God's Boundary-Breaking Mercy', *The Bible Today* 24 (January 1986), 24–29.

Kasper, W., *Jesus the Christ* (New York: Paulist Press, 1976/London: Burns & Oates, 1977), pp. 89–99.

Kasper, W., 'Zur historischen Problematik der Wunder Jesu', *Renovatio* 32 (1976), 78–79.

Kasper, W., 'Zur naturwissenschaftlichen Problematik der Wunder Jesu', *Renovatio* 32 (1976), 133–135.

Kasper, W., 'Zur theologischen Bedeutung der Wunder Jesu', *Renovatio* 32 (1976), 172–173.

Kaufmann, Y., 'Magie et miracles' in *Connaître la Bible* (Paris: P.U.F., 1970), pp. 80–90.

Kay, B., and Rogerson, J., *Miracles and Mysteries in the Bible* (Philadelphia: The Westminster Press, 1978).

Keck, L. E., 'Mark 3:7–12 and Mark's Christology', *Journal of Biblical Literature* 84 (1965), 341–358.

Kee, H. C., 'The Terminology of Mark's Exorcism Stories', *New Testament Studies* 14 (1967–68), 232–246.

Kee, H. C., 'Aretalogy and Gospel', *Journal of Biblical Literature* 92 (1973), 402–422.

Kee, H. C., *Aretalogies, Hellenistic 'Lives', and the Sources of Mark* (Berkeley: Center for Hermeneutical Studies in Hellenistic and Modern Culture, 1975).

Kee, H. C., 'Myth and Miracle: Isis, Wisdom and the Logos of John' in *Myth, Symbol and Reality* (ed. A. Olson; Notre Dame/London: University of Notre Dame Press, 1980), pp. 145–164.

Kee, H. C., *Miracle in the Early Christian World. A Study in Socio-Historical Method* (New Haven, Conn.: Yale University Press, 1983).

Kelley, J., 'God at Work', *The Way* 18 (1978), 163–173.

Kertelge, K., 'Zur Interpretation der Wunder Jesu. Ein Literaturbericht', *Bibel und Leben* 9 (1968), 140–153.

Kertelge, K., *Die Wunder Jesu im Markusevangelium. Eine redaktions-geschichtliche Untersuchung* (Munich: Kösel Verlag, 1970).

Kertelge, K., 'Begrunden die Wunder Jesu den Glauben?', *Trierer Theologische Zeitschrift* 80 (1971), 129–140.

Kertelge, K., 'Die Überlieferung der Wunder Jesu und die Frage nach dem historischen Jesus' in *Rückfrage nach Jesus. Zur Methodik und Bedeutung der Frage nach dem historischen Jesus* (Quaestiones Disputatae 63; Freiburg: Herder, 1974), pp. 174–193.

Kertelge, K., 'Die Wunder Jesu in der neueren Exegese', *Theologische Berichte* 5 (1976), 71–105.

Kertelge, K., 'Die Wunder Jesu in der neueren Exegese', *Theologisches Jahrbuch* (1981), 67–93.

Kirchschläger, W., 'Exorzismus in Qumran?', *Kairos* 18 (1976), 135–153.

Kirchschläger, W., 'Wie über Wunder reden?', *Bibel und Liturgie* 51 (1978), 252–254.

Kirchschläger, W., 'Leid und Krankheit in der neutestamentlichen Verkündigung', *Arzt und Christ* 27 (1981), 6–20.

Kirchschläger, W., *Jesu exorzistisches Wirken aus der Sicht des Lukas. Ein Beitrag zur lukanischen Redaktion* (Klosterneuberg: Österreichisches Katholisches Bibelwerk, 1981).

Klein, G., 'Wunderglaube und Neues Testament' in *Ärgernisse. Konfronta-tionen mit dem Neuen Testament* (Munich: Kösel Verlag, 1970), pp. 13–57.

Kleinman, A., *Patients and Healers in the Context of Culture* (Berkeley/London: University of California Press, 1980).

Knoch, O., 'Die Wunder Jesu. Biblische Gesichtspunkte', *Theologie der Gegenwart* 24 (1981), 203–211.

Koch, D. A., *Die Bedeutung der Wundererzählungen für die Christologie des Markusevangeliums* (Beihefte zur ZNW 42; Berlin: W. de Gruyter, 1975).

Koester, H., 'One Jesus and Four Primitive Gospels' in *Trajectories Through Early Christianity* (ed. J. M. Robinson and H. Koester; Philadelphia: Fortress Press, 1971), pp. 158–204.

Kolenkow, A. B., 'Beyond Miracles, Suffering and Eschatology' in *Society of Biblical Literature 1973 Seminar Papers*, pp. 155–202.

Kolenkow, A. B., 'A Problem of Power: How Miracle Doers Counter Charges of Magic in the Hellenistic World' in *Society of Biblical Literature 1976 Seminar Papers* (ed. G. McRae; Missoula, Mont.: Scholars Press, 1976), pp. 105–110.

Kolenkow, A. B., 'Healing Controversy as a Tie Between Miracle and Passion Material for a Proto-Gospel', *Journal of Biblical Literature* 95 (1976), 623–638.

Kolenkow, A. B., 'Relationships between Miracle and Prophecy in the Greco-Roman World and Early Christianity' in *Aufstieg und Niedergang der Römischen Welt* II.23/2 (Berlin: W. de Gruyter, 1980), pp. 1470–1506.

Kolping, A., *Wunder und Auferstehung Jesu Christi* (Theologische Brennpunkte 20; Bergen-Enkheim: Kaffke, 1969).

Kopec, E., 'Über den Motivationswert der Wunder', *Collectanea Theologica* 46 (1976), special fascicle, 45–57.

Koppelmann, F., *Jesus nicht Christus. Doch Wunder und Gegenwart der Gotteswelt* (Berlin: Buchhandlung Johannesstift, 1973).

Kremer, J., 'Besessenheit und Exorzismus. Aussagen der Bibel und heutige Problematik', *Bibel und Liturgie* 48 (1975), 22–28.

Kümmel, W. G., 'Jesusforschung seit 1965. IV. Bergpredigt—Gleichnisse— Wunderberichte', *Theologische Rundschau* 43 (1978), 105–161.

Kümmel, W. G., 'Jesusforschung seit 1965. IV. Bergpredigt—Gleichnisse— Wunderberichte (mit Nachträge) (Schluss)', *Theologische Rundschau* 43 (1978), 233–265.

Küng, H., 'Die Gretchenfrage des christlichen Glaubens? Systematische Überlegungen zum neutestamentlichen Wunder', *Theologische Quartalschrift* 152 (1972), 214–233.

Kunath, S., *Antike Parallelen zu den Wundergeschichten im Neuen Testament* (Göttinger Quellenhefte 4; Göttingen: Vandenhoeck & Ruprecht,1976).

Laflamme, R., 'Le miracle dans l'économie de la Parole', *Laval Théologique et Philosophique* 20 (1964), 214–246.

Lamarche, P., 'Les miracles de Jésus selon Marc' in *Les Miracles de Jésus* (ed. X. Léon-Dufour; Parole de Dieu; Paris: Éditions du Seuil, 1977), pp. 213–226.

Lampe, G. W. H., 'Miracles in the Acts of the Apostles' in *Miracles. Cambridge Studies in Their Philosophy and History* (ed. C. F. D. Moule; London: A. R. Mowbray & Co., Ltd, 1965), pp. 163–178.

Lampe, G. W. H., 'Miracles and Early Christian Apologetic', *ibid*, pp. 203–218.

Langevin, P.-E., 'La signification du miracle dans le message du Nouveau Testament', *Science et Esprit* 27 (1975), 161–186.

Lapointe, R., 'Qu'est-il des miracles?', *Église et Theologie* 6 (1975), 77–96.

LaRoncière, J. de, *Des miracles. Contestations et constatations* (Paris: Téqui, 1979).

Latourelle, R., 'Miracles and Revelation', *Theology Digest* 12 (1964), 99–103.

Latourelle, R., 'Authenticité historique des miracles de Jésus: Essai de critériologie', *Gregorianum* 54 (1973), 225–262.

Latourelle, R., 'Autenticità storica dei miracoli di Gesù', *Rassegna di Teologia* 15 (1974), 81–102.

Latourelle, R., *Miracles de Jésus et théologie du miracle* (Paris: Éditions du Cerf, 1985).

Latourelle, R., 'Originalité et Fonctions des miracles de Jésus', *Gregorianum* 66 (1985), 641–653.

Lattke, M., 'New Testament Miracle Stories and Hellenistic Culture of Late Antiquity', *Listening* 20 (1985), 54–64.

Lawton, J. S., *Miracles and Revelation* (London: Lutterworth, 1959/New York: Association Press, 1960).

Légasse, S., 'L'historien en quête de l'événement' in *Les Miracles de Jésus* (ed. X. Léon-Dufour; Parole de Dieu; Paris: Éditions du Seuil, 1977), pp. 109–145.

Légasse, S., 'Les miracles de Jésus selon Matthieu', *ibid.*, pp. 227–247.

Legrand, L., 'Christ's Miracles as "Social Work" ', *Indian Ecclesiastical Studies* I,1 (1962), 43–64.

Lentzen-Deis, F., 'Die Wunder Jesu. Zur neueren Literatur und zur Frage nach der Historizität', *Theologie und Philosophie* 43 (1968), 392–402.

Léon-Dufour, X., 'Parler de miracle aujourd'hui', *Etudes* no. 344 (1976), 437–454.

Léon-Dufour, X. (ed.), *Les Miracles de Jésus* (Parole de Dieu; Paris: Éditions du Seuil, 1977).

Léon-Dufour, X., 'Approches diverses du miracle', *ibid.*, pp. 11–39.

Léon-Dufour, X., 'Les miracles de Jésus selon Jean', *ibid.*, pp. 269–286.

Léon-Dufour, X., 'Structure et fonction du récit de miracle', *ibid.*, pp. 289–353.

Léon-Dufour, X., 'Conclusion', *ibid.*, pp. 355–374.

Léon-Dufour, X., 'Autour du *semeion* johannique' in *Die Kirche des Anfangs. Festschrift H. Schürmann* (ed. R. Schnackenburg; Leipzig: St. Benno-Verlag, 1977), pp. 363–378.

Liefeld, W. L., 'The Hellenistic "Divine Man" and the Figure of Jesus in the Gospels', *Journal of the Evangelical Theological Society* 16 (1973), 195–205.

Limbeck, M., 'Jesus und die Dämonen', *Bibel und Kirche* (1975), 7–11.

Lindars, B., 'Elijah, Elisha and the Gospel Miracles' in *Miracles. Cambridge Studies in Their Philosophy and History* (ed. C. F. D. Moule; London: A. R. Mowbray & Co., Ltd, 1965), pp. 63–79.

Linton, O., 'The Demand for a Sign from Heaven (Mk 8, 11–12 and par.)', *Studia Theologica* 19 (1965), 112–129.

Loader, W. R. G., 'Son of David, Blindness, Possession and Duality in Matthew', *Catholic Biblical Quarterly* 44 (1982), 570–585.

Lohse, E., 'Glaube und Wunder. Ein Beitrag zu der Theologia Crucis in den synoptischen Evangelien' in *Theologia Crucis—Signum Crucis. Festschrift E. Dinkler* (ed. C. Andresen and G. Klein; Tübingen: J. C. B. Mohr, 1979), pp. 335–350.

Lohse, E., *The First Christians. Their Beginnings, Writings and Beliefs* (Philadelphia: Fortress Press, 1983), pp. 48–52.

Londis, J. J., 'Miracles and Credibility', *Religious Studies* 16 (1980), 457–463.

Long, B. O., 'The Social Setting for Prophetic Miracle Stories', *Semeia* 3 (1975), 46–63.

Loos, H. van der, *The Miracles of Jesus* (Leiden: E. J. Brill, 1965).

McCasland, S. V., *By the Finger of God. Demon Possession and Exorcism in Early Christianity in the Light of Modern Views of Mental Illness* (New York: Macmillan, 1951).

McCasland, S. V., 'Signs and Wonders', *Journal of Biblical Literature* 76 (1957), 149–152.

McDonald, A. H., 'Herodotos on the Miraculous' in *Miracles. Cambridge Studies in Their Philosophy and History* (ed. C. F. D. Moule; London: A. R. Mowbray & Co., Ltd, 1965), pp. 81–92.

McGinley, L. J., *Form-Criticism of the Synoptic Healing Narratives: A Study in the Theories of Martin Dibelius and Rudolf Bultmann* (Woodstock, Md: Woodstock College Press, 1944).

Mackay, B. S., 'Plutarch and the Miraculous' in *Miracles. Cambridge Studies in Their Philosophy and History* (ed. C. F. D. Moule; London: A. R. Mowbray & Co., Ltd, 1965), pp. 93–112.

McKenzie, J. L., 'Signs and Power: The New Testament Presentation of Miracles', *Chicago Studies* 3 (1964), 5–18.

McNamara, K., 'The Nature and Recognition of Miracles', *Irish Theological Quarterly* 27 (1960), 294–322.

MacRae, R., 'Miracle in *The Antiquitates* of Josephus' in *Miracles. Cambridge Studies in Their Philosophy and History* (ed. C. F. D. Moule; London: A. R. Mowbray & Co., Ltd, 1965), pp. 127–148.

Maeder, A., 'Der Archetyp des Heilers und die Heilung', *Antaios* 2 (1961), 299–317.

Maertens, J.-T., 'La structure des récits de miracle dans les synoptiques', *Studies in Religion/Sciences Religieuses* 6 (1976–77), 253–266.

Maertens, J.-T., 'The Structure of the Synoptic Miracle Accounts', *Theology Digest* 26 (1978), 153–159.

Maher, M., 'Recent Writings on the Miracles', *New Blackfriars* 56 (658; 1975), 165–174.

Maillot, A., *Les miracles de Jésus et nous* (Cahiers du Réveil; Tournon: Réveil, 1977).

Mann, U., *Das Wunderbare: Wunder, Segen und Engel* (Handbuch systematischer Theologie 17; Gütersloh: Mohn, 1979).

Mark, J., 'Myth and Miracle or the Ambiguity of Bultmann', *Theology* 66 (1963), 134–140.

Martins Terra, J. E., *O Milagre* (São Paulo: Loyola, 1981).

Martorell, J., *Los milagros de Jesús* (Series Academica 2; Valencia: Facultad de Teología 'San Vicente Ferrer', 1980).

Martucci, J., 'Les récits de miracle: influence des récits de l'Ancien Testament sur ceux du Nouveau', *Science et Esprit* 27 (1975), 133–146.

Marxsen, H., 'Zur Wunderfrage' in *Der Streit um die Bibel* (Gladbeck-Westfalen: Schriftenmissions-Verlag, 1965), pp. 43–59.

Masure, E., 'Le miracle comme signe', *Revue des sciences philosophiques et théologiques* (1959), 274–276.

Meeks, W. A., 'The Divine Agent and His Counterfeit in Philo and the Fourth Gospel' in *Aspects of Religious Propaganda in Judaism and Early Christianity* (ed. E. Schüssler-Fiorenza; Notre Dame, Ind.; Notre Dame University Press, 1976), pp. 43–67.

Melinsky, M. A. H., *Healing Miracles. An Examination from History and*

Experience of the Place of Miracles in Christian Thought and Medical Practice (London: A. R. Mowbray & Co., Ltd, 1968).

Menoud, P., 'La signification du miracle dans le Nouveau Testament', *Revue d'Histoire et de Philosophie Religieuses* 28–29 (1948–49), 173–192.

Menoud, P., 'Miracle et sacrement dans le Nouveau Testament', *Verbum Caro* 6 (1952), 139–154.

Mensching, G., *Das Wunder im Glauben und Aberglauben der Völker* (Leiden: E. J. Brill, 1957).

Merli, D., 'Glauben und Vertrauen in den Wundererzählungen der Evangelien. Überlegungen zu einem biblischer Grundbegriff', *Bibel und Leben* 14 (1973), 210–215.

Merli, D., *Fiducia e fide nei miracoli evangelici* (Quaderni della rivista 'Bibbia e Oriente' 5; Genoa: Studio e Vita, 1973).

Metzger, B. M., *Index to Periodical Literature on Christ and the Gospels* (Leiden: E. J. Brill, 1962), nos 275–337.

Metzger, B. M., *The New Testament: Its Background, Growth, and Content* (Nashville: Abingdon Press, 1965/Cambridge: Lutterworth Press, 1969), pp. 132–135.

Minette de Tillesse, G., *Le secret messianique dans l'évangile de Marc* (Lectio Divina 47; Paris: Éditions du Cerf, 1968), pp. 39–73.

Mischo, J., 'Parapsychologie und Wunder', *Zeitschrift für Parapsychologie* 12 (1970), 37–89, 137–162; 13 (1971), 24–40.

Moiser, J., 'The Structure of Matthew 8–9: A Suggestion', *Zeitschrift für die neutestamentliche Wissenschaft* 76 (1985), 117–118.

Molinari, P., 'Saints and Miracles', *The Way* 18 (1978), 287–299.

Moule, C. F. D. (ed.), *Miracles. Cambridge Studies in Their Philosophy and History* (London: A. R. Mowbray & Co., Ltd, 1965).

Moule, C. F. D., 'The Vocabulary of Miracle', *ibid.*, pp. 235–238.

Moule, C. F. D., 'The Classification of Miracle Stories', *ibid.*, pp. 239–243.

Mourlon Beernaert, P., 'Jesus Christ and Health. The Testimony of the Gospels', *Lumen Vitae* 41 (1986), 35–48.

Mullin, R., *Miracles and Magic. The Miracles and Spells of Saints and Witches* (London: A. R. Mowbray & Co., Ltd, 1979).

Murray, F., 'Preaching the Miracles', *Worship* 42 (1968), 364–368.

Mussner, F., *The Miracles of Jesus. An Introduction* (Notre Dame, Ind.: University of Notre Dame Press/Shannon: Ecclesia Press, 1970).

Mussner, F., 'Ipsissima facta Jesu?', *Theologische Rundschau* 68 (1972), 177–185.

Mussner, F., 'Zur Diskussion über die "ipsissima facta"', *Theologie der Gegenwart in Auswahl* 15 (1972), 125–200.

Navone, J. J., 'Biblical Conflict with Magic and Sorcery', *The Bible Today* no. 64 (February 1973), 1053–1057.

Neidl, F., 'Zum gegenwartigen Verständnis der Wunder Jesu', *Entschluss* (November 1972), 60–62.

Neil, W., 'Expository Problems: the Nature Miracles', *Expository Times* 67 (1955–56), 369–372.

Neirynck, F., 'The Miracle Stories in the Acts of the Apostles. An Introduction' in *Les Actes des Apôtres. Traditions, redaction, théologie* (ed. J. Kremer; Louvain: Leuven University Press, 1982), pp. 169–213 [= *Evangelica...* (Louvain: Leuven University Press, 1982), pp.

835–880].

Nicholls, W., 'Physical Laws and Physical Miracles', *Irish Theological Quarterly* 27 (1960), 49–56.

Nicoll, M., *De nieuwe mens. Een interpretatie van enige gelijkenissen en wonderen van Christus* (Wassenaar: Servire, 1970).

Nielsen, H. K., 'Ein Beitrag zur Beurteilung der Tradition über die Heilungstätigkeit Jesu' in *Probleme der Forschung* (ed. A. Fuchs; SNTU 3; Vienna/Munich: Herold Verlag, 1978), pp. 58–90.

Nock, A. D., 'Paul and the Magus' in *Essays on Religion and the Ancient World* (ed. Z. Stewart; Cambridge, Mass.: Harvard University Press, 1972), pp. 308–330.

Noorda, S., 'Illness and Sin, Forgiving and Healing' in *Studies in Hellenistic Religions* (ed. M. J. Vermaseren; Études preliminaires aux religions orientales dans l'empire romain 78; Leiden: E. J. Brill, 1979).

O'Bréartúin, L., 'The Theology of Miracles', *Ephemerides Carmeliticae* 20 (1969), 3–51.

O'Connell, P., 'Miracles: Sign and Fact', *The Month* 36 (1966), 53–60.

Odegard, D., 'Miracles and Good Evidence', *Religious Studies* 18 (1982), 37–46.

Ogawa, A., 'Le problème de l'actualisation chez Matthieu', *Annual of the Japanese Biblical Institute* 3 (1977), 84–131.

Olson, S. N., 'Christ for All of Life: Mark's Miracles for 1985', *Currents in Theology and Mission* 12 (1985), 90–99.

Ory, A., *Mirabilia: De mirakelverhalen in het licht van de functionele exegese* (Sint-Truiden: privately published, 1978).

Paliard, C., 'Les miracles et nous', *Journal de la vie. Aujourd'hui la Bible* 130 (March 1973), 20.

Parker, P., 'Early Christianity as a Religion of Healing', *The Saint Luke's Journal of Theology* 19 (1976), 142–150.

Passian, R. E., *Neues Licht auf alte Wunder. PSI klärt Bibelwunderstreit* (Flensburg: Schroeder, 1982).

Pater, W. de, 'Wonder en wetenschap: een taalanalytische benadering', *Tijdschrift voor Theologie* 9 (1969), 11–53.

Perry, M. C., 'Believing and Commending the Miracles', *Expository Times* 73 (1961–62), 340–343.

Pesch, R., *Jesu ureigene Taten? Ein Beitrag zur Wunderfrage* (Quaestiones Disputatae 52; Freiburg: Herder, 1970).

Pesch, R., 'Zur theologischen Bedeutung der "Machtstaten" Jesu', *Theologische Quartalschrift* 152 (1972), 203–213.

Pesch, R., and Kratz, R., *So liest man synoptisch* II: *Wundergeschichten: Exorzismen, Heilungen, Totenerweckungen* (Frankfurt am Main: J. Knecht, 1976).

Pesch, R., and Kratz, R., *So liest man synoptisch* III: *Wundergeschichten: Rettungswunder, Normenwunder, Fernheilungen* (Frankfurt am Main: J. Knecht, 1976).

Petzke, G., *Die Traditionen über Apollonius von Tyana und das Neue Testament* (Studia ad Corpus Hellenisticum Novi Testamenti 1; Leiden: E. J. Brill, 1970).

Petzke, G., 'Historizität und Bedeutsamkeit von Wunderberichten. Möglichkeiten des religionsgeschichtlichen Vergleiches' in *Neues Testament und*

Christliche Existenz. Festschrift H. Braun (ed. H. D. Betz and L. Schottroff; Tübingen: J. C. B. Mohr, 1973), pp. 367–385.

Petzke, G., 'Die historische Frage nach den Wundertaten Jesu', *New Testament Studies* 22 (1975–76), 180–204.

Pilch, J. J., 'Healing in Mark: A Social Science Analysis', *Biblical Theology Bulletin* 15 (1985), 142–150.

Pilch, J. J., 'The Health Care System in Matthew', *Biblical Theology Bulletin* 16 (1986), 102–106.

Pittenger, N., 'On Miracles I', *Expository Times* 80 (1968–69), 104–107.

Polhill, J. B., 'Perspectives on the Miracle Stories', *Review and Expositor* 74 (1977), 389–399.

Prenter, R., 'The Miracles of Jesus' in *The Gospel as History* (ed. V. Vatja; Philadelphia: Fortress Press, 1975), 15–19.

Price, R. M., 'Conversion and the Miraculous', *Journal of Psychology and Theology* 9 (1981), 26–36.

Propper, T., 'Thesen zum Wunderverständnis' in *Bittgebet: Testfall des Glaubens* (ed. G. Greshake and G. Lohfink; Mainz: Matthias-Grünewald Verlag, 1978), pp. 71–91.

Ramsey, I. T., *Religious Language* (London: SCM Press/New York: Macmillan, 1957), pp. 144–150.

Ramsey, I. T., *et al.*, *The Miracles and the Resurrection: Some Recent Studies* (London: SPCK, 1964).

Reese, J., 'God Heals through Jesus' in *Jesus, His Word and Work* (New York: Pueblo Publishing Company, 1978), pp. 81–90.

Reiser, W., *Taten und Wunder Jesu* (Arbeit am Evangelium 1; Basel: Reinhardt, 1969).

Reitzenstein, R., *Hellenistische Wundererzählungen* (Stuttgart: Teubner, 1963).

Remus, H., 'Does Terminology Distinguish Early Christian from Pagan Miracles?', *Journal of Biblical Literature* 101 (1982), 531–551.

Remus, H., ' "Magic or Miracle?" Some Second Century Instances', *Second Century* 2 (1982), 127–156.

Renner, R., *Die Wunder Jesu in Theologie und Unterricht* (Lahr, Schwarzwald: Schauenburg, 1966).

Reumann, J., *Jesus in the Church's Gospels* (Philadelphia: Fortress Press, 1968), pp. 199–217.

Richardson, N., *The Panorama of Luke* (London: Epworth Press, 1982).

Riga, P., 'Sign of Glory. The Use of "Semeion" in St John's Gospel', *Interpretation* 17 (1965), 402–424.

Robbins, V. K., '*Dunameis* and *Semeia* in Mark', *Biblical Research* 18 (1973), 5–20.

Robinson, B., 'The Challenge of the Gospel Miracle Stories', *New Blackfriars* 60 (1979), 321–335.

Robinson, J. A. T., *But That I Can't Believe!* (London: Collins, 1967), pp. 30–33.

Robinson, J. M., 'The Miracles Source of John', *Journal of the American Academy of Religion* 39 (1971), 339–348.

Rochais, G., *Les récits de résurrection des morts dans le Nouveau Testament* (SNTS Monograph Series 40; Cambridge: Cambridge University Press, 1981).

Rodé, F., *Le miracle dans la controverse moderniste* (Paris: Beauchesne, 1965).

Rohrbach, H., *Mit dem Unsichtbaren leben: unsichtbare Mächte und die Macht Jesu* (Wuppertal: R. Brockhaus, 1976).

Roloff, J., *Das Kerygma und der irdische Jesus. Historische Motive in den Jesus-Erzählungen der Evangelien* (Göttingen: Vandenhoeck & Ruprecht, 1970), pp. 141–207.

Ross, J. P., 'Some Notes on Miracle in the Old Testament' in *Miracles. Cambridge Studies in Their Philosophy and History* (ed. C. F. D. Moule; London: A. R. Mowbray & Co., Ltd, 1965), pp. 43–60.

Ruegg, U., 'Zur Theologie der Wundergeschichten' in *Wunder Jesu* (ed. A. Steiner and V. Weymann; Basel: Reinhardt Verlag, 1978), pp. 42–48.

Ruegg, U., 'Wundergeschichten. Gottes Interesse am ganzen Menschen', *Reformatio* 30 (1981), 643–647.

Rybolt, J. E., 'Proclaiming Healing to the People', *The Bible Today* no. 81 (December 1975), 573–578.

Ryrie, C. C., *The Miracles of Our Lord* (Nashville: Thomas Nelson Publishers, 1984).

Sabourin, L., 'The Miracles of Jesus. I: Preliminary Survey', *Biblical Theology Bulletin* 1 (1971), 59–80.

Sabourin, L., 'Old Testament Miracles', *Biblical Theology Bulletin* 1 (1971), 227–261.

Sabourin, L., 'Hellenistic and Rabbinic "Miracles" ', *Biblical Theology Bulletin* 2 (1972), 281–307.

Sabourin, L., 'The Miracles of Jesus. II: Jesus and the Evil Powers', *Biblical Theology Bulletin* 4 (1974), 115–175.

Sabourin, L., 'Miracles of Jesus. III.: Healings, Resuscitations, Nature Miracles', *Biblical Theology Bulletin* 5 (1975), 146–200.

Sabourin, L., *The Divine Miracles Discussed and Defended* (Rome: Catholic Book Agency, 1977).

Sabourin, L., 'He Has Worked Marvels', *The Way* 18 (1978), 243–251.

Sanders, E. P., *Jesus and Judaism* (Philadelphia: Fortress Press/London: SCM Press, 1985), pp. 157–173.

Schadewaldt, H., 'Asklepios und Christus', *Die medizinische Welt* 31 (1967), 1755–1761.

Scharbert, J., 'Was versteht das Alte Testament unter Wunder?', *Bibel und Kirche* 22 (1967), 37–42.

Schedl, C., 'Die Zehn Wunder nach Matthäus' in *Talmud, Evangelium, Synagoge* (Innsbruck: Tyrolia-Verlag, 1969), pp. 291–335.

Scheffczyk, L., 'Die ambivalente Situation bezüglich der Wunderfrage heute', *Münchener Theologische Zeitschrift* 32 (1981), 292–295.

Schellong, D., 'Hinweis und Widerspruch. Zum Verständnis der Wunder Jesu', *Zeitenwende. Die Neue Furche* 45 (1974), 390–407.

Schenke, L., *Die Wundererzählungen des Markusevangeliums* (Stuttgarter Biblische Beiträge 3; Stuttgart: Verlag Katholisches Bibelwerk, 1974).

Schierse, F. J., *Die Wunder Jesu in Exegese und Verkündigung* (Düsseldorf: Patmos, 1967).

Schierse, F. J., 'Wunder in der Verkündigung', *Bibel und Kirche* 29 (1974), 10–13.

Schille, G., *Die urchristliche Wundertradition. Ein Beitrag zur Frage nach dem irdischen Jesus* (Stuttgart: Calwer, 1967).

Schillebeeckx, E., *Jesus—An Experiment in Christology* (New York: Vintage Books, 1981), pp. 179–200.

Schilling, B., 'Die Frage nach der Entstehung der synoptischen Wunder-geschichten in der deutschen neutestamentlichen Forschung', *Svensk Exegetisk Årsbok* 35 (1970), 61–78.

Schlier, H., *Principalities and Powers in the New Testament* (Quaestiones Disputatae 3; New York: Herder and Herder, 1964).

Schmidt, L., 'Wunderauslegung im Unterricht', *Der evangelische Erzieher* 15 (1963), 136–147, 193–196.

Schmutzler, S., 'Die Wunder Jesu im kirchlichen Unterricht', *Die Christenlehre* 15 (1962).

Schnackenburg, R., 'Miracles in the New Testament and Modern Science' in *Present and Future. Modern Aspects of New Testament Theology* (The Cardinal O'Hara Series 3; Notre Dame/London: University of Notre Dame Press, 1966), pp. 44–63.

Schneider, G., 'Hat Jesus Wunder gewirkt?' in *Anfragen an das Neue Testament* (Essen: Ludgerus, 1973), pp. 71–83.

Schnyder, C., 'Kann man heute an Wunder glauben? Auseinandersetzung mit Wundergeschichten aus dem 1. Jahrhundert n. Chr.' in *Wunder Jesu* (ed. A. Steiner and V. Weymann; Basel: Reinhardt Verlag, 1978), pp. 49–58.

Schoffeleers, M., 'Christ as the Medicine-man and the Medicine-man as Christ: a tentative history of African Christological Thought', *Man and Life* 8 (1982), 11–28.

Schoonenberg, P., 'Jesus' Signs' in *Covenant and Creation* (London: Sheed and Ward, 1968/Notre Dame, Ind.: University of Notre Dame Press, 1969), pp. 150–186.

Schubert, K., 'Wunderberichte und ihr Kerygma in der rabbinischen Tradition', *Kairos* 24 (1982), 31–37.

Schütz, C., 'Die Wunder Jesu' in *Mysterium Salutis* III/2 (ed. J. Feiner; Einsiedeln: Benziger, 1969), pp. 97–123.

Schwank, B., 'Wunderbericht und Wunderkritik in den neutestamentlichen Schriften', *Erbe und Auftrag* 50 (1974), 259–273.

Schwarz, H., *Das Verständnis des Wunders bei Heim und Bultmann* (Arbeiten zur Theologie 11.6; Stuttgart: Calwer Verlag, 1966).

Schweizer, E., *The Good News According to Mark* (Richmond, Va.: John Knox Press, 1970/London: SPCK, 1971), pp. 107–122.

Schweizer, E., *Jesus* (Richmond, Va.: John Knox Press/London: SCM Press, 1971), pp. 43–45.

Scott, B. B., 'How to Mismanage a Miracle: Reader-Response Criticism' in *Society of Biblical Literature 1983 Seminar Papers* (ed. R. K. Richards; Chico, Cal.: Scholars Press, 1983), pp. 439–449.

Seckler, M., 'Plädoyer für Ehrlichkeit im Umgang mit Wundern', *Theologische Quartalschrift* 151 (1971), 337–345.

Segalla, G., 'La cristologia nella tradizione sinottica dei miracoli', *Teologia* 5 (1980), 41–66.

294   *The Miracle Stories of the Synoptic Gospels*

Segalla, S., 'La cristologia soteriologica dei miracoli nei Sinottici', *Teologia* 5 (1980), 145–182.

Senior, D., *Jesus. A Gospel Portrait* (Dayton: Pflaum Press, 1975), pp. 113–131.

Sider, R. J., 'The Historian, the Miraculous and Post Newtonian Man', *Scottish Journal of Theology* 25 (1972), 309–319.

Siegmund, G., 'Theologie des Wunders', *Theologische Revue* 58 (1962), 290–298.

Sklba, R. J., 'Penetrating the Mystery of Divine Healing', *The Bible Today* no. 81 (December 1975), 579–585.

Slusser, D. M., 'The Healing Miracles in Mark', *Christian Century* 87 (19; 1970), 597–599.

Smith, D. M., 'The Milieu of the Johannine Miracle Source' in *Jews, Greeks, and Christians. Festschrift W. D. Davies* (ed. R. Hammerton-Kelly and R. Scroggs; Leiden: E. J. Brill, 1976), pp. 164–180.

Smith, G., 'Jewish, Christian, and Pagan Views of Miracle under the Flavian Emperors' in *Society of Biblical Literature 1983 Seminar Papers* (ed. R. K. Richards; Chico, Cal.: Scholars Press, 1983), pp. 341–348.

Smith, M., 'Prolegomena to a Discussion of Aretalogies, Divine Men, the Gospels and Jesus', *Journal of Biblical Literature* 90 (1971), 174–199.

Smith, M., *Jesus the Magician* (San Francisco: Harper and Row, 1978/Wellingborough: Aquarian Press, 1985).

Smith, M., 'On the History of the "Divine Man" ' in *Paganisme, Judaïsme, Christianisme: Mélanges offerts à Marcel Simon* (ed. A. Benoit *et al.*; Paris: de Boccard, 1978), pp. 335–345.

Smith, R. D., *Comparative Miracles* (St Louis: B. Herder Book Co., 1965).

Sneck, W. J., 'Neo-Pentecostals and Healing', *The Way* 18 (1978), 263–271.

Snoy, T., 'Les miracles dans l'évangile de Marc. Examen de quelques études récentes', *Revue Théologique de Louvain* 3 (1972), 449–466; 4 (1973), 58–101.

Soares Prabhu, G., 'The Miracles of Jesus Today', *Jeevadhara* 27 (1975), 189–204.

Söhngen, G., 'Wunderzeichen und Glaube' in *Die Einheit der Theologie. Gesammelte Abhandlungen, Aufsätze, Vorträge* (Munich: Kösel Verlag, 1952), pp. 265–285.

Songer, H. S., 'Demonic Possession and Mental Illness', *Religion in Life* 36 (1967), 119–127.

Speigl, J., 'Die Rolle der Wunder im vorkonstantinischen Christentum', *Zeitschrift für Katholische Theologie* 92 (1970), 287–312.

Speigl, J., 'Early Christian Attitudes toward Miracles', *Theology Digest* 19 (1971), 254–257.

Splett, J., 'Hegel über das Wunder', *Theologie und Philosophie* 41 (1966), 520–535.

Stanley, D. M., 'Salvation and Healing', *The Way* 10 (1970), 298–317.

Stanley, D. M., 'Believe the Works', *The Way* 18 (1978), 272–286.

Staudinger, F., 'Die neutestamentlichen Wunder in der Verkündigung', *Erbe und Auftrag* 44 (1968), 355–366.

Staudinger, H., and Schluter, J., *Am Wunder glauben? Gottes Allmacht und moderne Welterfahrung* (Herderbücherei 1258; Freiburg: Herder, 1986).

Steiner, A., 'Wundergeschichten als literarische Gattung' in *Wunder Jesu* (ed. A. Steiner and V. Weymann; Basel: Reinhardt Verlag, 1978), pp. 24–34.

Steiner, A., and Weymann, V. (eds), *Wunder Jesu* (Bibelarbeit in der Gemeinde: Themen und Materialien 2; Basel: Reinhardt Verlag, 1978).

Steinhauser, M. G., 'Healing Stories in the Gospels', *Liturgy* 25 (1980), 27–30.

Steinmetz, F.-J., '"Sie sahen die Wunder, die er tat" (Apg 8,6). Ereignis und Bedeutung religiöser Krafttaten in unseren Zeit', *Geist und Leben* 46 (1973), 99–114.

Stolz, F., 'Zeichen und Wunder. Die prophetische Legitimation und ihre Geschichte', *Zeitschrift für Theologie und Kirche* 69 (1972), 125–144.

Sturch, R. L., 'The Markan Miracles and the Other Synoptists', *Expository Times* 89 (1977–78), 375–376.

Suhl, A., *Die Wunder Jesu. Ereignis und Überlieferung* (Gütersloh: Mohn, 1968).

Suhl, A. (ed.), *Der Wunderbegriff im Neuen Testament* (Wege der Forschung 295; Darmstadt: Wissenschaftliche Buchgesellschaft, 1980).

Suriano, T. M., 'Christian Faith and the Miracles of Jesus', *The Bible Today* no. 92 (November 1977), 1358–1364.

Sweet, J. P. M., 'The Theory of Miracles in the Wisdom of Solomon' in *Miracles. Cambridge Studies in Their Philosophy and History* (ed. C. F. D. Moule; London: A. R. Mowbray & Co., Ltd, 1965), pp. 113–126.

Sweet, J. P. M., 'Miracle and Faith. II: The Miracles of Jesus', *Epworth Review* 3 (1976), 81–91.

Tagawa, K., *Miracles et Évangile. La pensée personnelle de l'évangéliste Marc* (Études d'histoire et de philosophie religieuses 62; Paris: P.U.F., 1966).

Talbert, C., 'The Concept of Immortals in Mediterranean Antiquity', *Journal of Biblical Literature* 94 (1975), 419–436.

Talbert, C, 'Miracle in Luke-Acts and in the Lukan Milieu' in *Reading Luke. A Literary Theological Commentary on the Third Gospel* (New York: Crossroad, 1984), pp. 241–246.

Taymans, F., 'Le miracle, signe du surnaturel', *Nouvelle Revue Théologique* 77 (1955), 222–245.

Taymans, F., 'Faith, Miracles and Reason' in *Faith, Reason and the Gospel* (ed. J. J. Heaney; Westminster, Md: Newman Press, 1964), pp. 299–310.

Tenzler, J., 'Tiefenpsychologie und Wunderfrage. Der kognitive Teilbeitrag der Tiefenpsychologie zur Exegese biblischer Wunder', *Bibel und Kirche* 29 (1974), 6–10.

Ternant, P., 'Les miracles de Jésus dans les Évangiles', *Catéchistes* 53 (1963), 35–54.

Ternant, P., 'Les signes de foi', *Assemblées du Seigneur* 75 (1965), 38–74.

Theissen, G., *The Miracle Stories of the Early Christian Tradition* (Edinburgh: T. & T. Clark/Philadelphia: Fortress Press, 1983).

Thouless, R. H., 'Miracles and Psychical Research', *Theology* 72 (1969), 253–258.

Tiede, D. L., *The Charismatic Figure as Miracle Worker* (SBL Dissertation Series 1; Missoula, Mont.: Society of Biblical Literature, 1972).

Trocmé, E., *Jesus and His Contemporaries* (London: SCM Press, 1973)/*Jesus as Seen by His Contemporaries* (Philadelphia: The Westminster Press, 1973), pp. 97–109.

Vandré, R., *Wundergeschichten im Religionsunterricht* (Göttingen: Vandenhoeck & Ruprecht, 1975).

Verweyen, H., 'Die historische Rückfrage nach den Wundern Jesu', *Trierer Theologische Zeitschrift* 90 (1981), 41–58.

Verweyen, H., 'Einheit und Vielfalt der Evangelien am Beispiel von Wundergeschichten (inbesonders Mk 5, 25–34 parr.)', *Didaskalia* 11 (1981), 3–24.

Vögtle, A., 'Jesu Wunder einst und heute', *Bibel und Leben* 2 (1961), 234–254.

Vögtle, A., 'Jesu Wundertaten vor dem Hintergrund ihrer Zeit' in *Die Zeit Jesu* (ed. H. J. Schultz; Kontexte 3; Stuttgart: Kreuz-Verlag, 1966), pp. 83–90.

Vögtle, A., 'Wunder und Wort in urchristlicher Glaubenswerbung (Mt 11,2–5/Lk 7,18–23)' in *Das Evangelium und die Evangelien. Beiträge zur Evangelienforschung* (Düsseldorf: Patmos, 1971), pp. 219–252.

Vogels, W., 'Les gens amenaient des infirmes à Jésus', *Prêtre et Pasteur* 84 (1981), 458–467.

Wansbrough, H., 'Event and Interpretation VII: Jesus the Wonderworker', *Clergy Review* 55 (1970), 859–867.

Ward, B., *Miracles and the Medieval Mind. Theory, Record and Event 1000–1215* (London: Scolar Press/Philadelphia: University of Pennsylvania Press, 1982).

Warfield, B. B., *Miracles: Yesterday and Today* (Grand Rapids: Eerdmans, 1965).

Weder, H., 'Wunder Jesu und Wundergeschichten', *Verkündigung und Forschung* 29 (1984), 25–49.

Weeden, T. J., 'The Heresy That Necessitated Mark's Gospel', *Zeitschrift für die neutestamentliche Wissenschaft* 59 (1968), 145–158.

Weiser, A., *Was die Bibel Wunder nennt. Ein Sachbuch zu den Berichten der Evangelien* (Stuttgart: Verlag Katholisches Bibelwerk, 1975).

Weissmahr, B., *Gottes Wirken in der Welt. Ein Diskussionsbeitrag zur Frage der Evolution und des Wunders* (Frankfurter Theologische Studien; Frankfurt: J. Knecht, 1973).

Weissmahr, B., 'Wunder als Zeichen Gottes? Fundamentaltheologische Überlegungen', *Theologie der Gegenwart* 24 (1981), 212–218.

Wenham, D., and Blomberg, C., *Gospel Perspectives*, vol. 6: *The Miracles of Jesus* (Sheffield: JSOT Press, 1985).

Wenisch, B., *Geschichten oder Geschichte? Theologie des Wunders* (Salzburg: Verlag St. Peter, 1981).

Weymann, V., 'Schwierigkeiten mit Wundern' in *Wunder Jesu* (ed. A. Steiner and V. Weymann; Basel: Reinhardt Verlag, 1978), pp. 35–41.

Wibbing, S., *Wunder und christliche Existenz heute: Überlegungen für Unterricht und Predigt* (Taschenbücher Siebenstern 751; Gütersloh: Mohn, 1979).

Wilkinson, J., 'A Study of Healing in the Gospel according to John', *Scottish Journal of Theology* 20 (1967), 442–461.

Wilkinson, J., *Health and Healing: Studies in New Testament Principles and Practice* (London: Handsel, 1980).

Wills, J., 'Miracles and Scientific Law', *Review and Expositor* 59 (1962), 137–145.

Wilms, F. E., *Wunder im Alten Testament* (Regensburg: Pustet Verlag, 1979).

Winkelmann, M., *Biblische Wunder. Kritik, Chance, Deutung* (Pfeiffer-Werkbücher 140; Munich: Pfeiffer, 1977).

Wire, A. C., 'The Structure of the Gospel Miracle Stories and Their Tellers', *Semeia* 11 (1978), 83–113.

Wire, A. C., 'The Miracle Story as the Whole Story', *South East Asian Journal of Theology* 22 (1981), 29–37.

Witmer, J. A., 'The Doctrine of Miracles', *Bibliotheca Sacra* 130 (1973), 126–134.

Witt, O., 'Biblische Krankenheilung heute?' in *Studia Anglicana* (Wuppertal: R. Brockhaus, 1972), pp. 101–107.

Wood, C. M., 'The Events in Which God Acts', *Heythrop Journal* 22 (1981), 278–284.

Woods, G. F., 'The Evidential Value of the Biblical Miracles' in *Miracles. Cambridge Studies in Their Philosophy and History* (ed. C. F. D. Moule; London: A. R. Mowbray & Co., Ltd, 1965), pp. 19–32.

Worsley, P., 'Non-Western Medical Systems', *Annual Review of Anthropology* 11 (1982), 315–348.

Yamauchi, E. M., 'Magic in the Biblical World', *Tyndale Bulletin* 34 (1983), 169–200.

Youngblood, D. A., 'The Miracles of the Gospels', *The Bible Today* no. 39 (December 1968), 2723–2730.

Ypma, S., 'Het bijbels wonder', *Kerk en Theologie* 32 (1980), 35–40.

Zehrer, F., 'Das Problem der Wunder Jesu', *Theologisch-praktische Quartalschrift* 122 (1974), 233–243.

Zeilinger, F., 'Zum Wunderverständnis der Bibel', *Bibel und Liturgie* 42 (1969), 27–43.

Zeller, D., 'Wunder und Bekenntnis. Zum Sitz im Leben urchristlicher Wundergeschichten', *Biblische Zeitschrift* 25 (1981), 204–222.

Zuck, J. E., 'Tales of Wonder: Biblical Narrative, Myth, and Fairy Stories', *Journal of the American Academy of Religion* 44 (1976), 299–308.

—— 'Beweise oder Zeichen? Bemerkungen um eine Neuinterpretation der "Wunder" Jesu', *Herder Korrespondenz* 26 (1972), 509–514.

—— *Les miracles de l'évangile. Cahiers Évangile* 8 (Paris: Le Service biblique Évangile et Vie, 1974).

—— *Ziende blind? Bijbelse wonderverhalen exegetisch en catechetisch toegelicht* (Antwerp: Patmos, 1976).

—— 'Les miracles dans l'Évangile', *Fêtes et Saisons* no. 377 (August–September 1983).

II. On particular miracle stories

1. The healing of a demoniac at the synagogue (Mk 1:21–28; Lk 4:31–37)

Argyle, A. W., 'The Meaning of *exousia* in Mark 1:22, 27', *Expository Times* 80 (1968–69), 343.

Bächli, O., ' "Was habe ich mit dir zu schaffen?" Eine formelhafte Frage im A.T. und N.T.', *Theologische Zeitschrift* 33 (1977), 69–80.

Brière, J., 'Le cri et le secret. Signification d'un exorcisme. Mc 1,21–28', *Assemblées du Seigneur* 35 (1973), 34–46.

Burkill, T. A., *New Light on the Earliest Gospel. Seven Markan Studies* (Ithaca, N.Y./London: Cornell University Press, 1972), pp. 16–17.

Busse, U., *Die Wunder des Propheten Jesus* (Stuttgart: Verlag Katholisches Bibelwerk, 1977), pp. 66–90.

Dewey, J., *Markan Public Debate* (Chico, Cal.: Scholars Press, 1980), pp. 172–179.

Dideberg, D., and Mourlon Beernaert, P., ' "Jésus vint en Galilée." Essai sur la structure de Marc 1,21–45', *Nouvelle Revue Théologique* 98 (1976), 306–323.

Dideberg, D., and Mourlon Beernaert, P., ' "Jesus came into Galilee": the structure of Mark 1:21–45', *Theology Digest* 25 (1977), 111–116.

Flusser, D., *Die rabbinischen Gleichnisse und der Gleichniserzähler Jesus*. I. Teil: *Das Wesen der Gleichnisse* (Berne/Frankfurt am Main: P. Lang, 1981), pp. 210–215.

Fridrichsen, A., *The Problem of Miracle in Primitive Christianity* (Minneapolis: Augsburg Publishing House, 1972), pp. 111–113.

Guillemette, P., 'Mc 1,24 est-il une formule de défense magique?', *Science et Esprit* 30 (1978), 81–96.

Guillemette, P., 'Un enseignement nouveau, plein d'authorité. Étude de Mc 1,21–28', *Novum Testamentum* 22 (1980), 222–247.

Kee, H. C., 'The Terminology of Mark's Exorcism Stories', *New Testament Studies* 14 (1967–68), 232–246, esp. 242–243.

Kertelge, K., *Die Wunder Jesu im Markusevangelium* (Munich: Kösel Verlag, 1970), pp. 50–60.

Kirchschläger, W., *Jesu exorzistisches Wirken aus der Sicht des Lukas* (Klosterneuburg: Österreichisches Katholisches Bibelwerk, 1981), pp. 27–44.

März, C. P., *Das Wort Gottes bei Lukas* (Erfurter Theologische Schriften 11; Leipzig: St. Benno-Verlag, 1974), pp. 38–41.

Minette de Tillesse, G., *Le secret messianique dans l'Évangile de Marc* (Paris: Éditions du Cerf, 1968), pp. 77–83.

Mussner, F., 'Ein Wortspiel in Mk 1,24?', *Biblische Zeitschrift* 4 (1960), 285–286.

Osiek, C., 'The Jewish-Christian Community at Capharnaum', *The Bible Today* 19 (January 1981), 36–39.

Pesch, R., 'Ein Tag vollmächtigen Wirkens Jesu in Kapharnaum (Mk 1,21–34, 35–39)', *Bibel und Leben* 9 (1968), 114–128, 177–195, 261–277.

Pesch, R., ' "Eine neue Lehre aus Macht." Eine Studie zu Mk 1,21–28' in *Evangelienforschung. Ausgewählte Aufsätze deutscher Exegeten* (ed. J. B. Bauer; Graz/Vienna/Cologne: Styria, 1968), pp. 241–276.

Pilch, J. J., 'Healing in Mark: A Social Science Analysis', *Biblical Theology Bulletin* 15 (1985), 142–150.

Rice, G. E., 'Luke 4:31–44: Release for Captives', *Andrews University Seminary Studies* 20 (1982), 23–28.

Robinson, B., 'The Challenge of the Gospel Miracle Stories', *New Blackfriars* 60 (710–711; July-August 1979), 321–334.

Schille, G., *Die urchristliche Wundertradition* (Stuttgart: Calwer Verlag, 1967), pp. 28–29.

Schramm, T., *Der Markus-Stoff bei Lukas* (SNTS Monograph Series 14; Cambridge: Cambridge University Press, 1971), pp. 85–91.

Schweizer, E., ' "Er wird Nazoräer heissen" (zu Mc 1,24; Mt 2,23)' in *Judentum—Urchristentum—Kirche. Festschrift J. Jeremias* (ed. W. Eltester; Berlin: A. Töpelmann, 1960), pp. 90–93.

Stein, R. H., 'The "Redaktionsgeschichtlich" Investigation of a Markan Seam (Mc 1:21f.)', *Zeitschrift für die neutestamentliche Wissenschaft* 61 (1970), 70–94.

Suhl, A., 'Überlegungen zur Hermeneutik an Hand von Mk 1,21–28', *Kairos* 26 (1984), 28–38.

Tagawa, K., *Miracles et Évangile. La pensée personnelle de l'évangéliste Marc* (Paris: P.U.F., 1966), pp. 82–92.

Talbert, C., 'The Lukan Presentation of Jesus' Ministry in Galilee: Luke 4:31 – 9:50', *Review and Expositor* 64 (1967), 485–497.

Thissen, W., *Erzählung der Befreiung. Eine exegetische Untersuchung zu Mk 2,1 – 3,6* (Forschung zur Bibel 21; Würzburg: Echter Verlag, 1976), pp. 267–276.

Trevijano, R., 'El trasfondo apocalíptico de Mc 1,24.25; 5,7.8 y par', *Burgense* 11 (1970), 117–133.

Urman, D., 'New Finds: The Site of the Miracle of the Man with an Unclean Spirit', *Christian News from Israel* (1971), 72–76.

2. The healing of Peter's mother-in-law (Mk 1:29–31 and parallels)

Busse, U., *Die Wunder des Propheten Jesus* (Stuttgart: Verlag Katholisches Bibelwerk, 1977), pp. 57–90.

Dietrich, W., *Das Petrusbild der lukanischen Schriften* (BWANT 94; Stuttgart: Kohlhammer, 1972), pp. 19–23.

Fuchs, A., 'Entwicklungsgeschichtliche Studie zu Mk 1,29–31 par. Mt 8,14–15 par. Lk 4,38–39', *Studien zum Neuen Testament und seiner Umwelt* 6–7 (1981–82), 21–76.

Gaide, G., 'De l'admiration à la foi. Mc 1,29–39', *Assemblées du Seigneur* 36 (1974), 39–48.

Gerhardsson, B., *The Mighty Acts of Jesus according to Matthew* (Lund: Gleerup, 1979), pp. 40–41.

Held, H. J., 'Matthew as Interpreter of the Miracle Stories' in *Tradition and Interpretation in Matthew* (ed. G. Bornkamm, G. Barth and H. J. Held; Philadelphia: The Westminster Press/London: SCM Press, 1963), pp. 169ff., 231ff.

Hengel, R. and M., 'Die Heilungen Jesu und medizinisches Denken' in *Der Wunderbegriff im Neuen Testament* (ed. A. Suhl; Darmstadt: Wissenschaftliche Buchgesellschaft, 1980), pp. 338–373, esp. 348–351.

Kertelge, K., *Die Wunder Jesu im Markusevangelium* (Munich: Kösel Verlag, 1970), pp. 60–62.

Kirchschläger, W., 'Fieberheilung in Apg 28 und Lk 4' in *Les Actes des Apôtres. Traditions, rédaction, théologie* (ed. J. Kremer; Louvain: Leuven University Press, 1979), pp. 509–521.

Kirchschläger, W., *Jesu exorzistisches Wirken aus der Sicht des Lukas* (Klosterneuburg: Österreichisches Katholisches Bibelwerk, 1981), pp. 55–69.

Lamarche, P., 'La guérison de la belle-mère de Pierre et le genre littéraire des évangiles', *Nouvelle Revue Théologique* 87 (1965), 515–526.

Lamarche, P., 'La guérison de la belle-mère de Pierre (Mc 1,29–31)' in *Révélation de Dieu chez Marc* (Paris: Beauchesne, 1976), pp. 47–60.

Léon-Dufour, X., 'La guérison de la belle-mère de Simon-Pierre' in *Études d'Évangile* (Parole de Dieu; Paris: Éditions du Seuil, 1965), pp. 123–148.

Longstaff, T. R. W., 'Mark 1:29–31: The Healing of Peter's Mother-in-Law' in *Evidence of Conflation in Mark? A Study of the Synoptic Problem* (SBL Dissertation Series 28; Missoula, Mont.: Scholars Press, 1977), pp. 129–140.

Loos, H. van der, *The Miracles of Jesus* (Leiden: E. J. Brill, 1965), pp. 551–555.

Pesch, R., 'Die Heilung der Schwiegermutter des Simon-Petrus. Ein Beispiel heutiger Synoptikerexegese' in *Neuere Exegese—Verlust oder Gewinn?* (Freiburg: Herder, 1968), pp. 143–175.

Praeder, S. M., 'Acts 27:1 – 28:16: Sea Voyages in Ancient Literature and the Theology of Luke-Acts', *The Catholic Biblical Quarterly* 46 (1984), 683–706, esp. 702–703.

Rigato, M. L., 'Tradizione e redazione in Mc 1,29–31 (e paralleli). La guarigione della suocera di Simon Pietro', *Rivista Biblica* 17 (1969), 139–174.

Schenke, L., *Die Wundererzählungen des Markusevangeliums* (Stuttgart: Verlag Katholisches Bibelwerk, 1974), pp. 109–129.

Suhl, A., 'Die Wunder Jesu. Ereignis und Überlieferung' in *Der Wunderbegriff im Neuen Testament* (ed. A. Suhl; Darmstadt: Wissenschaftliche Buchgesellschaft, 1980), pp. 500–502.

Thissen, W., *Erzählung der Befreiung. Eine exegetische Untersuchung zu Mk 2,1 – 3,6* (Würzburg: Echter Verlag, 1976), pp. 276–280.

Weiser, A., *Was die Bibel Wunder nennt* (Stuttgart: Verlag Katholisches Bibelwerk, 1977), pp. 39–46.

3. The healing of a leper (Mk 1:40–45 and parallels)

Boismard, M.-E., 'La guérison du lépreux (Mc 1,40 et par.)', *Salmanticensis* 28 (1981), 283–291.

Bruners, W., *Die Reinigung der zehn Aussätzigen und die Heilung des Samariters, Lk 17,11–19* (Forschung zur Bibel 23; Stuttgart: Verlag Katholisches Bibelwerk, 1977), pp. 370–380.

Burkill, T. A., *New Light on the Earliest Gospel. Seven Markan Studies* (Ithaca, N.Y./London: Cornell University Press, 1972), pp. 21–22.

Cave, C. H., 'The Leper: Mark 1:40–45', *New Testament Studies* 25 (1978–79), 245–250.

Danker, F. W., 'Mark 1:45 and the Secrecy Motif', *Concordia Theological Monthly* 37 (1966), 492–499.

Edwards, G. E., *Jesus and the Politics of Violence* (New York: Harper & Row, 1972), pp. 76–77.

Elliott, J. K., 'The Conclusion of the Pericope of the Healing of the Leper and Mark 1,45', *Journal of Theological Studies* 22 (1971), 153–157.

Elliott, J. K., 'Is *ho exelthōn* a Title for Jesus in Mark 1,45?', *Journal of Theological Studies* 27 (1976), 402–405.

Elliott, K., 'The Healing of the Leper in the Synoptic Parallels', *Theologische Zeitschrift* 34 (1978), 175–176.

Fossion, A., 'From the Bible Text to the Homily. Cure of a Leper (Mk 1,40–45)', *Lumen Vitae* 35 (1980), 279–290.

Fusco, V., 'Il segreto messianico nell' episodio del lebbroso (Mc 1,40–45)', *Rivista Biblica* 29 (1981), 273–313.

Geysels, L., and Verbeke, J., 'De genezing van een melaatse (Mc 1,40–45)' in *Ziende blind? Bijbelse wonderverhalen exegetisch en catechetisch toegelicht* (Antwerp: Patmos, 1977), pp. 163–177.

Held, H. J., 'Matthew as Interpreter of the Miracle Stories' in *Tradition and Interpretation in Matthew* (ed. G. Bornkamm, G. Barth and H. J. Held; Philadelphia: The Westminster Press/London: SCM Press, 1963), pp. 213–215, 255–257.

Helmer, F., 'Die Heilung eines Aussätzigen (Mk 1,40–45)', *Erbe und Auftrag* 55 (1982), 310–313.

Herranz Marco, M., 'La curación de un leproso según San Marcos (Mc 1,40–45)', *Estudios Bíblicos* 31 (1972), 399–433.

Kertelge, K., *Die Wunder Jesu im Markusevangelium* (Munich: Kösel Verlag, 1970), pp. 62–75.

Kingsbury, J. D., 'Retelling the "Old, Old Story": The Miracle of the Cleansing of the Leper as an Approach to the Theology of Matthew', *Currents in Theology and Mission* 4 (1977), 342–349.

Kirchschläger, W., *Jesu exorzistiches Wirken aus der Sicht des Lukas* (Klosterneuburg: Österreichisches Katholiches Bibelwerk, 1981), pp. 221–227.

Masson, C., 'La guérison du lépreux (Marc 1,40–45)' in *Vers les sources d'eau vive* (Lausanne: Payot, 1961), pp. 11–19.

Minette de Tillesse, G., *Le secret messianique dans l'Évangile de Marc* (Lectio Divina 47; Paris: Éditions du Cerf, 1968), pp. 41–51, 64–69.

Mussner, F., *The Miracles of Jesus* (Notre Dame, Ind.: University of Notre Dame Press/Shannon: Ecclesia Press, 1970), pp. 28–38.

Neirynck, F., 'Papyrus Egerton 2 and the Healing of the Leper', *Ephemerides Theologicae Lovanienses* 61 (1985), 153–160.

Paul, A., 'La guérison d'un lépreux. Approche d'un récit de Marc (1,40–45)', *Nouvelle Revue Théologique* 92 (1970), 692–704.

Pesch, R., *Jesu ureigene Taten? Ein Beitrag zur Wunderfrage* (Quaestiones Disputatae 52; Freiburg: Herder, 1970), pp. 52–113.

Pilch, J. J., 'Biblical Leprosy and Body Symbolism', *Biblical Theology Bulletin* 11 (1981), 108–113.

Ryrie, C. C., 'The Cleansing of the Leper', *Bibliotheca Sacra* 113 (1956), 262–267.

Sabourin, L., *The Divine Miracles Discussed and Defended* (Rome: Catholic Book Agency, 1977), pp. 74–76.

Schenke, L., *Die Wundererzählungen des Markusevangeliums* (Stuttgarter Biblische Beiträge; Stuttgart: Verlag Katholisches Bibelwerk, 1974), pp. 130–145.

Schramm, T., *Der Markus-Stoff bei Lukas* (Cambridge: Cambridge University Press, 1971), pp. 91–99.

Standaert, B., *L'Évangile selon Marc. Composition et Genre littéraire* (Nijmegen: Stichting Studentenpers, 1978), pp. 126–134.

Suhl, A., *Die Funktion der alttestamentlichen Zitate und Anspielungen im Markusevangelium* (Gütersloh: Mohn, 1965), pp. 120–123.

Tagawa, K., *Miracles et Évangile. La pensée personnelle de l'évangéliste Marc* (Paris: P.U.F., 1966), pp. 20–21, 165–166.

Telford, G. B., 'Mark 1:40–45', *Interpretation* 36 (1982), 54–58.

Theobald, M., 'Die Anfänge der Kirche. Zur Struktur von Lk 5,1 – 6,19', *New Testament Studies* 30 (1984), 91–108.

Thissen, W., *Erzählung der Befreiung. Eine exegetische Untersuchung zu Mk 2,1 – 3,6* (Würzburg: Echter Verlag, 1976), pp. 288–295.

Van Linden, P., *Knowing Christ Through Mark's Gospel* (Chicago: Franciscan Herald Press, 1977), pp. 39–50.

Zeller, D., 'Die Heilung des Aussätzigen (Mk 1,40–45). Ein Beispiel bekennender und werbender Erzählung', *Trierer Theologische Zeitschrift* 93 (1984), 138–146.

Zimmermann, H., *Neutestamentliche Methodenlehre: Darstellung der historisch-kritische Methode* (Stuttgart: Verlag Katholisches Bibelwerk, 1967), pp. 237–242.

4. The healing of the paralytic (Mk 2:1–12 and parallels)

Baumgarten, A. I., 'The Name of the Pharisees', *Journal of Biblical Literature* 102 (1983), 411–428.

Best, E., 'Mark ii,1–12', *Biblical Theology* 3 (1953), 41–46.

Betz, O., and Grimm, W., *Wesen und Wirklichkeit der Wunder Jesu* (Frankfurt am Main: P. Lang, 1977), pp. 36–39.

Booyer, G. H., 'Mk 2:10a and the Interpretation of the Healing of the Paralytic', *Harvard Theological Review* 47 (1954), 115–120.

Borsch, F. H., *Power in Weakness. New Hearing for Gospel Stories of Healing and Discipleship* (Philadelphia: Fortress Press, 1983), pp. 9–21.

Bouwman, G., *De Derde Nachtwake* (Tielt: Lannoo, 1968), pp. 191–194.

Budesheim, T. L., 'Jesus and the Disciples in Conflict with Judaism', *Zeitschrift für die neutestamentliche Wissenschaft* 62 (1971), 190–209.

Burkill, T. A., *Mysterious Revelation* (Ithaca, N.Y.: Cornell University Press, 1963), pp. 123–135.

Calloud, J., 'Toward a Structural Analysis of Mark', *Semeia* 16 (1979), 133–165.

Ceroke, C. P., 'Is Mk 2,10a a Saying of Jesus?', *The Catholic Biblical Quarterly* 22 (1960), 369–390.

Clark, D. J., 'Criteria for Identifying Chiasm', *Linguistica Biblica* 35 (1975), 63–72.

Cook, M. J., *Mark's Treatment of the Jewish Leaders* (Leiden: E. J. Brill, 1978), pp. 29–51.

Delorme, J., 'Marc 2,1–13—ou l'ouverture des frontières', *Sémiotique et Bible* 30 (1983), 1–14.

Dewey, J., 'The Literary Structure of the Controversy Stories in Mark 2:1–3:6', *Journal of Biblical Literature* 92 (1973), 394–401.

Dewey, J., *Markan Public Debate. Literary Technique, Concentric Structure, and Theology in Mark 2:1 – 3:6* (SBL Dissertation Series 48; Chico, Cal.: Scholars Press, 1980).

Diedhou, J. C., 'Catechesis of the Young in Senegal: a Gospel Example (Luke 5:17–26)', *Lumen Vitae* 40 (1985), 314–321.

Dormeyer, D., ' "Narrative Analyse" von Mk 2,1–12. Möglichkeiten und Grenzen einer Verbindung zwischen "Generativer Poetik" und Didaktik neutestamentlicher Wundererzählungen', *Linguistica Biblica* 31 (1974), 68–88.

Doughty, D. J., 'The Authority of the Son of Man (Mk 2:1 – 3:6)', *Zeitschrift für die neutestamentliche Wissenschaft* 74 (1983), 161–181.

Dunn, J. D. G., 'Mark 2:1 – 3:6: a Bridge between Jesus and Paul on the Question of Law', *New Testament Studies* 30 (1984), 395–415.

Duplacy, J., 'Marc 2,10. Note de syntaxe' in *Mélanges bibliques rédigés en l'honneur de A. Robert* (Paris: Bloud & Gay, 1955), pp. 420–427.

Dupont, J., 'Le paralytique pardonné', *Nouvelle Revue Théologique* 82 (1960), 940–958.

Elliott, J. H., 'Man and the Son of Man in the Gospel of Mark' in *Humane Gesellschaft* (ed. T. Rendtorff and A. Rich; Zurich: Zwingli Verlag, 1970), pp. 50–58.

Feuillet, A., 'L'*exousia* du Fils de l'Homme (d'après Mc 2,10.28 et par.)', *Recherches de Science Religieuse* 42 (1954), 161–192.

Fridrichsen, A., *The Problem of Miracle in Primitive Christianity* (Minneapolis: Augsburg Publishing House, 1972), pp. 128–134.

Gerhardsson, B., *The Mighty Acts of Jesus according to Matthew* (Lund: Gleerup, 1979), pp. 75–77.

Gnilka, J., 'Das Elend vor dem Menschensohn (Mk 2,1–12)' in *Jesus und der Menschensohn. Festchrift A. Vögtle* (Freiburg: Herder, 1975), pp. 196–209.

Greeven, H., 'Die Heilung des Gelähmten nach Matthäus', *Wort und Dienst* N.F. 4 (1955), 65–78.

Hallbäck, G., 'Materialistische Exegese und strukturale Analyse. Ein methodologischer Vergleich anhand von Markus 2, 1–12', *Linguistica Biblica* 50 (1982), 7–32.

Hay, L. S., 'The Son of Man in Mark 2:10 and 2:28', *Journal of Biblical Literature* 89 (1970), 69–75.

Hofius, O., 'Vergebungszuspruch und Vollmachtsfrage. Mk 2,1–12 und das Problem priesterlicher Absolution im antiken Judentum' in *'Wenn nicht jetzt, wann dann?' Aufsätze fur Hans-Joachim Kraus* (ed. H.-G. Geyer *et al.*: Neukirchen-Vluyn: Neukirchener Verlag, 1983), pp. 115–127.

Hultgren, A. J., *Jesus and His Adversaries. The Form and Function of the*

Conflict Stories in the Synoptic Tradition (Augsburg Publishing House, 1979), pp. 106–109, 151–174.

Kamphaus, F., *The Gospels for Preachers and Teachers* (London: Sheed and Ward, 1968), pp. 120–127.

Kertelge, K., *Die Wunder Jesu im Markusevangelium* (Munich: Kösel Verlag, 1970), pp. 75–82.

Kertelge, K., 'Die Vollmacht des Menschensohnes zur Sündenvergebung (Mk 2,10)' in *Orientierung an Jesus* (ed. P. Hoffmann; Freiburg: Herder, 1973), pp. 205–214.

Kilpatrick, G. D., 'Jesus, His Family and His Disciples', *Journal for the Study of the New Testament* 15 (1982), 3–19.

Klauck, H.-J., 'Die Frage der Sündenvergebung in der Perikope von der Heilung des Gelähmten (Mk 2,1–12 par.)', *Biblische Zeitschrift* N.S. 25 (1981), 223–248.

Kolenkow, A. B., 'Healing Controversy as a Tie between Miracle and Passion Material for a Proto-Gospel', *Journal of Biblical Literature* 95 (1976), 623–638.

Kuhn, H. W., *Ältere Sammlungen im Markusevangelium* (Göttingen: Vandenhoeck & Ruprecht, 1971), pp. 53ff.

Lange, J., *Das Erscheinen des Auferstandenen im Evangelium nach Matthäus* (Würzburg: Echter Verlag, 1973), pp. 55–64.

Leal, J., 'Qui dedit talem potestatem hominibus (Mt 9,8)', *Verbum Domini* 44 (1966), 53–59.

Leroy, H., 'Vergebung als Heilung. Zur jesuanischen Sicht der Vergebung', *Diakonia* 14 (1983), 79–84.

Maisch, I., *Die Heilung des Gelähmten. Eine exegetisch-traditions-geschichtliche Untersuchung zu Mk 2,1–12* (Stuttgarter Bibelstudien 52; Stuttgart: Verlag Katholisches Bibelwerk, 1971).

Mead, R. T., 'The Healing of the Paralytic—A Unit?', *Journal of Biblical Literature* 80 (1961), 348–354.

Minette de Tillesse, G., *Le secret messianique dans l'Évangile de Marc* (Lectio Divina 47; Paris: Éditions du Cerf, 1968), pp. 116–122, 242–248.

Muhlack, G., *Die Parallelen von Lukas-Evangelium und Apostelgeschichte* (Frankfurt am Main: P. Lang, 1979), pp. 15–38.

Neirynck, F., 'Les accords mineurs et la rédaction des évangiles. L'épisode du paralytique (Mt ix,1–8/Lc v,17–26, par. Mc ii,1–12)', *Ephemerides Theologicae Lovanienses* 50 (1974), 215–230.

Nützel, J. M., *Jesus als Offenbarer Gottes nach den lukanischen Schriften* (Forschung zur Bibel 39; Würzburg: Echter Verlag, 1980), pp. 228–230.

Rasco, E., ' "Cuatro" y "la fe": ¿quiénes y de quién? (Mc 2,3b.5a)', *Biblica* 50 (1969), 59–67.

Ringe, S. H., *Jesus, Liberation and the Biblical Jubilee* (Overtures to Biblical Theology; Philadelphia: Fortress Press, 1985), pp. 71–74.

Rolland, P., 'Jésus connaissait leur pensées', *Ephemerides Theologicae Lovanienses* 62 (1986), 118–121.

Schenk, W., ' "Den Menschen". Mt 9:8', *Zeitschrift für die neutes-tamentlichen Wissenschaft* 54 (1963), 272–275.

Schramm, T., *Der Markus-Stoff bei Lukas* (Cambridge: Cambridge University Press, 1971), pp. 99–103.

Standaert, B., *L'Évangile selon Marc. Composition et Genre littéraire* (Nijmegen: Stichting Studentenpers, 1978), pp. 175–180, 270–272.

Stock, A., 'Chiastic Awareness and Education in Antiquity', *Biblical Theology Bulletin* 14 (1984), 23–27.

Thissen, W., *Erzählung der Befreiung: Eine exegetische Untersuchung zu Mk 2,1 – 3,6* (Forschung zur Bibel 21; Würzburg: Echter Verlag, 1976).

Trautmann, M., *Zeichenhafte Handlungen Jesu* (Forschung zur Bibel 37; Würzburg: Echter Verlag, 1980), pp. 234–257.

Tucket, C., 'The Present Son of Man', *Journal for the Study of the New Testament* 14 (1982), 58–81.

Wibbing, S., *Wunder und christliche Existenz heute* (Gütersloh: Mohn, 1979), pp. 112–124.

Winkelmann, M., *Biblische Wunder. Kritik, Chance, Deutung* (Munich: Pfeiffer, 1977), pp. 133–138.

Winstanley, M. T., 'Paralytics and the Kingdom: A Marcan Reflection', *Review for Religious* 39 (1980), 894–899.

5. Healing of the man with the withered hand (Mk 3:1–6 and parallels)

Bennett, W. J., Jr, 'The Herodians of Mark's Gospel', *Novum Testamentum* 17 (1975), 9–14.

Betz, O., and Grimm, W., *Wesen und Wirklichkeit der Wunder Jesu* (Frankfurt am Main: P. Lang, 1977), pp. 33–35.

Borsch, F. H., *Power in Weakness. New Hearing for Gospel Stories of Healing and Discipleship* (Philadelphia: Fortress Press, 1983), pp. 67–84.

Cope, O. L., *Matthew. A Scribe Trained for the Kingdom of Heaven* (CBQ Monograph Series 5; Washington, D.C.: Catholic Biblical Association of America, 1976), pp. 32–52.

Derrett, J. D. M., 'Christ and the Power of Choice (Mark 3,1–6)', *Biblica* 65 (1984), 168–188.

Dewey, J., *Markan Public Debate* (Chico, Cal.: Scholars Press, 1980), pp. 100–105, 111–112.

Dietzfelbinger, C., 'Vom Sinn der Sabbatheilungen Jesu', *Evangelische Theologie* 38 (1978), 281–298.

Duprez, A., 'Les récits évangéliques de miracles', *Lumière et Vie* 23 (119; 1974), 49–69.

Gerhardsson, B., *The Mighty Acts of Jesus according to Matthew* (Lund: Gleerup, 1979), pp. 77–81.

Hultgren, A. J., *Jesus and His Adversaries* (Minneapolis: Augsburg Publishing House, 1979), pp. 82–84, 154–157.

Kertelge, K., *Die Wunder Jesu im Markusevangelium* (Munich: Kösel Verlag, 1970), pp. 82–85.

Longstaff, T. R. W., 'Mark 3:1–6: The Man with the Withered Hand' in *Evidence of Conflation in Mark? A Study in the Synoptic Problem* (SBL Dissertation Series 28; Missoula, Mont.: Scholars Press, 1977), pp. 153–167.

Loos, H. van der, *The Miracles of Jesus* (Leiden: E. J. Brill, 1965), pp. 436–440.

Martin, F., 'Est-il permis le sabbat de faire le bien ou le mal?', *Lumière et Vie* 32 (164; 1983), 69–79.

Mourlon Beernaert, P., 'Jésus controversé. Structure et théologie de Marc 2,1 – 3,6', *Nouvelle Revue Théologique* 95 (1973), 129–149.

Sauer, J., 'Traditionsgeschichtliche Überlegungen zu Mk 3,1–6', *Zeitschrift für die neutestamentliche Wissenschaft* 73 (1982), 183–203.

Thissen, W., *Erzählung der Befreiung: Eine exegetische Untersuchung zu Mk 2,1 – 3,6* (Forschung zur Bibel 21; Würzburg: Echter Verlag, 1976), pp. 74–89, 157–159.

Tilborg, S. van, *The Jewish Leaders in Matthew* (Leiden: E. J. Brill, 1972), pp. 73–74.

Trautmann, M., *Zeichenhafte Handlungen Jesu* (Forschung zur Bibel 37; Würzburg: Echter Verlag, 1980), pp. 278–317.

Wibbing, S., *Wunder und christliche Existenz heute* (Gütersloh: Mohn, 1979), pp. 124–128.

6. The stilling of the storm (Mk 4:35–41 and parallels)

Achtemeier, P., 'Person and Deed. Jesus and the Storm-Tossed Sea', *Interpretation* 16 (1962), 169–176.

Achtemeier, P., 'Toward the Isolation of Pre-Markan Miracle Catenae', *Journal of Biblical Literature* 89 (1970), 265–291, esp. 274–275.

Allen, R. J., *Our Eyes Can Be Opened. Preaching the Miracle Stories of the Synoptic Gospels Today* (Washington, D.C.: University Press of America, 1982), pp. 35–43.

Best, E., *Following Jesus. Discipleship in the Gospel of Mark* (Sheffield: JSOT Press, 1981), pp. 230–234.

Betz, O., and Grimm, W., *Wesen und Wirklichkeit der Wunder Jesu* (Frankfurt am Main: P. Lang, 1977), pp. 56–57, 68–70, 82–83.

Bornkamm, G., 'The Stilling of the Storm in Matthew' in *Tradition and Interpretation in Matthew* (ed. G. Bornkamm, G. Barth and H. J. Held; Philadelphia: The Westminster Press/London: SCM Press, 1963), pp. 52–57.

Coogan, M. D., 'An Ancient Near Eastern Myth and its Transformation: The Storm God and the Sea', *The Bible Today* 7 (October 1975), 457–463.

Duplacy, J., 'Et il y eut un grand calme. La tempête apaisée (Matthieu 8,23–27)', *Bible et Vie Chrétienne* 74 (1967), 15–28.

Faricy, R., 'The Power of Jesus over Sea and Serpent', *The Bible Today* 21 (July 1983), 260–267.

Fischer, K. M., and Wahlde, U. C. von, 'The Miracles of Mark 4:35 – 5:43. Their Meaning and Function in the Gospel Framework', *Biblical Theology Bulletin* 11 (1981), 13–16.

Gerhardsson, B., *The Mighty Acts of Jesus according to Matthew* (Lund: Gleerup, 1979), pp. 53–55, 62, 90.

Glöckner, R., *Biblischer Glaube ohne Wunder?* (Einsiedeln: Johannes Verlag, 1979), pp. 129–130.

Glöckner, R., *Neutestamentliche Wundergeschichten und das Lob der Wundertaten Gottes in den Psalmen* (Mainz: Matthias-Grünewald

Verlag, 1983), pp. 60–79.

Heil, J. P., *Jesus Walking on the Sea. Meaning and Gospel Functions of Matt 14:22–33, Mark 6:45–52 and John 6:15b–21* (Analecta Biblica 87; Rome: Biblical Institute Press, 1981), pp. 85–103, 118–131.

Hengel, M., *The Charismatic Leader and His Followers* (Edinburgh: T. & T. Clark, 1981), pp. 3–15.

Hilgert, E., *The Ship and Related Symbols in the New Testament* (Assen: Van Gorcum, 1962), pp. 84ff., 97ff.

Hilgert, E., 'Symbolismus und Heilsgeschichte in den Evangelien. Ein Beitrag zu den Seesturm- und Gerasenererzählungen' in *Oikonomia. Heilsgeschichte als Thema der Theologie. Festschrift O. Cullmann* (ed. F. Christ; Hamburg-Bergstedt: H. Reich, 1967), pp. 51–56.

Iersel, B. M. F. van, and Linmans, A. J. M., 'The Storm on the Lake, Mk iv,35–41 and Mt viii,18–27 in the Light of Form-Criticism, "Redaktionsgeschichte" and Structural Analysis' in *Miscellanea Neotestamentica* II (ed. T. Baarda *et al.*; Leiden: E. J. Brill, 1978), pp. 17–48.

Kamphaus, F., *The Gospels for Preachers and Teachers* (London: Sheed and Ward, 1968), pp. 127–135.

Kertelge, K., *Die Wunder Jesu im Markusevangelium* (Munich: Kösel Verlag, 1970), pp. 91–100.

Kirchschläger, W., *Jesu exorzistisches Wirken aus der Sicht des Lukas* (Klosterneuburg: Österreichisches Katholisches Bibelwerk, 1981), pp. 71–89.

Klauck, H.-J., *Allegorie und Allegorese in synoptischen Gleichnistexten* (Münster: Aschendorff, 1978), pp. 340–348.

Klemm, H. G., 'Das Wort von der Selbstbestattung der Toten. Beobachtungen zur Auslegungsgeschichte von Mt viii.22 par.', *New Testament Studies* 16 (1969–70), 60–75.

Kratz, R., *Rettungswunder. Motiv-, traditions- und formkritische Aufarbeitung einer biblischen Gattung* (Europäische Hochschulschriften 23/123; Frankfurt/Berne: P. Lang, 1979).

Lamarche, P., 'La tempête apaisée (Mc 4,35–41)' in *Révélation de Dieu chez Marc* (Paris: Beauchesne, 1976), pp. 61–77.

Lamote, J., 'De stormstilling (Mc 4.35–41 en par.): Geloven in drievoud' in *Ziende blind? Bijbelse Wonderverhalen exegetisch en catechetisch toegelicht* (Antwerp: Patmos, 1977), pp. 243–258.

Léon-Dufour, X., 'La tempête apaisée', *Nouvelle Revue Théologique* 97 (1965), 897–922 [= *Études d'Évangile* (Paris: Éditions du Seuil, 1965), pp. 150–182].

Léon-Dufour, X., 'Exégèse du Nouveau Testament. Évangiles Synoptiques: histoire et interprétation', *Recherches de Science Religieuse* 53 (1965), 600–642, esp. 600–612.

Linskens, J., 'The Stilling of the Tempest in the Gospel of Saint Matthew (8:23–27)', *The Sower* 5 (1963), 163–173, 205–216.

McHugh, J., 'The Origins and Growth of the Gospel Traditions. II: Two Nature Miracles', *Clergy Review* 58 (1973), 83–95.

Magass, W., ' "Er aber schlief" (Mt 8,24). Ein Versuch über die Kleinigkeit (meloč)', *Linguistica Biblica* 29–30 (1973), 55–59.

Meye, R. P., *Jesus and the Twelve* (Grand Rapids: Eerdmans, 1968), pp. 63–73.

Meye, R. P., 'Psalm 107 as "Horizon" for Interpreting the Miracle Stories of Mark 4:35 – 8:26' in *Unity and Diversity in New Testament Theology* (ed. R. A. Guelich; Grand Rapids: Eerdmans, 1978), pp. 1–13.

Peterson, E., 'Das Schiff als Symbol der Kirche in der Eschatologie' in *Frühkirche, Judentum und Gnosis. Studien und Untersuchungen* (Freiburg: Herder, 1959), pp. 92–96.

Priebe, D. A., 'Communicating the Text Today', *Dialog* 7 (1968), 266–274.

Riebl, M., *Auferstehung Jesu in der Stunde seines Todes?* (Stuttgart: Verlag Katholisches Bibelwerk, 1978), pp. 68–69.

Riebl, M., 'Nachfolge Jesu nach Ostern. Eine didaktisch aufbereitete Auslegung von Mt 8,23–27', *Bibel und Liturgie* 55 (1982), 221–225.

Rivera, L. F., 'La liberación en el éxodo. El éxodo de Marcos y la revelación del líder (4,35 – 8,30)', *Revista Bíblica* 33 (1971), 13–26.

Robinson, B., 'The Challenge of the Gospel Miracle Stories', *New Blackfriars* 60 (1979), 321–335, esp. 329–331.

Ruegg, U., 'Zum Vertrauen befreit. Jesus mit seinen Jünger im Sturm (Markus 4,35–41)' in *Wunder Jesu. Bibelarbeit in der Gemeinde* (ed. A. Steiner and V. Weymann; Basel: F. Reinhardt, 1978), pp. 113–126.

Schille, G., 'Die Seesturmerzählung. Markus 4:35–41 als Beispiel neutestamentlicher Aktualisierung', *Zeitschrift für die neutestamentliche Wissenschaft* 56 (1965), 30–40.

Schille, G., *Die urchristliche Wundertradition* (Stuttgart: Calwer Verlag, 1967), pp. 32–34.

Schmithals, W., *Wunder und Glaube. Eine Auslegung von Markus 4,35 – 6,6a* (Biblische Studien 59; Neukirchen-Vluyn: Neukirchener Verlag, 1970).

Schramm, T., *Der Markus-Stoff bei Lukas* (Cambridge: Cambridge University Press, 1971), pp. 124–125.

Schwarz, G., '*Aphes tous nekrous thapsai tous heautōn nekrous*', *Zeitschrift für die neutestamentliche Wissenschaft* 72 (1981), 272–276.

Soares Prabhu, G. M., 'And There was a Great Calm. A "Dvani" Reading of the Stilling of the Storm (Mk 4,35–41)', *BibleBhashyam* 5 (1979), 295–308.

Standaert, B., *L'Évangile selon Marc. Composition et Genre littéraire* (Nijmegen: Stichting Studentenpers, 1978), pp. 135–140.

Steinhauser, M. G., *Doppelbildworte in den synoptischen Evangelien* (Forschung zur Bibel 44; Würzburg: Echter Verlag, 1981), pp. 96–121.

Suriano, T. M., ' "Who Then Is This?"…Jesus Masters the Sea', *The Bible Today* no. 79 (1975), 449–456.

Thurston, B. B., 'Faith and Fear in Mark's Gospel', *The Bible Today* 23 (September 1985), 305–310.

Tilborg, S. van, *The Jewish Leaders in Matthew* (Leiden: E. J. Brill, 1972), pp. 128–131.

Vandré, R., *Wundergeschichten im Religionsunterricht* (Göttingen: Vandenhoeck & Ruprecht, 1979), pp. 64–70.

7. The raising of a widow's only son (Lk 7:11–17)

Belle, G. van, 'Buitenbijbelse wonderverhalen' in *Ziende blind? Bijbelse wonderverhalen exegetisch en catechetisch toegelicht* (Antwerp: Patmos,

1976), pp. 38–42.

Betz, O., and Grimm, W., *Wesen und Wirklichkeit der Wunder Jesu* (Frankfurt am Main: P. Lang, 1977), pp. 39–40.

Brodie, T. L., 'Towards Unravelling Luke's Use of the Old Testament: Luke 7.11–17 as an *Imitatio* of I Kings 17.17–24', *New Testament Studies* 32 (1986), 247–267.

Busse, U., *Die Wunder des Propheten Jesus* (Stuttgart: Verlag Katholisches Bibelwerk, 1977), pp. 161–175.

Campbell, D. K., 'The Prince of Life at Nain', *Bibliotheca Sacra* 115 (1958), 341–347.

Dillon, R. J., *From Eye-Witnesses to Ministers of the Word* (Analecta Biblica 82; Rome: Biblical Institute Press, 1978), pp. 117ff.

Glöckner, R., *Neutestamentliche Wundergeschichten und der Lob der Wundertaten Gottes in den Psalmen* (Mainz: Matthias-Grünewald Verlag, 1983), pp. 50–51.

Juel, D., *Luke-Acts. The Promise of History* (Atlanta: John Knox Press, 1983/London: SCM Press, 1984), pp. 41–43.

Kilian, R., 'Die Totenerweckungen Elias und Elishas—eine Motivwanderung', *Biblische Zeitschrift* 10 (1966), 44–56.

Kluge, J., ' "Die Auferstehung des Jünglings zu Nain" oder "Der Auferstehungsglaube und die Frage nach Leben und Tod." Zwei Unterrichtsmodelle zu Lk 7,11–17' in *Tod und Leben* (ed. R. Kakuschke; Göttingen: Vandenhoeck & Ruprecht, 1978), pp. 202–220.

Muhlack, G., *Die Parallelen von Lukas-Evangelium und Apostelgeschichte* (Frankfurt am Main: P. Lang, 1979), pp. 55–63.

Petzke, G., 'Historizität und Bedeutsamkeit von Wunderberichten. Möglichkeiten und Grenzen des religionsgeschichtlichen Vergleiches' in *Neues Testament und christliche Existenz* (ed. H. D. Betz and L. Schottroff; Tübingen: J. C. B. Mohr, 1973), pp. 367–385.

Rochais, G. *Les récits de résurrection des morts dans le Nouveau Testament* (SNTS Monograph Series 40; Cambridge: Cambridge University Press, 1981), pp. 18–38.

Schmitt, A., 'Die Totenerweckung in 2 Kon 4,8–37', *Biblische Zeitschrift* 19 (1975), 1–25.

Schnyder, C., 'Zum Leben befreit. Jesus erweckt den einzigen Sohn einer Witwe vom Tode (Lukas 7,11–17)' in *Wunder Jesu. Bibelarbeit in der Gemeinde* (ed. A. Stein and V. Weymann; Basel: F. Reinhardt, 1978), pp. 77–88.

Schulze, W., 'Lk 7:11–17: Jüngling, ich sage dir, steh auf!', *Am Tisch des Wortes* N.S. 162 (1977), 76–81.

Schweizer, E., *Neues Testament und Christologie im Werden* (Göttingen: Vandenhoeck & Ruprecht, 1982), pp. 66–67.

Stallmann, M., 'Versuch einer katechetischen Meditation über die Auferweckung des Jünglings von Naim' in *Die biblische Geschichte im Unterricht* (Göttingen: Vandenhoeck & Ruprecht, 1963), pp. 149–157.

Vogels, W., 'A Semiotic Study of Luke 7:11–17', *Église et Théologie* 14 (1983), 273–292.

Wibbing, S., *Wunder und christliche Existenz heute* (Gütersloh: Mohn, 1979), pp. 129–135.

8. *The healing of ten lepers (Lk 17:11–19)*

Bailey, J. H., *The Miracles of Jesus for Today* (Nashville: Abingdon Press, 1977), pp. 88–98.

Betz, H. D., 'The Cleansing of the Ten Lepers (Luke 17:11–19)', *Journal of Biblical Literature* 90 (1971), 314–328.

Betz, O., and Grimm, W., *Wesen und Wirklichkeit der Wunder Jesu* (Frankfurt am Main: P. Lang, 1977), pp. 39–40.

Bours, J., 'Vom dankbaren Samariter: Eine Meditation über Lk 17,11–19', *Bibel und Leben* 1 (1960), 193–198.

Bruners, W., *Die Reinigung der zehn Aussätzigen und die Heilung des Samariters, Lk 17,11–19. Ein Beitrag zur lukanischen Interpretation der Reinigung von Aussätzigen* (Forschung zur Bibel 23; Stuttgart: Verlag Katholisches Bibelwerk, 1977).

Busse, U., *Die Wunder des Propheten Jesus. Die Rezeption, Komposition und Interpretation der Wundertradition im Evangelium des Lukas* (Forschung zur Bibel 24; Stuttgart: Verlag Katholisches Bibelwerk, 1977), pp. 313–327.

Busse, U., *et al.* (eds), *Jesus zwischen arm und reich. Lukas-evangelium* (Stuttgart: Verlag Katholisches Bibelwerk, 1980), pp. 126–128.

Charpentier, E., 'L'étranger appelé au salut. Lc 17,11–19', *Assemblées du Seigneur* 59 (1974), 68–79.

Dillon, R. J., *From Eye-Witnesses to Ministers of the Word* (Analecta Biblica 82; Rome: Biblical Institute Press, 1978), pp. 35–36.

Glöckner, R., *Biblische Glaube ohne Wunder?* (Einsiedeln: Johannes Verlag, 1979), pp. 84–85.

Glöckner, R., *Neutestamentliche Wundergeschichten und das Lob der Wundertaten Gottes in den Psalmen* (Mainz: Matthias-Grünewald Verlag, 1983), pp. 125–160.

Glombitza, O., 'Der dankbare Samariter. Luk xvii.11–19', *Novum Testamentum* 11 (1969), 241–246.

Nützel, J. M., *Jesus als Offenbarer Gottes nach den lukanischen Schriften* (Forschung zur Bibel 39; Würzburg: Echter Verlag, 1980), pp. 205–206.

Pesch, R., *Jesu ureigene Taten? Ein Beitrag zur Wunderfrage* (Quaestiones Disputatae 52; Freiburg: Herder, 1970), pp. 114–134.

Pilch, J. J., 'Biblical Leprosy and Body Symbolism', *Biblical Theology Bulletin* 11 (1981), 108–113.

Sabourin, L., *The Divine Miracles Discussed and Defended* (Rome: Catholic Book Agency, 1977), pp. 115–117.

Strelan, J. G., 'Preparing to Preach: Reflections on Luke 17:11–19', *Lutheran Theological Journal* 16 (1982), 83–87.

Unnik, W. C. van, 'L'usage de *sōzein* sauver et ses dérivés dans les évangiles synoptiques' in *La Formation des Évangiles* (Bruges: Desclée, 1957), pp. 178–194.

Vandré, R., *Wundergeschichten im Religionsunterricht* (Göttingen: Vandenhoeck & Ruprecht, 1979), pp. 116–120.